INDIGENOUS
LEGAL RELATIONS in
AUSTRALIA

INDIGENOUS
LEGAL RELATIONS in
AUSTRALIA

Larissa Behrendt
Chris Cunneen
Terri Libesman

OXFORD
UNIVERSITY PRESS
AUSTRALIA & NEW ZEALAND

253 Normanby Road, South Melbourne, Victoria 3205, Australia

Oxford University Press is a department of the University of Oxford.
It furthers the University's objective of excellence in research,
scholarship, and education by publishing worldwide in

Oxford New York

Auckland Cape Town Dar es Salaam Hong Kong Karachi
Kuala Lumpur Madrid Melbourne Mexico City Nairobi
New Delhi Shanghai Taipei Toronto

With offices in

Argentina Austria Brazil Chile Czech Republic France Greece
Guatemala Hungary Italy Japan Poland Portugal Singapore
South Korea Switzerland Thailand Turkey Ukraine Vietnam

OXFORD is a trademark of Oxford University Press
in the UK and in certain other countries

National Library of Australia Cataloguing-in-Publication data

Behrendt, Larissa.
Indigenous legal relations in Australia / Larissa Behrendt,
Chris Cunneen, Terri Libesman.

ISBN 9780195562019 (pbk.)

Includes bibliographical references and index.

1. Aboriginal Australians–Legal status, laws, etc. 2. Aboriginal Australians,
Treatment of. Aboriginal Australians– 3. Government relations. Indigenous peoples
(International law)
I. Cunneen, Chris, 1953-
Libesman, Terri.

342.940872

Edited by Puddingburn Publishing Services
Cover design and Text design by Kerry Cooke, eggplant communications
Cover image: 'Return to Sender', 2005, by Adam Hill
Typeset by Linda Hamley, Melbourne
Proofread by Natasha Broadstock
Indexed by Puddingburn Publishing Services
Printed by Ligare Book Printers, Australia

Contents

About the Authors

Chris Cunneen is the NewSouth Global Professor of Criminology at the University of New South Wales, Sydney, Australia. He has published widely in the area of juvenile justice, restorative justice and Indigenous legal issues. His books include *The Critical Criminology Companion* (Federation Press 2008); *Juvenile Justice: Youth and Crime in Australia* (Oxford University Press 2007); *Conflict, Politics and Crime* (Allen & Unwin 2001); *Faces of Hate* (Federation Press 1997) and *Indigenous People and the Law in Australia* (Butterworths 1995).

Larissa Behrendt is a Professor of Law and Director of Research at the Jumbunna Indigenous House of Learning. She is a Judicial Member and Alternate Chair of the Serious Offenders Review Council and a Land Commissioner of the Land and Environment Court. She is a board member of the Museum of Contemporary Art, a Director of the Bangarra Dance Theatre, and the Chair of National Indigenous Television Ltd.

Terri Libesman is a Senior Lecturer in the Faculty of Law at the University of Technology, Sydney. She researchers and writes with respect to Indigenous children's well-being. She is currently researching cultural care planning for Indigenous children in out of home care with the peak Indigenous children's organisation, the Secretariat of the National Aboriginal and Islander Child Care (SNAICC) and providing advice to the Northern Territory Emergency Response Review Board on the human rights implications of the intervention in the Northern Territory.

Robynne Quiggin is solicitor director at Vincent-Quiggin Legal and Consulting Services. She specialises in Indigenous legal issues relating to Indigenous heritage, the arts, consumer issues and human rights. Robynne teaches part time at several universities. She is a member of the National Indigenous Arts Reference Group, the Commonwealth Consumer Affairs Advisory Council, the National Indigenous Consumer Strategy Reference Group, the Indigenous Financial Services Network and is currently a board member of the Indigenous Consumer Assistance Network, as well as Gadigal Information Services incorporating Koori Radio.

Preface

When Prime Minister Kevin Rudd delivered an apology to members of the Stolen Generation on 13 February 2008, it was indeed a historic occasion. It was a significant day because the apology was long overdue. Having been a key finding in the 1997 *Bringing Them Home* report, the most comprehensive study of the impact of the removal policy on Aboriginal people who were taken away and the families who lost their children, it made the recommendation that an official policy should be made by all governments.

But it was also an important moment because it sent a strong message that there was renewed potential for a new era in the relationship between Indigenous and non-Indigenous Australians. The apology indicated to Aboriginal people that, after the problematic policies of the Howard era, there was an opportunity for things to be different. It certainly indicated that there is an opportunity now for a renewed dialogue about the unfinished business of reconciliation.

The purpose of this book is to introduce students and readers to the major issues facing Aboriginal and Torres Strait Islander people in their contact with Anglo-Australian law and legal institutions. It also seeks to engage readers in some key debates around Aboriginal and Torres Strait Islander issues such as a treaty, a bill of rights, reparations for the Stolen Generation and changes to the Constitution.

The book is divided into four Parts: the law of the colonisers; equality before the law: criminalisation; law, land and culture; and, law, rights and governance.

There are a number of common themes that run through this book.

The importance of history

We recognise that it is impossible to understand the contemporary situation which Indigenous people face in their contact with law without a strong understanding of colonial and more recent history in Australia. The effects of colonial law and policy from the assertion of sovereignty, to the drafting of the Australian Constitution, to the creation of legal regimes of 'protection' and the forced removal of Indigenous children are manifest today. The absences in that colonial history also reverberate today, through for example the failure to negotiate a treaty with Aboriginal and Torres Strait Islander peoples. The history of this colonial legacy is contested. This contest is manifest in contemporary legal issues addressed across this book. It is particularly magnified when historical events, such as the Stolen Generations or proof of native title, are contested in court.

Our task in this book is not to judge the past by the present (a familiar catch-cry of conservative commentators). Rather it is to be able to understand through a knowledge of the past, the present situation in which Indigenous people find themselves vis-à-vis the Australian state. The legal and political history of Australia provides us with a roadmap for understanding the dynamics of contemporary Indigenous struggle and the patterns of racism and disadvantage still firmly entrenched within the Australian politic. How could we, for example, understand the current demands for reparation and compensation for stolen wages and stolen children without an understanding of the profound impacts of colonial law and policy?

The pervasiveness of racial discrimination

Many Aboriginal and Torres Strait Islanders continue to feel that issues of racism are prevalent in their experience of everyday life, whether it is in the provision of services or in the negative stereotypes that still pervade Australian society about Indigenous people and their communities. That racism continues to be a defining experience for Aboriginal and Torres Strait Islander people stands in stark contrast to social research that shows that more and more Australians are resistant to having their society characterised as racist.

This book shows how discrimination on the basis of race has been an undeniable historical experience for Aboriginal people and documents the many ways in which laws continue to operate differently and to offer less protection to Aboriginal and Torres Strait Islander people. It also explores how law can play a role in providing a framework for recognising Aboriginal and Torres Strait Islander peoples' rights and thereby contribute to processes which can address racism and promote more substantive equality in family, community and public life.

International human rights standards

International human rights standards either explicitly or implicitly permeate the discussion in most chapters of this book. Human rights principles provide a framework for discussing issues including diverse subjects such as the possibilities of rights protection through, for example a bill of rights, and the international principles for reparations (the Bassiouni principles) for the Stolen Generations. Conventions to which Australia is already a state party such as the UN Convention on the Rights of the Child underpin the discussions on child protection and juvenile justice.

The UN Declaration on the Rights of Indigenous Peoples has a place of particular importance when discussing human rights. This is especially the case with Indigenous claims to self-determination. The right to self-determination is a principle that underpins many of the discussions in this book, from for example the role of Indigenous organisations in deciding the future of Indigenous children through to the establishment of effective governance structures more generally for Indigenous people.

The importance of Indigenous decision-making

The right to self-determination connects directly to a further theme explored throughout this book, and that is the importance of Indigenous decision-making. The possibilities for understanding and developing Indigenous decision-making are explored in varied contexts. On the one hand there is discussion of the attempts by government to create Indigenous modes of decision-making through bodies like the National Aboriginal Consultative Committee in the late 1970s to the creation of the elected ATSIC in the late 1980s and the government appointed National Indigenous Council in 2004. The book also explores Indigenous modes of governance which have been developed using both imposed structures, such as corporations and statutory bodies such as land councils, and within independent organisations such as the Aboriginal Provisional Government. Indigenous peoples claiming the right to participate in decision making and control their future are evident in political groups both within and independent of government structures throughout Australian history. The book also contemplates the necessary requirements for new modes of Indigenous governance and representation in the post-National Indigenous Council and new Labor government environment.

The importance of Indigenous political struggle

We noted that it is impossible to understand the contemporary situation which Indigenous people face in their contact with law without a strong understanding of history. It is equally impossible without an understanding of Indigenous political struggle. It is not possible to understand the importance and limitations of the constitutional changes of 1967 without understanding the Indigenous political struggle against racial discrimination and social and political exclusion. Nor could we understand the establishment of the Royal Commission into Aboriginal Deaths in Custody or the National Inquiry into the Separation of Aboriginal and Torres Strait Islander Children from Their Families without understanding the role of Indigenous organisations in forcing government to confront the effects and ongoing trauma of deaths in custody, imprisonment and the removal of children.

The limitations of Anglo-Australian law

Another theme throughout this book is the limitations of Australian law in resolving the complex contemporary and historical problems that continue to exist. For example, Australian law recognises native title to land, but does so in a way that prioritises the property interests of non-Indigenous people. Another example is customary law. Australian governments, courts and law reform bodies still engage in a 'recognition' debate over Indigenous law, and have done so for centuries now, but always in a context that prioritises Australian over Indigenous law.

A further example is racial discrimination. Australian law prohibits racial discrimination, except when the legislature decides that it is permissible to discriminate and suspends the legislation. While perhaps the overt forms of direct racial discrimination are now less frequent, we know that the legislation has not served Indigenous people well in countering the myriad forms of indirect and institutionalised discrimination that permeate social and economic life. Nor has the prohibition on discrimination impacted on the way governments construct legislation, such as the mandatory sentencing laws in the Northern Territory in the late 1990s, which have a clearly foreseeable discriminatory impact.

This book is concerned with the experiences of Aboriginal and Torres Strait Islander people under the Anglo-Australian legal system but it raises a broader question. When assessing how well a legal system works, the true test is how well it works for the socio-economically disadvantaged, the culturally distinct and the historically marginalised. If a legal system cannot protect those who are the most vulnerable within the community, it raises questions about how secure everyone's rights are and how it can be improved. Aboriginal and Torres Strait Islander people provide a litmus test as to how well our legal system works to protect those who are less well off within the community.

Table of Cases

Table of Statutes

PART 1

The Law of the Colonisers

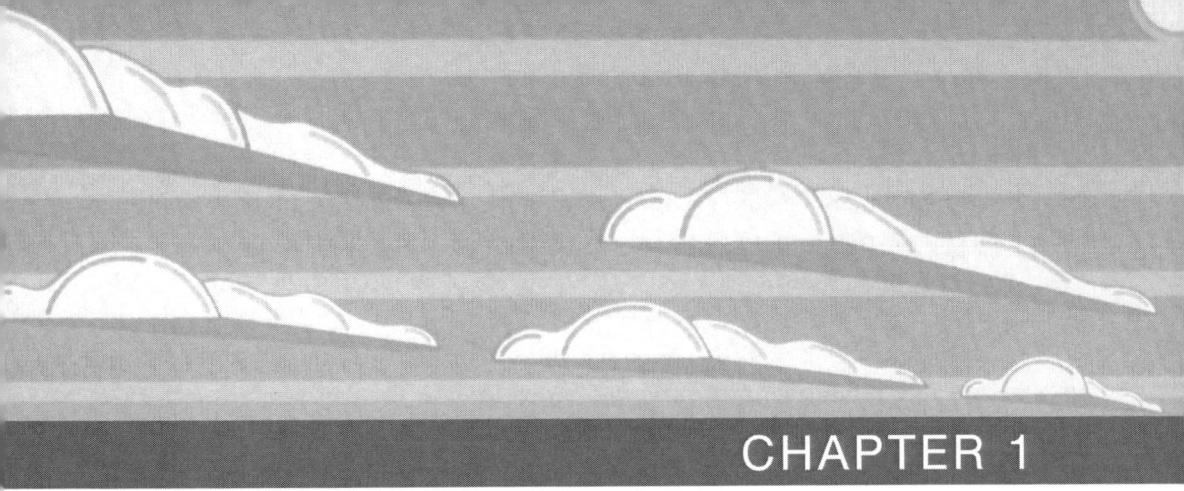

CHAPTER 1

Dispossession and Colonisation

Introduction

In September 2007 the Draft Declaration on Indigenous Peoples Rights was voted upon and overwhelmingly adopted by 143 countries at the General Assembly of the United Nations. Australia was one of four countries to vote against adoption of the Declaration. The Declaration affirms the rights of Indigenous peoples to their culture, land, natural resources and self-government. But as Ellison has guided us, to understand this story, we need to go back to the beginning (Ellison 1952: 9). The beginning takes us to history and mythology, the events and their retelling in stories, artwork, documents, monuments and national holidays that are foundational to Australia's past, present and future. These stories are contested in our national imagination and this contest is evident in the legal history of Australia's colonisation. This is a contest about might and its relation to power and authority. It as a contest about morality and justice, greed and inequity, and pluralism and reconciliation. The history wars, that is contests about how Australia was colonised, are highly emotional battles (Rowley 1970; Attwood 1996; Markus 1994; Reynolds 1981; Read 1992; Windshuttle 2002). This is not surprising. They are battles about identity and legitimacy. They are battles about a past which is difficult to reconcile with the basic tenets of human rights which have been widely accepted by the international community since the Second World War. The understanding that imperialism offends foundational international human rights principles of self-determination is evident in United Nations resolutions and support for processes of decolonisation, in particular with respect to the European colonies which had majority non-European populations (General Assembly Resolution 1514 (xv), 14 December 1960)). These processes however left a gaping moral and practical hole. What of Indigenous peoples who form a minority in post-colonial democracies? Over the last two decades, the United Nations has attempted to address the position of Indigenous peoples with the recognition of Indigenous peoples' rights to land, culture and a distinct identity in a number of treaties including the International Covenant on Civil and Political Rights, the International Convention on the Elimination of all forms of Discrimination and the Convention on the Rights of the Child (Anaya 2004). The Declaration of Indigenous Peoples Rights is the most comprehensive international statement with respect to Indigenous peoples' rights (see Chapter 14 for a discussion of contemporary domestic and international human rights issues with respect to self-determination). Australia has lagged behind comparable democracies such as Canada, New Zealand and the USA in recognising native title and Indigenous peoples' rights more generally. It continues to be slow and ambivalent in its willingness to recognise the broader political and legal implications of prior Indigenous occupation. The recognition of native title in 1992 exposed but left unresolved the legitimacy of Australia's constitutional foundations. These are discussed in this chapter with respect to the dispossession of Indigenous peoples by law and war in the late nineteenth and twentieth centuries and some reference is made to cases which contest Aboriginal jurisdiction in the twenty-first century.

Captain Cook is an iconic symbol of Australia's foundation as a nation. The contest between competing understandings of Australia's identity and legitimacy are evident in competing Indigenous and mainstream versions of this story (Beaglehole 1955; Healy 1997; Rose 1984; Nugent 2008). Accounts of Captain Cook's conduct on his landing at Botany Bay in 1770 vary from compassionate commander to aggressive transgressor and thief depending on the period that the story is recounted in and who it is recounted by. Some accounts bear a resemblance to the events which are recorded, while others embellish the story with details which are not accounted for in the record and still others use Captain Cook allegorically to convey an understanding of the process of colonisation more broadly. The stylised accordance of significance to this foundational story is also evident in the legal history of colonisation, aspects of which will be recounted below. The events of the past and the principles of justice and legitimacy, which they either support or undermine, are of ongoing material significance in terms of the current experiences of Indigenous Australians as well as in terms of the moral legitimacy of the nation. This history is crucial to the current relationship which Indigenous peoples have with the law in all spheres of life. Contemporary legacies of the past, and how they impact on Indigenous peoples' relationship with the law, are discussed in the subsequent chapters.

DISCUSSION QUESTION

- Research and discuss Indigenous and non-Indigenous stories with respect to Captain Cook's landing at Botany Bay.

Dispossession post-*Mabo*

Justice Brennan claimed in *Mabo v Queensland (No 2)* (1992) 175 CLR 1 that the common law could not be complicit in the violent and unjust dispossession of Aboriginal and Torres Strait Islander peoples. This was one reason offered for recognising native title and purporting to end the era of terra nullius. This claim is problematic for a number of reasons. The *Mabo* decision, while bold in descriptors of past wrong, is timid and evasive in its exploration of the implications of recognition of prior ownership by Indigenous peoples. Most troublesome is its failure to address the implications of its own recognition of an existing system of laws within Aboriginal and Torres Strait Islander communities. How can Aboriginal and Torres Strait Islander peoples' laws be acknowledged for the purpose of recognising native title while simultaneously denied for all other purposes? How can the common law take the moral high ground with its recognition of prior ownership while leaving this title completely vulnerable to extinguishment by governments? Although the recognition of native title had not been challenged in the High Court before *Mabo (No 2)* in 1992, it would be disingenuous to suggest that the common law was not implicated in the regulation of Aboriginal and Torres Strait Islander peoples in a way that was fundamental to their dispossession and control. (For a discussion of native title see Chapter 9). Indigenous peoples have had the law applied to them in discriminatory ways for as long as Anglo law has operated in Australian colonies. The status of Indigenous peoples was ambiguous at the time of colonisation and as the early case law discussed below suggests, the legal characterisation of Indigenous peoples appears to be closely tied to the needs and capacities of the colonial powers.

The legal process of dispossession

In English law a legal distinction is made between the acquisition of territory and the acquisition of land. It is this distinction which enabled the High Court of Australia in *Mabo (No 2)* to recognise Indigenous peoples' right to native title without fundamentally reviewing the legitimacy with which Australia was colonised. While technically and legally this distinction could be made, the recognition of Aboriginal and Torres Strait Islander peoples' original ownership of land inevitably leads to questions about the legitimacy of the colonisation of Australia which remain unanswered. If recognising native title addresses the myth of terra nullius with respect to title, what about the parallel presumptions about Indigenous Australians with respect to the acquisition of sovereignty? While the common law sustains a distinction between territorial sovereignty and the acquisition of land, this distinction is not part of Indigenous laws and social organisation.

At the time of colonisation the method for acquisition of colonies was outlined both in international and municipal, that is English, law. English law however gave the Crown the prerogative to acquire new territories and it did not require this acquisition to be made in compliance with international law. It is the intention of the Crown, which is ascertained by its own acts and surrounding circumstances, which determines if sovereignty has been attained for the purpose of English law. Classification of how a territory has been colonised determines the law operating in a colony and the power of the Crown to legislate in the colony. In conquered or ceded territories, local law remained in place to the extent that it was not 'unconscionable' or incompatible with the acquired sovereignty. The Crown however had the power to make laws which were not incompatible with existing law until a representative legislative assembly was established. In settled colonies, which were classified as those being uninhabited or virtually uninhabited, English law accompanied colonisation to the extent that it was suitable to the local circumstances (McNeil 1989: 109–133).

However these simple classifications with clear consequences did not in fact have easy or obvious application in many colonial contexts including Australia. As the discussion of case law below illustrates, a mix of customary and English law was applied to Aboriginal and Torres Strait Islander peoples for at least the first 40 years of colonisation. The relationship between the common law and customary law still remains contested and ambiguous as is evident in the development of native title law, the controversy surrounding the revocation of customary law considerations in sentencing in criminal matters and the development of alternative court and decision-making processes with respect to dispute resolution relevant to Indigenous peoples in the criminal justice system (see Chapters 5, 7 and 9). While there was no single definition of what constituted an 'uninhabited' country, one of the clearest indicators used by colonial courts was the lack of an established system of law as understood by colonial courts. Lord Watson made the following assessment of New South Wales in *Cooper v Stuart* (1889) 14 App Cas 286 at 291–292:

> There is a great difference between the case of a colony acquired by conquest or cessation, in which there is an established system of law, and that of a colony which consisted of a tract of territory practically unoccupied, without settled inhabitants or settled law, at the time when it was peacefully annexed to the British dominions. The Colony of New South Wales belongs to the latter class.

This decision was made on presumptions with respect to Aboriginal society rather than evidence. The presumptions with respect to a lack of law and with respect to peaceful settlement were clearly wrong. The question of whether Indigenous law continued/s to operate once British sovereignty had been declared, while ambiguous in parts of the nineteenth century, has been categorically rejected by the High Court in contemporary cases both before and after *Mabo (No 2)*.

DISCUSSION QUESTION

- Should laws be based on a factual foundation or is the established and long-standing acceptance of a law sufficient to give it legitimacy?

Context of colonisation

The disregard for Aboriginal and Torres Strait Islander peoples' occupation of Australia at the time of colonisation appears to be founded in a combination of expedience and racist philosophical and political ideas. Theories about race at the time of colonisation were both influenced by and contributed to colonial expansion. During the period of European exploration from the sixteenth century onwards, ideas about different races were developed to explain the different peoples who were encountered in the 'new world'. From the 1750s, racial theories ostensibly based on scientific evidence developed typologies which divided people into races. These typologies were developed with notions of 'civilised' and 'barbaric' races which formed a chain of human evolution. This chain of human evolution, which placed Europeans at the top of the hierarchy and Indigenous peoples in a state of nature, also influenced legal thinking. This is evident in the frequent reference to Aboriginal peoples as barbaric and uncivilised in the nineteenth-century cases discussed below.

It is likely that Cook and Banks believed that there were few Indigenous people along the coast and even fewer inland. Australia was colonised at a time when the ideas of John Locke influenced understandings of property ownership. Locke's ideas provided a useful justification for the imperial project which required dispossession of Indigenous peoples. Locke argued that if there was no sign of agriculture then the natives must still be living in a state of nature. This view coincided with the mid-eighteenth-century writings of Sir William Blackstone in his *Commentaries on the Laws of England* (1807) which were influential in providing legal arguments to justify colonisation. Blackstone argued that there were two types of colonies: either those that were 'desert and uncultivated' which were discovered and occupied by colonial powers; or those which were already cultivated and were gained through conquest or ceded by a treaty to the colonial power. While Australia was colonised as a settled colony, as the cases discussed below illustrate, these categorisations did not fit neatly with experience on the ground. While Australia was classified as settled, in practical terms it was recognised that Aboriginal peoples had systems of laws which governed relations between them. More than half a century after colonisation the application of the Anglo criminal law between Aboriginal people, with respect to the most serious of criminal offences murder, remained unsettled. The paucity of cases brought against Aboriginal peoples for crimes committed in the colony also evidences a more complex experience of race relations than the simple categorisation as a settled colony would suggest.

Contested sovereignty

The idea of a single body of law applying to Indigenous and other Australians has been contested in Australian courts at least since 1828 with the case of *R v Ballard* discussed below. The contemporary judiciary's obsession with a singular sovereignty seems to be founded in what could be considered to be an outdated understanding of nation states as operating almost exclusively autonomously. This defies the experience of globalisation which has impacted on the autonomy of all nations. It defies the development of international law which has, since the Declaration of Human Rights, attempted to balance the human rights of individuals with recognition of states' autonomy and independence. In more recent years international human rights law has developed jurisprudence which attempts to balance not only individual but also collective minority and Indigenous peoples' rights with state rights. For a discussion of the gradual response of international human rights jurisprudence to Indigenous peoples claims to be recognised see Chapter 14. Australian courts have however been very slow to accept that recognising legal pluralism, in particular the distinct identity of Indigenous peoples, will not cause the sky to fall in. It could in fact strengthen the Australian political system and provide greater, rather than less, certainty and security.

DISCUSSION QUESTION

- Discuss ways in which sovereignty for nation states is different in the twenty-first century compared with the nineteenth century.

The rule of law

The position of Aboriginal people, as British subjects, at the time of colonisation was at best ambiguous. Two basic tenets of the rule of law have been denied to Aboriginal and Torres Strait Islander people consistently from the time of colonisation, the first being that laws should not be exercised arbitrarily and the second that law should sustain a normative order and thereby contribute to the maintenance of law and order within communities. It is plain from the evidence of frontier violence and the role of police in this violence that laws were arbitrarily applied to Aboriginal communities. The ongoing arbitrary exercise of laws with respect to Aboriginal and Torres Strait Islander people is evident in discussion throughout this book but it is particularly pronounced in the Protection era (see Chapter 2). As outlined below in cases from *R v Murrell* (1836) to *Wik Peoples v Queensland* (1996), the failure of the courts to recognise Aboriginal law and custom has denied Aboriginal peoples a fundamental way of maintaining social cohesion and reinforcing understood community standards of behaviour. Both these denials have ongoing repercussions for Indigenous peoples in terms of their right to equality and law and order within their communities.

Governor Phillip's original instructions from the Colonial Office in Britain distinguished Aboriginal people from 'our subjects' but required Governor Phillip to provide legal protection to Aboriginal people. What ensued was a combination of attempts to manage and pacify Aboriginal resistance to the taking of their land and violence against their communities. This took many forms including military-style responses to resistance and officials turning a blind eye to vigil anti-responses by colonists to threats or incursions from Aboriginal groups. The Royal Commission into Aboriginal Deaths in Custody reported on some of the responses to Aboriginal resistance which breached the rule of law:

> In 1797, Governor Hunter declared Aboriginal people a danger and sent out armed parties to pacify them. By 1816 [Governor] Macquarie had made a martial law-style proclamation. He banned Aboriginal meetings, the carrying of weapons (including those used for hunting), abolished their own system of punishments and reconciliation, and entitled settlers and the military troops to use Force of arms; on armed Aboriginal people or unarmed groups of six or more. (Johnston 1991: (2)13)

Declarations and proclamations such as these suggest the difficulty which colonial governments had maintaining law and order and their acute awareness of Indigenous resistance to their dispossession from their lands. The extent to which officials and colonists recognised Indigenous peoples' prior ownership of their land and their resistance to being dispossessed is not reflected in legal doctrine. It was particularly detached from cases such as *Cooper v Stuart* (1889) (referred to above) which were heard in the House of Lords, divorced from evidence or practical experience of the frontier.

DISCUSSION QUESTION

- Discuss arguments with respect to how recognition of Indigenous peoples' laws and customs could strengthen or abrogate from the application of the rule of law.

'Quietening' the frontier

Although colonial governments did not officially endorse violence against Aboriginal peoples, it was often condoned. While the doctrine of settlement enabled the colonial government to grant Aboriginal land, at a practical level it usually had to be taken by force. The response of numerous governors to groups of Aboriginal people, including declarations of martial law and banning of Aboriginal meetings, is indicative of the level of fear which conflict over land generated amongst colonists. Aboriginal people were often dispersed or 'quietened' by native or general police. There are many accounts of killings and massacres by both civilians and police (see Elder 1988; Evans, Saunders and Cronin 1988; Reynolds 1989; Markus 1990). Some such as the Coniston massacre in the Northern Territory took place in the twentieth century (Markus 1990: 135–136). While prosecution of violent offenders was rare, there are some examples such as the trial and execution of the perpetrators of the Myall Creek massacre in 1838.

CASE

The massacre at Waterloo Creek

Detailed accounts of the extensive and indiscriminate killing by the New South Wales Mounted Police, under the command of Major James Nunn at Waterloo Creek in 1838, reached Governor Gipps in Port Phillip by the time Nunn returned from his expedition. It is estimated that he and his troops killed 40 or 50 Aborigines in a single encounter at Waterloo Creek. Bruce Elder describes the aftermath of the massacre:

> ... and then his men engaged in a typical frontier style mopping-up operation which meant that any Aborigine they came into contact with, they killed. After the

massacre they hunted the survivors through the riverbank scrub, shooting and slashing at them. Those Aborigines who tried to swim to freedom were shot mid stream. The creek ran with blood. The women who had been at the camp were captured and forced to lead the troopers to other camps where similar massacres occurred. Nunn kept no record. The details and the scale remained imprecise. ... Somewhere between the Gwydie and the Namoi, Nunn left the niceties of British law behind him ... he was lionised all the way back to Sydney (Elder 1988:70).

While Nunn was not prosecuted, the perpetrators of the Myall Creek massacre, which occurred less than a year later, were brought to justice. Elder interprets this prosecution as a sign of Governor Gipps' intolerance of indiscriminate frontier violence. Others have argued that it was easier for Governor Gipps to prosecute the ex-convict stockmen who were responsible for the Myall Creek massacre than the police who were responsible for more extensive killings. Historian David Neal points out the equivocal position which Governor Gipps faced with respect to addressing police violence on the frontier. The first problem was that he depended on the police to protect colonists, the second was that colonisation by definition required the quashing of resistance and protection of white land holders. David Neal suggests that the mix of law and power at the frontier 'was heavily weighted towards the latter and, in the case of Nunn, it clearly spilled over into lawlessness (Neal 1991: 154).

The use of Aboriginal people as police and their involvement in violent attacks or assisting perpetrators has caused considerable controversy. The Queensland Mounted Police, which was under the command of European officers, has been described as the most lethal force used against Aboriginal people. According to a Queensland Police Department history of the group, they were recruited and deployed to ensure that they were working against groups who were alien to them and a long distance from their own home, which made it difficult for them to dessert (Richards 2008).

The police in Australia carried out paramilitary functions which in other colonial countries were carried out by the military. The role of police at the frontier and later in implementing 'protection' and assimilation policies, which involved child removal and forcing people off their lands, have had an enduring impact on many Aboriginal and Torres Strait Islander peoples' perceptions of police and more broadly the failure of the rule of law for them (see Chapter 2). The memory of massacres and the mistreatment of Aboriginal and Torres Strait Islander people, some of which occurred in the relatively recent past, are a living part of many communities' oral histories and memory.

Dispossession by law

While limited attempts in the nineteenth century were made to present the appearance of Aboriginal and Torres Strait Islander people as being equal before the law, the formal status and rights of Aboriginal and Torres Strait Islander people remained and to some extent, as later chapters in this book illustrate, remain unequal. Opinions among colonists, Indigenous peoples, governors and others were diverse. As discussed above some recognised the injustice of violent dispossession while others treated Aboriginal people with utter disregard. The following letter to the *Launceston Advertisor* of 6 September 1831 raises the ambivalent status of Aboriginal people:

> Are these unhappy people, the subjects of our King, in a state of rebellion or are they an injured people, whom we have invaded and with whom we are at war?
>
> Are they within the reach of our laws; or are they to be judged by the law of nations?
>
> Are they to be viewed in the light of murderers, or as prisoners of war?
>
> Have they been guilty of any crime under the laws of nations which is punishable by death, or have they only been carrying on a war in their own way?
>
> Are they British subjects at all, or a foreign enemy who has never been subdued and which resists our usurped authority and domination? (Reynolds 1989: 11–12)

As early as 1829, we see questions about the recognition of Indigenous laws raised in Australian courts. The following cases look at whether the Supreme Court of New South Wales has jurisdiction to try disputes between Aborigine people. The court had already determined in *R v Lowe* (1827) Supreme Court of New South Wales Forbes CJ, and Stephen J, 23 May 1827, that Aboriginal people in conflict with Europeans were subject to its jurisdiction.

CASE STUDY

R v Ballard

Supreme Court of New South Wales (Forbes CJ and Dowling J) 13 June 1829, AILR Vol 3 No 3 1998

In 1829 in *R v Ballard* the Supreme Court of New South Wales was asked by the Attorney-General if an Aboriginal person could be prosecuted for the alleged murder of another Aboriginal person at the Domain near Sydney. Chief Justice Forbes and Justice Dowling in separate judgments held that, 'it had always been the policy of the judges and the government of New South Wales not to interfere in disputes between Aborigines' at 412. Chief Justice Forbes in his judgment notes at 413:

> I believe it has been the practice of the Courts of this country, since the colony was settled, never to interfere with or enter into the quarrels that have taken place

between or amongst the native themselves ... But I am not aware that British laws have been applied to the aboriginal natives in transactions solely between themselves, whether of contract, tort or crime ... It may be a question admitting of doubt, whether any advantages could be gained, without previous preparation, by engrafting the institutions of our country, upon the natural system which savages have adopted for their own government ... If their institutions, however barbarous or abhorrent from our notions of religion and civilisation, become matured into a system and produced all the effects upon their intercourse, that a less objectionable course of proceeding (in our judgement) could produce, then I know not upon what principle of municipal jurisdiction it would be right to interfere with them ... With these general observations, I am of opinion that this man is not amenable to English law for the act he is supposed to have committed.

Justice Dowling in a short separate judgment noted at 414:

Until the aboriginal natives of this Country shall consent, either actually or by implication, to the interposition of our laws in the administration of justice for acts committed by themselves upon themselves, I know of no reason human, or divine, which ought to justify us in interfering with their institutions even if such interference were practicable.

While both judgments are plainly racist and characterise Aboriginal people as 'savages' and less 'civilised' than their British colonisers, they also clearly recognise that Aboriginal peoples exist with their own system of laws governing relations between them. Paradoxically while some judges in more contemporary courts have acknowledged the subtle and complex system of laws governing Aboriginal and Torres Strait Islander peoples they have refused to find space within the common law for recognition of the operation of these laws.

Less than a decade after the decision in *Ballard* was handed down the full bench of the Supreme Court of New South Wales, including Chief Justices Forbes and Justice Dowling whose decisions in *Ballard* are discussed above, concurred with Justice Burton in a decision which completely reversed the findings in *Ballard*.

R v Murrell

Supreme Court of New South Wales (Forbes CJ, Dowling and Burton JJ) 11 April 1836, Sydney AILR Vol 3 No 3 1998

In *R v Jack Congo Murrell*, the Aboriginal defendant was charged with murder and his counsel argued that the court had no jurisdiction to try him. Murrell's counsel Mr

Stephens argued before the Full Bench of the New South Wales Supreme Court that Aboriginal people had their own laws and customs which governed relations between them:

> The reason why subjects of Great Britain are bound by the laws of their country is that they are protected by them; the natives are not protected by those laws, they are not admitted as witnesses in Courts of Justice, they cannot claim any civil rights, they cannot claim recovery of, or compensation for, those lands which have been torn from them, and which they have probably held for centuries. They are not therefore bound by laws which afford them no protection (at 415).

Justice Burton delivering the opinion of the court found that Aboriginal people were:

> ... entitled to be regarded by civilised nations as a free and independent people, and are entitled to the possession of those rights which as such are valuable to them, yet the various tribes had not attained at the first settlement of the English people amongst them to such a position in point of numbers and civilisation, and to such a form of Government and laws, as to be entitled to be recognised as so many sovereign states governed by law of their own (at 416).

He went on to hold that the land from the far north extremity known as Cape York, to the southern extremity of territory known as New South Wales and embracing all the country inland to the west as far as 129 degrees and including all the islands to the East in the Pacific have been taken into 'actual possession by the King of England'.

Justice Burton concluded his judgment with the opinion:

> ... that the greatest possible inconvenience and scandal to this community would be consequent if it were to be holden by this Court that it has no jurisdiction in such a case as the present—to be holden in fact that crimes of murder and others of almost equal enormity may be committed by those people in our Streets without restraint so they be committed only upon one another! and that our laws are no sanctuary to them (at 416).

Only five years after *Murrell* was handed down, the question of the New South Wales Supreme Court's jurisdiction to try criminal matters between Aboriginal people was raised again in *R v Bonjon*.

R v Bonjon

Supreme Court of New South Wales (Willis J) 16 September 1841, Melbourne AILR Vol 3 No 3 1998.

Bonjon, a Wadora man, was charged with the shooting murder of Yammowing, of the Colijon people, at Geelong in Port Phillip. The case was heard before Justice Willis, a single judge of the Supreme Court of New South Wales. Bonjon's council Mr Barry argued that occupation did not give the Crown authority over Indigenous inhabitants as subjects unless there was a treaty or agreement between them and they elected to come under English law. He argued at 417 that: 'Aborigines have their own modes of punishments under their own regulations. Their regulations, like those of all societies, extend to murder. The Aborigines live in self-governing communities. English law then, was not the only law in the colony, and it could not be imposed upon them by terror.' Mr Coke, the Crown prosecutor, argued that it was lawful for a civilised country to occupy the territory of uncivilised persons, so long as they are left land for subsistence. He argued that the Crown brought the law of England to New South Wales and that Aboriginal people are protected by the law and that they are bound to obey it.

Justice Willis starts his considerably longer judgment than those in *Murrell* or *Ballard's* case with reference to the report of the Select Committee of the House of Commons on the Aborigines where British settlements are made of 1834. He emphasised statements from the Report which recognised Aboriginal peoples' civil rights and that Europeans have entered their lands uninvited. Justice Willis cited from the Report at 419:

> Europeans have entered their borders uninvited, and when there, have not only acted as if they were the undoubted lords of the soil, but have punished the natives as aggressors if they evinced a disposition to live in their own country. If they have been found upon their own property (and this is said with reference to the Australian Aborigines) they have been hunted as thieves and robbers—they have been driven back into the interiors as if they were dogs or kangaroos.

Justice Willis then went on to provide a history of the colonisation of New South Wales and he looked comparatively at how 'uncivilised' tribes have been treated in other British colonies. He provided a rendition of Captain Cook's arrival at Botany Bay and then suggested that the numbers, intellect and social organisation of the Aboriginal people were misunderstood. He then provided evidence from the former Attorney-General of New South Wales to the Senate Committee referred to above, which suggested that New South Wales Aborigines had laws which should have been operative. The New South Wales Attorney-General noted that an interpreter could not be found for court hearings and that 'we ought forthwith to begin, at least, to reduce the laws and usages of the Aboriginal tribes to language, print them, and direct our courts of justice to respect these laws in proper cases' at 420. Justice Willis went on to describe his perceptions of Aboriginal languages, culture and ceremonies. He also referred to the illegal attempt by John Batman in 1835 to treat with Aboriginal people for 600,000 acres of land. While he noted how the terms of this illegal agreement were unjust, he also commented that it was to be 'regretted' that the Government had not made a treaty with the Aboriginal people of Port Phillip.

Justice Willis then posed what he perceived to be the central question before him, at 422:

> Whether the Sovereignty thus asserted within the limits defined by the Commission of His Excellency the Governor legally excludes the aborigines, according to the law of nations, as acknowledged and acted upon by the British Government, from the rightful sovereignty and occupancy of a reasonable portion of the soil, and destroys their existence as self-governing communities, so entirely as to place them, with regard to the prevalence of law among themselves, in the unqualified condition of British subjects or whether it has merely reduced them to the state of dependant allies, still retaining their own laws and usages, subject only to such restraints and qualified control as the safety of colonists and protection of the aborigines required, (subject to that right of pre-emption of their lands, which is undoubted) is the point upon which the present question mainly rests.

Justice Willis went on to review overseas authorities including the judgments by Chief Justice Marshall of the US Supreme Court which recognised Indigenous peoples in America as domestic dependant nations. Justice Willis concluded at 425:

> I repeat that I am not aware of any express enactment or treaty subjecting the Aborigines of this colony to English colonial law, and I have shown that the Aborigines cannot be considered as Foreigners in a Kingdom which is their own. From these premises rapidly indeed collected, I am at present strongly led to infer that the Aborigines must be considered and dealt with, until some further provision be made, as distinct though dependant tribes governed among themselves by their own rude laws and customs. If this be so I strongly doubt the propriety of my assuming the exercise of jurisdiction in the case before me.

Justice Willis was aware that the Governor and Chief Justice did not approve of his judgment in *Bonjon's* case. He therefore sent his judgment to the Law Officers of the Crown in London for an opinion. The Colonial Office dealt with his request curtly and it was simply noted that the matter had already been decided in *Murrell's* case. As John Hookey notes, Justice Willis' 'independence of mind was so little appreciated in New South Wales that by June 1843 he was removed from office' (1984: 5).

These nineteenth-century cases, like many of the letters to editors in contemporary newspapers, reflect a diversity of views about the morality and legal consequences of colonisation. They illustrate how legal pluralism, through the recognition of the operation of Aboriginal and Torres Strait Islander laws and customs coexisting with

British law, was considered a possibility. They also illustrate an awareness of the different manner in which colonised minority Indigenous peoples were accorded rights in comparative overseas jurisdictions.

DISCUSSION QUESTION

- In what ways do you think Australia's legal history and contemporary race relations would have been altered if *Ballard* and *Bonjon* rather than *Murrell* were followed as precedent?

Pluralism revisited in the twentieth century

The manner and extent of recognition of Aboriginal and Torres Strait Islander laws and customs by the common law and more broadly in mainstream Australian law have been raised more recently in a number of areas including native title and criminal law (see Chapters 7 and 9). The contemporary significance of questions of the coexistence of Aboriginal and mainstream laws and customs and more broadly the just resolution of the foundations and ongoing basis for colonisation are discussed in Chapters 12, 13, 14 and 15.

In *R v Wedge* [1976] 1 NSWLR 581, Wedge was charged with murder. He claimed that the court had no jurisdiction to hear the matter because he was an Aboriginal person and a member of a sovereign people. Rath J followed the decision in *Murrell's* case and held that upon settlement there was only one sovereign, namely the King of England and only one law, namely English law. Upon settlement, the Aboriginal people in the colony became the subjects of the King and, as such, were not only entitled to the protection of the law but were liable for breaches of the law.

In *Coe v Commonwealth* (1979) 53 ALJR 403, Coe attempted to raise fundamental questions about the basis on which Australia was colonised and the implications which this has for Aboriginal peoples' land and civil rights. Coe claimed that prior to colonisation Aboriginal people enjoyed exclusive sovereignty over Australia and that after conquest their law and ownership of land continued. He sought a declaration restraining the Commonwealth from interfering with Aboriginal possession of lands which they still held and an order for compensation for lands which had been wrongfully taken away. The hearing in the High Court focused on the refusal by Mason J to allow Coe to amend his statement of claim. The Court, with four judges sitting, divided equally as to whether to allow the statement of claim to be amended and so Coe's appeal failed and the substantive issues were not heard. However Gibbs J reiterated the view that Australia's sovereignty could not be challenged in a domestic court. He said at 409:

> If the amended statement of claim intends to suggest either that the legal foundation of the Commonwealth is insecure, or that the powers of the parliament are more limited than is provided in the Constitution, or that there is an Aboriginal nation which has sovereignty over Australia, it cannot be supported … The contention that there is in Australia an Aboriginal nation exercising sovereignty, even of a limited kind, is quite impossible in law to maintain.

This view has been sustained in cases heard after *Mabo (No 2)* where the Crown's absolute title to land rather than sovereignty was successfully challenged. The sovereignty of the Crown, although not challenged by the plaintiffs, was confirmed in *Mabo (No 2)* in 1992. Since *Mabo (No 2)* the High Court's opinion that sovereignty is non-justiciable in a domestic court has been reaffirmed in *Coe v Commonwealth (the Wiradjuri claim)* (1993) 68 ALJR 110, *Walker v New South Wales* (1994) 182 CLR at 45 and *Wik Peoples v Queensland* (1996) 187 CLR 1. In *Walker v New South Wales* Mason J at 48 refers to a statement which he made in *Coe v Commonwealth*:

> *Mabo (No 2)* is entirely at odds with the notion that sovereignty adverse to the Crown resides in the Aboriginal people of Australia. The decision is equally at odds with the notion that there resides in the Aboriginal people a limited kind of sovereignty embraced in the notion that they are a 'domestic dependant nation' entitled to self-government and full rights (save the right of alienation) or that as a free and independent people they are entitled to any rights and interests other than those created or recognised by the laws of the Commonwealth, the State of New South Wales and the common law.

We see in these cases the limited capacity of Australian courts and law to recognise Indigenous peoples' law. This is despite awareness as indicated in *Ballard* and *Bonjon's* cases from a very early time of the possibility of a domestic dependant nation status and subsequently other forms of limited self-determination. International human rights law and indeed domestically our federal system of laws provide examples of how pluralism within the legal system can exist without undermining the Australian state or fracturing what in *Mabo (No 2)* is described as the skeleton of the common law. As discussed in Chapters 13 and 14, recognition of Aboriginal and Torres Strait Islander peoples' prior sovereignty offers an opportunity for just coexistence and reconciliation between Indigenous and non-Indigenous Australians. As discussed above, the High Court has reaffirmed in cases as recent as *Mabo (No 2)* and *Wik Peoples v Queensland* that questions pertaining to Australia's sovereignty are not justiciable in a domestic court. This is perhaps because of a limited conception of sovereignty as singular and indivisible. As discussions with respect to self-determination in Chapter 14 suggest, a complex and nuanced understanding of self-determination has been developed with respect to Indigenous peoples in international law over the past 30 years. These more divisible understandings of a limited exercise of internal jurisdiction had been conceptualised in the 1830s by Chief Justice Marshall of the US Supreme Court. More broadly the idea of nation states as islands of sovereignty no longer holds sway in a globalised and interdependent world. With some flexibility and imagination, Indigenous peoples' prior sovereignty could be recognised in a manner which enhances rather than fractures Australia's democratic system of governance. Such recognition is not precluded by our history or the shaky legal grounds on which Australia was colonised. Rather it provides a way of addressing what clearly was in practice an ambivalent exercise of authority over Aboriginal and Torres Strait Islander peoples in the nineteenth century and offers a way forward in the twenty-first century.

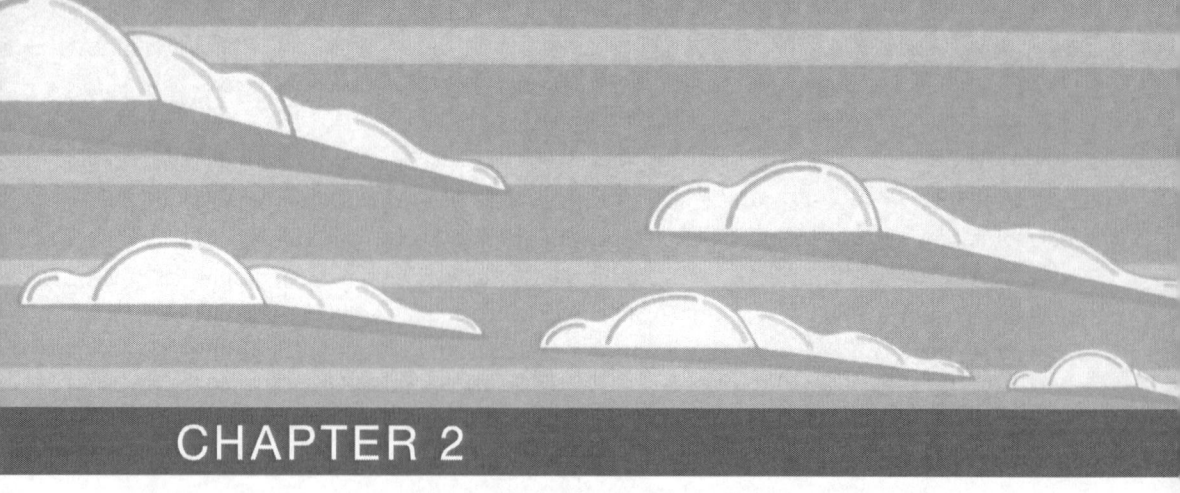

CHAPTER 2

Warfare to Welfare: Genocide to Racial Discrimination

The purpose of this chapter is to provide an understanding of the transformation in the legal relationship between Indigenous people and Anglo-Australian law during the late nineteenth and early twentieth centuries and the entrenchment of racial discrimination which characterised much of the twentieth century.

The chapter begins with a discussion of the 'protection' period and furthers our understanding of how the law was used to entrench racial discrimination and exclusion systematically. The chapter surveys the state policies of protection and the subsequent development of assimilation policies.

The chapter uses a number of case studies to explore the issues of protection and assimilation. Two relatively brief case studies discuss medical exclusions and compulsory examinations, and the restrictions placed on Aboriginal people's right to vote during the period from Federation to the early 1960s. Two more extensive case studies examine the Stolen Generations through the lens of the National Inquiry into the Separation of Aboriginal and Torres Strait Islander Children from Their Families and the management by governments of Indigenous people's money and the Stolen Wages issue.

The protection era

Government policies of 'protection' were introduced at differing times across Australia during the latter part of the nineteenth and the early twentieth centuries. At various times during the early colonial period, measures were taken to 'protect' Aboriginal people. For example in South Australia, there was provision for a 'Protector of Aborigines' from the time of the establishment of the colony in 1836. The role of the Protector was to afford Aboriginal people 'protection in the undisturbed possession of their property rights to such lands as may be occupied in any special manner'. He was also to 'make them friendly to the settlers, induce them to labour, lead them to civilisation and religion' (Rowley 1972a: 77).

Victoria

More comprehensive protection legislation was introduced in Victoria with the *Aborigines Protection Act 1869*. Victoria was the first colonial government to put in place an extensive bureaucratic system for the control of Aboriginal people. The Board for the Protection of Aborigines was given power over 'fullbloods' and 'half castes' habitually associating with 'fullbloods'. The Board could decide where people lived, control their employment and take custody of children. A system of work certificates was introduced and from 1871 wages could be paid to local 'guardians' appointed by the Board (Kidd 2007: 118). By the end of the nineteenth century however, Australian states were introducing far more comprehensive 'protection' legislation which enabled more extensive regulation of the lives of Aboriginal people. A central feature of the regulation of Aboriginal people was their segregation from non-Aboriginal society. It is this far-reaching legislation centred around segregation which is normally referred to as heralding the 'protection era'.

Queensland

The Queensland *Aboriginal Protection and Restriction of the Sale of Opium Act* became law in 1897. This Act remained in place for 40 years and was copied in large part by Western Australia and South Australia which also implemented it in Northern Territory. The legislation defined in strict racial terms who was to be subject to the Act.

4   Every person who is —
   (a)   An aboriginal inhabitant of Queensland; or
   (b)   A half-caste who, at the commencement of this Act, is living with an aboriginal as wife, husband, or child; or
   (c)   A half-caste who, otherwise than as wife, husband, or child, habitually lives or associates with aboriginals;
   shall be deemed to be an aboriginal within the meaning of this Act.

The Act was extensive in its powers over Aboriginal people, including directing where Aboriginal people were to live. Superintendents were placed in charge of reserves and Protectors of Aborigines were established for various districts. Section 31 of the Act enumerated 17 areas of regulation including:

- the manner in which Aborigines were moved to reserves;
- the power of protectors;
- the care, custody and education of children;
- the transfer of orphaned or deserted 'half-caste' children into orphanages;
- the conditions under which children could be placed out to service;
- the maintenance of discipline on reserves and the imprisonment for up to three months of any Aboriginal or 'half-caste' in breach of disciplinary regulations;
- the authorisation for a protector to summarily imprison an Aboriginal or 'half-caste' for up to 14 days for committing a crime or for being grossly insubordinate;
- the prohibition of Aboriginal rites or customs that, in the opinion of the Minister, 'are injurious to the welfare of aboriginals living upon a reserve' and the ambit provision 'for all other matters and things that my be necessary to give effect to this Act'.

As a result of the legislation, the lives of Aboriginal people[1] from birth to death could be controlled by officials. There were no avenues of appeal against these administrative decisions. Legal rights became dependent on racial origin, and were to remain that way for much of the twentieth century (Rowley 1972a: 183).

Western Australia

Early legislation in Western Australia was primarily concerned with the regulation and control of Aboriginal labour. The *Aborigines Protection Act 1886* established the Aborigines Protection Board and provided for management of reserves and some medical care and rations. However the major part of the Act dealt with employment relations.

The *Aborigines Act 1905* was the main 'protection' legislation. It created the new office of Chief Protector and the Aborigines Department. Protectors (who were police officers) were established in various districts. It expanded legislative power over Aboriginal people and had various provisions designed to stop cohabitation between Aboriginal and non-Aboriginal people.

---

1   When the Queensland *Aborigines Protection Act* was first introduced in 1897, it was argued by the Government Resident for the Torres Strait that the Islanders should be exempt from its provisions. The Torres Strait Islands had been annexed by Queensland in the 1870s. By 1904 the control of Torres Strait Islanders passed to the Chief Protector and they became subject to the same legislation as Aboriginal people.

Northern Territory

Prior to 1911 the Northern Territory was administered by South Australia. The first protection legislation was the *Northern Territory Aborigines Act 1910* passed by the South Australian Parliament. The legislation established a Northern Territory Aboriginals Department with a duty to 'exercise a general supervision and care over all matters affecting the welfare of the Aboriginals, and to protect them against injustice, imposition and fraud': s 6(6). A Chief Protector of Aboriginals for the Northern Territory was to be appointed. The Chief Protector was to be the legal guardian of every Aboriginal and every 'half-caste child'. The Chief Protector was given power to confine any Aboriginal or 'half-caste' to an Aboriginal reserve. An Aboriginal woman could not marry a non-Aboriginal man without the written permission of the Chief Protector. Aboriginal people could not be employed without a licence.

The *Aboriginals Ordinance 1911* further extended the powers of the Chief Protector to include the 'care, custody, or control of any aboriginal or half-caste if in his opinion it is necessary or desirable in the interests of the aboriginal or half-caste for him to do so'. Any place could be declared a prohibited area and Aboriginal people could be forbidden to be in such an area.

The legislation clearly allowed for extreme regulation. One historian has given the following example.

> In 1932 Cook [the Chief Protector] required each Aborigine in the Darwin district to be finger printed, subjected to compulsory medical inspection, and issued with a bronze numbered disk, the numbers providing the key to the detailed records kept by government. The disks had a hole in the middle and were supplied with red tape to enable them to be worn around the neck or on a hat. Disks were necessary for admission to picture shows and to make withdrawals from trust accounts (Markus 1990: 100).

Despite the benevolent title of the 'protector' it was always clear in whose interests such regulations were used. Chief Protector Cook had stated that: '... the native actually has become an intruder in a white man's country. Politically the Northern Territory must always be governed as a white man's country, by the white man for the white man' (Markus 1990: 90).

South Australia

The South Australian legislation, the *Aborigines Act*, was introduced in 1911 and was influenced by the earlier legislation in Queensland and Western Australia. It established an Aborigines Department and a Chief Protector to administer it. The duty of the department was to 'exercise a general supervision and care over all matters affecting the welfare of the aboriginals, and to protect them against injustice, imposition and fraud'.

The Chief Protector had wide powers over Aboriginal people and those defined as 'half-caste'. The legislation gave the power to segregate Aboriginal people on reserves.

New South Wales

A protector was appointed in New South Wales in 1881 and a Board for the Protection of Aborigines was established in 1883. The *Aborigines Protection Act* was introduced in 1909. Like the legislation in other states, the 1909 Act provided the legislative power to exert extensive control over the movement and lives of Aboriginal people. Amendments to the legislation (*Aborigines Protection Amending Act 1915* (NSW)) increased the Board's powers to remove Aboriginal children without court supervision and to restrict Aborigines to reserves (*Aborigines Protection Amendment Act 1918* (NSW)).

Much of the administrative power in the legislation derived from the use of regulations. Section 20 of the Act enabled regulations to be made covering an extensive array of social and economic activities. The broad use of regulations was also typical of protection legislation in other states. The use of regulations meant there was no requirement for parliamentary approval. The regulations became law simply through proclamation.

A national system of protection and the intensification of control

By 1911, all states and territories with the exception of Tasmania had passed Protection Acts with an emphasis on segregation and restriction. Aboriginal and Torres Strait Islander people throughout mainland Australia and the Torres Strait had their legal status formally and drastically reduced. No protection legislation was enacted in Tasmania as the official position was that there were no longer any Aborigines living there.

The protection legislation remained intact for the first half of the twentieth century. The legislation had been built on the assumption that Aboriginal people were 'a dying race'. However, by the 1920s, it was apparent that the so-called 'half-caste' population was increasing. For instance in 1929 the Annual Report of the Chief Protector in Western Australia noted the 'increasing half-caste population more than balances the diminishing full-blood people' (cited in Rowley 1972b: 7).

Increasingly the so-called 'half-caste' Aboriginal population became defined as a major social and racial problem that required even more restrictive and racist legislation. In Queensland the *Aboriginals Protection and Restriction of the Sale of Opium Act* was amended in 1934 to make sexual intercourse between an Aboriginal woman and a non-Aboriginal man an offence punishable by six months' imprisonment or a fine of £50.

Protection legislation generally became obsessed with the classification of Indigenous people on the basis of their racial composition, and there was a raft of new or amended protection legislation introduced throughout Australia during the period of the 1930s.

Wearne has described the situation on Queensland reserves at the height of the protection legislation as follows.

> On the reserves, enormous power to control and direct was given by the Act to the superintendent. Aboriginal courts on reserves could consist of the superintendent sitting alone—and he need not have legal training. So broad and ill-defined were his powers that he could hear as an offence almost any matter of which he disapproved. Representation by counsel—a fundamental right, not a privilege, in British law—required the permission of the court (ie the superintendent). Appeal to the visiting Justice against the superintendent's decision would invite almost certain retaliation. The newly established Aboriginal police force, also under the superintendent's control, was wide open to manipulation by him through police 'trusties', and, hence, to abuse of individuals at his direction. His responsibility also extended to the reserve gaol. So not only did the superintendent represent the authority of the Protector/Director; under the Act, he was appointed policeman, judge and gaoler—a situation which completely negates the normal process and principles of justice. Thus residents of reserves were to a very large extent at the mercy of a powerful official who may, or may not, use his wide discretionary authority wisely and justly (Wearne 1980: 15).

The effect of protection policies and their administration was to establish a powerful instrument in the discrimination of Aboriginal people on the basis of their 'race'. Protection legislation racially segregated Aboriginal people from Australian citizens and then proceeded to criminalise certain types of behaviour. For example, the criminalisation of Indigenous people for alcohol offences and their subsequent incarceration began with the introduction of the Western Australian protection legislation in 1905 (Haebich 1992: 110). Typically under the protection legislation, police were given specific powers in relation to Aboriginal people in public places and on reserves. The Queensland legislation allowed for Aboriginal people to be detained in prison indefinitely if they were considered 'uncontrollable'.

Although the Acts were couched in the language of protection, essentially the model for administration and maintenance of control were the institutions of the criminal justice system (often through police as guardians or protectors) and by way of penal sanctions built around the deprivation of liberty. The extensive regulation of the lives of Aboriginal people and the corresponding legislative denial of basic human rights became inextricably linked with the day-to-day administration of Aboriginal affairs. The breadth of discretion afforded superintendents and protectors meant there was 'very little restraint on their exercise of power' (Chesterman and Galligan 1997: 41).

The right to vote

The constitutional issues in relation to Indigenous people are the subject of Chapter 13; here we draw on the issue of the right to vote as a case study in the exclusionary processes in place during much of the twentieth century in Australia. At the time of Federation, both Queensland and Western Australia had legislation in place which explicitly prevented Aboriginal people from voting (*Election Act 1885* (Qld) and *Constitution Acts Amendment Act 1899* (WA)). In New South Wales and Victoria, denying the vote to those residents deemed in receipt of charitable aid such as residents of government stations achieved a similar result (see, for example, *Parliamentary Electorates and Elections Act 1893* (NSW)).

Section 4 of the *Commonwealth Franchise Act 1902* (Cth) expressly barred Aboriginal people from voting in the federal elections:

> No aboriginal native of Australia, Asia, Africa or the Islands of the Pacific except New Zealand shall be entitled to have his name placed on an Electoral Roll unless so entitled under section forty–one of the Constitution.

Entitlement to vote by virtue of s 41 of the Constitution arose where Aboriginal people were entitled to state franchise (for example, Aborigines in South Australia). However, such provisions were nullified in practice when Commonwealth electoral officers removed such franchisees from the electoral rolls (Chesterman and Galligan 1997: 89). The 1902 Act set the Commonwealth legislative paradigm 'with the exclusionary category "aboriginal native" being enshrined throughout subsequent naturalisation and pension legislation' (Chesterman and Galligan 1997: 91).

The *Nationality and Citizenship Act 1948* (Cth) established the legal construct of 'Australian citizen'. Indigenous people by virtue of being born in Australia were automatically entitled to Australian citizenship. However, the Act changed nothing in relation to citizenship rights for Indigenous people: voting restrictions remained as did restrictions on social security entitlements (Chesterman and Galligan 1997: 119). The *Commonwealth Electoral Act 1949* continued to allow Aboriginal people the right to vote in national elections if they were eligible to vote in state elections or had been members of the defence force. Aboriginal people had voting rights in South Australia, Victoria and New South Wales. Restrictions on voting remained in Western Australia, Queensland and the Northern Territory.

Aboriginal activists' tireless struggle for full citizenship rights (see Chapter 13) and mounting domestic and international scrutiny and criticism over Australia's treatment of Aboriginal people provided the momentum for the Menzies Government's decision to initiate a parliamentary inquiry into the extension of the federal vote to all Aborigines (Chesterman 2001: 36–39). In 1961 the parliamentary committee reported its findings and recommended that the federal right to vote be extended immediately to all Aboriginal people in Australia (Chesterman 2001: 39).

The *Commonwealth Electoral Act 1962* withdrew the requirement of enrolment in state elections, thus giving Aboriginal people the right to vote in federal elections irrespective of which state they lived in. Queensland was the last state to give Aboriginal people the right to vote in state elections. Even then the Queensland *Election Acts Amendment Act 1965* exempted Aboriginal people from compulsory enrolment and made it an offence for any person to influence 'a Torres Strait Islander or an Aboriginal Inhabitant of Australia in the free exercise of his choice whether or not to enrol as an elector' (s 26A(3)). McCorquodale has commented on this section of the legislation thus:

> Penalty applies as much to attempts to persuade to enrol as to refrain from so doing.
> A particularly naked and cynical perversion by statute of the right to participate in
> the Western democratic processes (McCorquodale 1987a: 61).

Nationally, voting for Indigenous people was not compulsory and little attempt was made to enrol Indigenous people. It was not until 1983 that Indigenous people had the same voting obligations as non-Indigenous people in Australia.

DISCUSSION QUESTIONS

- What are some of the ways personal, family and social life were controlled under protection legislation? What are the implications for the enjoyment of citizenship rights?
- What are the implications of the exclusion of Aboriginal people from citizenship rights in terms of nation-building, the constitution and sovereignty?

Assimilation and integration

The move towards an 'assimilationist' policy began in the late 1930s. The first Commonwealth–State Native Welfare Conference was held in Canberra in 1937. The meeting was dominated by the protectors of Western Australia (AO Neville), Queensland (JW Bleakley) and the Northern Territory (Dr Cook). The view adopted was that the destiny of non-fullblood Aboriginal people lay in their 'ultimate absorption' into white society (NISATSIC 1997: 32, also Rowley 1972a: 319–321).

The introduction of the policy of assimilation was delayed because of the Second World War. After 1945, policy development occurred at different times—usually when it suited particular state or territory interests. By 1951 all Australian governments at least claimed that they were acting in accordance with an assimilationist policy, and by the 1961 Native Welfare Conference an agreed definition on assimilation was formulated.

> The policy of assimilation means that all Aborigines and part-Aborigines are expected eventually to attain the same manner of living as other Australians and to live as members of a single Australian community enjoying the same rights and privileges, accepting the same responsibilities, observing the same customs and influenced by the same beliefs, as other Australians (cited in Rowley 1972b: 399).

The legislation during the era of 'assimilation' varied greatly from one state to another and often went through a period of transformation between 1940 and 1972, even within particular states. Broadly speaking, however, the legislation touched on similar areas and was based on a similar philosophy regarding the place of Aboriginal people within Australian society. The move to assimilation led to new forms and types of surveillance. For instance in New South Wales, district officers were introduced in the late 1940s to assist and supervise Aboriginal people moving away from the reserves and into towns. District officers focused on Aboriginal households to see whether they performed to the standards and cultural requirements of non-Aboriginal society.

In Western Australia the *Natives (Citizenship Rights) Act 1944* allowed for certain Aboriginal people to be granted citizenship rights. A 'native' could apply for a Certificate of Citizenship if the person could show that they had 'dissolved tribal and native associations for two years prior to the date of application' or were 'otherwise a fit and proper person to obtain a certificate'. The magistrate issuing the certificate had to be satisfied that 'the applicant has adopted the manner and habits of civilised life'. A certificate could be suspended or cancelled by a magistrate upon complaint from the Commissioner of Native Affairs or any other person, or upon conviction for two offences. Such certificates for exemption from the Aboriginal Acts were also available in other states including South Australia, Queensland and New South Wales.

As McCorquodale noted in relation to the Western Australian legislation:

> The Act indicates full supremacist notions of white stereotypes ('civilised life') and of black ('he has dissolved tribal and native association'). It is hard to conceive of any other democracy where two convictions for any offence (eg being on a reserve without permission) could result in loss of citizenship rights. The Act also renders an Aborigine a non-Aborigine upon granting of a certificate, and renders him/her subject to reclassification. The parallels with Nazi Germany … and South Africa are obvious (McCorquodale 1987a: 99).

In Queensland the *Aboriginal and Torres Strait Islander Affairs Act 1965* introduced the principle of assimilation. It replaced the Department of Native Affairs with the

Department of Aboriginal and Islanders Affairs. It also repealed some of the earlier 'protection' provisions. The protector director was no longer the legal guardian of Aboriginal people under 21 years of age, nor was his permission required for marriage. Aboriginal people were given state voting rights and allowed access to liquor off reserves. Superintendents of reserves were now called 'managers'. Police 'protectors' were replaced by 'district officers' who were clerks of the court (who in rural areas were often police). In 1971 the *Aborigines Act* and the *Torres Strait Islander Act* were introduced. Both Acts reiterated the government's policy of assimilation. While the 1971 legislation was an improvement on the 1965 Act, it was still substantially a re-enactment of the earlier legislation in modified terms. Garth Nettheim (1973: 113) noted that the 1971 legislation could be criticised on three broad grounds:

- lack of consultation with the people most directly affected, namely the Aborigines and Islanders themselves;
- excessive delegation by parliament of powers to the administration with inadequate limitations and little real prospect of any effective review; and
- major and minor violations of international human rights standards.

The policy of assimilation was not inconsistent with maintaining discriminatory legislation aimed at controlling Indigenous people. Such legislation could be justified on the grounds of providing the necessary 'tuition' for Aboriginal people to be able to enjoy equality. As Beckett (1988: 23) noted, 'the goal of eventual entry into the community [was used] as a justification for segregating Aborigines on settlements, and the goal of eventual citizenship as justification for curtailing their civil rights'.

Certainly during the decades following 1945, legislation governing Aboriginal and Torres Strait Islander people remained highly restrictive—even if there was a growing espousal of assimilationist philosophy.

Medical exclusions and compulsory examinations

Compulsory medical examinations for Aboriginal people were introduced as part of protection legislation and centred around fears of leprosy. These examinations first began in 1911 in South Australia, and then were extended throughout the 1930s to New South Wales, Queensland and Western Australia (Saggers and Gray 1991: 84). Under ss 24 and 25 of the *Aborigines Act 1911* (SA), special provisions were created for a 'separate system of lock-hospitals and for the segregated treatment of Aborigines within public hospitals as well as for compulsory examinations' (Rowley 1972b: 58). These provisions were retained in both the 1934 and the 1939 Protection Acts. In 1962, the South Australian Parliament passed the *Aboriginal Affairs Act 1962* (SA) which included the power to order those classified as 'Aboriginal' with contagious

CASE STUDY

diseases to undergo medical procedures. These provisions remained in place until 1968 (Chesterman and Galligan 1997: 181, 187). According to Saggers and Gray (1991: 80) health regulations were used until the 1940s to exclude Aboriginal children from Western Australian state schools.

The ability to force Aboriginal people to undergo medical examinations and procedures remained in place until the repeal of the legislation in various states in the 1960s. The idea of compulsory medical examinations has since re-emerged in 2007 in the Northern Territory.

There was resistance to assimilation among the non-Aboriginal community. For example, in New South Wales in February 1940 there was a strike by parents at Collarenebri school against the proposal that 20 Aboriginal children should be admitted as students (Rowley 1972b: 80, see also Goodall 1996). The segregation of Aboriginal people existed in many social activities. Theatres had roped off special sections, hotels refused drinks, hospitals had separate 'wards' (usually the verandah for Aborigines), and Aboriginal women were prohibited from using maternity wards for childbirth.

In her study of Walgett in 1945, Marie Reay noted that, in general, the rationale or ideology behind restricted Aboriginal access to various institutions and leisure activities was usually couched in terms of the claim that Aboriginal people were 'unclean' (Reay 1945: 298). Reay's study of Collarenebri gave a clear indication of the policies of segregation which existed in living areas, entertainment, education, hospitalisation and burial.

> The chief means of entertainment in Collarenebri are the cinema and dancing. Films are shown in a hall built for that purpose, and, in summer in an open air theatre. In both the Aborigines are required to sit in a separate block of seats ... This segregation is ostensibly based on the Aborigines' alleged dirtiness. Aborigines are not permitted to attend dances held in the Town Hall ... Again the exclusion is ostensibly based on hygienic grounds, but the following statement by a middle-aged white woman is probably nearer the true reason: 'We see enough of them in the street without having them at dances, too'. Nevertheless, Aborigines are not permitted to hire the hall for holding dances of their own (Reay 1947: 7–8).

The segregation and denial of civil rights were fought against by Aboriginal people continually during the course of the twentieth century. The establishment of the Australian Aboriginal Progressive Association (AAPA) during the 1920s (Goodall 1996: 149–170), and the Freedom Ride in February 1965 (Perkins 1975) are two examples of this resistance: see Chapter 13 for further discussion.

DISCUSSION QUESTIONS

- What is meant by assimilation?
- Does it imply a new relationship between Aboriginal people and Anglo-Australian law?
- In terms of the rule of law what are some of the continuities and differences between protection and assimilation regimes?

The Stolen Generations

The National Inquiry into the Separation of Aboriginal and Torres Strait Islander Children from Their Families (NISATSIC) was established by the Federal Labor Government in May 1995 and conducted by the Human Rights and Equal Opportunity Commission (HREOC). The Inquiry was the outcome of a long battle for recognition of the issue of forced separations by Indigenous people and their organisations, including SNAICC (Secretariat of the National Aboriginal and Islander Child Care), New South Wales Link-Up, and Aboriginal legal services, particularly in Western Australia and Darwin (D'Souza 1998: 2).

The terms of reference of the Inquiry required that it investigate and assess the effects of past laws, practices and policies which resulted in the separation of Indigenous children from their families by compulsion, duress or undue influence. The Inquiry was also required to examine the adequacy of services available for those affected by separation; to examine the principles relevant to compensation; and to examine current laws, practices and policies with respect to contemporary separations, and advise of changes required taking into account the principle of self-determination.

The effects

The Inquiry estimated that 10 per cent of Indigenous children were removed from their families and communities under state-sanctioned policies and removal practices in Australia between 1910 and 1970 (NISATSIC 1997: 18). Today, most Indigenous families continue to be affected in one or more generations by the forcible removal of children during this time (NISATSIC 1997: 37). The Inquiry considered a number of different effects of the experiences of forced removal.

Separation from primary care giver

Separation from the primary care giver can give rise to problems of attachment and the development of psychiatric disorders. Separation also can affect developmental

CASE STUDY

stages and learning skills, particularly where infants are required to transfer attachment to a large number of ever-changing adults because of institutionalisation and multiple foster parents. These problems also manifest themselves with the ability to develop successful future relationships (NISATSIC 1997: 182–185).

Institutionalisation

The effects of early institutionalisation have been to discourage personal attachments, and to retard intellectual and social development. Institutionalisation made it difficult to develop a sense of self-worth and a sense of personal identity. A common response, particularly for boys, was juvenile offending. Children were regularly told their parents were dead (when they were not), or that the parents had voluntarily given up their children (NISATSIC 1997: 186–192).

Abuse and denigration

Typically for Aboriginal children who were removed their Aboriginality was either hidden and denied, or denigrated. Many of the children were exposed to substandard living conditions and many experienced repeated sexual abuse. A survey by the Western Australian Aboriginal Legal Service of 483 Aboriginal people forcibly removed showed that 62 per cent had been physically abused. Further some one in six witnesses to the Inquiry who had been removed also reported sexual abuse or exploitation (NISATSIC 1997: 194). Racism was also a key part of the denigration—the assimilation policy demanded that children reject their Aboriginality and their families.

Separation from the Indigenous community

The effect of separating Indigenous children from their communities meant the loss of cultural knowledge, the loss of language and the loss of Indigenous identity. It has also prevented or limited Indigenous people who were removed from successfully asserting their native title rights (NISATSIC 1997: 202–211).

The effects on family and community

Forcible separation affected parents and families, as well as the children removed. The traumatisation of having a child forcibly taken, sometimes secretively and often with no further contact possible, was never adequately dealt with for these parents. On a wider level, removals from communities deprived those communities of the right to reproduce and perpetuate themselves.

Inter-generational effects

The effects of removal have been inter-generational as the children who were removed grew up and had their own families—but in a context where they had never experienced a nurturing parental role (NISATSIC 1997: 212–232). The survey by the

Western Australian Aboriginal Legal Service referred to above found that one-third of 483 Aboriginal people forcibly removed subsequently had children of their own removed (NISATSIC 1997: 226).

Self-harm, high rates of suicide, domestic violence, alcohol abuse, depression and mental illness have been the long-term effects of the unresolved grief and trauma caused by the forced removal of Indigenous children.

The findings

The Inquiry found that the basic safeguards which protected non-Indigenous families were cast aside when it came to Indigenous children. The main components of forced removal were deprivation of liberty; deprivation of parental rights; abuses of power; breach of guardianship duties; and violation of international human rights. The Inquiry was careful not to evaluate past actions of government through contemporary values of today. It evaluated the actions of government on the basis of prevailing legal values at the time (NISTASIC 1997: 249).

Deprivation of liberty

In regard to deprivation of liberty, the Inquiry found that 'the taking of Indigenous children from their homes by force and their confinement to training homes, orphanages ... [etc] amounted to deprivation of liberty and [unlawful] imprisonment' (NISATSIC 1997: 253). The safeguard of court scrutiny before detention was denied Indigenous children. Removal was permitted by the order of a public servant at the same time that the removal of non-Indigenous children required a court order.

Deprivation of parental rights

In regard to deprivation of parental rights, it was found that in some jurisdictions legislation stripped Indigenous parents of their parental rights and made a Chief Protector the legal guardian of all Indigenous children. This was contrary to the common law which safeguarded parental rights: a parent could only forfeit their parental rights if a court found misconduct or that state guardianship was in the child's best interest (NISATSIC 1997: 255).

Abuses of power

Although legislation authorised the removal of Indigenous children, some protectors and inspectors resorted to kidnapping or trickery to take the children from their parents. There are many examples of children being taken directly from school or a hospital without their parents' knowledge (NISATSIC 1997: 257). These actions were abuses of power—actions beyond what was authorised by the legislation.

Breach of duty of care and guardianship duties

Furthermore, protectors and protection boards had a duty of care and protection to those over whom they exercised control. The report identifies at least three ways in which guardianship and statutory duties were failed with Indigenous children.

First, there was a failure to provide the contemporary standard of care for Indigenous children to the same level as non-Indigenous children. Although standards of care for non-Indigenous children were far from satisfactory, Indigenous children experienced appalling standards of care—brutal punishments, cold, hunger, fear, sexual abuse, and so forth. Second, there was a failure to protect Indigenous children from harm, from abuse and from exploitation. Many of the children were verbally, physically, emotionally or sexually abused. Third, there was a failure to consult or involve parents in decisions about the child. Many children were falsely told their parents were dead.

Violation of international human rights standards

The main international human rights obligations imposed on Australia and breached by a policy of forced removals were prohibitions on racial discrimination and genocide. The policy of forced removal continued to be practised after Australia had voluntarily subscribed to treaties outlawing both racial discrimination and genocide, which was from the mid-1940s onwards (NISATSIC 1997: 266).

The legislative regimes created for the removal of Indigenous children were different and inferior to those established for non-Indigenous children. They were racially discriminatory and remained in place until 1954 in Western Australia, 1957 in Victoria, 1962 in South Australia, 1964 in Northern Territory and 1965 in Queensland. In addition, government officials knew they were in breach of international legal obligations (NISATSIC 1997: 270). The Inquiry found that the policy of forcible removal of Indigenous children could be properly called genocide and breached international law at least from December 1946 when the United Nations General Assembly adopted a resolution declaring genocide already a crime under international law (NISATSIC 1997: 275). The Inquiry found that there was the requisite intention to commit genocide and that a process to carry out the genocide was put in place, namely the forcible transfer of children from one population to another.

> Official policy and legislation for Indigenous families and children was contrary to accepted legal principle imported into Australia as British common law and, from late 1946, constituted a crime against humanity. It offended accepted standards of the time and was the subject of dissent and resistance. The implementation of the legislation was marked by breaches of fundamental obligations on the part of officials and others to the detriment of vulnerable and dependent children whose parents were powerless to know their whereabouts and protect them from exploitation and abuse (NISATSIC 1997: 275).

In summary, the Inquiry found that the policy of forced removal of Indigenous children was contrary to prohibitions on racial discrimination and genocide, and was contrary to accepted legal principle found in the common law. Finally, the removals had led to other forms of criminal victimisation including widespread sexual and physical assault (NISATSIC 1997: 277–278).

The Inquiry made 54 recommendations and these were based on the principle of reparation. The approach of the Inquiry was to consider international provisions for responding to and redressing gross violations of human rights (NISATSIC 1997: 278–280) (see Chapter 4). In summary, the main recommendations centred around:

- acknowledgment and apology
- guarantees against repetition
- measures of restitution
- measures of rehabilitation, and
- monetary compensation.

The Inquiry recommended that reparation be available for all who suffered because of forcible removal including the individuals who were removed, family members who suffered, communities that suffered cultural and community disintegration, and the descendants of those forcibly removed. For further discussion of the recommendations and the former Howard Government responses, see Cunneen and Libesman (2000a), and the Senate Legal and Constitutional References Committee (2000).

DISCUSSION QUESTION

- What are the implications of child removal policies for Aboriginal understandings of the rule of law?

Stolen Wages

CASE

Throughout the nineteenth and twentieth centuries, various Australian governments put in place legislative and administrative controls over the employment, working conditions and wages of Indigenous workers. These controls allowed for the non-payment of wages to some workers, the underpayment of wages, and the diversion of wages into trust and savings accounts. In December 2006 the Senate Standing

Committee on Legal and Constitutional Affairs released the report of its inquiry into what has become known as Indigenous 'Stolen Wages'. The Committee found:

> ... compelling evidence that governments systematically withheld and mismanaged Indigenous wages and entitlements over decades. In addition, there is evidence of Indigenous people being underpaid or not paid at all for their work. These practices were implemented from the late 19th century onwards and, in some cases, were still in place in the 1980s. Indigenous people have been seriously disadvantaged by these practices across generations (Senate Standing Committee on Legal and Constitutional Affairs 2006: 4).

Typically state protection legislation set out controls on Indigenous workers whereby they could only be employed under a permit granted by a protector. Minimum wages were set for Indigenous workers with a permit. For example in Queensland the wage was set at less than one-eighth the 'white wage'. Protectors could instruct the employer to pay the wages of the Indigenous worker directly to the protector. Monies held by the protector were to be deposited in the worker's name in a government bank account where accounts of expenditure were to be kept. Some small percentage of the worker's wage could be given to the worker as pocket money, either by the employer or the protector. In Queensland further deductions could be taken from the wages of Indigenous workers to be placed in an Aboriginal Provident Fund (later the Aboriginal Welfare Fund) which was established for the 'relief of natives'.

In the Northern Territory protectors could direct an employer to pay a portion of Aboriginal workers' wages to the protector to be subsequently held in a trust account. However, it was also the case that after 1933 employers of Aboriginal workers could be exempted from paying *any* wages if the protector was satisfied the employer was maintaining the relatives and dependants of the Aboriginal employee.

In New South Wales the focus of control of the Aborigines Protection Board was the apprenticeship (or indenture) of Aboriginal children. The power of the Board to apprentice Aboriginal children 'on such terms and conditions as it may think under the circumstances of the case are desirable' continued until 1969 (cited in Senate Standing Committee on Legal and Constitutional Affairs 2006: 15). The protection legislation established the wages for Aboriginal apprentices and directed that a small percentage be given as pocket money to the apprentice and the remainder go into a trust account to be paid out to the apprentice at the end of their apprenticeship.

The Commonwealth Government also controlled Indigenous people's access to money through social security provisions.

> For the most part, Aboriginal people were prohibited from receiving allowances, such as the child endowment payment, maternity allowance and old-age pension, when they were first introduced. Subsequent amendments to legislation meant that, although an Aboriginal person may have been entitled to a payment, there was

provision for the allowance to be paid 'indirectly' to a third party, such as a mission or a government authority, on their behalf. In some cases, evidence suggests that social security entitlements were re-directed into trust accounts administered by state government Aboriginal welfare authorities (Senate Standing Committee on Legal and Constitutional Affairs 2006: 30).

Indigenous entitlement to various social security provisions was limited and conditional. For example, 'nomadic' Aboriginal people were not entitled to child endowment (which was introduced in 1941) until the restrictions were removed in 1966. Maternity allowances were introduced in 1912, but specifically excluded 'women who are Asiatics, Aboriginal natives of Australia, Papua or the Islands of the Pacific' (Senate Standing Committee on Legal and Constitutional Affairs 2006: 34). The 1942 maternity allowance legislation continued to exclude 'nomadic' or 'primitive' mothers until the provisions were repealed in 1966.

For those Aboriginal people who were entitled to child endowment, state governments diverted the funds. For example, Queensland had its missions and settlements defined as 'institutions' so that bulk quarterly endowment payments were received on behalf of settlement mothers. State government grants to the missions and settlements were reduced by the amount of the incoming endowment revenue (Senate Standing Committee on Legal and Constitutional Affairs 2006: 31). Similar diversion of entitlements occurred with maternity allowances, invalid, old age and widows' pensions.

There is evidence that on pastoral stations in Western Australia and the Northern Territory, the station itself received child endowment, old age and other pensions 'on behalf' of Aboriginal employees and their families. These were regarded as a form of station subsidy.

The Inquiry found that governments had put in place compulsory regimes for the regulation of Indigenous money, including compulsory contributions to savings and trust fund accounts. However, governments failed to ensure that Indigenous people received the money they were entitled to, and failed to ensure that the savings and trust fund accounts were properly protected from misappropriation and fraud (Senate Standing Committee on Legal and Constitutional Affairs 2006: 41).

> Misuse of money included misappropriation by governments, fraud by protectors and employers, and non-payment or underpayment of wages by employers. Although the protection boards, protectors and governments were under obligations to keep proper records and account for all Indigenous monies, these obligations were often not complied with (Senate Standing Committee on Legal and Constitutional Affairs 2006: 49).

Examples of misappropriation of Indigenous money included in Queensland using Indigenous savings accounts and trust funds to pay for expenses related to the administration and maintenance of reserves, such as infrastructure costs. In South Australia money was used to pay rent back to the government authority, for medical expenses, clothes and other items.

The Senate Standing Committee on Legal and Constitutional Affairs received many allegations of fraud and noted the difficulty of proving these allegations. However, the Committee also noted the widespread and long-running nature of the complaints concerning fraud and the poor administration of the finances of Indigenous people under various Protection Acts. In Queensland the government commissioned an independent report on the Stolen Wages issue in 1991. The report noted that until 1965 control mechanisms in the Savings Bank were ineffective in guarding against errors, fraud and misappropriation. 'Large frauds on the Savings Bank were detected from time to time, and the Department admitted that, even in these cases, the extent of the fraud could only be reliably determined by the admissions of the persons involved in the frauds' (Senate Standing Committee on Legal and Constitutional Affairs 2006: 52). In the early part of the twentieth century police fraud of the accounts was debated in parliament and a thumb-printing and witnessing procedure was introduced to try and safeguard against fraudulent practices. In the Northern Territory a 1919 Royal Commission into the administration of the territory showed the ease with which Aboriginal trust funds could be defrauded (Senate Standing Committee on Legal and Constitutional Affairs 2006: 76). In New South Wales there were two investigations in the late 1930s which considered the management of Indigenous monies (Senate Standing Committee on Legal and Constitutional Affairs 2006: 74).

In addition to misappropriation of Indigenous money and the commission of fraud, there was also the non-payment and underpayment of wages to Indigenous workers. The Committee noted that 'by far most evidence' of mismanagement related to this issue. In Queensland the government was well aware at least from the 1930s to the 1960s that Indigenous workers were not receiving their 'pocket money'. Indeed the government rejected the auditor's recommendations to tighten controls on the system (Senate Standing Committee on Legal and Constitutional Affairs 2006: 55). In New South Wales, Aboriginal apprentices often were not paid their savings when they reached the age of 21.

The effects of the Stolen Wages of Indigenous people and subsequent immiseration arising from this exploitation, are fundamental to understanding the contemporary situation of Indigenous people in Australia. The submission to the Inquiry by the historian Anna Haebich begins to capture some of the long-term impacts:

> Aboriginal people played a major role in building the [Western Australian] state economy ... It was the state government's discriminatory employment system that prevented Aboriginal workers from benefiting from the Australian labour system, which was hailed around the world as an exemplary model for protecting worker's wages and rights. Instead, Aboriginal people were subject to a disabling system

which denied them proper wages, protection from exploitation and abuse, proper living conditions, and adequate education and training. So while other Australians were able to build financial security and an economic future for their families, Aboriginal workers were hindered by these controls. Aboriginal poverty in Western Australia today is a direct consequence of this discriminatory treatment (cited in Senate Standing Committee on Legal and Constitutional Affairs 2006: 68).

The inter-generational impact of government policy in the realm of financial controls over Indigenous people is probably as great as the impact of the policies of Aboriginal child removal. Indeed the control of Indigenous labour and its exploitation at times were directly connected to the removal of children—such as in the case of Indigenous child apprentices and domestic workers in New South Wales.

There are many barriers to Indigenous people receiving compensation. Records and files have been lost or are missing, and the complexity and number of records involved in trying to piece together information for any one individual is daunting. It has become clear in Western Australia, Queensland and New South Wales that many records are either missing or were never created. For example, in Western Australia, the Aboriginal Legal Service estimated that as a result of archival destruction some 21 per cent of the 15,400 personal dossier files created between 1926 and 1959 have been deliberately destroyed (Senate Standing Committee on Legal and Constitutional Affairs 2006: 84).

DISCUSSION QUESTIONS

- What issues do Stolen Wages raise in relation to government's administration of Indigenous affairs?
- What legal remedies might be available?

Genocide in Australia

The genocide of Indigenous people in Australia is a contentious matter that involves both historical and legal issues. The United Nations Convention on the Prevention and Punishment of the Crime of Genocide 1948 was ratified by Australia on 8 July 1949 and entered into force on 12 January 1951. There is no Australian domestic legislation implementing the Genocide Convention. The definition of genocide in Article II of the Convention is as follows:

Genocide means any of the following acts committed with intent to destroy, in whole or in part, a national, ethnical, racial or religious group, as such:

(a)   Killing members of the group;

(b)   Causing serious bodily or mental harm to members of the group;

(c)   Deliberately inflicting on the group conditions of life calculated to bring about its physical destruction in whole or in part;

(d)   Imposing measures intended to prevent births within the group;

(e)   Forcibly transferring children of the group to another group.

In *Kruger v Commonwealth* (1997) 190 CLR 1, the plaintiffs claimed that the *Aboriginal Ordinance 1918* (NT) violated an implied constitutional right of freedom from genocide. The High Court found there was no such implied constitutional right (see also Chapter 13). Only Gaudron J expressly acknowledged that the acts encompassed in the definition of genocide were 'so fundamentally abhorrent to the principles of the common law' that the Commonwealth's power to pass such laws might be constrained. All six justices held that in authorising the removal and detention of Aboriginal children, the *Aboriginal Ordinance* did not authorise acts of genocide as defined in the Convention. The intention of the Ordinance was beneficial. The question before the Court was whether the Ordinance authorised genocide, not whether acts undertaken were in fact genocidal.

In *Nulyarimma v Thompson* (1999) 96 FCR 153, the Full Federal Court considered an appeal from an earlier decision where a charge of genocide against the then Prime Minister John Howard and others had been dismissed. The charge arose from their support for the 1998 Native Title amendments. The second situation considered in *Nulyarimma* arose from a charge against the Commonwealth and others for genocide relating to the failure to proceed with a World Heritage listing of lands of the Arabunna people. The majority of the Federal Court found that the international crime of genocide was not incorporated into Australian domestic law. Merkel J (dissenting) found that international customary law on genocide formed part of the common law. The Federal Court also found that the plaintiffs had not proved the necessary intention to commit genocide. In particular it was found that cultural genocide falls outside the definition of genocide.

Both *Nulyarimma* and *Kruger* confirmed that genocide is not a crime under Australian common law (Saul 2000). Furthermore, the proof of intention will be key to any successful argument of genocide. This was further confirmed in the *Sumner* case argued in the South Australia Supreme Court in relation to the Ngarrindjeri people and the construction of the Hindmarsh Island Bridge: *Sumner v United Kingdom of Great Britain* [2000] SASC 91.

As noted above, the National Inquiry into the Separation of Aboriginal and Torres Strait Islander Children from Their Families found that removal policies constituted genocide. The forced transfer of children was defined in the Genocide Convention as constituting physical genocide and not as cultural genocide (NISATSIC 1997: 271–273; Storey 1997: 13). In addition to being a prescribed act in the Convention, the forced transfer of children was undertaken with the intent to destroy the particular group. The fact that protectors and administrators may have believed that the 'breeding out' of Aboriginality through forced removal of children was in the best interests of the children, and a historical and scientifically based inevitability, does not preclude a determination that the actions amounted to genocide (NISASTIC 1997: 273–274; Storey 1998: 13).

However, one of the problems with the NISATSIC analysis is the failure to distinguish between the pre-1945 policy of 'breeding out' Aboriginality and the post-War period of assimilation. Indeed one of the Inquiry's Commissioners, Sir Ronald Wilson, was to state later: 'I think it was a mistake to use the word genocide … once you latch onto the term "genocide", you're arguing about the intent and we should never have used it' (*The Bulletin*, 12 June 2001, p 27).

As we argue in the next chapter, this does not effect an argument for compensation or reparation. One might argue that there was no evidence that forcible child removal was a genocidal policy at any time in Australian history and still not undermine the argument for reparation. Essentially the justification relies on several planks: the breach of common law duties; the breach of statutory duties; criminal actions; and the breach of international human rights standards. Each of these 'planks' is itself comprised of different duties and obligations, breaches of which might give rise to redress.

Australian historians have also considered the issue of genocide within the context of colonisation and frontier violence (Moses 2005). Moses considers the development of a genocidal government policy in Queensland during the latter half of the nineteenth century. At the forefront of this policy was the Native Police (see Chapter 1). The use of the Native Police as part of government terror 'transformed local genocidal massacres by settlers into an official state-wide policy' (Moses 2000: 102). In relation to the removal of Aboriginal children, it has been Manne's (2001, 2005) argument that the genocidal moment in Australian policy was during the 1930s and culminating in the 1937 Commonwealth–State conference referred to earlier in this chapter. At this moment, 'genocidal thought and administrative practice touched' (Manne 2001: 40).

DISCUSSION QUESTIONS

- Should we distinguish between intention and motive in genocide? Can mixed motives lead to genocide?
- Was destruction of Indigenous people's culture, and therefore a genocidal effect, inevitable?
- What is ethnocide? How does it differ from genocide?

Conclusion

In summarising the periods of protection and assimilation, the Royal Commission into Aboriginal Deaths in Custody found:

> Aboriginal people [were denied] the right to live by their own rules, to decide on their own policies. They were denied the freedom to run their own economic and family life. They were also denied the right to own land, to earn a secure living as farmers, merchants, or in the labour market at their own discretion, to earn a family wage, to receive welfare benefits, to live where they pleased. Under various policies their private, reproductive lives were under scrutiny by government and missionary officials. They could not necessarily marry the person they chose, fraternise with people of their choice, speak to people of a certain colour skin, live in a particular street or on a particular reserve. They could not decide how many people they shared their house with. They were not eligible for old age pension, for workers compensation, for maternity allowances or for child endowment. Even when legislation on such matters changed in the 1940s and 1950s, it was often the manager of the mission or reserve rather than the individual who was paid this money. They could not run their own bank accounts. Anyone who objected could end up exiled hundreds of kilometres away or imprisoned for an unknown time (Johnston 1991: (2) 518).

The late nineteenth and twentieth centuries saw the suspension of the rule of law and the denial of basic citizenship rights in relation to Indigenous people in Australia. There was extensive regulation of Indigenous people and the active disruption of familial, social and cultural life—generally conducted in the name of racially defined and discriminatory policies. Although firmly located within the boundaries of Anglo-Australian law, Indigenous people did not enjoy the protections, rights and benefits bestowed on other subjects and citizens.

Ostensibly law and policy sought to protect and to assimilate Aboriginal people in their own best interests. Yet the reality of government administration was one where the interests of Aboriginal people were barely visible. The protection and assimilation policies and the specific case studies presented here in relation to stolen children and stolen money show the fraud, the misappropriation, the abuse of powers and the widespread use of institutions and penal sanctions lay at the heart of colonial policy.

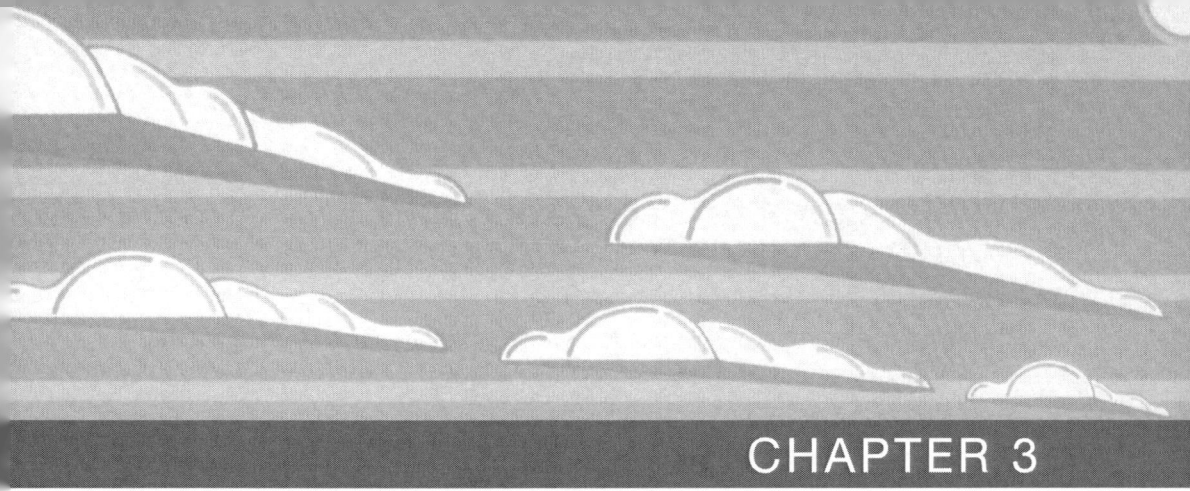

CHAPTER 3

Reparation and Redress

The purpose of this chapter is to consider the issues of reparation and redress for the historical injustices outlined in previous chapters. In particular we explore the potentials and the limitations of the law in addressing injustices that have arisen as a consequence of the colonial experience. The chapter considers two examples in particular: the attempt by the Stolen Generations to receive compensation by way of litigation, and the processes established to provide compensation for stolen wages and missing trust funds. The chapter begins by raising the question of contemporary responsibility for past injustices, the nature of those injustices and the international human rights context for responding to historical injustices and gross violations of human rights.

Justifications for reparation and compensation

Our understanding of whether there is a sense of responsibility for the past and for historical injustices fundamentally affects our view on whether compensation and reparation are necessary or appropriate. There are many possible justifications for reparation and compensation and these include obligations which may be historical, moral or legal. We derive a particular social identity from our family, our community, our nation. We acquire joint commitments as members of more enduring plural entities like nations. Since a nation is an ongoing, intergenerational, plural subject, joint commitment means sharing responsibility for its past. These responsibilities are trans-individual because we are a product of these broader social relations and commitments, and trans-generational because the obligations exist over time.

> [The] justification for historical obligations is grounded in a conception of society or nation as an intergenerational community. Its institutions and moral relationships persist over time and through a succession of generations, and it depends for its moral and political integrity on its members accepting trans-generational obligations and honouring historical entitlements ... Members of such societies make, or think that they would be justified in making, moral demands on their successors. For example, they, or those who represent them, make commitments that are supposed to be binding on posterity and they think that their successors ought to honour those commitments (Thompson 2002: xviii).

There are many specific moral and legal obligations for reparation for historical injustices that relate to the circumstances and context of the specific injustice. For example, there may be legal obligations that arise from treaties which were signed generations previously. These obligations are based on legal assumptions about the binding nature of a contract or promise—they are binding on future generations of citizens of the state parties. The Treaty of Waitangi in New Zealand is an example of a treaty signed with Indigenous people in the nineteenth century which has force today through the Waitangi Tribunal (Ward 1999). Obligations might also arise from historical title, for example a persisting entitlement to land which demands a process for return or compensation. Recognition of native title could be considered in this light (see Chapter 9). Responsibility for past wrongs might also arise because of current benefits derived from past wrongs. This is an argument about unjust enrichment which means that current beneficiaries of a past injustice have a legal obligation for reparation or compensation. This argument has been used in the USA in relation to reparation for slavery (Robinson 2001; Westley 1998).

As we demonstrated in the previous chapter, during the period of protection legislation and the post-1945 assimilation period, there were numerous legislative controls placed on Indigenous peoples which were basic violations of human rights and related to the view that Aboriginal people were a racially distinct and inferior group. These included restrictions on movement, residence, education, health care, employment, voting, and welfare/social security entitlements. Prior to the introduction of the *Racial Discrimination Act 1975* (Cth), these actions were not unlawful by domestic legal standards. However, they were racially discriminatory, offended international human rights principles and there is an arguable moral obligation for reparation. In addition to these legislative controls, there were at times negligent, corrupt and dishonest practices by those who were responsible for the administration of Indigenous affairs. There were a number of massacres of Aboriginal people in central Australia and the Kimberleys in the early part of the twentieth century. The survivors and descendants of these atrocities also arguably have a case for reparation and compensation.

Justifications for reparation and compensation to the Stolen Generations

There are a number of arguments which might justify reparations to the Stolen Generations. These include:

Moral responsibility

As noted in the previous chapter the effects of forcible removal gave rise to institutionalisation, abuse and denigration, separation from parents and removal from the Indigenous community, and inter-generational negative effects on individuals, families and communities. These negative effects arose as a direct consequence of government policy and practice. It has been argued that 'the consequences of removal and their continuing effects on the well-being of Indigenous communities raise a moral obligation on governments to make meaningful and adequate reparations' (PIAC 2000: 10).

Promoting social justice and equality of outcomes

The evidence shows that those who were removed were generally worse off in relation to social, economic, health, education and criminal justice indicators compared to other Indigenous Australians who were not removed (NISATSIC 1997: 12–16). In this context reparations might be seen in line with successive federal government attempts to promote social justice outcomes for Indigenous people.

CASE STUDY

Violations of international human rights and common law rights

The NISATSIC found that forcible removal involved breaches of a number of basic human rights including prohibitions against genocide and racial discrimination. Forcible removal also breached common law rights including prohibitions against deprivation of liberty; deprivation of parental rights; abuses of power and breach of guardianship duties. It could be argued that reparation is a way of remedying these wrongs as an alternative to litigation.

Reconciliation

It has been argued that reconciliation requires adequate redress for past wrongs. The former Governor-General Sir William Deane stated in the inaugural Lingiari lecture in 1996, that:

> The present plight ... of so many Aborigines must be acknowledged as largely flowing from what happened in the past ... Theoretically, there could be national reconciliation without any redress at all of the dispossession and other wrongs sustained by the Aborigines. As a practical matter, however, it is apparent that recognition of the need for appropriate redress for present disadvantage flowing from past injustice and oppression is a pre-requisite of reconciliation (cited in NISATSIC 1997: 4).

DISCUSSION QUESTION

- Do current generations have responsibility to redress past wrongs?

Developing international law principles on reparation

The process of developing principles and guidelines on the right to reparation for victims of violations of international human rights law has been gaining momentum for more than a decade and a half. It is uncontroversial, in international or domestic law, to state that a where a right has been violated it should be remedied. However, the questions of 'who' and 'how' with respect to violations of international human rights law have always been difficult.

The Bassiouni-Van Boven principles have developed in response to these important questions of how to provide remedy and repair to victims of gross abuses of human rights. It is expected that these principles will be adopted eventually by the United Nations General Assembly. The Van Boven principles were first developed in the 1990s—these were the principles that were utilised by the NISATSIC (1997: 280–283).

In 1998 the Commission on Human Rights appointed Bassiouni to further revise the principles developed by Van Boven taking into account the views and concerns expressed by states, inter-governmental and non-governmental organisations. His final report was submitted in 2000 and forms the Basic Principles and Guidelines on the Right to Remedy and Reparation for Victims of Violations of International Human Rights and Violations of Humanitarian Law.

The Bassiouni Principles and Guidelines cover:

- matters relating to victims (for example a victim can be a person or collective group);
- removing legislative barriers (for example, statutes of limitations should not unduly restrict the ability of a victim to pursue a claim against a perpetrator);
- removing procedural barriers (for example, the legal or administrative procedures designed to provide justice and reparation should avoid the retraumatisation of victims);
- providing access to justice (for example, facilitating victims' ability to utilise remedies);
- ensuring non-discrimination (for example, ensuring that victims are not discriminated against on the basis of race or gender); and
- providing reparations (see below).

The bulk of the Bassiouni Principles and Guidelines address the right to adequate, effective and prompt reparation. Ultimate responsibility for reparation lies with states; a state is to provide reparation for its own violations and in the event that another party is responsible and unwilling or unable to meet their obligations to repair, the state should endeavour to provide assistance, including reparation.

The basic purpose of reparation is to promote justice and the basic principle underpinning the quantum of reparation is a proportional response to the gravity of the violations and the harms that have been caused. The forms of reparation are restitution, compensation, rehabilitation and satisfaction and guarantees of non-repetition.

Restitution

Restitution should, whenever possible, restore the victim to the original situation. Restitution can include the restoration of social status, identity, return to one's place of residence, restoration of employment and return of property (Principle 22).

Compensation

Compensation should be provided for any economically assessable damage: physical or mental harm, including pain, suffering and emotional distress; lost opportunities, including employment, education and social benefits; material damages and loss of earnings; harm to reputation or dignity; and costs required for legal or expert assistance, medicines and medical services, and psychological and social services (Principle 23).

Rehabilitation

Rehabilitation should include, as appropriate, medical and psychological care as well as legal and social services (Principle 24).

Satisfaction and guarantees of non-repetition

Satisfaction and guarantees of non-repetition include cessation of continuing violations, verification of the facts and full public disclosure of the truth, the search for the whereabouts of the disappeared; apology, including public acknowledgment of the facts and acceptance of responsibility; commemorations and tributes to the victims; and inclusion of an accurate account of the violations that occurred in educational material at all levels (Principle 25).

DISCUSSION QUESTION

* What particular legal problems might be posed by reparations?

The apology to the Stolen Generations

An essential part of reparations is an acknowledgment and apology for past wrongs. A national apology was one of the key recommendations from the NISATSIC report, and was steadfastly refused for a decade under the Howard Government (Cunneen and Libesman 2000a). One of the first acts of the Rudd Labor Government was to issue an apology on behalf of the Australian Parliament to the Stolen Generations.

> Today we honour the Indigenous peoples of this land, the oldest continuing cultures in human history.
>
> We reflect on their past mistreatment.
>
> We reflect in particular on the mistreatment of those who were Stolen Generations—this blemished chapter in our nation's history.

The time has now come for the nation to turn a new page in Australia's history by righting the wrongs of the past and so moving forward with confidence to the future.

We apologise for the laws and policies of successive Parliaments and governments that have inflicted profound grief, suffering and loss on these our fellow Australians.

We apologise especially for the removal of Aboriginal and Torres Strait Islander children from their families, their communities and their country.

For the pain, suffering and hurt of these Stolen Generations, their descendants and for their families left behind, we say sorry.

To the mothers and the fathers, the brothers and the sisters, for the breaking up of families and communities, we say sorry.

And for the indignity and degradation thus inflicted on a proud people and a proud culture, we say sorry.

We the Parliament of Australia respectfully request that this apology be received in the spirit in which it is offered as part of the healing of the nation.

For the future we take heart; resolving that this new page in the history of our great continent can now be written.

We today take this first step by acknowledging the past and laying claim to a future that embraces all Australians.

A future where this Parliament resolves that the injustices of the past must never, never happen again.

A future where we harness the determination of all Australians, Indigenous and non-Indigenous, to close the gap that lies between us in life expectancy, educational achievement and economic opportunity.

A future where we embrace the possibility of new solutions to enduring problems where old approaches have failed.

A future based on mutual respect, mutual resolve and mutual responsibility.

A future where all Australians, whatever their origins, are truly equal partners, with equal opportunities and with an equal stake in shaping the next chapter in the history of this great country, Australia.

Prime Minister Rudd, Parliament of Australia, 13 February 2008

The Prime Minister's speech at the time of the apology clearly acknowledged that governments were responsible for the policies that led to the forced removal of Indigenous children. He stated:

The uncomfortable truth for us all is that the parliaments of the nation, individually and collectively, enacted statutes and delegated authority under those statutes that made the forced removal of children on racial grounds fully lawful ... We, the parliaments of the nation, are ultimately responsible, not those who gave effect to our laws, the problem lay with the laws themselves. As has been said of settler societies elsewhere, we are the bearers of many blessings from our ancestors and therefore we must also be the bearer of their burdens as well (http://www.pm.gov.au/media/Speech/2008/speech_0073.cfm)

Redress through litigation: Stolen Generations

One strategy in the search for legal remedies for the Stolen Generations has been through the use of litigation. Many of the claims by members of the Stolen Generations seek to establish civil liability through a variety of causes of action including negligence, breach of fiduciary and/or statutory duties as well as wrongful imprisonment. Exceptions to this include Valerie Linow's application for criminal compensation before the New South Wales Victims' Compensation Tribunal and the *Kruger* plaintiffs, who claimed that the Northern Territory Aboriginals Ordinance violated certain constitutional rights. With the exceptions of Linow and Trevorrow, these claims have been unsuccessful. We briefly review the major cases. For more extensive discussion see Cunneen and Grix (2004).

Joy Williams

In 1993, Joy Williams commenced proceedings against the New South Wales Government claiming damages for negligence, wrongful imprisonment and breach of fiduciary duty. In addition, an application was made under the *Limitation Act 1969* (NSW) for an order extending the time within which proceedings could be commenced. Initially the court declined to extend the limitation period on the grounds that it was 'neither just nor reasonable' to do so (*Williams v Minister, Aboriginal Land Rights Act 1983* (unreported) at [36]), although this decision was subsequently reversed by a majority of the New South Wales Court of Appeal: *Williams v Minister, Aboriginal Land Rights Act 1983 (No 1)* (1994) 35 NSWLR 497.

Williams alleged that the Aborigines Welfare Board (AWB) had committed trespass in taking her to and keeping her at the Bomaderry Children's Home. She was four weeks old at the time. She further alleged that the AWB had failed to adequately supervise her during her residence at the Bomaderry and Lutanda Children's Homes. Had the AWB provided adequate supervision during this time, they would have been alerted to the fact that her behaviour was exhibiting symptoms of an attachment disorder and as such, she would have been referred to a Child Guidance Clinic. Child Guidance Clinics were available at that time and employed suitably qualified professionals to work with and treat disturbed and/or difficult children (Cody 2001: 156). There was also evidence that she had not received any 'visits, letters or supervision' from the AWB in the 12 years that she lived at the Lutanda Children's Home (Cody 2001: 156). Joy Williams alleged that in the absence of appropriate treatment and care for her welfare, she developed the psychiatric disorder, Borderline Personality Disorder.

Joy Williams alleged that the conduct of the AWB placed it in breach of a duty of care, in breach of a statutory duty and in breach of a fiduciary duty to her. In addition, these breaches had caused her losses and damage for which the defendants were liable. Evidence was provided as to her experiences after leaving the Lutanda Children's Home. These included periods of unemployment, substance abuse, psychiatric care and imprisonment. She further alleged that her own lack of parenting had resulted in an inability to form relationships and to raise her three children. The plaintiff claimed damages by way of economic loss, general damages and exemplary or aggravated damages.

Abadee J found against the plaintiff in all areas, and ordered costs against her: *Williams v Minister, Aboriginal Land Rights Act 1983 (No 2)* (1999) 25 Fam LR 86 (*Williams No 2*). The New South Wales Court of Appeal upheld the decision: *Williams v Minister Aboriginal Land Rights Act and State of New South Wales (No 3)* (2000) Aust Torts Reports ¶ 81-578 (*Williams No 3*).

Lorna Cubillo and Peter Gunner

In 1996, Lorna Cubillo and Peter Gunner each commenced proceedings against the Commonwealth in the High Court claiming damages for wrongful imprisonment and deprivation of liberty, negligence, breach of statutory duty and breach of fiduciary duty. In addition, an order was sought pursuant to s 44 of the *Limitation of Action Act 1981* (NT) extending the time within which proceedings could be commenced. The proceedings were subsequently remitted to the Federal Court and the parties consented to having the matters heard together.

In response, the Commonwealth filed a notice of motion seeking summary dismissal of both actions. On 30 April 1999, O'Loughlin J delivered an interlocutory judgment in which he declined to make the orders sought by the Commonwealth. In doing so, he remarked: '… these cases are of such importance—not only to the individual applicants and to the larger Aboriginal community, but also to the nation as a whole—that nothing short of a determination on the merits … is warranted': *Cubillo v Commonwealth* (1999) 89 FCR 528 at [203].

The plaintiffs' closing submission sets out the basis of their claim:

> By the actions of the Commonwealth, Lorna Cubillo and Peter Gunner were removed as young children from their families and communities. They were taken hundreds of kilometres from the countries of their birth. They were prevented from returning. They were made to live among strangers, in a strange place, in institutions which bore no resemblance to a home. They lost, by the actions of the Commonwealth, the chance to grow among the warmth of their own people, speaking their people's

languages and learning about their country. They suffered lasting psychiatric injury. They were treated as orphans when they were not orphans. They lost the culture and traditions of their families. Decades later, the Commonwealth of Australia says in this case that it did them no wrong at all: *Cubillo v Commonwealth (No 2)* (2000) 103 FCR 1 at [2] (*Cubillo (No 2)*).

Specifically, the plaintiffs alleged that they had been forcibly removed from their families and detained in institutions against their will pursuant to a state-sanctioned policy whereby 'part-Aboriginal' children were removed from their families. They acknowledged that the Aboriginals Ordinance of that time gave the Director of Native Affairs the power to remove and detain part-Aboriginal children if, in the Director's opinion, it was necessary or desirable in the interests of the child to do so. However, the plaintiffs alleged that the Director had not exercised this power properly, for their individual best interests had not been taken into account. Further, the plaintiffs alleged that the conduct of the Director, in failing to provide for their custody, maintenance and education as required by the Ordinance, constituted a breach of the statutory duty owed to each of them. As a result of these and other breaches, the plaintiffs had suffered losses and damages for which they sought compensation. They each claimed general damages as well as aggravated and exemplary damages.

O'Loughlin J found against the plaintiffs and the decision was later upheld in an appeal to the Full Federal Court: *Cubillo v Commonwealth* (2001) 112 FCR 455. See Clarke (2001) and van Krieken (2001) for extensive discussions of O'Loughlin J's decision.

Alec Kruger and others

In 1995, the plaintiffs commenced legal proceedings in which they challenged the constitutional validity of the *Aboriginals Ordinance Act 1918* (NT). The Ordinance provided for the appointment of a Chief Protector of Aborigines and conferred extensive powers on that position including, under s 6(1), the discretion to undertake the care, custody and control of any 'aboriginal or half-caste'. Section 16 empowered the Chief Protector to remove any 'aboriginal or half-caste' to any reserve or 'aboriginal institution' so defined to include mission stations, schools, reformatories, orphanages or other institutions declared to be an 'aboriginal institution' for the purposes of the Ordinance. Finally, s 7(1) provided that the Chief Protector and later, the Director of Native Affairs, be the legal guardian of all Aboriginal people.

The plaintiffs advanced several reasons for challenging the constitutional validity of the relevant provisions of the Ordinance. First, the detention powers of the Ordinance invalidly conferred a judicial power on a non-judicial body in contravention of the 'separation of power' doctrine enshrined in Chapter III of the Constitution. Second, the plaintiffs claimed that the Ordinance infringed their implied constitutional right to legal equality. In addition, they claimed that the Ordinance violated their implied constitutional right to freedom of movement and association as well as an implied constitutional right to freedom from genocide. The plaintiffs further contended that the Ordinance violated the express protection of freedom of religion enshrined in s 116 of the Constitution.

The plaintiffs further argued that a breach of these implied constitutional rights, guarantees and freedoms gave rise to a right of action to recover damages from the Commonwealth. They also relied upon causes of action recognised by the common law; that is, the tort of wrongful imprisonment and deprivation of liberty. The plaintiffs sought damages in regard to the losses they had suffered in personal, spiritual as well as financial terms and further, in regard to their potential land claim entitlements (Buti 1998: 234).

The High Court handed down its decision in *Kruger v Commonwealth* (1997) 71 ALJR 126 and rejected the plaintiffs' claims on all grounds.

Crimes Compensation Tribunals: Linow

Some members of the Stolen Generations have sought compensation for crimes committed against them while wards of the state or in foster care under criminal injuries compensation schemes. People seeking compensation under these schemes generally need to prove that the relevant crime occurred and that harm occasioned to them was a result of that crime. Some members of the Stolen Generations in Victoria have successfully made claims under the criminal injuries compensation schemes for sexual assaults and were awarded approximately $4,000 each (Cornwall 2002: 47). Obviously, not all claims succeed. For example, in 1999 the New South Wales Victims Compensation Tribunal rejected Judy Stubbs' claim for compensation for removal from her family and subsequent abuse (Cunneen and Grix 2003: 14).

Valerie Linow's claim is an example of successful use of the process. She lodged an application in the New South Wales Victims Compensation Tribunal (VCT) for compensation in relation to sexual assaults between May and October 1958. These events were well outside of the two-year limitation period provided under s 26(1) of the *Victims Support and Rehabilitation Act 1996* (NSW). Leave was granted for the matter to be determined by the Tribunal. Linow's claim was determined by an assessor on the documentary evidence provided and her application for compensation was dismissed (New South Wales Victims Compensation Tribunal 2002a).

However, an appeal was allowed and the determination of the compensation assessor was set aside accordingly. The Chairperson of the VCT stated that he was satisfied that Linow had suffered an injury as required by s 5(1)(c) of the *Victims Support and Rehabilitation Act 1996* (NSW) (New South Wales Victims Compensation Tribunal 2002b). Further, the Chairperson was satisfied that this injury, which included the diagnosed disorders, was caused either as a direct result of the sexual assaults or as a result of the sexual assaults in combination with 'other stressors' (New South Wales Victims Compensation Tribunal 2002b). It is clear from the facts set out in the determination that the 'other stressors' included Linow's removal from her family at age two. The compensable injury of sexual assault category 3 was established and Linow was awarded $35,000 accordingly.

> I have got my justice after 45 years. I'm free because it was tormenting me all the time. I feel like I am reborn. I can go forward and leave this dreadful past behind ... It's not the money that's important to me. It is the knowledge and recognition that this happened to Aboriginal people. No one could pay any amount for what happened to us because we lost a lot (cited in Jopson 2002).

One of the reasons for the success of Valerie Linow's claim was that her sexual assaults and beatings had been reported by her to police and the Aborigines Welfare Board.

Limitations of litigation

There are various and, at times, unique difficulties confronting Stolen Generation claimants before the courts. Some of the major limitations of the litigation process include:

- the problem Indigenous people have in overcoming statutory limitation periods, when these events occurred many decades ago;
- the lack of constitutional protections;
- the problem of establishing specific liability for harms that have been caused;
- the difficulty of locating evidence, particularly when governments were lax in recording matters involving Indigenous people;
- the emotional and psychological trauma experienced by claimants in the hostile environment of an adversarial court system;
- the enormous financial cost;
- the length of time involved before the outcome of litigation is finalised; and
- overcoming the judicial view that 'standards of the time' justified removal in the best interests of the child.

Below we touch on some of the major reasons for the failure of Stolen Generations cases. For a fuller discussion of these and other socio-legal limitations of Stolen Generations litigation, see Cunneen and Grix (2004).

The limit of constitutional protections

In the *Kruger* case the majority of the High Court rejected the existence of a number of implied constitutional rights (see also Chapter 12). The majority also found that the Northern Territory Ordinance did not authorise acts of genocide.

Wrongful imprisonment

Plaintiffs were not generally successful in proving trespass and wrongful imprisonment. In *Williams (No 2)* at [674], Abadee J found that Williams had become a ward shortly after her birth, on application by her mother. Williams' placement in institutions was with the consent of her mother and as such, was held to be lawful. In regard to Peter Gunner's action for wrongful imprisonment, O'Loughlin J found that the Director of Native Affairs had not unlawfully removed him from Utopia Station but rather, that his removal was the result of his mother having given her 'informed' consent as evidenced by a thumb print on a consent form: *Cubillo (No 2)* at [788].

Breach of statutory duty

Similarly, plaintiffs have not generally been successful in arguing a breach of statutory duty. Abadee J held that there was no actionable statutory duty because the provisions of the *Aborigines Protection Act 1909* (NSW) were not intended to confer a right of action in tort having reference to the nature, scope and terms of the legislation: *Williams (No 2)* at [681]. Even if this duty was owed, his Honour held that there had been no such breach by the defendants. O'Loughlin J held that Cubillo and Gunner did have private rights of action for breach of statutory duty available to them: *Cubillo (No 1)* at [96]. However, he ultimately rejected the plaintiffs' claims for breach of statutory duty in relation to the Director's guardianship powers because of the absence of any evidence as to the actions of the Director being beyond power, that is, being 'exercised for a malicious purpose or for an objective that was foreign to the mandates of the legislation': *Cubillo (No 2)* at [1190].

Negligence

In relation to common law duty of care and findings of negligence, Abadee J declined to impose a duty of care on the state. He supported this conclusion in part, by taking into account the public policy considerations set out in the 'novel categories of negligence' cases: *Williams (No 2)* at [771]. In particular, his Honour considered it unsatisfactory to impose a common law duty of care upon a third party for harm caused in circumstances where no such duty would arise as between a parent and child. To do so, in Abadee J's view, would be to impose a 'higher duty' on third parties (*Williams No 2*) at [787]) which might, in turn, have wider ramifications for the exercise of statutory powers by public authorities in a social welfare context.

In *Cubillo (No 2)*, O'Loughlin J accepted that once the plaintiffs came into the care of the Director of Native Affairs, a duty of care arose from the exercise of those powers conferred by the Ordinance to ensure their safety and well-being (Clarke 2001: 276). His Honour found however, that the Director had not breached his duty of care to

Lorna Cubillo in relation to the conditions at the Retta Dixon Home which, although 'not good … were not so bad as to create a cause of action': *Cubillo (No 2)* at [1267]. By way of contrast, in regard to Peter Gunner's claim, O'Loughlin J found that the Director had failed to ensure that reasonable standards were maintained at St Mary's Hostel. However, the duty of care was owed by the Director alone, and the Commonwealth could not be held vicariously liable for its breach.

Fiduciary duty

Stolen Generation plaintiffs identified a variety of fiduciary duties allegedly owed to each of them by respective governments. These included duties to have regard to and to act in the plaintiff's best interests; to avoid conflict between its interests and the interests of the plaintiffs; to properly supervise the institutions or individuals into whose care the plaintiffs were placed; and to advise the plaintiffs to obtain independent advice (see *Cubillo (No 2)* at [1277]).

However the courts have been reluctant in Australia to expand the range of fiduciary obligations. In regard to the imposition of fiduciary duties on the relationship of guardian and ward, O'Loughlin J considered himself bound by the decision in *Paramasivam v Flynn* (1998) 90 FCR 489:

> In Anglo-Australian law, the interests which [these] equitable doctrines … have hitherto protected are economic interests … Here, the conduct complained of is within the purview of the law of tort, which has worked out and elaborated principles according to which various kinds of loss and damage, resulting from intentional or negligent wrongful conduct, is to be compensated. That is not a field on which there is any obvious need for equity to enter: *Cubillo (No 2)* at [1291]; see also Clarke 2001: 285.

In *Williams (No 2)*, Abadee J stated at [733]: 'Any extension of the law to protect other than economic interests had to be justified in principle with regard to the particular interests protected by equitable doctrines. In my view no such principle exists to warrant extension into a case such as the present'.

Evidentiary hurdles

Litigation presents very particular evidentiary hurdles for members of the Stolen Generations. Government records are likely to paint a picture in which the removal and subsequent treatment of Indigenous children complied with 'their best interests' and met the standards of the time. Protection laws are characterised as benign in their intent, as 'beneficial' laws—even if discriminatory. 'Government records, not surprisingly, fail to reveal the level of abuse, deprivation and racism …' (PIAC 2000: 16–17).

The onus is on members of the Stolen Generations to show that the removals, detentions or other exercises of statutory power were unlawful. The claimants are placed in a position whereby they must counteract the official version of history. The task of counteracting this official portrayal is made more difficult when the events occurred 50 years or more ago and witnesses are difficult to locate, no longer alive or fail to remember relevant facts. In addition the experience of removal, institutionalisation and isolation meant that many children never made complaints about abuse, particularly sexual abuse, and hence no records exist to substantiate their story (PIAC 2000: 17).

Statute of limitations

Time limits (or statutory limitation periods) apply to claims for damages arising from negligence, wrongful imprisonment and breaches of statutory duties. This has proven to be a significant problem confronting Stolen Generation claimants. Although the courts in *Cubillo* and *Williams* deferred making a final decision on the question of limitations until after the substantive issues had been considered, both 'ultimately concluded that there would be "overwhelming prejudice" to the defendant if time limits were waived' (Cornwall 2002: 46). Those litigants who succeed in having the limitation period extended will be selected on criteria such as the availability of records and witnesses, criteria 'unrelated to the underlying justice of the situation' (PIAC 2000: 16).

Successful litigation: *Trevorrow*

Bruce Trevorrow was removed from his family when he was 13 months old and placed with a foster parent without the consent of his family. The removal occurred after his father had organised his son's attendance at hospital. Bruce would not see his father again and it would be 10 years before he saw his mother or siblings.

The causes of action pleaded by the plaintiff were that his removal was not authorised by law and was beyond power. The plaintiff alleged he was the subject of misfeasance in public office and was falsely imprisoned. It was contended that the State of South Australia was his statutory legal guardian at relevant times. It was also said that the plaintiff's removal from his parents' care, his placement in foster care, and his return to his natural family involved breaches of duty: *Trevorrow v South Australia (No 5)* (2007) 98 SASR 136; [2007] SASC 285 (1 August 2007) (*Trevorrow*) at [5].

Gray J found at [1228]–[1233] that:

> The plaintiff, as an infant and as a child, was dealt with by the State without lawful authority in a manner that affected his personal well being and freedom. He was the subject of misfeasance in public office. He was falsely imprisoned. He was the subject of breaches of the common law duty of care owed by the State.

At the time of the relevant events it was reasonably foreseeable that there was a material risk of injury, loss and damage if the plaintiff was taken from his natural family and placed in care. The foreseeability of the risk and the magnitude of the damage that might follow was compounded by the manner of the removal and by the conduct following thereafter. The parents of the plaintiff were unaware of what was occurring. They did not consent [to his removal] …

When the decision was taken to return the plaintiff to his natural family, there was a need for particular care and support. Again there was a foreseeable risk of damage if the return was not handled with care …

The Crown Solicitors of the time gave advice that the powers to remove Aboriginal children from their parents were limited. It is significant that at relevant times the State, through its Cabinet, was aware of these advices and the requests for legislative change to provide the authority to remove Aboriginal children from their natural families in an unrestricted manner …

I am satisfied that the conduct of the State, amounting to misfeasance in public office, together with the false imprisonment of the plaintiff, has been a material cause of the plaintiff's long-term depression …

Gray J awarded damages in favour of the plaintiff for $525,000. The South Australian Government has appealed the decision on points of law but is not seeking to overturn damages. The *Trevorrow* case has implications for both South Australia and Australia more generally. In 1958 the South Australian Secretary of the Aborigines Protection Board estimated that approximately 300 Aboriginal children were removed from their families despite the fact that it was known there was no legal authority or power to do so. The broader implications of *Trevorrow* for the rest of Australia is that the decision is 'authority for the proposition that by the mid 1950s it was reasonably foreseeable that the separation of infant Aboriginal children from their families and placement in long term non Indigenous foster care created real risks for the health of those children' (Richardson 2007: 5).

DISCUSSION QUESTIONS

- Discuss the advantages and disadvantages of litigation in the Stolen Generations cases.
- Is the extent of harm related to successful redress? What limitations do these cases show in the judiciary's capacity to deal with historical evidence compared to documentary evidence?

Compensation and redress through a Tribunal: a Stolen Generations Reparations Tribunal

The NISATSIC had recommended the establishment of a National Compensation Fund for the Stolen Generations. More recently the Public Interest Advocacy Centre (PIAC) has, in consultation with Indigenous people, developed a proposal for a Reparations Tribunal (Cornwall 2002). This proposal was also endorsed by a Senate Committee inquiry into government responses to the Stolen Generations (Senate Legal and Constitutional References Committee 2000).

Recommendations for a Compensation and Reparations Tribunal

The NISATSIC had recommended the establishment of a National Compensation Fund as a statutory alternative to litigation, and to avoid inequity among states as to their approach to compensation. The Inquiry recommended a Board to administer the fund and that it be comprised of a majority of Indigenous people. The procedural principles applied to the Compensation Fund should include widest possible publicity; free legal advice and representation for claimants; no limitation period; independent decision-making including participation of Indigenous people; minimum formality; not bound by rules of evidence; and cultural appropriateness (NISATSIC 1997: 307–311).

The Inquiry argued that credible claims of forced removal should be compensated for by a minimum lump sum. The burden of proof should be on Government to rebut otherwise credible claims and a defence should be that the removal was in the best interests of the child. Further compensation should be available where claimants can prove on the balance of probabilities that particular harm or loss was suffered. The Inquiry recommended 10 heads of damage for compensation: racial discrimination; arbitrary deprivation of liberty; pain and suffering; physical, sexual and emotional abuse; disruption of family life; loss of cultural rights and fulfilment; loss of native title rights; labour exploitation; economic loss; and loss of opportunities. Finally, the Inquiry recommended that the National Compensation Fund would not displace claimants' common law rights to seek damages in the courts. However, a claimant who was successful in one forum would not be entitled to proceed in the other (NISATSIC 1997: 311–313).

PIAC developed and extended the original NISATSIC proposal to the establishment of a Reparations Tribunal. In cases where Indigenous people can establish that they were forcibly removed they would still be entitled to a minimum lump sum payment (compensation). In addition people forcibly removed and their families, communities and descendants should be entitled to reparations. Reparations might include a range of remedies determined by the Tribunal. They could potentially include such things as acknowledgments and memorials, cultural and language centres, the provision of counselling services and so on. The Reparations Tribunal would adopt procedural principles that enable the victims of these abuses to have their matters heard in a dignified and sympathetic manner. These would include informal procedures, relaxed rules of evidence, legal representation and interpreters where required and the capacity to determine group or representative claims. The Tribunal would have a majority of Indigenous members and a life span of 10 years.

The proposed Reparations Tribunal broadens the concept of a tribunal only ordering monetary compensation to one able to establish wider reparations packages. The PIAC proposal consciously draws on the experience in other countries, including the South African Truth and Reconciliation Commission. Support for a national Reparations Tribunal has been forthcoming from the Senate Legal and Constitutional References Committee (2000). The Committee recommended that a Reparations Tribunal be established to address the need for a process of reparations including monetary compensation (recommendation 7) and that the PIAC proposal be used as a general 'template' for the recommended tribunal (recommendation 8) (Senate Legal and Constitutional References Committee 2000: xviii, 238–261).

It has been proposed that the Reparations Tribunal would have three broad divisions with corresponding functions.

- A Hearing Division which would assist people to find government and church records, and to put together family histories and genealogies. It would also provide a forum to hear people's stories.
- A Rehabilitation and Reparations Division which would make decisions about entitlement to reparations for individuals, families, groups and communities. People might seek a package of reparations that best meets their needs.
- A Recommendations Division which would focus on providing solutions to current government and church practices. These might include issues such as making recommendations on improving relevant record keeping by government and churches; or negotiating with churches to keep former institutions as museums; or making recommendations to prevent the current high level of removals of Indigenous children through welfare and juvenile justice practices (PIAC 2000).

A Reparations Tribunal will have to settle some difficult issues, including who is eligible for reparations; how the issue of consent will be dealt with, and what evidence will determine a forcible removal; the assessment of compensatory damages (if they differ from a lump-sum payment); procedural issues, in particular the burden and onus of proof; who would be the respondents (Commonwealth, states, churches); and the appeal mechanisms to be put in place. However, these are not insurmountable problems and they have already been considered in some detail (PIAC 2000; Senate Legal and Constitutional References Committee 2000; Cornwall 2002).

Compensation and Repayment Schemes (1): ex gratia payments to the Tasmanian Stolen Generations

Separate from the arguments for a national reparations tribunal, the Tasmanian Government has established a compensation fund for Aboriginal people forcibly removed from their families in that state. The Tasmanian Government initiated legislation to create a $5 million Stolen Generations Fund to provide payments to eligible members of the Stolen Generations. The *Stolen Generations of Aboriginal Children Act 2006* provides for ex gratia payments to be made to members of the Stolen Generations in Tasmania.

The amount each eligible person is entitled to receive is determined by the legislation. There are three categories of eligible applicants. The first category relates to Aboriginal people who are living and were removed either as a ward or child of the state between 1935 and 1975. The second category relates to Aboriginal people who are living and were removed between 1935 and 1975 by a Tasmanian government agency without the consent of their parents or guardians, or in circumstances where undue influence or duress was applied. In both categories the child must have been removed for more than 12 continuous months and have not been in the care of an Aboriginal family in that period. The third category creates eligibility for compensation for the children of deceased persons who would have otherwise satisfied the requirements of categories one and two.

Eligible children of a deceased member of the Stolen Generations are entitled to $5,000 each, with a maximum of $20,000 for a family group. After claims from children are paid, the balance remaining in the fund is to be shared equally by eligible members of the Stolen Generations. The amount each eligible person will receive will not be known until the number of successful applicants has been determined. There is no process for public hearings. The Stolen Generations Assessor determines the validity of the applications for an ex gratia payment. The Stolen Generations Assessor's decision is final—there is no appeal or review process available. The Act became operational on 15 January 2007. The application period is now closed.

Compensation and Repayment Schemes (2): the Aboriginal Trust Fund Repayment Scheme (NSW)

The New South Wales Government began the Aboriginal Trust Fund Repayment Scheme (AFTRS) in 2004 with a process of consultation on how to repay unpaid wages and other payments made into the Aboriginal Trust Fund operated by the New South Wales Aborigines Protection Board and later the Aborigines Welfare Board between 1900 and 1969. The AFTRS commenced operation in 2005. The main features of the scheme are:

- the repayment of wages and other money placed in the Aboriginal Trust Fund which has not been repaid, indexed to its current value;
- no cap on repayment amounts;
- claims to be paid where there is reliable evidence of money being paid into the Aboriginal Trust Fund and where there is no evidence, or no reliable evidence, that the money was paid out. Oral evidence may be accepted where gaps in written records exist;
- claims may be made by individuals who had their money placed into the Aboriginal Trust Fund (or their authorised representative), or, where the direct claimant is deceased, their descendants may make a claim;
- claimants are not required to sign an indemnity; and
- the provision of practical support and counselling for claimants (Senate Standing Committee on Legal and Constitutional Affairs 2006: 111–112).

Evidence provided to a Senate Inquiry indicated that repayments had varied between $1,000 and $24,000. However, there was potential for gross under-estimation of money owed to Indigenous people because there was no questioning of whether the amount in the trust fund reflected the actual amount that should have been paid from wages (Senate Standing Committee on Legal and Constitutional Affairs 2006: 115). PIAC has successfully appeared before the AFTRS Panel to argue that interim assessments for their clients were based on incomplete and inaccurate records.

Compensation and Repayment Schemes (3): the Queensland Underpayment of Award Wages Process and the Queensland Indigenous Wages and Savings Reparations Scheme

In 1999 the Queensland Government introduced a scheme to provide a payment of $7,000 to Indigenous workers who had been employed on reserves after 1975 and paid at lower rates than non-Indigenous workers. This scheme (the Underpayment of Award Wages Process—UAWP) was a response to a successful claim by Palm Island Indigenous people to the Human Rights and Equal Opportunity Commission that they had been racially discriminated against because they were paid at a lower rate than they would have been if they were not Indigenous. The Commission had found in their favour and awarded the Palm Island claimants $7,000 each (*Bligh v State of Queensland* [1996] HREOCA 28).

The UAWP scheme applied for the period 1975 (when the Commonwealth *Racial Discrimination Act* was introduced) to 1986 (when award wages were paid to all Indigenous workers on Queensland reserves). Applications closed on 31 January 2003, and the Queensland Government has reportedly paid out $40 million to Indigenous workers under the scheme (Senate Standing Committee on Legal and Constitutional Affairs 2006: 93).

One of the criticisms of the UAWP scheme was that it only applied to Indigenous workers on government-run reserves, and not people working on church-operated missions. The *Baird* case challenged this in the Full Federal Court which ruled that the calculation and payment of grants by the Queensland Government to the church missions was based on the payment of below-award wages to Indigenous workers, and was thus in breach of the *Racial Discrimination Act*: *Baird v Queensland* (2006) 156 FCR 451; [2006] FCAFC 162.

In 2002 the Queensland Government made an offer of a one-off payment through the Queensland Indigenous Wages and Savings Reparations Scheme for Indigenous workers who could show that their wages and savings had been controlled under the Queensland Protection Acts. The offer included $55.4 million for payments to individuals, a written apology from the government to all living persons who had their wages and savings controlled under an Act and who were eligible to make a claim for compensation, and a statement in parliament to publicly recognise past injustices on the basis of race.

The eligibility criteria for the one-off payment distinguished between individuals claiming the reparations offer. In order to be eligible, claimants had to be born before either 31 December 1951 or 31 December 1956 and have had their wages or savings controlled under a Protection Act. The former received a capped payment of $4,000 and the latter a capped payment of $2,000. The reasoning for the difference was that those eligible for the larger payment had their wages and saving more tightly controlled under the pre-1965 protection legislation.

The Queensland scheme has been widely criticised for the paucity of the capped amount of reparations money, for the fact that claimants must sign an indemnity clause releasing government from any further liability, and the fact that the scheme will not receive written or oral evidence about the amount owed. The Queensland Aboriginal and Islander Legal Service Secretariat (QAILSS) had proposed a scale of payments depending on the length of time the person had worked, ranging from $25,000 to $45,000 (Senate Standing Committee on Legal and Constitutional Affairs 2006: 100). In terms of the reliance on written records, where there is no written record of a person under the Protection Acts, they are not eligible for the reparations offer. The difficulties associated with missing records, and the extent and complexity of the archives when locating records relating to individuals were ignored. The Senate Standing Committee noted that: 'Many witnesses considered it was unfair to place such a reliance on the documentary records, particularly when it was the responsibility of the Queensland Government, and not the individual worker, to keep and maintain the records' (Senate Standing Committee on Legal and Constitutional Affairs 2006: 108).

DISCUSSION QUESTIONS

- Balance the advantages and disadvantages of reparations packages compared to individual litigation as a means of redress. Is there a benefit to retaining both options?

Conclusion

This chapter began by looking at the justifications for reparation and compensation for Indigenous people and some of the areas that might be covered by a reparations approach. It was noted that there is an international human rights approach to ensuring proper remedies for the victims of gross violations of human rights.

The discussion on Stolen Generations cases shows some of the inherent problems with using litigation as a way of responding to historical injustices. Many similar problems are also evident in relation to litigation in other areas (for example, lack of documentary evidence, missing wages and trust funds).

At the moment the response to historical injustices is a complex ad hoc and piecemeal approach to what were essentially common problems across the nation. A member of the Stolen Generations in Tasmania may receive an ex gratia payment. Following the *Trevorrow* case there may be a great likelihood of receiving compensation in South Australia. Elsewhere in Australia the Stolen Generations receive nothing. Indigenous people who lost money through stolen wages and trust funds may receive a small amount of money in Queensland, a potentially larger amount in New South Wales and nothing elsewhere.

Current approaches seeking redress are also piecemeal in the sense that they ignore some gross violations of human rights. There are significant areas of racial discrimination which, while lawful until 1975, provide a profound moral argument for reparations. As detailed in the previous chapter 'protection' legislation introduced significant restrictions on movement, residence, education, health care, employment, marriage and other civil rights including voting. Further, there has been no attempt to seek compensation and reparations in relation to relatively recent mass killings such as the massacres in the early part of the twentieth century like Coniston in Central Australia in 1928. Finally, and perhaps most importantly, the compensation or reparation schemes that do exist do not provide an opportunity for Indigenous people to 'tell their story'. They do not provide the opportunity for the recording of history and the acknowledgment of what occurred which are fundamental to the longer term processes of reconciliation.

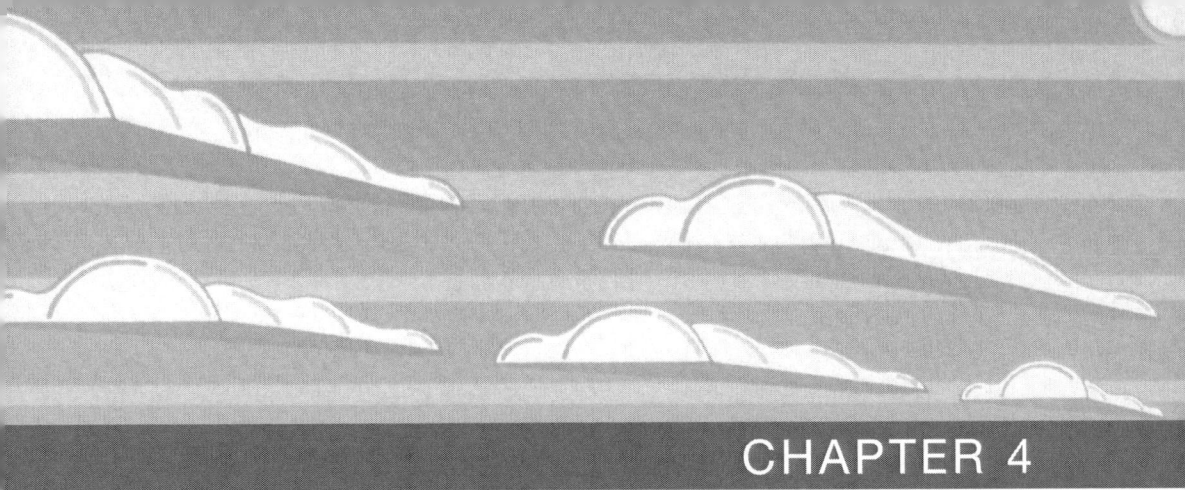

CHAPTER 4

Contemporary Aboriginal and Torres Strait Islander Children's Welfare

> The state is still undermining our right to bring up our own children, and to have a say over the course of their lives. and judicial systems still discriminate against us and view our family cultures as somehow pathological. They still deny the right of our children to grow up within their own culture. With all that we know about the long term effects of removing Aboriginal and Torres Strait Islander children from their families and communities, Australians cannot allow this to continue (Dodson 1997).

Introduction

At the time of the National Inquiry into the Separation of Aboriginal and Torres Strait Islander Children from Their Families (NISATSIC), Indigenous children were placed in out-of-home care at six times the rate of all children. In 2005–2006 Indigenous children were seven times more likely to be placed in out-of-home care than all children. Indigenous children remain significantly over-represented in all stages of contact with child protection departments in Australia (Australian Institute of Health and Welfare 2006a). However this contact does not suggest either effective or comprehensive responses to Indigenous children's well-being. Systemic problems which are closely tied to the history and current legacy of colonial relations between Aboriginal and Torres Strait Islander peoples and mainstream communities underpin this over-representation (Cunneen and Libesman 2000b). One of the most destructive colonial policies, which has particular significance for child welfare departments, was the forced and unjustified removal of Aboriginal and Torres Strait Islander children from their families (see Chapter 3). The trauma of this and other colonial policies is experienced inter-generationally by Aboriginal and Torres Strait Islander communities. This trauma is often compounded by current and repeated traumatic experiences including violence, sexual abuse, substance abuse and related problems both experienced and witnessed by many Indigenous children (Aboriginal Child Sexual Assault Taskforce 2006; Robertson 2000; Atkinson 2002).

Child welfare in Australia is primarily a state and territory responsibility. The peak Indigenous children's organisation, the Secretariat of National Aboriginal and Torres Strait Islander Child Care (SNAICC), has been calling for national legislation with respect to Indigenous children's well-being for more than two decades. The NISATSIC called upon the Council of Australian Governments (COAG) to facilitate a national response to its recommendations for a new framework for Indigenous children's welfare. This has not occurred and each state and territory has reviewed and reformed its child welfare legislation separately.

The over-representation of Indigenous children in child welfare departments has been a problem which governments and communities have attempted to address in all Australian jurisdictions and in other countries with parallel histories of colonisation of minority Indigenous peoples. This chapter will discuss Aboriginal and Torres Strait Islander children's welfare within a human rights framework. It will consider what needs to be addressed to provide effective child welfare services to Indigenous children, how the United Nations Convention on the Rights of the Child applies to child welfare issues facing Indigenous children, the findings and recommendations made by NISATSIC for reform of contemporary child welfare, reforms to Australian child welfare legislation which have been made over the last decade and a comparative case study of legislative reform in Manitoba, Canada.

What needs to be addressed?

In all Australian jurisdictions it has been recognised that the delivery of children's services by government departments has not provided good outcomes for Indigenous children and families (NISATSIC 2007). It has also been recognised that a case-based focus, that is looking at each child's situation in isolation from the broader community issues, has not been successful (Gungil Jinibah Centre 1994; Cunneen and Libesman 2002). This is not surprising when one considers the many structural inequalities which face whole communities and which are out of the individual's control (see Systemic inequality below). It is widely believed that Indigenous organisations and workers, because of their experience and understanding of the issues which families are facing, provide more effective services to Indigenous families. Muriel Bamblett, CEO of the Victorian Child Care Agency and chairperson of SNAICC comments: 'In order to prevent the next stolen generations we need commitments by state, territory and federal governments to strengthen the resource base of Aboriginal and Torres Strait Islander agencies to deliver the culturally-embedded child and family programmes that we know work for our people' (Bamblett 2007: 10).

In some Indigenous communities the devastation of colonial policies is such that law and order has broken down. Many other Indigenous communities have to struggle to maintain their cultural authority and the laws and traditions which sustain it. The active suppression of Aboriginal and Torres Strait Islander languages, laws and culture have been extensively documented (NISATSIC 2007; Chesterman and Galligan 1997). This denial of laws and cultural norms affects a continuum of life in communities, from disciplining children to substance abuse. This is exacerbated by the introduction of the worst of Western culture including drugs, pornography and gambling which further undermine the authority of parents, grandparent and elders in communities. If the underlying causes of violence and child abuse which are experienced in some Indigenous families and communities are to be addressed then support for the culture, laws and traditions which nurture and provide order and stability in communities is needed (Libesman 2007). Consultations with Indigenous family carers in focus groups across the country with respect to Aboriginal and Torres Strait Islander parenting needs and practices, and with respect to risks and strengths experienced in the raising of Aboriginal children, consistently raise the themes of loss of respect for elders and ways of disciplining children, racism and discrimination experienced in all spheres, the influence of 'Americanism' on children, the challenge of engaging children who are disaffected and the value of cultural revitalisation for children's well-being (Borg and Paul 2005).

In addition to support for the revitalisation of Indigenous law and culture many Aboriginal and Torres Strait Islander communities need to develop community and personal capacities. This is also a legacy of policies of paternalism, discrimination and the denial of citizenship entitlements which many Indigenous communities have experienced inter-generationally. The history of the arbitrary deprivation of control over all aspects of Aboriginal and Torres Strait Islander peoples' lives, and in particular loss of control over family life, is discussed in Chapter 3. Many families, both Indigenous and non-Indigenous, who have contact with child welfare systems live lives which are chaotic and characterised by a lack of control over the adverse events which impact on them. Gaining Indigenous control over children, families and communities is therefore in layered ways, which are embedded both in current and historical experiences, an important part of fostering Indigenous children's well-being.

DISCUSSION QUESTION

- Discuss the relationship between cultural control and law and order.

Systemic inequality

In all jurisdictions in Australia, Indigenous children are more likely to come into contact with child welfare departments as a result of neglect rather than abuse (Australian Institute of Health and Welfare 2006a). Neglect is directly tied to poverty. Poverty and marginalisation from the mainstream economy are also a legacy of colonial relations experienced by Indigenous communities. If child protection legislation is to be effective it needs to understand, facilitate and complement policy which addresses the underlying causes of Indigenous children's over-representation in child protection systems. The systemic disadvantage facing Indigenous families is evidenced by the following statistical analysis. The statistics reveal the extreme poverty and disadvantage of Indigenous Australians. They have been chosen to give a representative picture of some of the key factors affecting Indigenous children as compared to all children.

Child welfare

The proportion of Indigenous children, and therefore their families, involved in the child welfare system in Australia far outweighs the proportion of non-Indigenous children who have been the subject of intervention by child welfare authorities. However comparisons between states and territories should be viewed with caution as the different jurisdictions have different ways of collecting these statistics and have different definitions of and criteria for making child protection findings. Jurisdictions with lower Indigenous child protection rates may not be doing a better job than those with higher rates. The difference can reflect poor collection of Indigenous status in some jurisdictions or a failure to provide adequate child protection services compared with jurisdictions where there are higher rates of involvement with Indigenous children.

Child protection substantiations

Nationally, in 2004–2005, 4,887 Indigenous children were the subject of child protection substantiation. A substantiated finding means that a child welfare department has investigated a complaint and found that a child has been abused or neglected. The substantiation rate for Indigenous children was 24.0 per 1,000 children, for children aged 0–16 years. The substantiation rate for non-Indigenous children was 6.7 per 1,000 children, for children aged 0–16 years in the same period (Steering Committee for the Review of Government Service Provision 2006: Chapter 15 at 15.9 and table 15A). As such, the rate of Indigenous children subject to child protection substantiations was more than three times greater than the rate within non-Indigenous child populations (Service Provision 2006: chapter 15 at 15.9 and table 15A). A child protection order is made by a Children's Court when it has found that a child has been abused or neglected. Here, the rate of Indigenous children subject to care and protection orders is more than five times greater than the rate for non-Indigenous children.

Out-of-home care

Nationally at 30 June 2005, 5,678 Indigenous children and 18,017 non-Indigenous children were in out-of-home care. The rate of children in out-of-home care per 1,000 children in the population aged 0–17 years was 26.4 for Indigenous children and 3.9 for non-Indigenous children (Steering Committee for the Review of Government Service Provision 2006: chapter 15 at 15.9 and table 15A). This makes the rate of Indigenous children in out-of-home care more than seven times greater than the national rate of non-Indigenous children in out-of-home care arrangements. At 30 June 2004, for those jurisdictions that provided data, 68 per cent of Indigenous children in out-of-home care were placed in accordance with the 'child placement principle', however this proportion ranged from 40 per cent in Tasmania to 81 per cent in Western Australia (Australian Bureau of Statistics 2005: 214, table 11.6). For discussion of the child placement principle see below.

Early school leaving

The following statistics represent the national school retention rates of Indigenous compared with non-Indigenous children in 2004. Retention rates for non-Indigenous school students from Year 7/8 to Year 10 was 98.5 per cent compared with 86.4 per cent for Indigenous children. The retention rate of non-Indigenous full-time school students to Year 12 was 76.8 per cent compared with 39.5 per cent for Indigenous

CASE STUDY

children. Thus there is a differential of -37.3 between Indigenous and non-Indigenous children retained in school to Year 12.

Juvenile detention

The over-representation of Indigenous compared with all children at all stages of the juvenile justice system is discussed in Chapter 5.

Underemployment rates and annual household income

Indigenous people continue to experience lower levels of employment (and higher levels of unemployment) than non-Indigenous people, with Indigenous adults in 2002 being more than twice as likely to be unemployed (13 per cent) as non-Indigenous adults (4.6 per cent). The average gross household income of Indigenous people was $394 per week in 2002, equal to 59 per cent of that of non-Indigenous adults in 2002 ($665) (Australian Bureau of Statistics 2004: 29). More recent 2003–2004 statistics on household income distribution does not separate Indigenous compared with all households.

Homelessness/overcrowding

Many Aboriginal and Torres Strait Islander families live in inadequate and overcrowded houses which lack basic services such as running water, electricity or sewerage connections. The Australian Bureau of Statistics reports, 'Using the Canadian National Occupancy Standard definition of overcrowding, 15 per cent of households with Indigenous person(s) were considered overcrowded (i.e. requiring at least one extra bedroom), compared to 4 per cent of other households. In households with Indigenous person(s), overcrowding increased with remoteness. In major cities, about 11 per cent of all households with Indigenous person(s) require at least one extra bedroom, compared with 42 per cent of households with Indigenous person(s) in very Remote areas of Australia' (Australian Bureau of Statistics 2003: 37). The most accurate statistics in relation to homelessness are still those collected as part of the 2001 National Census. It is information which is difficult to collect for an array of reasons. In 2001, the national rate of Indigenous homelessness was 176 per 10,000, however this rate varied across jurisdictions. The highest rates of Indigenous homelessness were found in the Northern Territory and South Australia. Nationally, the rate of homelessness for Indigenous Australians was 3.5 times higher than the rate for non-Indigenous Australians. Victoria had the largest gap between Indigenous and non-Indigenous Australians, with the rate of Indigenous homelessness being more than five times the rate for non-Indigenous people (Chamberlain and Mackenzie 2003: 47).

Life expectancy

The latest available estimates of life expectancy at birth for the Indigenous population are for the period 1996–2001. At the national level, Indigenous life expectancy at birth for 1996–2001 is estimated at 59.4 years for males and 64.8 years for females. This is well below the 76.6 years and 82.0 years for non-Indigenous males and females respectively, for the period of 1998–2000 (Australian Bureau of Statistics 2005a: 78, table 9.8).

The Commonwealth is the only level of government with the resources to comprehensively respond to the systemic and structural problems which undermine efforts to repair past harms and prevent ongoing inequities in Indigenous compared with all children's well-being. As outlined above, all governments have failed to address the lack of adequate infrastructure including insufficient and inadequate housing, health, education and other services pertaining to Indigenous peoples' well-being. In 2007 the Howard Liberal Government embarked on a controversial intervention into Aboriginal communities in the Northern Territory. While the stated objective of the intervention was to address child sexual abuse, the motivation for the intervention and its likely impact on Indigenous children's well-being are highly contested. This will be discussed later in this chapter. In November 2007, the Howard Government was voted out of office after 10 years in power. The Rudd Labor Government now has the opportunity to act decisively to implement a human rights framework for addressing Indigenous children's well-being and to redress the huge disparities between Indigenous and other children in Australia.

DISCUSSION QUESTION

- What is the relationship between systemic inequality and legal responses to child protection?

A human rights approach to Indigenous children's well-being

A human rights approach can provide an effective framework for Indigenous children's welfare because it is an approach which recognises and supports two essential matters. A human rights approach addresses the structural inequality and poverty which many Indigenous communities face. It therefore sees as essential the need to address all those indicators of inequality discussed above. However a human rights approach does not simply frame Indigenous people as a subset of those sections of the community which are poor and disadvantaged. A human rights approach also supports Indigenous children's right to their cultural identity and recognises the relationship between children's best interests and support for their culture, and those laws, traditions and activities which support a secure and safe identity (Libesman 2007). The Convention on the Rights of the Child (CROC) provides a framework within which children's civil, political, economic, social and cultural rights are articulated. There are frequent references in CROC to the importance of cultural, ethnic and linguistic rights. Article 30 of CROC requires that:

> In those States in which ethnic, religious or linguistic minorities or persons of indigenous origin exist, a child belonging to such a minority or who is indigenous shall not be denied the right, in community with other members of his or her group, to enjoy his or her own culture, to profess and practise his or her own religion, or to use his or her own language.

Article 30 of CROC is the only article in a human rights treaty which Australia has ratified which specifically refers to Indigenous people. It provides a strong basis for the recognition of Indigenous children's cultural rights. A human rights approach is consistent with a community development approach to children's well-being and support for greater Indigenous participation and control over their children's well-being. This is an approach which many Aboriginal and Torres Strait Islander organisations and individuals have called for.

The Convention on the Rights of the Child

Australia is a signatory to CROC and this means that all government departments, both state and federal, should comply with it. CROC is a treaty which is interpreted and monitored by the Committee on the Rights of the Child. The participation of Indigenous and other diverse groups in the development of CROC offers the potential for standards which are inclusive of Indigenous children and communities to develop. Indigenous people can participate in the development of CROC by providing information when their government provides their state report on compliance every three years and by contributing to the Committee's development of General Comments which become part of the law of CROC. Particular attention has been paid by the Committee to Indigenous children's rights. In addition to responding to country reports, the Committee held a General Day of Discussion on Indigenous children's rights in 2003. This resulted in the Committee recognising among other matters the importance of Indigenous participation in all decision-making which has relevance to Indigenous children and recognising the importance of land to Indigenous peoples and to Indigenous children's identity (recommendation 4).

Articles in CROC

CROC provides a framework within which children's civil, political, economic, social and cultural rights are articulated. There are 42 substantive articles in CROC. These articles relate to Indigenous children's rights in three ways: through general principles, through specific rights of Indigenous children, and through rights applicable to all children. CROC addresses many of the issues which face Aboriginal and Torres Strait Islander children in Australia. Issues which are addressed in CROC include: the right to survival and development; the right to a name, nationality and to be cared for by parents; the right to one's identity; the right to protection from all forms of physical, mental and sexual abuse; protection from discrimination; and respect for the views of the child.

Cultural rights recognised in CROC

There are frequent references in CROC to the importance of cultural, ethnic and linguistic background in addition to Article 30 which specifically includes Indigenous children (Cohen 1998). These references include Article 8 which addresses identity rights, Article 14 which addresses the right to freedom of thought and religion, Article 20 which addresses cultural continuity in temporary and permanent out-of-home care placements, and Article 29 which addresses the need to develop respect for a child's cultural identity, language and religion in their education. This theme of recognition for Indigenous and minority cultures provides a context for the interpretation of the other articles in CROC including Article 3 which provides that the best interests of the child must be a primary consideration in all decision-making with respect to the child. The best interests of the child, or a similar requirement, is the overriding principle in all state and territory child welfare legislation in Australia. Therefore how the best interest is defined is crucial to the weight and respect given to cultural security.

Australia's 2005 periodic report to the Committee on the Rights of the Child

The Committee on the Rights of the Child looked at Australia's report and made recommendations with respect to Australia's compliance with CROC in September 2005. The Committee expressed concerns and made recommendations with respect to many matters. Some of their concerns and recommendations with respect to Indigenous child welfare included: the discriminatory disparities in the provision and accessibility of services provided to Indigenous compared with other children; the need to fully implement the recommendations from *Bringing Them Home* (see below); the significant over-representation of Indigenous children in out-of-home care and the need to fully implement the Aboriginal child placement principle; the need to overcome, in a 'time bound manner' the disparity in the nutritional status between Indigenous and non-Indigenous children; the need to provide affordable housing and raise the standard of living of Indigenous children; and that an evaluation of the new arrangements for the administration of Indigenous affairs take place soon, in order to assess whether the abolition of ATSIC has been in the best interests of Indigenous children (Committee on the Rights of the Child 2005).

The value of CROC for Indigenous children

CROC provides a framework for the setting of standards for accountability by Indigenous and non-Indigenous organisations which work with Indigenous children. This framework includes mechanisms for the ongoing interpretation and review of these standards by an expert committee (Cohen 1993). The human rights framework provided by CROC is compatible with a capacity building and whole community approach to Indigenous children's well-being (Libesman 2007a). It is a respectful framework which acknowledges the value of Indigenous culture. The Committee on the Rights of the Child's work also complements that of other human rights monitoring bodies and forums (see Chapter 14). CROC and other international human rights law provide a useful yardstick with which to measure government departments, community organisations, and others involved with children. These principles could provide safeguards for Indigenous and all children, regardless of whether an Indigenous or non-Indigenous agency is working with the community.

DISCUSSION QUESTION

* Discuss some of the benefits and limitations of an international human rights framework for setting standards for local Aboriginal and Torres Strait Islander communities' needs.

Bringing Them Home

Indigenous organisations and individuals made many submissions to the Stolen Generations Inquiry with respect to contemporary child welfare. These submissions made three things clear. The first was that current child welfare legislation and administration was not serving Indigenous communities. Not a single submission to the National Inquiry was satisfied with the child welfare services in their state or territory. The second was that there was acknowledgment of the need for child welfare services and a call on governments to address the current needs of Aboriginal and Torres Strait

Islander children and families. The third was that Indigenous communities and families wanted more control over their children's well-being and welfare (NISATSIC 1997).

What *Bringing Them Home* recommended

Bringing Them Home's two-tiered recommendations with respect to child welfare enable both the structural inequality and poverty which many Indigenous communities face and the cultural safety and security of Indigenous children to be addressed. Both these issues are essential for securing Aboriginal and Torres Strait Islander children's fundamental human rights including their safety, dignity and security. The Inquiry recognised that different communities have different levels of capacity and aspirations with respect to controlling child welfare. The Report's recommendations are founded on fundamental human rights including recognition of the best interests of the child, participation rights, principles of non-discrimination, and principles of recognition of cultural and personal identities.

Self-determination

The NISATSIC recommended that national legislation be negotiated and adopted between Australian governments and key Indigenous organisations that would enable binding agreements to be made between governments and communities and give Indigenous people the opportunity to fully participate in decisions which affect their children (Recommendation 43). This recommendation provides that agreements should allow for the transfer of responsibility and control for Indigenous children's welfare to Indigenous organisations to the extent that communities have the capacity and want to take responsibility for child welfare. It is also recognised that adequate funding and resources must be provided to support the measures adopted by communities and that the human rights of Aboriginal and Torres Strait Islander children must be protected, regardless of whether an Aboriginal and Torres Strait Islander or non-Indigenous organisation or a government department is involved with the child.

Other child welfare recommendations made by NISATSIC

Other child welfare recommendations made by the NISATSIC include that minimum standards legislation for the treatment of all Aboriginal and Torres Strait Islander children and young people be negotiated by the Council of Australian Governments (COAG) and peak Aboriginal and Torres Strait Islander organisations (Recommendation 44). It was also recommended that benchmark standards be established for defining the best interests of the child (Recommendation 46). This requirement recognises the pivotal role which the best interest standard plays in most child welfare legislation.

The appropriateness of this standard for Aboriginal and Torres Strait Islander children is dependent on the knowledge and experiences of those defining what constitutes the best interests of a child and the weight which should be accorded to the different factors included. The Inquiry also recommended that requirements be established for consultation with accredited Aboriginal and Torres Strait Islander organisations (Recommendation 49). This recommendation recognises that a process needs to be in place both for identifying relevant organisations to consult with and for the consultation process itself, to ensure that it is thorough and in good faith. The Inquiry recommended that decision-makers ascertain if a child is Aboriginal or Torres Strait Islander when they come to the attention of any statutory organisation (Recommendation 49). This recommendation was made in recognition of the fact that many children were and continue to have contact with child welfare departments without recognition of their cultural background and specific cultural needs. This compromises the effectiveness of services provided to the child and their family and opportunities are lost for securing the child's well-being at an early stage of contact. While an Aboriginal and Torres Strait Islander child placement principle had been recognised in a number of jurisdictions prior to the National Inquiry, placement of children in out-of-home care is the most severe child welfare intervention and usually takes place after a department has already had considerable contact with the family. The importance of consultation and participation at all stages of contact with a child is recognised in the recommendation that accredited Aboriginal and Torres Strait Islander organisations be consulted at each stage of decision-making with respect to the child (Recommendation 49). The Inquiry also recommended that legislative recognition be given to the Aboriginal and Torres Strait Islander child placement principle, including the order of priority for the placement of children and that wherever possible their ongoing contact with their family is ensured (Recommendation 51).

These recommendations develop minimum standards for the immediate protection of Indigenous children and a longer term framework for addressing underlying and structural problems. This two-tiered approach recognises that immediate reform is necessary but that there also needs to be a longer term commitment of resources and that a process is required for capacity building within communities. This is in contrast to the federal government's approach in the Northern Territory which is discussed below. It is disappointing that the Commonwealth has failed to fulfil its role in implementing the recommendations from the NISATSIC. The Committee on the Rights of Child in its response to the Australian Government's periodic report in 2005 called on the state to fully implement the recommendations from the NISATSIC. While all states and territories have reviewed and reformed their child welfare legislation over the last decade, some more than once, none have implemented Recommendation 43 which addresses principles of self-determination as applied to contemporary child welfare and juvenile justice. They have nonetheless all made some progress in terms of reforming their child welfare legislation as it applies to Indigenous children. However there needs to be a considerable funding injection to enable these legislative reforms to be transformed into policy and practice. These reforms should be stepping stones towards greater capacity building within Indigenous children's organisations and towards a process of Indigenising child welfare as it serves Aboriginal and Torres Strait Islander communities. With the election of the Rudd Labor Government in November 2007, the potential for greater flexibility and cooperation between the federal government and state and territory governments has arisen.

DISCUSSION QUESTIONS

- What is the relationship between principles of self-determination and Aboriginal and Torres Strait Islander children's well-being?
- Why do you think state, territory and the federal governments have failed to implement Recommendation 43 of NISATSIC which addresses principles of self-determination with respect to Indigenous child welfare?

Australian child welfare legislation

As mentioned above, since *Bringing Them Home* was released a decade ago all states and territories have reviewed their child welfare legislation, some more than once. The reform processes have generally included a review of the child protection systems as they relate specifically to Indigenous children and families. They have all also acknowledged the importance of Indigenous identity for Indigenous children's welfare. The following provides an overview of reforms and how they compare with the recommendations from the NISATSIC and more generally a human rights perspective.

It is beyond the scope of this chapter to provide an overview of service delivery, or policy and programs with respect to Indigenous child welfare. However legislative reform cannot bring about improvements without parallel programs for addressing the social and economic factors which underpin child abuse and neglect and resources for effective support for Indigenous children's well-being. Many of the reforms discussed are directed towards greater recognition of Aboriginal and Torres Strait Islander peoples' involvement in decision-making affecting Indigenous children. They more broadly reflect recognition of the importance of culture and Indigenous identity for effective child protection and the well-being of Indigenous children. This is consistent with an international trend of capacity building and devolving responsibility for Indigenous children's well-being to Indigenous agencies and communities (Libesman 2004a). The reforms reflect the influence of both the recommendations from the NISATSIC and the ongoing advocacy by Indigenous children's organisations.

Aboriginal and Torres Strait Islander child placement principle

In all jurisdictions an Aboriginal and Torres Strait Islander child placement principle has been implemented in legislation. This principle provides an order of placement for Indigenous children who need to be placed in out-of-home care. The principle is an acknowledgment of the importance of Indigenous culture and family connection for Indigenous children and also in recognition of the destructive impacts which the history of assimilationist policies has had on Indigenous people.

In each jurisdiction the Aboriginal and Torres Strait Islander child placement principle has a similar descending order of placement preference for children who need to be in out-of-home care. The first preference is with the child's extended family or kinship group, the second preference with their local community and the third preference with another Indigenous family in the area. If it is not practicable or in the best interests of the child, then they will be placed with a non-Indigenous family. There is also a requirement in each jurisdiction that relevant Aboriginal or Torres Strait Islander organisations, and in some jurisdictions that the extended family, be consulted about the child's placement. In each jurisdiction children who are placed with non-Indigenous carers are to be assisted to keep in contact with their family, language and culture and in most jurisdictions the aim is to reunite the children who are placed in non-Indigenous care with their families and communities. An innovative provision in the *Children, Youth and Families Act 2005* (Vic) is the requirement that the Secretary must prepare and monitor the implementation of a cultural plan for each Aboriginal child placed in out-of-home care under a guardianship to the Secretary order (s 176).

While it is a great achievement to have legislative recognition of the Aboriginal and Torres Strait Islander child placement principle in all jurisdictions in Australia there is still a long way to go before the principle is in fact achieved. The Committee on the Rights of the Child expressed concern about the full implementation of this principle in their 2005 Report on Australia's compliance with the Convention on the Rights of the Child (para 39). Placement of children in out-of-home care is a measure of last resort and, as NISATSIC recommended, effective and culturally appropriate support for families and communities needs to occur a long time before out-of-home care is considered. This need has been legislatively recognised in child welfare legislation in a number of jurisdictions as will be discussed below. The placement principle is subject in most jurisdictions to the best interests of the child or similar guiding principles. This means that the effectiveness of the principle and its relevant application to Indigenous children is dependent on the full participation of Indigenous communities in the decision-making so that the best interests, or other general principles, incorporate Aboriginal and Torres Strait Islander experience.

A related matter is the process for participation and consultation with relevant family and Indigenous organisations. Most legislation provides for consultation but not all legislation provides guidance as to the weight which is to be given to these opinions and the process which is to guide the consultations. In some jurisdictions such as Victoria, Queensland and South Australia there is a process for designating appropriate organisations for the purpose of consultation with respect to placement and other decisions, and in other jurisdictions such as New South Wales there is no formal process for designating and identifying who should be consulted with (*Children, Youth and Families Act 2005* (Vic) s 12; *Child Protection Act 1999* (Qld) s 6(1); *Child Protection Act 1993* (SA) s 5).

A final matter which impacts on the placement of children in out-of-home care is the resurgence in a focus on stability and the early permanent placement of children who cannot live with their parents in out-of-home care. Two countervailing trends are occurring nationally and internationally in child welfare. The first is about family reunion and support for capacity building within families and communities. The second is a trend towards early permanent placements in out-of-home care. This usually involves setting short time frames within which a permanent decision needs to be made as to whether the child could be placed back with a parent or whether in the court's view there is no 'realistic possibility' of reunion. The trend towards early permanent placements has caused considerable concern within Indigenous communities in many parts of the world including Australia. The peak Indigenous children's organisation SNAICC believes that Indigenous children should always retain the possibility of reuniting with their families (SNAICC 2005). While Indigenous and all children have a need for stability and security, the impact of loss of culture and identity for children who are permanently placed away from their family is also significant. In Australia, there have been different ways of accommodating Indigenous communities' concerns about permanently placing children in each jurisdiction. The *Children, Youth and Families Act 2005* (Vic) has dealt effectively with these two competing needs. Section 323 provides that where an Aboriginal child is to be placed solely with a non-Aboriginal person, an Aboriginal agency must recommend the placement.

Principles of self-determination and participation

The New South Wales and Western Australian child welfare legislation and the current Northern Territory Bill have a 'self-determination' provision, all in a similar format, which provides that :

> Aboriginal and Torres Strait Islanders should be *allowed* to participate in the protection and care of their children with as much self-determination as possible [the *Children and Young Person's Care and Protection Act 1998* (NSW) s 11; the *Children and Community Services Act 2004* (WA) s 13; the *Care and Protection of Children and Young People Bill 2007* (NT) s 11].

While this provision is a step towards recognising the types of principle outlined in recommendation 43 from NISATSIC it has significant limitations. The provision is unclear and does not provide a definition of the term 'self-determination'. Rather than involving Aboriginal and Torres Strait Islander organisations as partners, their involvement is at the discretion of the Minister, who can outsource programs and discuss strategies with Aboriginal and Torres Strait Islander communities. Further, the provision fails to provide legislative safeguards as to how, and by whom, resources and programs should be designed and implemented.

In Victoria the legislation provides for a more far-reaching involvement of Indigenous organisations in the provision and administration of care and protection services. Section 18 of the *Children Youth and Families Act 2005* (Vic) provides for the delegation of most of the Secretary's functions to the principal officer of an Aboriginal agency. This provides extensive opportunity for the involvement of Indigenous agencies in all spheres of Indigenous children's welfare and well-being, up to and including guardianship responsibilities for children. However these are delegated powers and they are dependent on the Secretary exercising his or her discretion.

Participation

In all states and territories the legislation requires that Indigenous organisations, and in some jurisdiction also family, must participate in all significant decisions which involve Aboriginal children and in some jurisdictions such as Queensland they must be consulted about all other decisions (*Child Protection Act 1999* (Qld) s 6(1)). In Tasmania submissions made by Indigenous organisations must be taken into account. In South Australia there is a requirement that consultations take place in a manner that is as sympathetic to Aboriginal traditions as is possible (*Child Protection Act 1993* (SA) s 5). In most other jurisdictions, the terms and conditions of the consultation process are at the Minister's discretion, for example the *Children and Young Person's Care and Protection Act 1998* (NSW) s 12. In Victoria, there is provision that decisions about Aboriginal children should involve a meeting convened by an Aboriginal convenor who has been appointed by an Aboriginal agency (*Children Youth and Families Act 2005* (Vic) s 12). There is however little structural support or guidance across the legislation for its implementation.

Concluding comments on state and territory legislative reform

While the reforms of state and territory legislation discussed incorporate Indigenous input into decisions about their children they do not develop an Indigenous pathway for participating in the care and protection of children. Rather they provide an avenue for Indigenous participation in the mainstream departmental process. If the well-being of Indigenous children is to be addressed then the structural disadvantages and poverty which many communities face has to be an integral part of longer term policy for Indigenous children's well-being. Legislative reform can facilitate change but it has to be complemented with social and economic reforms. Further, for these legislative reforms to be successful there needs to be adequate support for the Indigenous organisation involved in child welfare and more broadly children's well-being. This involves in most cases capacity building and more direct funding for service provision. These legislative reforms however do indicate a growing recognition that improving the well-being of Indigenous children requires inclusion of Indigenous people and understandings in all levels of decision-making, policy formation and service provision. The recommendations from *Bringing Them Home* provide a useful framework for advocating for further legislative and policy reform.

DISCUSSION QUESTION

- In what ways do you think the participation of family and the local community is both similar to and different for Indigenous compared with all children who have contact with child welfare departments?

Commonwealth intervention in the Northern Territory

In 2006 and 2007, there was considerable media attention given to child sexual abuse in Aboriginal communities, particularly after the revelations of a public prosecutor, Nanette Rogers, in the Northern Territory (Lateline 2006). While these 'revelations' shocked many, the issues have been raised over a long period of time with few effective responses (Aboriginal Child Sexual Assault Taskforce 2006; Robertson 2000; Queensland Domestic Violence Taskforce 1988). The release of the *Little Children are Sacred Report* in 2007, which looked at child sexual abuse in the Northern Territory, catalysed the former federal government's emergency response (Report of the Northern Territory Board of Inquiry into the Protection of Aboriginal Children from Sexual Assault 2007). While there is consensus that urgent action needs to be taken with respect to child sexual assault in Indigenous communities, there are very serious concerns about the Commonwealth's intervention. Although the Howard Government initially claimed to be responding to the *Little Children are Sacred Report* it failed to implement the Report's recommendations and has established an agenda which is not recommended either in this Report or the dozens of other reports of which we are aware, both nationally or internationally, which address child protection, child sexual assault or related community development issues. A second concern is the very limited reference to children in the composite set of five Acts which span 365 pages and enable the federal government's intervention (*Northern*

Territory National Emergency Response Act 2007 (Cth); *Appropriation (Northern Territory National Emergency Response and Other Measures Act (No 1) 2007–2008* (Cth); *Social Security and Other Legislation Amendment (Welfare Payment Reform Act) 2007* (Cth); *Families, Community Services and Indigenous Affairs and Other Legislation Amendment (Northern Territory National Emergency Response and Other Measures) Act 2007* (Cth); *Appropriation (Northern Territory National Emergency Response) Act (No 2) 2007–2008* (Cth)). A third concern is the speed with which the Howard Government passed these poorly drafted Bills through both Houses of Parliament without the opportunity for public scrutiny or debate. The Bills passed through the House of Representatives in one day and the Senate in the same week. Muriel Bamblett, chair person of SNAICC, made the following comment: 'SNAICC would like to believe the Prime Minister's intervention in the Northern Territory is motivated by genuine concern, but we have been calling for concerted national action on child abuse and neglect for many years' (Bamblett 2007). The election of the Rudd Labor Government offers the opportunity for the Northern Territory intervention to be reviewed and for more effective measures which address child sexual abuse and more broadly Indigenous children's well-being to be implemented. Although Labor in opposition did support the Northern Territory intervention they also expressed reservations with respect to the associated suspension of the *Racial Discrimination Act*.

Key concerns with the legislation include its punitive response to whole communities which will impact adversely on families who have done nothing wrong, the exemption of the intervention from the *Racial Discrimination Act 1975* (Cth), the undermining of fundamental legal principles such as the rule of law, and more broadly concerns that the intervention could make Aboriginal children less rather than more safe. The intervention includes measures which acquire and limit Aboriginal control over Aboriginal land, the quarantining of Aboriginal social security benefits, the abolition of the main source of Aboriginal employment in the Northern Territory, CDEP (Community Development Employment Projects), the taking over of Aboriginal councils and Aboriginal organisations and the acquisition of their assets, the removal of customary law considerations from sentencing in criminal matters, the regulation of alcohol and the banning of pornography on government computers.

Widespread concern has been expressed about amendments to the *Aboriginal Land Rights (Northern Territory) Act 1976* (Cth) and more broadly about the land reforms which are part of the intervention. Land reform aspects of the intervention include the compulsory acquisition of Aboriginal land held under various tenures, for lease to the Commonwealth for at least five years; the resumption of town camp leases; the abolition of the permit system to control entry onto Aboriginal lands; and the institution of free market principles such as market-based rents to housing. All these measures had been on the Howard Government's agenda for a number of years and all will derogate from Indigenous peoples' control over their land. The relationship between these amendments and child protection remains unexplained. The revocation of the requirement for members of the general public to obtain a permit to visit communities on Aboriginal land is a reform which has been lifted out of a report authored by John Reeves QC in 1998. Mr Reeves QC reviewed the *Aboriginal Land Rights (Northern Territory) Act 1976* (Cth) and made recommendations which included a breakdown of Northern Territory land councils into regional councils, the removal of permits for entry onto Aboriginal land and that the Northern Territory Government be enabled to resume Aboriginal land for public purposes. These recommendations did not get through the Senate, where the Howard Government at the time did not have a majority. The Reeves Report makes no reference to children. John Reeves QC was one of the eight members of the 'Northern Territory Response Taskforce' appointed to advise on and oversee the operational aspects of the intervention. In 2008 the Rudd Labor Government reinstated the permit system on Aboriginal lands.

The quarantining of social security income and the abolition of CDEP are intended to cut income sources to communities so that money will not be available to spend on substance abuse. It is notable that measures adopted by communities such as Tangentyere Council to set aside part of peoples' pension on a voluntary basis were not supported by the Howard Government and the Council has had to pay for the administration of this community initiative. The imposition of this quarantine to Aboriginal welfare recipients exclusively is racially discriminatory and when imposed, particularly without consultation, is likely to have the adverse effect of disempowering people and removing another aspect of control from them. Early evidence suggests that quarantining is creating extra work for shops and confusion among community members. The abolition of CDEP is particularly problematic and for many people will impose great financial and personal hardship. This is in addition to the impact that the loss of these jobs will have on community services such as night patrols and child care centres which are directly related to children's safety and well-being. The decision to abolish CDEP was made by the Howard Government with limited knowledge of what its impact will be on community services. The increase in unemployment in communities, both in terms of the loss of income and in terms of the loss of morale or purpose, will inevitably impact adversely on children's well-being. The Rudd Labor Government decided in 2008 to reinstate CDEP where it was abolished and to stop further closures of CDEP.

While there is a broad interest in addressing substance abuse and pornography in communities, the measures taken in the intervention do not seem to be well considered. They lack effective enforcement mechanisms with respect to licensees' provision of illegal alcohol to community members, and do not address addiction issues or how to prevent the transfer of substance abuse and associated violence to communities which are not covered by the intervention. Likewise the measures to prevent accessing pornography entail organisations keeping detailed records of computer usage with significant penalties for breaches. The outcome of this regulation is likely to be many breaches of the administrative requirements.

While the government's emergency intervention has been developed on the run and therefore unfolds in an ad hoc manner, it is in sharp contrast to the human rights approach advocated for in much of the research and literature nationally and internationally with respect to Indigenous child welfare. It is an approach that echoes the paternalism of the protectionist period, which has left a legacy of harm and loss which paradoxically is associated with contemporary child protection issues. The Commonwealth intervention contrasts sharply with the response in Manitoba, Canada to significant child protection concerns in First Nations communities. The process of reform in Manitoba is discussed below.

DISCUSSION QUESTIONS

- Discuss parallels between the polices which underpinned the removal of Aboriginal and Torres Strait Islander children from their families discussed in Chapter 3 and the intervention in the Northern Territory.
- Research measures which have been implemented in other states and territories that have been influenced by the Northern Territory intervention.
- Research how the Rudd Government has responded to the Northern Territory intervention.

CASE STUDY

Manitoba

The delivery of child welfare services in Manitoba, Canada has been reformed with a thorough and planned process for devolving responsibility for First Nations children to First Nations authorities across the province. Like Australia, Canada has a federal system of governance, with child welfare being the primary responsibility of provinces and territories. The Aboriginal Justice Inquiry released a report in 1991 which found that the Province was not delivering child welfare services to First Nations children in Manitoba effectively and that there should be an overhaul of the system (Aboriginal Justice Implementation Commission 1999). They recommended among other matters that child and family services be provided in a manner that respects Aboriginal peoples' unique status, and that their cultural and linguistic heritage be enshrined in legislation; that existing Indian agencies be expanded to enable them to offer services to band members living off reserves; and that an Aboriginal child and family service agency be established to handle all other Aboriginal child welfare cases in Manitoba (McKenzie and Morrissette 2003). The recommendations from this report catalysed the reforms which are part of the Aboriginal Justice Inquiry— Child Welfare Initiative outlined below.

The Aboriginal Justice Inquiry—Child Welfare Initiative negotiations were from the start a joint initiative between the Manitoba Metis Federation, the Assembly of Manitoba Chiefs, Manitoba Keewatinowi Okimakanakwere and the Province. The comprehensive inclusion of all parties in the negotiations has created a firm foundation for effective reform. The negotiations have resulted in shared responsibility between Aboriginal peoples and the province for child welfare. This initiative has resulted in the expansion of Aboriginal child welfare services which had already been established to service Aboriginal children on reserves and the establishment of new Aboriginal agencies to service Aboriginal children throughout Manitoba. The restructuring of child welfare in Manitoba commenced with the signing of Memorandums of Understanding and then Service Protocol Agreements between the province and the Manitoba Métis Federation, the Assembly of Manitoba Chiefs and the Manitoba Keewatinowin Okimakanak (Holnbeck et al 2003). The Manitoba initiative is different to all previous reforms in that the policy-making process was jointly developed, and the government, rather than being the primary policy maker, was one of four policy-making partners.

Under the *Child and Family Services Act 2003* (Manitoba) four umbrella child welfare authorities have been established. It is the responsibility of each Authority to develop policy and to fund local agencies to deliver culturally appropriate child support and protection services. The authorities are all working under the *Manitoba Child and Family Services Act 1985* (CSF) and the *Adoption Act 1997* while new, more culturally attuned, legislation is being developed. Two of the authorities are First Nations, there is also one Metis Child and Family Service Authority and a General Authority which is responsible for the delivery of services to other (non-Aboriginal) children and families. A Detailed Implementation Plan (DIP) was designed to provide a framework to implement the restructure of child welfare in Manitoba. A key feature of this plan is that it is a 'rolling document' designed to accommodate any changing circumstances. Caseloads, resources and assets are being transferred from the previous child welfare departments to the most culturally appropriate authority and their agencies. Under the old system non-Aboriginal agencies provided services to Aboriginal families. The General Authority and its associated agencies will be downsized as cases are transferred to the mandated First Nations and Metis authorities. This will only occur once the Aboriginal authorities and agencies are ready to assume these responsibilities.

The intake services are structured in such a way that the four authorities jointly manage the services but through designated agencies. In Winnipeg there is a joint intake response unit as the first point of contact and outside of Winnipeg a number of designated agencies are charged with the responsibility. There is a separate agency designed to provide emergency services, identify the authority which holds records and refer clients to the ongoing services. It is also envisaged that information sharing including information regarding abuse will take place and that common registries will be established for that purpose. Funding is also being transferred to the new authorities. The Manitoba Government provides funding to the authorities and this is then distributed to their agencies. An additional one-off payment was also made to cover additional expenses for things such as training, transitional costs, transfer of caseloads and other administrative costs.

A large body of opinion suggests that Aboriginal people have a right to define and deliver their own services (Aboriginal Justice Inquiry—Child Welfare Initiative 2003). The Manitoba restructure is based on the right of First Nations and Metis peoples to culturally appropriate services and the concepts of collaboration, participation and righting the wrongs of the past are at the core of the initiative (Blackstock and Trocme 2004). The restructured system was driven by First Nations and Metis peoples and it is unique in that regard. Another striking feature is that the Manitoba Government has been willing to share some aspects of its child welfare jurisdiction. The Manitoba initiative was developed as a five-phase plan with timelines that can be updated and amended to ensure that the reform is flexible and is not compromised by artificial constraints. The transfer stage appears to be well thought out with transfers being made on a region-by-region basis, with the aim that each authority and agency will have time to prepare and ensure they are ready to accept the responsibilities entrusted to them. This is particularly relevant to the Metis Authority because it had to be established from scratch, unlike the mandated First Nations agencies which have been set up in some form for over two decades. One of the benefits of the Manitoba initiative is that it is highly adaptable and can therefore be structured around regional differences. Although some issues may have been missed at the conceptual stage, the structure means it can more readily accommodate changes in the future. It also appears to offer a structure that can be adapted to other contexts and countries.

Conclusion

If the reform of child protection services to Indigenous communities is to be effective, Indigenous understandings need to permeate all aspects of legislation, service design and delivery. Fundamental improvement requires effective partnerships between child welfare departments and Indigenous agencies which facilitate a community development approach to Indigenous children's well-being. Contemporary Indigenous child welfare must be informed by the history of colonial policies and their impact on child welfare in Indigenous communities. This requires an integrated approach towards addressing individual and community trauma, building community capacity with a particular focus on children and families, and establishing processes and legislative structures for transferring responsibility, including resources, to community agencies. The Manitoba case study provides an example of such a process. It is very difficult for child welfare departments to relinquish power and resources. It is also very difficult for Indigenous communities to assume responsibility where this has been denied over a long period. However, a process of decolonising attitudes, establishing new Indigenous child protection structures and empowering Indigenous agencies through training and the provision of resources would, over a period of time, improve relations between mainstream and Indigenous agencies and facilitate the Indigenisation of child welfare.

PART 2
Equal before the Law: Criminalisation

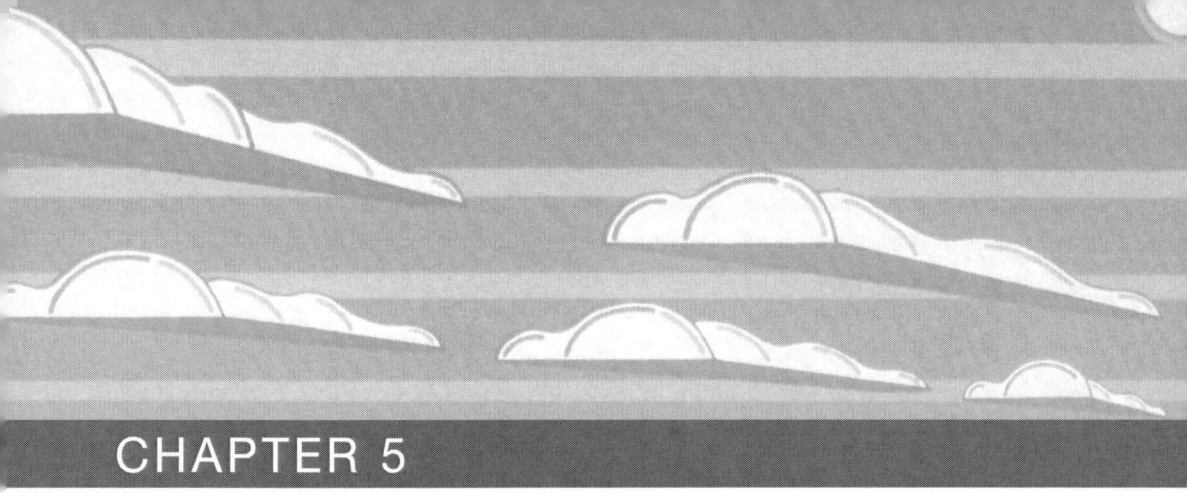

CHAPTER 5

Juvenile Justice

Introduction

This chapter, and the following two chapters, consider the contemporary relationship between Indigenous people and the institutions of the criminal law. We do this through an analysis of the juvenile justice system (Chapter 5), policing and criminalisation (Chapter 6) and courts, sentencing and punishment (Chapter 7). There is also a focus on reform and Indigenous programs in the community for dealing with offending behaviour including discussion of community justice groups and Indigenous courts.

As we saw in cases like *Bonjon* and *Murrell*, the interaction between Indigenous people and the criminal law has been subject to controversy from the early years of colonisation. In more recent times the Royal Commission into Aboriginal Deaths in Custody (Johnston 1991) provided an exhaustive examination of the role of the criminal law and the criminal justice system in the lives of Indigenous people in Australia. In this chapter we examine one part of the criminal justice system which deals specifically with children and young people. As will become evident, the importance of considering the impact of the criminal law on Indigenous children and young people is the long-term negative effects on individuals, families and communities.

We often speak of the *juvenile justice system* to distinguish it from the criminal laws, policies and procedures which apply to adults. There is not the space here to fully discuss all the distinctive features of juvenile justice (see Cunneen and White 2007). However, it is possible to identify key details.

- *Age.* A young person is defined as being between the age of 10 and 18 years in Australian jurisdictions. Children under the age of 10 years cannot be charged with a criminal offence. At 18 years of age, a young person is regarded as an adult by the criminal law.
- *Police discretion.* Police have greater discretion when dealing with young people because there is a greater range of diversionary options other than a court appearance.
- *Importance of the principle of diversion.* The importance of diverting young people from the formal justice system is recognised in international human rights law. The principle gives rise to specific alternatives to arrest, charge and court appearance.
- *Separate court.* The Children's Court determines most matters relating to young people. In serious indictable offences, the Children's Court acts as a committal court prior to the matter being transferred to a higher court.
- *Different sentencing principles.* The principle of rehabilitation is usually seen as foremost when sentencing young people. Compared to the sentencing of adults, the principles of retribution and deterrence are usually considered as less important with children and young people.
- *Different sentencing options.* The type and range of penalties applied in the Children's Court is different from the adult court system.
- *Different penal institutions.* Young people sentenced to detention are held in specific juvenile detention centres. However, in some cases a young person can be transferred into the adult correctional system, and in some cases young people serving a sentence in juvenile detention will remain in the juvenile system after they turn 18 years of age.

Figure 5.1 shows the process for juveniles from the time of police apprehension through to the use of diversionary alternatives or appearance in the Children's Court. No single jurisdiction in Australia operates exactly in this way, nor are all possible options canvassed in the diagram. Figure 5.1 provides an overview of the principal types of decisions which are made in the course of apprehending a young person, and most Australian jurisdictions approximate the process which is outlined.

Figure 5.1: Juvenile justice processes: from police apprehension to Children's Court

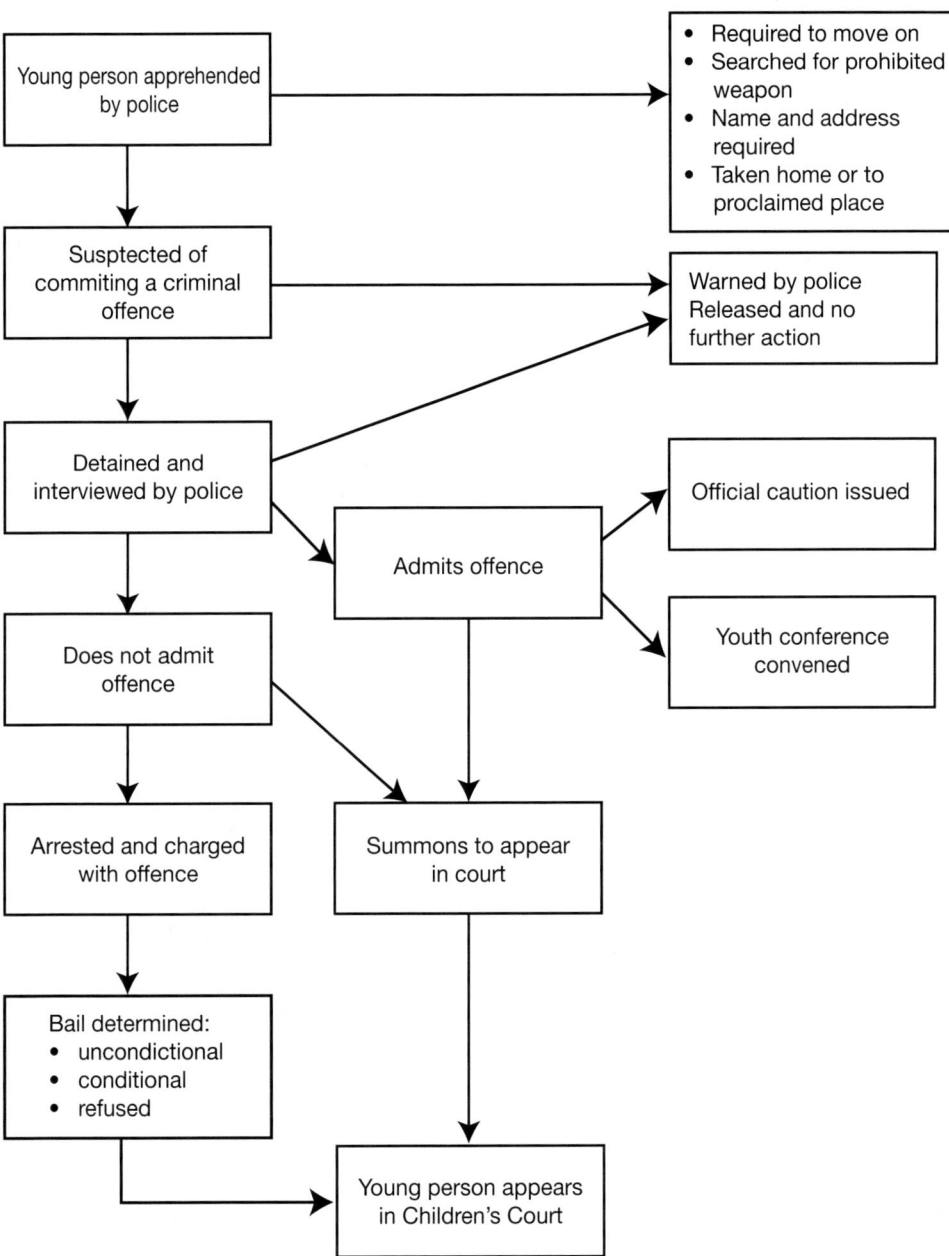

Each level of intervention involves decision-making, and the outcome of those decisions affect passage through the system. For example, the use of an option such as a warning, caution or conference diverts the young person away from a court appearance. The use of a summons to bring a young person before the court is less punitive than the use of arrest and charge which subsequently requires a bail determination.

As will become evident in our discussion in this chapter, at each stage of intervention Indigenous young people tend to receive the more punitive options. Thus, one result of the decisions which are made by authorities is that the level of over-representation actually increases as Aboriginal young people move through the system. Aboriginal youth are least over-represented in the least punitive stages of intervention (such as the use of a police caution) and most over-represented at the point of police custody or committal to an institution.

The extent of contact with juvenile justice agencies

One way to understand the extent of intervention by the criminal justice system into the lives of Aboriginal young people is to look at the number of juveniles who, at some time in their adolescence, come into contact with juvenile justice agencies. Research in South Australia has considered this question through the study of cohorts born in particular years. Morgan (1993) found that 55 per cent of Aboriginal youth born in 1972 either appeared in a Children's Court or before a youth panel during their juvenile years, while Skryzpiec and Wundersitz (2005) found for the 1984 cohort that this had decreased somewhat to 44 per cent. When broken down by sex, Skryzpiec and Wundersitz found that 63 per cent of Aboriginal boys and 27 per cent of Aboriginal girls had formal contact with the juvenile justice system. These figures can be compared to 24 per cent of non-Indigenous boys and 7 per cent of non-Indigenous girls (Skryzpiec and Wundersitz 2005: 5–6). The figures give some idea of the extensive formal contact of Aboriginal young people with juvenile justice agencies: a majority of Aboriginal male youth have formal contact at some stage of their adolescent years, as do more than one in four Aboriginal girls.

There is also evidence to suggest that Indigenous young people are more over-represented in the juvenile justice system than Indigenous adults are in the adult criminal justice system. For example, in Western Australia in 2000, 21 per cent of all adults arrested were Aboriginal, but 36 per cent of all juveniles arrested were Aboriginal (Ferrante, Fernandez and Loh 2001: 44). Nationally, Indigenous youth comprise 40 per cent of all young people held in police custody (Taylor and Bareja 2005: 27). As shown in Table 5.1 on 30 June 2005 there were 605 young people aged 10–17 in detention in Australia; of these 52.4 per cent (317) were Indigenous youth.

Table 5.1: Indigenous Young People Aged 10–17 years in Detention Centres in Australia as at 30 June 2005

State	Indigenous No	Non-Indigenous No	Indigenous Rate([1])	Non-Indigenous Rate([1])	Over-represenation([2])
NSW	112	105	364.6	15.1	24.1
VIC	20	43	303.8	8.1	37.4
QLD	54	44	188.1	10.4	18.1
WA	79	27	555.3	12.6	44.1
SA	26	33	470.6	21.1	22.3
TAS	8	27	205.9	52.7	3.9
NT	15	2	136.6	13.8	9.9
ACT	3	7	352.9	20.4	17.3
Australia	317	288	312.3	13.6	23.0

(1) Rate per 100,000 of the respective juvenile populations

(2) Over-representation measured by Indigenous rate per 100,000 divided by non-Indigenous rate

Source: Adapted from Taylor (2006: 17–23)

Figure 5.2: Indigenous juvenile over-representation in detention, Australia, 1994–2005

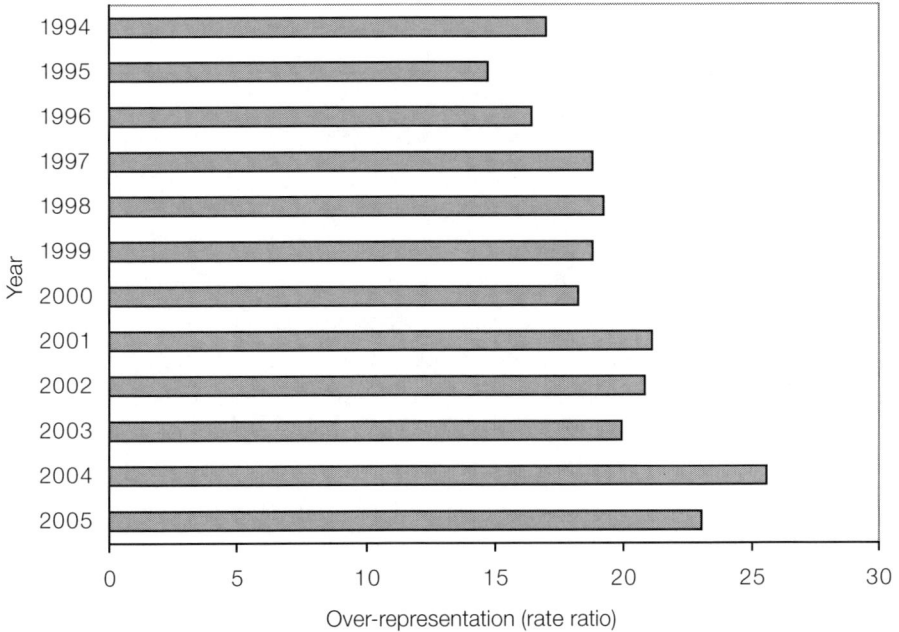

Table 5.1 shows that majority of young people incarcerated in New South Wales, the Northern Territory, Western Australia and Queensland are Indigenous. New South Wales has the greatest number of Indigenous young people in detention centres (112); the highest rate of Indigenous youth incarceration is in Western Australia (555.3 per 100,000).

In every jurisdiction in Australia, the rate of incarceration for Indigenous youth is much higher than the non-Indigenous rate. The level of over-representation is greatest in Western Australia where an Indigenous young person is 44 times more likely to be in a detention centre than a non-Indigenous youth. Nationally, Indigenous young people are 23 times more likely to be incarcerated than non-Indigenous youth.

Figure 5.2 shows that, despite attempts to reduce Indigenous over-representation in juvenile detention, the problem has generally worsened during the period 1994–2005.

Police decision-making and Indigenous youth

To a large extent, police determine which young people will enter the juvenile justice system, as well as the terms on which they enter. Police must continually decide whether to intervene and how to intervene. The evidence strongly suggests that police discretionary decisions work against the interests of Indigenous young people.

For example, there is considerable evidence that police intervene in situations involving Indigenous people, particularly 'street offences', in often unnecessary and provocative ways. The case study below illustrates how police actions can lead to tragic results for Indigenous youth.

The death of Daniel Yock

CASE STUDY

Daniel Yock died in police custody in Brisbane in November 1993. Nine Aboriginal young people (including Yock) aged between 15 and 18 years were in Musgrave Park in Brisbane. The older youths had bought some alcohol and were drinking. A police van began circling the park, driving slowly and observing the youths. When the group left the park the police van slowly followed them along the road. Although there was contradictory evidence, it appears that some verbal abuse and various gestures were directed at the police in the van, who called for assistance. Two other police cars responded. Police made a number of arrests for disorderly conduct. Yock was tackled to the ground by police during his arrest. He later died in the police van from a heart attack.

Police had considerable discretion as to how they might have proceeded. Perhaps, a warning to the young people would have been sufficient. Perhaps no intervention was necessary, and police contact with the Aboriginal police liaison officer would have been a better option. Irrespective of potential alternatives which were available, police *decided* to embark on the most confrontational approach possible in the circumstances.

The Royal Commission into Aboriginal Deaths in Custody noted in the early 1990s the effects of adverse police decisions:

> 14.4.8 The cases investigated by the Commission illustrate how the juvenile justice system prejudices the Aboriginal youth offender ... The complaint has frequently been made that young Aboriginals are unnecessarily or deliberately made the subject of trivial charges or multiple charges, with the result that the appearance of a serious criminal record is built up at an early age. This follows them through life, is a handicap against defending themselves or seeking mitigation if they are charged again, and also handicaps them in relation to employment and in other ways (Johnston 1991: (2) 275).

The Daniel Yock case occurred several years after the Royal Commission had reported and provides an example of situations that the Royal Commission into Aboriginal Deaths in Custody sought to avoid. Indeed, a number of recommendations were designed to encourage police to think about whether intervention was necessary in these situations and what alternative types of intervention might be appropriate rather than arrest and custody.

For further discussion of the Yock case see Criminal Justice Commission (1994), Cunneen (2001a: 134–135).

Curfews, parental responsibility and removal of young people from public places

There has also been a growing tendency to provide police with powers to remove children from public places under certain circumstances, and to hold parents 'responsible' for the actions of their children. An example of this type of legislation is the *Children (Protection and Parental Responsibility) Act 1997* (NSW). In relation to 'parental responsibility', the Act provides the power to require parents or guardians to attend court in matters involving their children, it allows the court to obtain undertakings from the parents in relation to their children's behaviour and creates an offence of 'wilful default' where parents are found to have contributed to their child's offence.

The *Children (Protection and Parental Responsibility) Act 1997* also increases police powers in public places. Police can remove unaccompanied young people under the age of 16 years from public places if they are considered to be 'at risk' (that is, in danger of harm or abuse, or about to commit an offence). The new police powers do not apply across the state; rather a local shire council must apply to become 'operational' under the legislation. This allows for differential application of the legislation, depending upon where people live.

The New South Wales Aboriginal Justice Advisory Council (AJAC) undertook research on the use of the 'removal' powers of the legislation in Ballina and Moree. In Ballina, the removal power was infrequently used by police. However, in Moree, where Aboriginal young people make up somewhere between 30 and 40 per cent of the youth population, the legislation was used far more frequently. Some 95 per cent of young people removed from public places were Indigenous. The AJAC concluded:

> The Act has sanctioned widespread police over-surveillance and control of young people. Young people have been incorrectly told there are curfews in place and that areas of the town are 'no go' zones. The Act has significantly changed behaviour patterns of young people and limited their freedoms to move around town (AJAC 1999a: 1).

The 'Northbridge Curfew' in Perth is another example of this type of differential policing which impacts disproportionately on Indigenous youth. The Western Australian Law Reform Commission found that:

> While ostensibly the Northbridge curfew applies to all children, statistics show that the majority of children dealt with pursuant to the curfew are Aboriginal. For example, 88 per cent of children dealt with by police in 2004 were Aboriginal (Law Reform Commission of Western Australia 2006: 210).

The policy on a curfew in the Northbridge entertainment area in Perth came into force in 2003 and relied on police powers already available under s 138B of the *Child Welfare Act 1947* (WA). The legislation authorises a police officer to apprehend an unsupervised child who is away from their usual place of residence, if the police officer believes the child to be in physical or moral danger, misbehaving or truanting from school. The Young People in Northbridge Policy prevents young people from being in the area unsupervised during particular hours: children under the age of 12 are prohibited after dark; children between 13 years and 15 years of age after 10 pm. Children 15 to 18 years of age may be apprehended at any time if their anti-social, offending or health-compromising behaviour places them or others at risk of harm (Law Reform Commission of Western Australia 2006: 210). Almost nine in every ten children removed under the curfew policy were Indigenous.

Stop and search powers

The problem of differential policing of Indigenous young people can also be seen in the way search powers have been used. The *Crimes Legislation Amendment (Police and Public Safety) Act 1998* (NSW) provides police with the power to search for prohibited implements (knives, scissors, and so on). Search powers of juveniles are used more frequently in Aboriginal communities. In Bourke and Brewarrina nearly 90 per cent, and in Moree 95 per cent, of searches were 'unsuccessful' in the sense that the young person was not carrying a prohibited implement at the time of the search (Chan and Cunneen 2000: 39).

The Pinkenba Incident

Three Aboriginal boys, aged 12, 13 and 14 years old, were detained by six police officers in a shopping mall in Fortitude Valley, Brisbane, some time after midnight on 10 May 1994. There was no evidence that the young people had committed any offence at the time they were detained. The boys were never charged with any criminal matter and were never taken to a police station. They were taken about 14 kilometres to an industrial wasteland and swamp in Pinkenba in three police cars.

The three youths later claimed they were terrorised by six police officers on the banks of a creek. The boys claimed that they were told to take off their clothes and shoes, and told they were going to be thrown in the creek. The children claimed that police threatened to cut off their fingers. Finally the six police drove off and left the children to find their way back to Fortitude Valley at around 4 am. The police officers were charged with unlawfully depriving the three Aboriginal young people of their liberty. The magistrate found that the police officers had no case to answer because there was no evidence that the children were held against their will. It was found that the children knew their legal rights and had voluntarily accompanied police. There was no dispute that they had been placed in the police cars, driven to Pinkenba, and 'dumped' there. The Pinkenba incident shows the way certain police are prepared to intervene and use a form of terror as a control tactic over what are perceived to be dissident and troublesome groups of Indigenous young people in public places. The courts provided no remedy for the injustice.

See Eades (1995a), Cunneen (2001a: 114–116).

CASE STUDY

Warnings and cautioning

When police suspect a young person of committing an offence, they have the option to warn the young person about their behaviour and take no further action. The use of a warning, by its nature, is a discretion which is largely unregulated and unsupervised. For example, s 14 of the *Young Offenders Act 1997* (NSW) provides that a young person can be dealt with by way of a warning for minor summary offences which do not involve violence. There is no systematic research on the use of warnings for Indigenous young people. However, evidence which shows that Indigenous young people are over-represented before the courts for offences such as offensive language strongly suggests that warnings are not being used as extensively as envisaged (Bargen 2000: 18).

Police have the power to issue a formal caution against a young person as an alternative to charging them with a criminal offence. The caution is a formal recorded warning to the young person about their criminal behaviour. If a caution is issued, the young person is not prosecuted and the matter does not proceed to court. There are various conditions that affect whether a caution can be issued. For example, there is a requirement that a young person admit the offence. In some jurisdictions young people with prior convictions are ineligible for a caution. Certain offences may also be excluded from cautioning such as serious indictable offences. Some legislation also establishes criteria: s 31 of the New South Wales *Young Offenders Act 1997* refers to the seriousness of the offence, the level of violence involved, the degree of harm caused and the offending history of the child as being important considerations to be taken into account when police are deciding whether to issue a caution.

Various studies over the last decade or so have found that Aboriginal young people do not receive the benefit of a police caution to the same extent as non-Aboriginal youth. For example, Luke and Cunneen's (1995) study in New South Wales found that some 5.7 per cent of Aboriginal young people were cautioned compared to 12.9 per cent of non-Aboriginal young people. Differential treatment was particularly evident in country areas, where two-thirds of Aboriginal interventions occur.

Even when young people had no prior record of either court appearance or caution, it was still found that Aboriginal first offenders had a greater chance of being prosecuted by police and thus a lower chance of receiving a police caution than non-Aboriginal youth (Luke and Cunneen 1995: 19–21). For example, Aboriginal girls with no prior record were less than half as likely as non-Aboriginal girls to receive a police caution (14 per cent compared to 30 per cent). This pattern of differential treatment was maintained when the offence type was held constant. For example, 15.5 per cent of Aboriginal female first offenders apprehended for minor theft were cautioned, compared to 36.8 per cent of non-Aboriginal females apprehended for the same offence (Luke and Cunneen 1995: 78).

More recent research in New South Wales since the introduction of the *Young Offenders Act 1997* shows that Indigenous young people are still less likely to receive a police caution than non-Indigenous youth (Chan et al 2004; Cunneen and Luke 2006). There is also evidence in other states that confirms that Indigenous young people are often only half as likely as a non-Indigenous youth to receive a diversionary option of a police caution (for further discussion of this research, see NISATSIC 1997:

513–516; Cunneen and White 2007: 155–156). There are two interconnected issues that arise. First, the failure to use cautions has the effect of entrenching Indigenous young people in the more punitive parts of the juvenile justice system. Second, it appears that cautioning can be an effective intervention given that the majority of young people cautioned at the beginning of their contact with juvenile justice agencies do not go on to have further contact with the juvenile justice system (Dennison et al 2006: 6).

Note on *WO (A Child) v The State of Western Australia*

'In 2005 the Western Australian Court of Criminal Appeal … took into account that the rate of referral to diversionary juvenile justice options is far less for Aboriginal children and, as a result, Aboriginal children come into contact with the formal criminal justice system at a much faster rate. Therefore, when making decisions based in part upon the offender's criminal record, it was held that a court must be careful to ensure that the cumulative effect of previous decisions is taken into account and that details of any past offending are closely examined' (Law Reform Commission of Western Australia 2006: 172).

CASE STUDY

Arrest or court attendance notice

If police decide not to caution but to proceed against a young person, there is a range of options available. The options vary somewhat from one jurisdiction to the next, however most have some form of 'conferencing' available as an alternative to a Children's Court appearance. We are going to leave the question of conferencing for the moment and return to it below. Let's assume for now that the police officer decides that it is appropriate that the young person be brought before the court to face criminal prosecution. This can be achieved either through arrest, custody and the determination of bail, or through the issue of a court attendance notice (also referred to as 'summons' or 'notice to appear').

The use of a court attendance notice is a less punitive way of bringing a young person before the courts on a criminal charge. Unlike proceeding by way of arrest, the use of a court attendance notice does not involve being detained or having bail determined. Research also indicates that Children's Courts are more likely to impose custodial sentences on young people brought before them by way of arrest than on the basis of a court attendance notice, because the process itself influences the court's view of the seriousness of the matter and the nature of the offender (Gale et al 1990).

In many states, the evidence shows Aboriginal young people are more likely to be proceeded against by way of arrest and bail, and to be held in police custody, and less likely to be issued with a court attendance notice than non-Aboriginal youth.

- In South Australia in 2005, 69 per cent of Aboriginal youth were brought into the juvenile justice system by way of arrest, compared to 44 per cent of non-Aboriginal youth (Office of Crime Statistics and Research 2006: 19).
- In Western Australia in 2004, a higher proportion of non-Aboriginal youth (31.5 per cent) were proceeded against by way of summons compared to Aboriginal young people (20.5 per cent). Conversely, a greater proportion of Aboriginal youth were arrested (Ferrante et al 2005: 46).
- In New South Wales in 2004, 45.7 per cent of Aboriginal young people were proceeded against by way of arrest compared to 17.1 per cent of non-Aboriginal youth (see also Figure 5.3) (Cunneen and Luke 2006: 63).
- In Queensland in 2004, 37 per cent of Indigenous young people were proceeded against by way of arrest compared to 19 per cent of non-Indigenous youth (Cunneen 2005: 46).

The evidence is very clear: throughout Australia, Aboriginal young people do not have the same benefits of less intrusive criminal justice processes. The one positive point to note is that in some jurisdictions, like New South Wales and Queensland, there has been a general move over recent years to use attendance notices instead of arrest. However, the trend has not been universal. In South Australia, the practice of arresting juveniles instead of using other methods has been on the increase over the last decade, rising from 27 per cent to 46 per cent of interventions (Office of Crime Statistics and Research 2006: 18).

Bail and remand

The purpose of bail is to ensure that the defendant will appear in court to face charges, and to protect any victim and/or the community from further offences. Generally, children have a greater right to bail than adults. The need to determine bail arises after the young person has been arrested and charged with a criminal offence. Bail does not arise when a person is proceeded against by way of a court attendance notice. Therefore, because Aboriginal young people are more likely to be proceeded with by way of arrest, they are more likely to face a bail determination. Two issues are important: first, whether bail will be refused and the young person held in custody; and second, if bail is granted, which conditions, if any, will be attached.

In the first instance, Aboriginal young people are more likely than non-Aboriginal young people to be refused bail by police. For example, it was found in Queensland that more than half, and sometimes more than two-thirds, of overnight detentions of young people in police watch-houses involved Indigenous youth. The major reason for such detention was the refusal of bail (NISATSIC 1997: 520). In New South Wales, Aboriginal young people are nearly 40 per cent more likely to be refused bail. However, the difference is not as great when prior criminal records are controlled for, except in rural areas, where Aboriginal first offenders are still twice as likely to be refused bail as non-Aboriginal first offenders (Luke and Cunneen 1995: 23–24).

The second issue of importance concerning bail is the nature of the conditions that are imposed when bail is granted. The Royal Commission into Aboriginal Deaths in Custody was particularly concerned with 'unreal conditions' that are imposed and then regularly broken. The result is that young people are recycled through the courts (Wootten 1991: 353). Onerous and oppressive bail conditions may include curfews and residential requirements amounting to banishment (Cunneen 1994: 139–141). Such conditions place enormous pressures on the young person and their family, and in the end may simply set up the young person for failure and further intervention.

There may also be specific requirements to meeting bail which disadvantage Indigenous young people. The Law Reform Commission of Western Australia (2006: 163) noted that the *Bail Act 1982* (WA) requires that a child under the age of 17 can only be released on bail if a responsible person signs an undertaking. This requirement may be difficult to meet with Aboriginal children arrested some distance from their homes and with family members unable to attend.

Changes to bail legislation

There has been a growing tendency to limit the presumption in favour of bail for repeat offenders, and this impacts negatively on Indigenous young people. For example, in New South Wales the following legislation has been introduced.

- The *Bail Amendment (Repeat Offenders) Act 2002* (NSW) removed the presumption in favour of bail for a very wide range of people: anyone on a bond or order who re-offends, anyone who has previously failed to appear, or has previously been convicted of an indictable offence.
- The *Justice Legislation Amendment (Non-association and Place Restriction) Act 2001* (NSW) allows a court to make a 'non-association order', prohibiting the offender from associating with specified person(s). The court may also make a 'place restriction order', prohibiting the offender from visiting a specified place or district.
- The *Law Enforcement Legislation Amendment (Public Safety) Act 2005* (NSW) came into effect in December 2005. The legislation removes the presumption in favour of bail for certain public order offences.

It is clear that there has been a much more punitive attitude towards refusing young people bail and detaining them in custody. Indigenous youth are more likely to have a prior offending history, to have had contact with police at an earlier age than non-Indigenous youth, and to be arrested for public order offences. In other words, they are more likely to fall into the category of those without a presumption in favour of bail.

These changes have had a significant impact on the detention of Indigenous young people. For example, in New South Wales between 2000 and mid-2005, the proportion of Indigenous young people on remand has risen from around 30 per cent to around 50 per cent of all remands over the period (Cunneen and Luke 2006: 127). In Queensland in 2004, 84 per cent of all admissions to detention that involved Indigenous young people were as a result of being remanded in custody. For the period 2000–2001 to 2003–2004, only 16 per cent of Indigenous young people remanded in custody were subsequently sentenced to detention (Cunneen 2005: 79).

DISCUSSION QUESTION

- Why are Indigenous young people more likely to be adversely affected by stricter bail legislation?

Youth justice conferencing

Youth justice conferencing has become a favoured option for diversion of young people from the courts in recent years. Conferences are intended to bring together young offenders and their support persons with the victim and their supporters to develop a sense of responsibility on the part of the offender for the offence. They are also intended to reach a mutually agreeable resolution (often referred to as an 'outcome plan') for the harm that has been caused by the offence and to reintegrate the offender back into the community. A successful conference is an alternative to a Children's Court appearance. Referral to a conference can be made by police and, in some jurisdictions, also by the court.

Various conferencing schemes exist in all Australian jurisdictions, although there are important differences between states and territories around eligibility criteria, referral processes and other procedures. In many jurisdictions, conferencing is established within specific legislation (for example, the relevant *Young Offenders Acts* in New South Wales, South Australia and Western Australia). Because conferencing has emerged as a major diversionary scheme for young people, it is important to consider whether the process has been successful in providing Indigenous young people with an effective diversionary alternative. The answer to this question is mixed.

The problem of referral

Indigenous young people are not being referred as frequently to conferences as non-Indigenous youth, although the difference varies from state to state and is perhaps not as pronounced as it was in the early years of conferencing. In the first few years of the *Young Offenders Act 1997* in New South Wales there were around 5,000 referrals to conferences and about 20 per cent of these referrals were Aboriginal young offenders. The rate of diversion was about 13 percentage points lower for Indigenous young people (Hennessy 1999). In more recent years, we have seen growth in the proportion of conferences involving Indigenous young people. In 2004–2005, 29 per cent of referrals to conferences involved Indigenous young people (New South Wales Department of Juvenile Justice 2005: 11). In fact, in 2004, an Indigenous young person was slightly more likely to be referred to a conference than a non-Indigenous young person. However, this also needs to be placed in the context of the relatively infrequent use of conferences compared to other interventions (see Figure 5.3). For data on Indigenous referrals in Western Australia, see Ferrante et al (2005: 54; 107; 116) and in South Australia the Office of Crime Statistics and Research (2006: 82–3).

The evidence suggests that the greater the police control of the referral process the less likely it is that Indigenous young people will benefit from conferencing. In states where there is the possibility of the Children's Court, as well as police, referring young people to a conference, there is less adverse discrimination. Courts appear more willing than police to refer Aboriginal youth, and this is reflected in the higher proportion of Aboriginal youth among court referrals to conferences in Western Australia (42.7 per cent of court referrals to conferences involved Indigenous young people compared to 31.6 per cent of police referrals: Ferrante et al 2005: 116), and in Queensland (59 per cent of all Indigenous conference referrals were made by the courts compared to 45 per cent for non-Indigenous referrals: Cunneen 2005: 62).

A worrying trend in some jurisdictions is that police referrals to conferences are declining. Police referrals of young people generally fell by 21 per cent in Western Australia in 2004 (Ferrante et al 2005: vii). In New South Wales, the proportion of police interventions resulting in a referral to a conference fell for both Indigenous and non-Indigenous young people between 2000 and 2004 to a point where they comprised 2.9 per cent of Indigenous interventions and 2.4 per cent of non-Indigenous interventions (Cunneen and Luke 2006: 63; see also Figure 5.3). In South Australia, the number of referrals has been on a slow but steady decline between 1995 and 2005 (Office of Crime Statistics and Research 2006: 27).

Thus law, policy and practice around the referral process will have a major impact on whether Aboriginal young people are likely to access conferencing programs. In addition, other policies will impact on access to programs. For example, in Western Australia conferencing is only available to first offenders, and in the Northern Territory for 'minor' offenders (Cunneen 1997: 304; Crosthwaite 1999; Jonas 2002). Yet we know that Indigenous young people come into the system at an earlier age, and are generally far more likely to have a record of previous convictions than non-Indigenous youth (Gale et al 1990, Luke and Cunneen 1995; Crime Research Centre 1995). These restrictions, coupled with restrictions on the type of matters which can be dealt by conferences

(Crime Research Centre 1995; Dodson 1996, Crosthwaite 1999), will structurally exclude many Indigenous young people from the process. Similarly in New South Wales, although the *Young Offenders Act 1997* has a presumption in favour of the use of the least restrictive form of sanction (s 7), police are also required to consider prior cautions, conferences or convictions when determining how to proceed with a young person.

Is conferencing culturally appropriate?

Questions can arise as to the cultural appropriateness of the conference format, the level of participation and satisfaction of Aboriginal people in the conference process, and the likelihood of successful completion of conference plans (Cunneen 1997; Urbis Keys Young 2001; Strang 2001).

One problem has been the assumption that conferencing as a form of restorative justice is inherently consistent with Indigenous culture (for further discussion see Cunneen 1997; Blagg 1997; Blagg 1998). The presumed applicability of the conferencing model to traditional Indigenous dispute resolution can grossly simplify Indigenous cultures in a number of ways. First, it assumes that Indigenous cultures are all the same and operate on a model that prioritises a simple confrontational meeting between offender and victim. Blagg (1997) has noted the extent to which Indigenous societies in Australia seek to avoid open conflict between victim and offender. Support for this view can be found in careful and extensive analysis of dispute management in Aboriginal communities such as that undertaken by Williams who discusses a variety of sanctions used by Yolngu people in Arnhemland including temporary exile, temporary internal exile, withdrawal and restitution (Williams 1987: 96–106). Many of these sanctions are based on avoidance rather than confrontation. Similarly, elders groups dealing with Indigenous young people in northern Queensland still rely on various forms of exile through the use of outstations. In central Australia, managing disputes and preparing for the intervention of the non-Indigenous criminal justice system may involve complex arrangements between various clan groups in the absence of the offender or the victim (Intjartnama 1994).

Second, conferencing assumes that Indigenous young people can operate effectively within an imposed model without suffering significant disadvantage because of cultural difference. These differences include inadequate understanding of Indigenous social structure, language barriers, different communication patterns and different spatial and temporal patterns which derive from cultural obligations (see Chapter 6). On the basis of observations of conferencing in South Australia, it has been suggested that 'the most striking aspect of the model developed *for* Indigenous people are the problems encountered with cultural difference' (Dodson 1996: 46).

Third, conferencing may fail to grasp adequately the relationship between Indigenous communities and non-Indigenous criminal justice bureaucracies. The demands of non-Indigenous law, practice and procedure can silence participation. This can occur through the police presence in a conference, through alienation from a process that does not understand and respect Indigenous structures and processes for inter-personal communication, or through undermining existing forms of Indigenous social control (Dodson 1996; Cunneen 1997).

Finally, the extent of consultation and negotiation with Indigenous people and Indigenous organisations in the development of conferencing programs has varied between different Australian jurisdictions. It appears that during the introduction of conferencing during the early to mid-1990s, very little negotiation took place with Indigenous people as to how the scheme would operate (see Cunneen 1997: 295–296). More recently there have been significant attempts to increase Indigenous participation, both as participants in conferences, as well as conference administrators and convenors (Bargen 1999).

Part of the problem has been that in most of Australia, conferencing has been an add-on feature to more punitive changes in juvenile justice legislation where serious and repeat offenders are ineligible for diversionary programs and are dealt with more punitively through sentencing regimes that are more akin to adult models. Indigenous young people are often seen as more difficult offenders and 'unresponsive' to alternatives such as conferencing. 'The courts may perceive Aboriginal youth to have "failed to respond" to diversionary options such as cautioning and family group conferences and consequently "up-tariff" them, that is, give them a more severe disposition than justified by the current offence alone' (Crime Research Centre 1995: 13).

Potential benefits

While we have emphasised some of the problems with conferencing, we also acknowledge some positive outcomes. Evidence is mixed on compliance. In Queensland, it suggests no difference in breach rates for Indigenous young offenders for failing to complete conferencing plans (Cunneen 2005a: 64). In South Australia Aboriginal youth were less likely to have a 'successful' conference than non-Aboriginal youth (18.4 per cent were unsuccessful compared to 10.8 per cent for non-Indigenous youth). The main reason was that Indigenous young offenders were less likely to attend the conference as required (Office of Crime Statistics and Research 2006: 5).

There appears to be no less satisfaction with the conferencing process by either Indigenous offenders or victims (Cunneen 2005a: 64; Trimboli 2000). Perhaps most importantly, research demonstrates that conferencing is more successful in reducing re-offending than the courts for both Indigenous and non-Indigenous participants (Luke and Lind 2002), although the impact is likely to be greatest among those with lower risks of re-offending (Hayes and Daly 2004).

Figure 5.3: Police interventions by type and Indigenous status, New South Wales, 2004

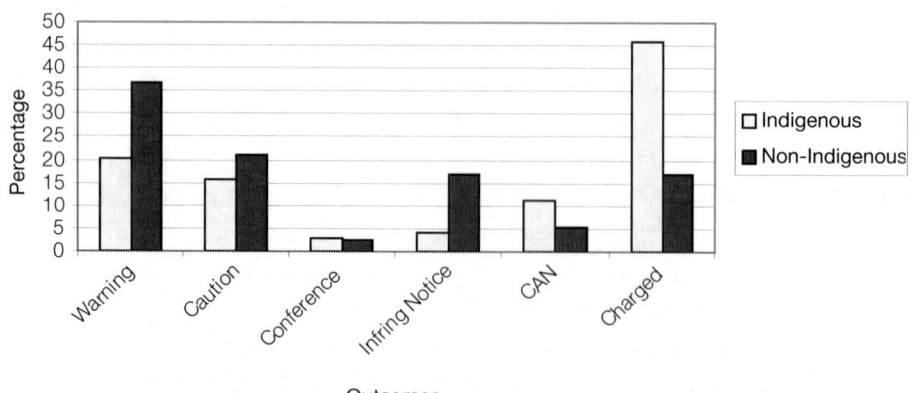

Note: CAN = Court Attendance Notice; Infring = Infringement.

Source: Cunneen and Luke (2006: 63)

The problem of police intervention and diversion

Figure 5.3 summarises the type of problems we have been discussing in relation to diversion. At the most punitive end of decision-making, Indigenous young people are most likely to be dealt with by way of arrest and charge, while at the least punitive end of decision-making, non-Indigenous young people are more likely to be dealt with by way of a warning.

DISCUSSION QUESTION

- Discuss the problems and benefits associated with tighter regulation of police discretionary decision-making involving young people.

Human rights principles and juvenile diversion

The United Nations Convention on the Rights of the Child (CROC) recognises the important principle of diverting young offenders from the formal processes of the criminal justice system. CROC was ratified by Australia in 1990. The principle of diversion is also confirmed in the United Nations Standard Minimum Rules for the Administration of Juvenile Justice 1985 (Beijing Rules). Article 40.3 of CROC establishes a clear preference for alternative diversionary measures over formal judicial proceedings:

> States Parties shall seek to promote the establishment of laws, procedures, authorities and institutions specifically applicable to children alleged as, accused of, or recognized as having infringed the penal law, and, in particular:
>
> (b)   Whenever appropriate and desirable, measures for dealing with such children without resorting to judicial proceedings, providing that human rights and legal safeguards are fully respected.

CROC also requires diversion at the point of police intervention. CROC states in Article 37(b) that the arrest of young people should be a measure of last resort and for the shortest period of time.[1]

The principles of non-discrimination and equality before the law are fundamental to the enjoyment of human rights. Article 2 of CROC prohibits discrimination and requires affirmative measures to diminish or eliminate conditions which give rise to discrimination. We have demonstrated that Indigenous children do not receive the same benefits of diversionary programs as other young people. Clearly, the adequate provision of diversionary programs and non-discrimination in access to those programs are critical to ensuring compliance with human rights.

The requirements of Article 30 of CROC are noted in Chapter 4. Article 30 accords special rights to Indigenous children and young people. It requires their protection through non-interference with the right to enjoy their own culture, practise their own religion and use their own language. Article 30 has an impact on the nature of diversionary programs. It requires that diversionary schemes be culturally appropriate or have the ability to be adapted in culturally appropriate ways.

Aboriginal elders and diversionary programs

There is some limited formal provision for direct involvement of Indigenous people or Indigenous organisations in the administration and decision-making of juvenile justice. For example, in some jurisdictions there is the possibility that Aboriginal elders can be involved in the issuing of police cautions to young offenders. The *Juvenile Justice Act 1992* (Qld) provides that that cautions can be delivered by a respected person from the Aboriginal and Torres Strait Islander community. However, it is difficult to ascertain how frequently this occurs in practice.

Some provisions also exist in legislation establishing conferences that they should be 'culturally appropriate'. According to the New South Wales *Juvenile Justice Act 1997*,

---

1   For further considerations relevant to the operation of diversionary alternatives, see HREOC (2001).

measures for dealing with children are to be culturally appropriate 'wherever possible' and the sanctions imposed should 'take into account the gender, race and sexuality' of the child (s 34(1)(a)(v) and s 34(1)(c)(iv)). The administrator of conferences, when choosing a convenor to run the conference, needs to consider whether it is possible to match the young person with a convenor from the same cultural background. Section 30(2)(c)(v) of the Tasmanian *Youth Justice Act 1997* provides that when conferences are held which involve Indigenous youth, then an elder or other representative of the young person's community must be invited.

The South Australian *Young Offenders Act 1993* lists in s 3(2) a number of statutory policies. Subsection (2)(e) provides for the proper regard of a youth's sense of racial, ethnic or cultural identity. However, there are no specific requirements in relation to either police cautions or family conferencing for culturally appropriate Indigenous participation. The Western Australian *Young Offenders Act 1994* requires that, when the person being dealt with is a 'member of an ethnic or other minority group', the conference team should include a person nominated by members of an ethnic or minority group, 'where practicable'.

These requirements pose several problems. What does 'culturally appropriate' mean? Who will decide what it is, when it is possible, and what processes will guarantee its implementation? There is no provision for Indigenous organisations and communities to make these decisions, nor decisions about the best interests of their children.

Juvenile justice reform

The two major national inquiries which considered Indigenous justice issues in the 1990s recommended substantial change to the way the juvenile justice operates in relation to Indigenous young people. The Royal Commission into Aboriginal Deaths in Custody (RCADIC) dealt extensively with the issue of Indigenous young people in the juvenile justice system. Many of the recommendations put forward were designed to deal with issues that are discussed in this chapter, and included an emphasis on the greater use of summons and diversionary mechanisms, realistic bail conditions, and the establishment of bail hostels. (See Chapter 6 for further discussion of the RCADIC.)

A fundamental recommendation in relation to young people was the need for negotiation between authorities and Aboriginal communities on the causes of offending and the development of suitable responses (Recommendation 62). Associated with this recommendation were two further recommendations (235 and 236) which required that the primary source of information about Aboriginal young people should derive from Aboriginal communities and organisations; and that Aboriginal community-based and devised strategies were the most successful way of operating programs for Aboriginal youth.

The Stolen Generations Inquiry was completed seven years after the RCADIC and its recommendations focus far more specifically on the importance of self-determination, as well as greater controls over decision-making in the juvenile justice system. The Inquiry noted that self-determination could take many forms from self-government to regional authorities, regional agreements or community constitutions—an issue we return to in more detail later in this book. Some communities or regions may seek the transfer of jurisdiction over juvenile justice matters to an Indigenous authority as essential to the exercise of self-determination. Other communities may wish to work with existing government departments in ways which provide greater control in decision-making for Indigenous organisations. Either way, the level of responsibility to be exercised by Indigenous communities must be negotiated with the communities themselves (NISATSIC 1997: 575–576).

Recommendation 43 is the key recommendation from the Stolen Generations Inquiry regarding Indigenous self-determination. It requires that national legislation be negotiated and adopted between Australian governments and key Indigenous organisations to establish a framework of negotiations for the implementation of self-determination. The national framework legislation should adopt principles that bind Australian governments to the Act; that allow Indigenous communities to formulate and negotiate an agreement on measures best suited to their needs in respect of their children and young people; that ensure adequate funding and resources are available to support the measures adopted by the community; and that ensure the human rights of Indigenous children are respected. Part (c) of recommendation 43 authorises negotiations to include the complete transfer of juvenile justice and/or welfare jurisdictions, the transfer of policing, judicial and/or departmental functions, or the development of shared jurisdiction where this is the desire of the community (NISATSIC 1997: 580).

Recommendation 44 of the Stolen Generations Inquiry requires the development of national legislation that establishes national minimum standards for the treatment of all Indigenous children and young people, irrespective of whether those children are dealt with by government or Indigenous communities and organisations. The recommended national minimum standards provide the benchmark for future developments. They include standards and rules covering:

- principles relating to the best interests of the child;
- the requirement for consultation with accredited Indigenous organisations thoroughly and in good faith when decisions are being made about an Indigenous young person, including decisions about diversion, bail, and other matters;
- minimising the use of arrest and maximising the use of court attendance notices;
- notification of an accredited Indigenous organisation whenever an Indigenous young person has been arrested or detained;

- protections during the interrogation process;
- minimising bail and detention in police cells;
- prioritising the use of Indigenous-run community-based sanctions;
- the consideration of relevant sentencing factors; and
- the minimisation of custodial sentences.

The development of national minimum standards recognises the need for immediate change in the level of control by Indigenous communities and organisations in the decisions that affect the future of their children and young people. Unfortunately, there has been an inadequate response to the recommendations of the Stolen Generations Inquiry (Cunneen and Libesman 2001).

Conclusion

Over the last decades, many Indigenous communities have grappled with developing alternative mechanisms for dealing with young people who offend. They include initiatives like night patrols, community justice groups and Indigenous courts; we deal more fully with these initiatives in the following chapters. Government departments also have had some successful programs like mentoring and specific alternatives to custody such as bail hostels. In some cases there have been successful interfaces between government departments and Indigenous community-based organisations such as the Koori Justice Worker Program in Victoria, community justice groups in Queensland, and Children's Courts initiatives involving elders in a number of states.

Unfortunately, many Indigenous community-based mechanisms have tended to be inadequately funded, and without a legislative framework. This has often limited their capacity to develop sustained solutions to problems. However, a key principle in these developments has been implementing self-determination at the grassroots level. Communities have continually sought their own solutions to the problem of the over-representation of Indigenous young people in the juvenile justice system (NISATSIC 1997; Dodson 1995, 1996).

A theme woven through this book is that Indigenous people have specific rights as distinct peoples of Australia. These rights are increasingly recognised in international law, and in particular and most importantly the right to self-determination. Further rights specifically in relation to Indigenous children can be found in the United Nations Convention on the Rights of the Child. A fundamental area for the application of self-determination must be in juvenile justice policy—particularly given the level of criminalisation of Indigenous youth and its long-term negative consequences on Indigenous communities.

CHAPTER 6

Criminalisation and Policing in Indigenous Communities

Introduction

There are two broad purposes to this chapter. The first is to build on the analysis provided in the previous chapter and to consider in more depth the processes of criminalisation of Indigenous people in Australia through policing and the criminal law. The second purpose is to reflect on contemporary Indigenous modes of policing and governance.

State policing in Indigenous communities is an important issue on any range of measures. For example, members of the Indigenous community of Palm Island were so impassioned after a death in police custody, they destroyed the local police station and courthouse. This should give us pause to reflect on community attitudes to criminalisation and the volatility of Aboriginal/police relations. The last national police custody survey (2002) showed that 26.3 per cent of police custodies in Australia involved Indigenous people. The rate of Indigenous custody was 2028.7 per 100,000 of the Indigenous population. Indigenous people were 17 times more likely to be held in police custody than non-Indigenous people in the Australia (Taylor and Bareja 2005: 22–23). Conversely, Indigenous victimisation rates are also high. The Steering Committee for the Report of Government Service Provision (SCROGSP) noted that, nationally, twice the proportion of Indigenous males and more than two-and-a-half times the proportion of Indigenous females reported being victims of physical or threatened violence than their non-Indigenous counterparts (SCROGSP 2005: Table 3A.11.2).

Clearly, policing and the criminal law play a large part in Indigenous people's lives. A recent report noted:

> Historically Aboriginal people have been subject to oppressive treatment by police. As a consequence, Aboriginal people often distrust and resent police officers. During the Commission's consultations many Aboriginal people complained about their treatment by police. The lack of respect by police for Aboriginal people generally, and for Elders and community leaders, was highlighted. Many Aboriginal people believe there is extensive racism within the police service. Lack of sensitivity by police towards Aboriginal victims and lack of appropriate support for victims of family violence were also mentioned. Many communities commented that young Aboriginal people were treated poorly by police. It is clear that relations between Aboriginal people and the police are still extremely strained (Law Reform Commission of Western Australia 2006: 192).

Problems with policing and criminalisation in Indigenous communities are well documented (Johnston 1991; Cunneen 2001a). The key driver to reform the relationship between Indigenous people, the police and the criminal justice system over the last several decades has been the Royal Commission into Aboriginal Deaths in Custody (RCADIC).

The Royal Commission into Aboriginal Deaths in Custody

The RCADIC was established in 1987 and reported to the federal parliament in 1991. It was generated by the activism from Aboriginal organisations including the Committee to Defend Black Rights and Aboriginal Legal Services, the families of those who had died in custody and their supporters. From the early 1980s there had been a number of deaths in police and prison custody which caused serious alarm among Aboriginal communities across the country. These included in particular the deaths of John Pat in Western Australia (who was a juvenile at the time and died after a pub brawl involving police), and Eddie Murray in New South Wales (picked up by police for public drunkenness and died from hanging in a police cell) (Cowlishaw 1991).

The RCADIC found that the high number of Aboriginal deaths in custody was directly relative to the over-representation of Aboriginal people in custody. However, failure by custodial authorities to exercise a proper duty of care was also exposed. The RCADIC found that there was little understanding of the duty of care owed by custodial authorities and there were many system defects in relation to exercising care. There were many failures to exercise proper care. In some cases, the failure to offer proper care directly contributed to or caused the death in custody (Johnston 1991: vol 1).

Commissioner Wootten in his report on New South Wales, Victoria and Tasmania noted that 'every one of the [18] deaths was potentially avoidable and in a more enlightened and efficient system … might not have occurred. Many of those who died should not or need not have been in custody at all' (Wootten 1991a: 7). He found that 'negligence, lack of care, and/or breach of instructions on the part of custodial authorities was found to have played an important role in the circumstances leading to 13 of the 18 deaths investigated' (Wootten 1991a: 63).

The RCADIC found that the most significant contributing factor to bringing Indigenous people into contact with the criminal justice system was their disadvantaged and unequal position within the wider society. The elimination of Indigenous disadvantage would only be achieved through empowerment, self-determination and reconciliation. The RCADIC also found that in the 99 deaths in custody investigated, the Aboriginality of the person played a significant and in some cases dominant role in the reason for the person being in custody and dying in custody. In almost half of the cases the person had been removed from their families as a child, and a similar proportion had been arrested for a criminal offence before they were 15 years old. In over 80 per cent of cases the person was unemployed. In general, those who died had early and repeated contact with the criminal justice system (Johnston 1991).

The RCADIC made 339 recommendations to achieve the ends of reducing custody levels, remedying social disadvantage and assuring self-determination. All Australian governments committed themselves to implementing the majority of recommendations.

The RCADIC also made specific recommendations designed to reduce the occurrence of deaths in custody including the removal of hanging points from cells; increasing the awareness by custodial and medical staff of issues concerning the proper treatment of both Indigenous and non-Indigenous prisoners; and a greater commitment to cross-cultural training for police, the judiciary and other criminal justice staff.

DISCUSSION QUESTION

- What criteria might we use to determine the success or failure of the RCADIC?

Public order and police powers

We noted above the results of the national police custody survey (2002) in terms of Indigenous over-representation. The survey also collected information on the most serious offence for which the person was in custody. The figures show that 23.5 per cent of Indigenous custodies resulted from public order offences (Taylor and Bareja 2005: 30). The second and third largest categories for Indigenous people were assault offences (16.2 per cent) and justice offences (breach of bail and other court orders) (11 per cent).

The RCADIC and minor offences

Many of the recommendations from the RCADIC dealt with diversion from police custody and this is not surprising given that two-thirds of all the deaths which were investigated occurred in police custody rather than prison. Furthermore, most Aboriginal people at the time of the RCADIC were in police custody for public drunkenness and street offences (Johnston 1991: vol 1, 12–13). The focus of recommendations in this regard was to decriminalise public drunkenness, provide sobering-up shelters, change practice and procedures relating to arrest and bail (particularly for minor offences) and to provide alternatives to the use of police custody.[1]

Public order offences and police powers to intervene in public places remain among the most contentious issues in the application of the criminal law and policing of Indigenous people. Criminal behaviour is behaviour which is legally defined as

---

1   Changes to police practice and legislation to enhance diversion from police custody are called for in recommendations 60–61, 79–91 and 214–233 (Johnston 1991: vol 5).

'wrong'. It is also socially defined behaviour. For example, possession and use of a drug such as heroin is a criminal offence, while possession and use of another drug, alcohol, by adults is legal. Behaviour which is criminal is not fixed, but changes with changing social attitudes. During the period of the late 1970s to the 1990s many states and territories in Australia decriminalised public drunkenness, although police still retain power to detain a person who is seriously intoxicated in public. Legislation abolishing the criminal offence of public drunkenness was passed in the Northern Territory in 1974, New South Wales in 1979, South Australia in 1984, Western Australia in 1989, the ACT in 1994 and in Tasmania in 2000. Public drunkenness remains a criminal offence in Victoria and Queensland (Drugs and Crime Prevention Committee 2001: 13–27).

Despite the decriminalisation of public drunkenness in most jurisdictions, many Indigenous people still come into contact with the criminal justice system because of the public consumption of alcohol. In part these problems are related to the use of protective detention, the use of local council by-laws prohibiting alcohol consumption and other restrictions such as the Northern Territory's law prohibiting alcohol consumption within two kilometres of licensed premises, and penalties associated with breaches of Queensland's alcohol management plans. Some alcohol restrictions only apply to Indigenous people or Indigenous communities (Race Discrimination Commissioner 1995; McRae et al 2003: 504–505; Cunneen 2005a).

Recommendations 80–84 of the RCADIC had called on governments to fund non-custodial alternatives for Indigenous people detained for drunkenness, and to place a statutory duty on police to use alternatives, and to negotiate with Aboriginal communities to find acceptable plans for public drinking.

The Callope decision

Callope pleaded guilty to two offences in the Magistrates Court at Weipa, namely that he had in his possession one can of beer in a public place which was a restricted area (the Napranum DOGIT Lands) declared under s 173H of the *Liquor Act 1992* as amended by the *Indigenous Communities Liquor Licences Act (2002)*. The second offence occurred the following day when he had in his possession one cask of red wine. The penalty imposed for the first offence was one month's imprisonment to be followed by probation for 40 weeks. For the second offence the penalty was six weeks' imprisonment with 42 weeks' probation. A special condition on each probation order was that the defendant undertake a substance abuse program. The sentences were to be served concurrently.

The magistrate's decision was appealed (*Callope v Senior Constable B Elsley*, District Court of Queensland, Cairns, 8 March 2005, White DCJ, File 510 of 2004, unreported). White J overturned the magistrate's decision and ordered Callope's

CASE STUDY

immediate release, taking into account the seven days he had served in custody prior to release on bail pending the appeal.

Callope's criminal history showed that, prior to the introduction of Alcohol Management Plans, his last appearance in court for any offence was 1988. Between 1988 and 2003 he was not convicted of offences of violence, public disorder, or any other type of offence. The 15-year period of not having contact with the criminal justice system changed with the introduction of the new legislation restricting alcohol possession. Once the legislation was in place, Callope was regularly before the courts. The offences discussed here were his third and fourth against the legislation. As Judge White noted, 'it is difficult to imagine a less serious example of this offence than the possession of one can of beer in circumstances in which there was no potential for the commission of the offence to undermine the purpose of the legislation' [which was to stem violence in Indigenous communities] (at 5).

For further discussion see Cunneen (2005a: 152–160). Also relevant is the Cape York Justice Study Report (Fitzgerald 2001) and various Queensland Government online resources on Alcohol Management Plans.

Move-on powers

Police have powers to request individuals in public places to 'move on' under certain conditions. The laws vary from one jurisdiction to another. In Western Australia move-on powers are found in s 50 of the *Police Act 1892*. The section came into operation in 2005. A police officer can order a person to leave a public place for up to 24 hours if the officer reasonably suspects the person is committing a breach of the peace or intends to commit an offence. Failure to comply with the order, without a reasonable excuse, can lead to a penalty of up to 12 months' imprisonment.

Discrimination and the use of move-on powers

There are numerous accounts to suggest that move-on notices are being issued to Aboriginal people in inappropriate circumstances and that Aboriginal people are being disproportionately affected by this law. It appears that in some cases Aboriginal people are being targeted by the police for congregating in large groups in public areas even though no one is doing anything wrong ...

The Commission is very concerned about the apparent discriminatory treatment of Aboriginal people with respect to move-on notices ... [B]ecause a move-on notice can be issued when a police officer reasonably suspects that the person is likely to commit an offence there is a large scope for misuse of police discretion (Law Reform Commission of Western Australia 2006: 209).

Move-on powers in New South Wales were introduced as a result of amendments in 1998 to s 28F of the *Summary Offences Act 1988*. They are now found in Part 14 of the *Law Enforcement (Powers and Responsibilities) Act 2002* (hereafter *LEPRA 2002*). They provide police with the power to direct a person to move on if the officer has reasonable grounds to believe that the person's behaviour or presence is causing obstruction, constituting harassment or intimidation, or is causing or likely to cause fear to another person. Failure to comply with the direction can lead to a fine of $220. Importantly they empower police to direct people to move on even in the absence of evidence that the person has committed or was likely to commit a criminal offence (Brown et al 2006: 853).

An Ombudsman's review of the move-on powers found that 22 per cent of people given directions in New South Wales were Indigenous people, and just over half of those were aged 17 years or younger (New South Wales Office of the Ombudsman 1999: 230). The Ombudsman noted the following:

> It is not clear why such high numbers of Aboriginal and Torres Strait Islander people are subject to s 28F directions. The impact of the 'move on' power was of particular concern to the Western Aboriginal Legal Service, which argued that the power
>
> ... brings otherwise law abiding persons into contact with the police and criminal justice system. The evil of this increased contact is highlighted in townships of high Aboriginal populations where relations between police and community have historically (and justifiably) been very poor.
>
> The legal service added that any increased contact may further exacerbate the tensions in police relations with Aboriginal communities (New South Wales Office of the Ombudsman 1999: 232).

An evaluation of the use of the legislation in areas with large Aboriginal populations shows wide disparity in the use of move-on powers. For example, police use of the move-on powers in Bourke and Brewarrina was at a rate 30 times higher than the state average (492.3 compared to 16.5 per 10,000 of the population) (Chan and Cunneen 2000: 32).

Offensive language and offensive behaviour

Offensive language and offensive behaviour are offences under state and territory law in Australia. For example, ss 4 and 4A of the *Summary Offences Act 1988* (NSW) prohibit offensive conduct and offensive language near or within view or hearing of a public place or school. As Brown et al (2006: 806) note, 'such provisions are inevitably open-ended, with the characterisation of the behaviour left to the discretion of the police in the first instance, and subsequently to the discretion of magistrates'.

In New South Wales, the maximum penalty for offensive conduct is three months' imprisonment and for offensive language a fine of $660. Aboriginal people are significantly over-represented in prosecutions for these types of offences. Research by the New South Wales Aboriginal Justice Advisory Committee found that in 1998 some 20 per cent of all prosecutions for these offences involved Aboriginal people, and 14.3 per cent of all Aboriginal people appearing in New South Wales Local Courts had at least one charge of offensive language or offensive conduct. In one out of four cases where an Aboriginal person was charged with offensive language or offensive conduct, they were also charged with offences against the police such as resisting arrest or assaulting police (AJAC 1999b; see also Jochelson 1997; New South Wales Anti-Discrimination Board 1982).

Commissioner Wootten from the RCADIC made the following observation about police use of and response to offensive language:

> Over and over again during this Commission there has been evidence about Aboriginals using the term 'cunts' in relation to police, usually with the result of a charge of offensive behaviour ... I have often been led to wonder how police could continue to remain offended by a term they heard so often and so routinely ... The evidence in the Gundy hearing gave several glimpses of the fact that, as one would expect, it is a term in common use amongst police themselves ...
>
> It is surely time that police learnt to ignore mere abuse, let alone simple 'bad language' ... Charges about language just become part of an oppressive mechanism of control of Aboriginals. Too often the attempt to arrest or charge an Aboriginal for offensive language sets in train a sequence of offences by that person and others—resisting arrest, assaulting police, hindering police and so on, none of which would have occurred if police were not so easily 'offended' (Wootten 1991a: 144–145).

The RCADIC recommended that the use of offensive language in circumstances of interventions initiated by police should not normally be occasion for arrest and charge (Recommendation 86). A review of the implementation of this recommendation found that, 'throughout Australia, Aboriginal people are being arrested, placed in police custody and, in some cases, imprisoned on the basis of behaviour that the police find offensive and which has been precipitated by police actions' (Cunneen and McDonald 1997: 8).

Some magistrates have questioned whether the use of the word 'fuck' in public constituted offensive language given its ubiquitous nature in social discourse. For example, New South Wales Magistrate Heilpern dismissed offensive language charges against an Aboriginal women in *Police v Butler* [2003] NSWLC at 1 (Moruya Local Court) and against an 18-year-old Aboriginal man in *Police v Dunn* (unreported, 27 August 1999, Dubbo Local Court). For further discussion see Brown et al (2006: 810, 817).

The use of arrest for minor offences

Police powers of arrest are found in the various Criminal Codes, Crimes Acts and related legislation in each state and territory in Australia. In New South Wales, for example, the powers of arrest are found in s 99, Pt 8 of the *LEPRA 2002* (NSW). Police have power to arrest a person if the person has committed or is committing an offence, or the police officer suspects on reasonable grounds that the person has committed an offence. Restrictions are placed on the use of arrest in s 99(3). Police should only proceed by way of arrest (instead of summons or court attendance notice) when it is necessary to ensure the person will attend court, to prevent the destruction of, or fabrication of evidence by the alleged offender, to stop the person from further offending, to stop the person from interfering with witnesses, or to preserve the safety or welfare of the person.

The RCADIC recommended that arrest be used as a last resort when deciding to commence criminal proceedings (Recommendation 87). This was a key recommendation to reduce the over-representation of Indigenous people in police custody. The problem for Indigenous people is that police tend to use arrest for minor offences, and they tend to use it more frequently in their apprehension of Indigenous people than they do with non-Indigenous people. A recent report on the Queensland Aboriginal and Torres Strait Islander Justice Agreement found that 52 per cent of Indigenous interventions involved the use of arrest compared to 36.5 per cent of non-Indigenous interventions. Conversely, more than half of non-Indigenous interventions were commenced by way of a 'notice to appear' (a type of summons) (Cunneen 2005a: 43).

In a matter involving charges against an Aboriginal man, Lance Carr, for resisting arrest, assaulting police and intimidating police, Magistrate Heilpern ruled that evidence from police should be excluded because it had been obtained as a result of an improper act. The improper act in this case was the arrest of Carr for offensive language in circumstances where the use of summons or court attendance notice would have been more appropriate. The Director of Public Prosecutions appealed the matter to the New South Wales Supreme Court, where the appeal was dismissed. Justice Smart noted that

> This Court ... has been emphasising for many years that it is inappropriate for powers of arrest to be used for minor offences where the defendant's name and address are known, there is no risk of him departing and there is no reason to believe that a summons will not be effective. Arrest is an additional punishment involving deprivation of freedom and frequently ignominy and fear. The consequences of the employment of the power of arrest unnecessarily and inappropriately and instead of issuing a summons are often anger ... and an escalation of the situation leading to the person resisting arrest and assaulting the police (*Director of Public Prosecutions v Carr* (2002) 127 A Crim R 151; [2002] NSWSC 194 at 35).

- Why are Indigenous people arrested so frequently for public order offences?

Problems with meeting bail conditions

We discussed in the previous chapter the problems associated with bail and Indigenous young people. We simply note here that there are a number of reasons why Aboriginal people may not meet bail conditions, including an inability to get to court because of a lack of available transport; communication barriers between Aboriginal defendants and their legal representatives; a lack of understanding of the bail process; unemployment and poverty; physical or mental disability; and prior offending histories. A report by the New South Wales AJAC (2000: 6–7) found that during 1999 in New South Wales Local Courts:

- almost half of all Aboriginal defendants (49.9 per cent) had their bail dispensed with compared with more than two-thirds of non-Aboriginal people (72 per cent);
- 38 per cent of Aboriginal defendants were on bail at the time their matter was finalised compared with 22 per cent of non-Aboriginal people;
- 10 per cent of Aboriginal defendants were refused bail, compared to 4 per cent for non-Aboriginal people;
- approximately 11 per cent of Aboriginal defendants who were bail refused and in custody on remand had their case dismissed by the court; and
- data for 2000–2001 showed that 45 per cent of Indigenous people remanded in custody did not receive a custodial sentence when their matter was finalised.

From over-policing to zero tolerance policing

The concept of over-policing is often used to refer to the *degree* of police intervention and the *nature* of police intervention in Indigenous communities (HREOC 1991: 90–94). The degree of intervention can be demonstrated through the number of police stationed in areas with large Aboriginal communities. In addition, over-policing can be seen in the nature of intervention through the use of particular policing *practices*—we have referred to some of these practices in relation to arrests for public order offences. In addition over-policing draws attention to the role police have played historically in the extensive regulation and surveillance of the lives of Aboriginal people through control over movement and social and familial relations during the period of protection legislation discussed in Chapter 2. In this sense, the notion of over-policing is grounded in the Indigenous experience of the criminal justice system, articulating an important part of the lived experience of being *policed*. For further discussion of the issue see Cunneen (2001b: 80–105).

A more recent phase in Australian policing has been the promotion in some jurisdictions of 'zero tolerance policing'. The idea behind zero tolerance policing is that a strong law enforcement approach to minor crime (in particular public order offences) will prevent more serious crime from occurring and will ultimately lead to falling crime rates. The approach relies on an analogy drawn by Wilson and Kelling regarding 'broken windows'. If one broken window is not repaired in a building, then others will be broken and the building vandalised, followed by other buildings, then the street, the neighbourhood, and so on. Similarly, according to Wilson and Kelling, if disorderly behaviour is not dealt with in a particular area, then more serious crime will be the result (Wilson and Kelling 1982). In this sense, zero tolerance policing is directly aimed at increasing arrest rates for minor offences such as public drunkenness, offensive language and behaviour, loitering and other similar offences.

The death of Thomas (TJ) Hickey

TJ Hickey died in the early hours of 15 February 2004 at the Sydney Childrens' Hospital after impaling himself on a metal fence while riding his bicycle in the inner Sydney suburb of Redfern. He was 17 years old. On the night following his death a serious riot erupted in Redfern between Aboriginal people and police.

The Coroner found that TJ's death was a death in custody, occurring as it did during police operations within the meaning of s 13A of the *Coroners Act 1980* (NSW). At the time of TJ's death there was a police operation in the vicinity arising from an earlier assault and robbery which had allegedly involved an Aboriginal offender. A number of vehicle patrols were active in the area at the time although they were not searching for TJ Hickey.

TJ had a criminal record for steal from the person, assault, breach of bail and break and enter. There was a warrant of apprehension for his arrest. His bail conditions precluded his going to 'The Block' residential area in Redfern which was where his mother lived. TJ was regarded by Redfern police as a 'High Risk Offender Profile'. His details were posted up on the noticeboard in the police lunchroom.

On the morning of his death TJ had left his girlfriend's house to meet his mother Gail Hickey at The Block (which was contrary to a condition of bail). TJ rode his bike into the middle of a police operation. Police denied pursuing or following TJ. He had, according to police, been discarded as a person of interest during their current operation. Some civilian witnesses and counsel for the family of the deceased argued

CASE STUDY

that police were indeed pursuing TJ when he had the accident on his bicycle which led to his death. The Coroner found that the police vehicle did not *pursue* the boy in terms of a *pursuit* within the meaning of the *NSW Police Safe Driving Policy,* but followed the boy some distance prior to the accident.

The subsequent riot after TJ's death received widespread publicity, with various 'causes' discussed by media and politicians, including alcohol, drugs and the hot summer weather. Little attention was paid to the long history of volatile conflict between Aboriginal people and the police in Redfern (Cunneen 1990a). The death of TJ Hickey sparked a riot, but did so in the context of constant complaints of police harassment, particularly of Aboriginal youth. Part of this harassment derives from a renewed focus on 'zero tolerance'-style police operations and the use of public order legislation that clearly targets young people.

It has been recognised that zero tolerance policing is likely to have an adverse effect on Indigenous communities by further increasing criminalisation for minor offences. For further discussion see Cunneen (1999). The flipside to zero tolerance policing has been the under-policing of family violence. Zero tolerance policing emphasises offences in public places—street offences. It diminishes the importance of interpersonal violent crime that occurs in the private sphere such as domestic violence.

DISCUSSION QUESTION

- Why do Indigenous deaths in custody lead to civil unrest? Are there any parallels in the non-Indigenous community?

Indigenous women and violence

There are numerous pressures on Indigenous women which limit their use of the legal system. The Aboriginal and Torres Strait Islander Social Justice Commissioner (hereafter ATSISJC) (2006: 7) notes that there are two main concerns for Indigenous women with criminal justice responses to family violence. First, the system is not effective in addressing the behaviour of the perpetrator in the longer term. Second, there is a range of barriers to the legal process, including access and cultural appropriateness. Often there is an inadequate police response. The Western Australian Chief Justice's Taskforce on Gender Bias found that Indigenous women were not protected by some police officers when they were assaulted and that some police failed to enforce domestic violence court orders (Malcolm 1994). Similarly, the Queensland Criminal Justice Commission (1996) in its consultations with Indigenous women was told that police provided inadequate responses when required to investigate violence against Indigenous women. It appears that many police view violence against Indigenous women as something which can be easily tolerated.

Yet the research data demonstrates that Indigenous women are:

- more than 10 times more likely to be a victim of homicide than other women in Australia;
- 45 times more likely than non-Indigenous women to be a victim of domestic violence (based on Western Australia data);
- 10.7 times more likely to be victims of violent crime than non-Indigenous women (based on Western Australia data);
- more than twice as likely to be the victim of sexual assault than non-Indigenous women (based on New South Wales data);
- seven times more likely to suffer grievous bodily harm in an assault than non-Indigenous women (based on New South Wales data); and
- 30 times more likely to hospitalised for assault than non-Indigenous women in Australia.

For sources and further information see ATSISJC (2002, 2003, 2006), Australian Institute of Health and Welfare (2006), Cunneen (2001a) and Memmot et al (2001).

R v Kina

Queensland Court of Appeal, 29 November 1993, No 221 of 1993, unreported

In 1988 Robyn Kina was sentenced to life imprisonment for the murder of her de facto husband, Anthony Black. After five years and two months in gaol, the Queensland Court of Appeal quashed the conviction of Kina declaring that there was a significant miscarriage of justice. The Court found that exceptional difficulties had arisen in communication between Kina and her legal representatives because of cultural, psychological and personal factors. These factors included her Aboriginality, the battered woman syndrome and the shameful (to her) nature of the relationship between Kina and Black. Kina had been denied satisfactory legal representation and the capacity to make informed decisions. Kina's trial in 1988 had lasted a matter of hours during which time she gave no evidence of the abuse, trauma or hardship she had suffered at the hands of Black.

Robyn Kina had grown up in a household where her father was violent towards his wife and children. From the time she was seven years old, Kina was sexually assaulted by her uncle. She engaged in sexual intercourse from a young age. She described herself as being alcoholic from the age of 14. There were a large number

CASE STUDY

of children in the family who were left with the father during Kina's early adolescence. Sometime from around the age of 12 Kina began prostituting herself for money to keep the household together. Kina met Black when she was in her mid-twenties. She was working as a prostitute at the time. During her relationship with Black she was constantly beaten, repeatedly tied up in bed, repeatedly forced to have anal sex with Black, and on several occasions forced to have sex with Black's workmates. In the week prior to Black's murder, he had raped her at least twice. On the day of his death he had demanded anal intercourse with Kina, which she refused. He then threatened to rape Kina's 14-year-old niece who was staying with them at the time.

Much of the discussion which emerged following the acquittal of Kina focused on the inadequacy of legal representation for Indigenous women, particularly its inability to consider how cultural difference can impact on access to justice, due process and equality before the law (ALRC 1994; Criminal Justice Commission 1996). There is also the issue that Kina had been criminally victimised continually from an early age without any recourse to legal protection or redress. In the end the only protection she could rely on was her own self-defence. The *Kina* case was an indictment of the inability of the law to deal with Indigenous women's experiences. From child sexual assault to rape as an adult, to a miscarriage of justice leading to imprisonment, Kina had received no protection from the law.

The *Kina* case shows all too clearly the direct links between victimisation, criminalisation and imprisonment. There have been other cases where Indigenous women have killed their partners after repeated abuse and the failure of legal protection: see *R v Hickey* (Supreme Court of New South Wales, 14 April 1992, unreported) and *R v Gilbert* (Supreme Court of Western Australia, Scott J, 4 November 1993, No 280 of 1993, unreported).

Cultural and communicative differences

We noted briefly in the previous chapter in the context of conferencing, that the legal process can raise particular communicative and cultural difficulties for Indigenous offenders and victims. Communication includes both verbal and non-verbal processes. Likewise, the 'silencing' of Indigenous people can occur through language and through broader cultural processes which misunderstand or fail to recognise the cultural context of Indigenous communication.

Language

There is an ill-founded expectation that Indigenous people speak 'English'. Yet linguists like Diana Eades (1995b, 2000) have shown that most Indigenous people in Australia speak a dialect of English which she refers to as Aboriginal English. This dialect has a number of varieties on a continuum from one close to standard English to a variety of the dialect which is close to Aboriginal Kriol. Aboriginal Kriol is itself a distinctive language. Speakers of Aboriginal English may also speak Aboriginal Kriol and one or more traditional Aboriginal languages.

The right to speak

Indigenous kinship relations can determine who should speak, and the subject matter about which particular people can speak. These restrictions can affect the giving of evidence or the participation is processes like mediation and conferencing.

Gratuitous concurrence

Gratuitous concurrence refers to the tendency of someone to agree to particular questions when being put by a person in authority, irrespective of whether 'yes' or 'no' is the correct answer, or indeed whether the question is understood.

Eye contact

Direct eye contact can be seen as rude and inappropriate among some Indigenous peoples. It can be misinterpreted as dishonesty or defiance within the mainstream culture.

Temporal and spatial definitions

Indigenous quantifying of time and space can be seen as imprecise in Western terms, with the result that Indigenous witnesses may seem vague or dishonest. Non-Indigenous people tend to be used to thinking in precise divisions of time, distance and quantity. Indigenous people are more likely to think in terms of social life or natural environment.

Hearing loss

The prevalence of hearing loss among Indigenous people can complicate further the cultural and linguistic problems identified above.

For further discussion of these issues see Eades (1995b, 2000), NSWLRC (2000: 221–237).

Police interviews and the Anunga Rules

After a suspect is apprehended, he or she is usually subjected to questioning by the police. If they make damaging admissions or confessions, then these may be used as evidence against them later, at their trial. It has long been recognised that suspects are particularly vulnerable at this time, and the law (attempting to safeguard the accused while giving the police reasonable scope to carry out their investigations) regulates the circumstances under which questioning may occur. In general police have the right to question a person when investigating a crime, and that person has the right to remain silent (although in certain circumstances the law may require they provide information). No adverse inference may be drawn from the exercise of this right to silence. For further discussion see Findlay et al (2005: 53–62).

To be admissible in court any confession or admission made to the police must be voluntary and not the result of duress, intimidation or violence. Even if a statement is found to be voluntary it may still be excluded in the exercise of the judge's discretion if it is considered that it would be unfair to the accused to receive it in evidence. In *R v Swaffield; Pavic v The Queen* (1998) 192 CLR 159 at 161, the High Court held that the admissibility of confessional evidence should be seen as 'turning first on the question of voluntariness, next on exclusion based on considerations of reliability and finally on an overall discretion which might take account of all the circumstances of the case to determine whether the admission of the evidence … is bought at a price which is unacceptable'. See also Findlay et al (2005: 198–202).

In 1976, as the culmination of a series of cases dealing with the admissibility of Aboriginal confessional evidence, Forster J enunciated the landmark Anunga Rules in *R v Anunga* (1976) 11 ALR 412 at 414–415. These rules are to provide guidance to police during interviews with Indigenous people. They are not laws, and breach of them does not automatically mean that evidence will be excluded.

(1) When an Aboriginal person is being interrogated as a suspect, unless he is as fluent in English as the average white man of English descent, an interpreter able to interpret in and from the Aboriginal person's language should be present …

(2) When an Aboriginal is being interrogated it is desirable where practicable that a 'prisoner's friend' (who may also be the interpreter) be present. The 'prisoner's friend' should be someone in whom the Aboriginal has apparent confidence …

(3) Great care should be taken in administering the caution … It is simply not adequate to administer it in the usual terms and say, 'Do you understand that?' or 'Do you understand you do not have to answer questions?'

(4) Great care should be taken in formulating questions so that so far as possible the answer which is wanted or expected is not suggested in any way …

(5) Even when an apparently frank and free confession has been obtained relating to the commission of an offence, police should continue to investigate the matter in an endeavour to obtain proof of the commission of the offence from other sources …

(6) Because Aboriginal people are often nervous and ill at ease in the presence of white authority figures like policemen it is particularly important that they be offered a meal …

(7)   It is particularly important that Aboriginal and other people are not interrogated when they are disabled by illness or drunkenness or tiredness …

(8)   Should an Aboriginal seek legal assistance reasonable steps should be taken to obtain such assistance …

(9)   When it is necessary to remove clothing for forensic examination or for the purposes of medical examination, steps must be taken forthwith to supply substitute clothing.

There is various case law where it has been held that failure to comply with the Anunga Rules *may* lead to the exclusion of evidence: see *Gudabi v The Queen* (1984) 52 ALR 133, and also McRae et al (2003: 528–529). Guidelines for interrogating Indigenous witnesses have been incorporated into various police instructions and standing orders. The extent to which they mirror the Anunga Rules varies; see, for example, the New South Wales Police Force's Code of Practice for CRIME (Custody, Rights, Investigation, Management and Evidence).[2] In some jurisdictions they have been incorporated into legislation (for example the Tasmanian *Criminal Law (Detention and Interrogation) Act 1995*).

Various commentators have noted that the Anunga Rules, police guidelines and even legislation requiring the presence of a third party during interrogation, are often not complied with and the incentives for encouraging compliance are sparse. For further discussion in relation to Indigenous people, see for example, Cunneen (1990b: 34–40), Goldflam (1995: 32–36) and Douglas (1998: 35–46). In addition the failure to provide interpreters for Indigenous people remains a critical issue (Eades 2000: 7–9, McRae et al 2003: 529–530; Cunneen 2005a).

Deaths in custody

Deaths in custody still occur at unacceptably high levels and there is strong evidence to suggest that the recommendations of the RCADIC are often ignored. Of the 54 deaths in custody in 2005, some 28 per cent involved Indigenous detainees. Half of the Indigenous deaths occurred in police custody. Non-Indigenous deaths were more likely to occur while in prison (Joudo 2006). The Indigenous rate of death in prison is slightly lower than the non-Indigenous rate (1.2 compared to 1.4 per 1,000). There are no comparable 'death rates' for police because of the lack of annual data on the number people in police custody.

The greater likelihood of Indigenous deaths occurring in police custody compared to non-Indigenous deaths reflects a consistent difference in location of Indigenous

---

2   Available online at http://www.police.nsw.gov.au/about_us/acts_and_legislations/legislation_list/code_of_practice_for_crime

deaths in custody which has been noted since the RCADIC (Johnston 1991). It is also an issue which has a particular gendered dimension to it—at the time of the Royal Commission nearly all Indigenous women who died in custody did so while detained by police (Cunneen and Kerley 1995).

Studies of Indigenous deaths in custody since the RCADIC continue to point to serious inadequacies in the implementation of the RCADIC recommendations designed to prevent deaths (Office of the ATSISJC 1996; Cunneen 2006b).

The death of Cameron Doomadgee in police custody

A recent controversial death in police custody involved 36-year-old Mulrunji (Cameron Doomadgee) who died in police custody on Palm Island in November 2004. Mulrunji was arrested for drunk and disorderly behaviour. He was a healthy man when arrested, was not known as a trouble-maker, and had not been previously arrested on Palm Island. The post-mortem examination revealed that Mulrunji suffered four broken ribs, a ruptured spleen and that his liver was almost cleaved in two. A riot occurred on the Island after the release of the autopsy results. During the riot the police station and local courthouse were destroyed.

The community's anger over the death of Mulrunji was vindicated by the Coroner's report into the death which was released in September 2006. Coroner Clements found that Mulrunji had punched Sergeant Hurley after being arrested and transported to the police station, and that Hurley had punched Mulrunji in response. Both men fell to the ground and Hurley lost his temper and hit Mulrunji several times after falling to the floor. 'I conclude that these actions of Senior Sergeant Hurley caused the fatal injuries' (Clements 2006: 27). After being beaten, Mulrunji was dragged away and deposited in the police cells. According to the Coroner, 'there was no attempt whatsoever to check on Mulrunji's state of health after the fall and its sequelae ... No attempt at resuscitation was made by any police officer even when there was a degree of uncertainty about whether Mulrunji had died' (Clements 2006: 27).

The Coroner found that the decision to arrest Mulrunji in the first instance for drunk and disorderly was an inappropriate use of police discretion and could easily have been addressed by means other than arrest. In other words, Mulrunji should never have been in police custody in the first place.

The Coroner was critical of the failure to check on the health of Mulrunji after the fall and the assault.

Mulrunji cried out for help from the cell after being fatally injured, and no help came. The images from the cell video tape of Mulrunji, writhing in pain as he lay dying on the cell floor, were shocking and terribly distressing to family and anyone who sat through that portion of the evidence. The sounds from the cell surveillance tape are unlikely to be forgotten by anyone who was in court and heard that tape played. There is clear evidence that this must have been able to be heard from the police station dayroom where the monitor was running. Indeed the timing of Senior Sergeant Hurley's visit to the cell suggests that the sounds were heard. But the response was completely inadequate and offered no proper review of Mulrunji's condition or call for medical attention. The inspections were cursory and dangerous even had Mulrunji been merely intoxicated. The so called arousal technique of nudging Mulrunji with a foot is not appropriate. It cannot be sanctioned (Clements 2006: 32).

The Coroner was highly critical of the investigation which failed to meet the standards of thoroughness, competency or impartiality. One investigating officer was a friend of Sergeant Hurley—the police officer most likely to be under investigation—and both investigating officers visited Hurley's house for dinner after the investigation had begun.

Initially the Director of Public Prosecutions decided against prosecuting Sergeant Hurley. After public pressure, an independent assessment of the evidence by former New South Wales Chief Justice, Sir Lawrence Street, found that a properly instructed jury could find a case of manslaughter against Sergeant Hurley and that he should face court. Hurley was later found not guilty.

Indigenous people in policing roles

Indigenous people can have a number of roles in policing. The most obvious role is as a fully sworn police officer. Other roles include community police, Aboriginal police/community liaison officers, or as 'special' police such as the pilot Queensland Aboriginal and Torres Strait Islander Police (QATSIP) program.

Aboriginal police/community liaison officers have been in existence for several decades. It appears that in more recent years there has been an improvement in training, employment conditions, and utilisation, at least in some states (Cunneen 2005a). However, there are also ongoing endemic problems including the basic difficulty of the role in providing a bridge between police and the community. Some issues recently identified in New South Wales include the failure to fill vacant positions promptly, the lack of females in the position and the lack of an obvious career path (New South Wales Ombudsman 2005: 14–15).

Indigenous community police emerged on the former reserves, and in general, exercise powers conferred on them through legislation which enables community councils to pass by-laws for the maintenance of peace and good order. The problems associated with the role and functions of the community police in Queensland for example, have been identified in reports by the RCADIC, and a number of coronial inquiries into Indigenous deaths in custody.[3] The main issues are the very limited powers of arrest, poor supervision by state police and a range of problems similar to those identified with community liaison officers including employment conditions and training.

In an attempt to resolve the problems with Indigenous community police, the Queensland Government piloted the transfer of management and control of Aboriginal and Islander community police to the Queensland Police Service (QPS). Officers were sworn is as 'special constables' and completed the accredited training course designed for Aboriginal community police, as well as additional operational training and training in the use of QPS information technology. An evaluation of the trial at Yarrabah, Woorabinda and Badu Island found at each of the sites, despite contextual differences, that the trial had been successful. However, it was most successful where there was an effective community justice system operating in the community concerned, and a local court to hear charges under the community by-laws (Cunneen 2005a: 183–186).

Indigenous policing and social control

Harry Blagg's (2005) work on Indigenous community justice mechanisms draws a distinction between community-*based* initiatives and community-*owned* initiatives. Community-based initiatives are often seen as extending government initiatives into a community setting. They may involve better service delivery of existing services. On the other hand, community-owned initiatives are ways of doing justice business that are driven by the community. They are essentially Indigenous solutions and extensions of Indigenous control over justice business. When properly supported and acknowledged, they are capacity-building and self-governance strategies. In this chapter we draw attention to two such initiatives: night patrols and community justice groups.

Night patrols

Indigenous night patrols are one of the longest running Indigenous community responses to reducing crime and maintaining order. They operate extensively in

---

3   The most recent being the *Coronial Findings in the Death of a Hope Vale Man in an Aboriginal Community Police Van*: http://www.justice.qld.gov.au/courts/coroner/findings/HopeVale.pdf. Accessed 30/8/06.

Western Australia, the Northern Territory and New South Wales. Other states, including Victoria, also have limited night patrols usually operating as part of other services. Night patrols work in different ways depending on a range of factors including demographic/geographic (urban, rural and remote); legislation in place to facilitate community governance; the local relationship with police; and so forth. Most night patrols operate through the work of volunteers, some have a paid coordinator, and some rely on work-for-the-dole funds. Sources of funds for vehicles and coordinators include police services, community services, corrective services, state departments of Aboriginal affairs and crime prevention funding.

Different night patrols may have varied client groups and different target offences or behaviour: young people, drug/petrol users, intoxicated persons, anti-social behaviour, domestic violence and so on. Night patrols may also be linked in with other Indigenous-operated programs such as community warden schemes, sobering-up shelters, community justice groups, law and justice groups and so forth.

Night patrols have been evaluated over many years and in different locations. Generally the evaluations have been positive; see Cunneen (2001a) and Blagg and Valuri (2004) for discussion of these evaluations.

Aboriginal community justice groups

In many parts of Australia, Indigenous communities have established community justice groups to deal with law and justice issues, often directly involving work with offenders. The composition of the groups and the type of work they undertake varies. Perhaps the most extensively documented and evaluated program has been the Kowanyama Justice Group (KJG), established in 1994 in Cape York in response to increasing calls by Aboriginal communities for local autonomy and self-management in matters concerning law, order, and justice. It is run by a community-elected group of elders (usually including three men and three women elected by the three main language groups in Kowanyama). The aims of the KJG include, among other things, to:

- address the issues of law and order in a way that the community understands to be right and in accordance with its own customs, laws, and understandings about justice;
- consult with magistrates about punishments and sanctions considered appropriate by Kowanyama people;
- recommend and, if appropriate, carry out certain kinds of community punishments for offenders;
- take action to prevent law and order problems in the community;
- work closely with the Aboriginal Council to put appropriate by-laws in place and help the Council make Kowanyama a more peaceful place;

- identify social and justice issues in the community;
- provide recommendations and advice to government departments and the Children's Court and the Department of Family Services about juvenile justice matters; and
- provide advice and assistance in setting up programs and supervising offenders.

The role of the community justice groups in Queensland has been extensively described and in some locations like Kowanyama, their work has been evaluated. For further extensive discussion of community justice groups in Queensland and proposals for Western Australia, see Cunneen (2005a: 130–141), LRCWA (2006: 97–113).

Community justice mechanisms, crime prevention and community control

Over the last two decades there have been significant Indigenous community justice initiatives, many of which have shown positive results or are promising in their potential impact. There are a number of themes that re-emerge in relation to successful initiatives. For example, in relation to drug and alcohol programs, there appears to be consensus that culturally appropriate and community-based programs that utilise multiple modes of intervention (that is, harm reduction, treatment and supply control) and involve the family and community in treatment are most successful.

The common themes in evaluations of Indigenous family violence programs include the need for holistic approaches, the utilisation of community development models which emphasise self-determination and community ownership, and the provision of culturally sensitive treatment which respects traditional law and customs and involves existing structures of authority such as elders, including women (Blagg 2000).

Blagg (2005) has summarised what he sees as the salient features of Aboriginal-owned community justice mechanisms. They include:

- a strong focus on achieving sustainability, durability and resilience in structures, processes and programs;
- a willingness to take into account Aboriginal law and culture in the way structures, processes and programs are devised and executed;
- a commitment to nurturing the necessary governance structures; and
- a process of capacity building, both in Aboriginal communities and in the government agencies that partner with them (Blagg 2005: 321).

Indigenous Justice Agreements

Most Australian states have negotiated and signed Justice Agreements with Indigenous people (as represented through AJACs). These Agreements vary between jurisdictions but can be seen to contain commonalities, and certainly set the policy framework within each state in relation to criminal justice issues.

The Queensland Justice Agreement can be used as an example. The long-term aim of the Agreement is to reduce Indigenous contact with the criminal justice system to parity with the non-Indigenous rate. A specific goal was to reduce by 50 per cent the rate of Aboriginal and Torres Strait Islander peoples incarcerated in the Queensland criminal justice system by 2011. It will achieve this goal through a range of 20 supporting outcomes and initiatives. Justice agencies, including police, have been required to report against these initiatives and outcomes. There is not space here to discuss each of these 20 initiatives, however they include such matters as:

- effective early intervention for Indigenous young people at risk of criminal justice intervention;
- effective diversionary strategies;
- safety and security for Indigenous people in custody;
- criminal justice policies, procedures and practices that are appropriate for Aboriginal and Torres Strait Islander people; and
- increased participation by Aboriginal and Torres Strait Islanders in the administration of justice including the development of their own solutions.

A recent evaluation of the Justice Agreement in Queensland found that there had been progress in meeting the aims of the Agreement. However, there was a need to resource and expand current initiatives. While the police service had introduced some innovative programs (like the Indigenous Licensing Program) one of the main failings was to ensure alternatives to arrest are used more equitably for Indigenous juveniles and adults (Cunneen 2005a).

Conclusion

State policing and criminalisation of Indigenous peoples in Australia remains a highly contested issue. Despite the work of the RCADIC, many recommendations aimed to reduce contact with police and unnecessary criminalisation for minor offences have not been implemented. More punitive approaches to law and order have seen increased police powers and greater use of public order offences. Meanwhile Indigenous deaths in police custody continue to occur too frequently and in controversial circumstances.

Underpinning high levels of criminalisation are specific problems which Indigenous people face in contact with the criminal justice system including cultural and communicative differences. Addressing these issues through, for example, the greater use of interpreters might go some way to ensuring equality before the law.

Indigenous women face particular problems in their contact with police. There are high levels of victimisation for assault, yet there are also significant limitations on the extent to which the law is used to provide protection. For some women the use of counter-violence is their only self-defence. And as we demonstrate further in the following chapter, Indigenous women cannot be easily categorised as either victim or offender.

This chapter concluded with a brief consideration of some Aboriginal community justice initiatives. There have been successes in reducing arrests and detention, as well as improvements in the maintenance of social harmony. The success of these programs has been reliant on the strength of the Aboriginal domain and the struggle for Indigenous autonomy. Indigenous assertion of autonomy and the struggle for self-determination have been productive of opening new spaces for the exercise of Indigenous governance over policing and criminal justice issues; they also provide us with the opportunity to re-think the possibilities of a postcolonial relationship between police and community (Cunneen 2005b).

CHAPTER 7

Courts, Sentencing and Punishment

Introduction

This chapter deals with a range of themes around courts, sentencing and punishment. To place the discussion in context we start with data on Indigenous imprisonment. As can be seen from Figure 7.1, Indigenous people have much higher rates of imprisonment than non-Indigenous people in every state and territory in Australia. Western Australia has the highest rate of Indigenous imprisonment in the nation at 2,688.4 per 100,000 of the population. This is 18.4 times the non-Indigenous rate of 144.8 per 100,000. There are also significant differences in the rate of imprisonment between states and territories: New South Wales has twice the rate of Indigenous imprisonment compared to Victoria, and Western Australia has nearly twice the rate of Indigenous imprisonment compared to South Australia, Queensland and the Northern Territory.

Figure 7.1: Imprisonment rates, by states and territories, 30 June 2006. Rate per 100,000 adult population (age standardised rate)

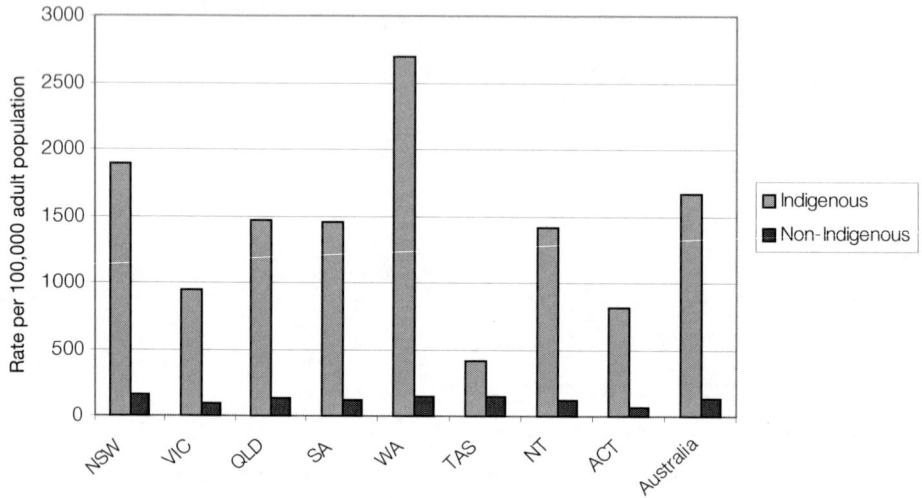

Australian states, territories and nation

Source: Adapted from ABS (2006: 14)

The level of Indigenous over-representation in adult imprisonment is shown in Table 7.1. For Australia as a whole, Indigenous people are 12.9 times more likely to be imprisoned than non-Indigenous people. As noted above Western Australia has the highest ratio of Indigenous over-representation in prison.

Table 7.1: Indigenous over-representation in adult imprisonment, Australia

NSW	VIC	QLD	SA	WA	TAS	NT	ACT	AUS
12.3	9.7	10.6	12.5	18.4	2.9	12.3	11.2	12.9

Based on Age Standardised Rates per 100,000 as at 30 June 2006.

Source: ABS (2006: 14)

Figure 7.2: Indigenous adult imprisonment. Rates per 100,000 adult population as at 30 June 1996 to 2006

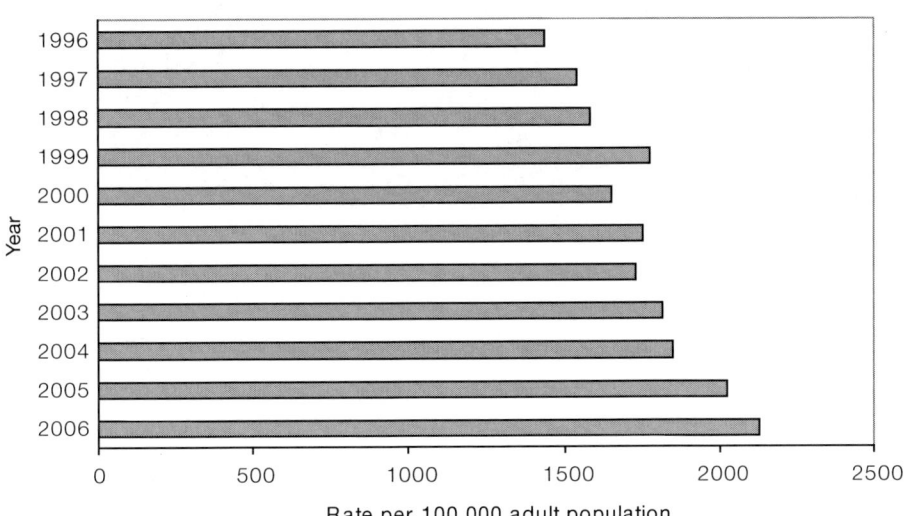

Rate per 100,000 adult population

Source: Adapted from ABS (2006: 33)

Figure 7.2 shows that Indigenous adult imprisonment rates have worsened during the last decade, having risen by 48 per cent since 1996.[1] This increase is despite the recommendations from the RCADIC which aimed to reduce Indigenous imprisonment.

Indigenous offences before the courts

The type of offences for which Indigenous people appear before the local Magistrates' Court[2] is shown in Table 7.2. While Indigenous people are over-represented for most offence categories before the courts, there are some noteworthy differences between the type of offences for which Indigenous people appear, compared to non-Indigenous people.

Indigenous people have higher proportions of 'acts intended to cause injury' (assaults), theft offences, public order offences and justice offences, than non-Indigenous people. Conversely non-Indigenous people have a much greater proportion of motor

---

1   We note that the general imprisonment rate for all Australians rose by 23.4 per cent during the same period (ABS 2006: 33).

2   Similar data for the higher courts is not available.

Table 7.2: Principal offence for persons found guilty in the New South Wales Local Court, 2005

Offence	Indigenous Persons		Non-Indigenous Persons		Total Persons		Indigenous Persons per Offence Type
	No	%	No	%	No	%	%
Homicide and related offences	1	0.0	41	0.0	42	0.0	2.4
Acts intended to cause injury	2,553	19.3	9,990	10.0	12,543	11.1	20.4
Sexual assault and related offences	20	0.2	193	0.2	213	0.2	9.4
Dangerous/ negligent acts endangering persons	174	1.3	4,484	4.5	4,658	4.1	3.7
Abduction	1	0.0	1	0.0	2	0.0	50.0
Robbery	10	0.1	29	0.0	39	0.0	25.6
Burglary and related offences	382	2.9	976	1.0	1,358	1.2	28.1
Theft (including motor vehicles)	1,348	10.2	6,715	6.7	8,063	7.1	16.7
Deception	183	1.4	3,385	3.4	3,568	3.2	5.1
Drug offences	728	5.5	5,203	5.2	5,931	5.2	12.3
Weapons	42	0.3	715	0.7	757	0.7	5.6
Property damage	761	5.7	3,649	3.6	4,410	3.9	17.3
Public order offences	1,582	11.9	5,657	5.7	7,239	6.4	21.9
Motor traffic offences	3,367	25.4	48,006	48.0	51,373	45.4	6.6
Justice offences	1,708	12.9	8,191	8.2	9,899	8.7	17.3
Miscellaneous	391	2.9	2,805	2.8	3,196	2.8	12.2
Total	**13,251**	**100.0**	**100,040**	**100.0**	**113,291**	**100.0**	**11.7**

Source: Adapted from New South Wales Bureau of Crime Statistics and Research (2006: 58–73)

traffic offences (nearly half of all non-Indigenous principal offences). In terms of the total number of offences, it is noteworthy that Indigenous people comprise 20.4 per cent of assaults and 21.9 per cent of public order offences.

Indigenous sentencing outcomes

Indigenous people (both adults and juveniles) have a greater likelihood of being sentenced to imprisonment than non-Indigenous offenders. For example in Western Australia in 2005, 11.1 per cent of Indigenous convictions in the adult Magistrates' Court resulted in imprisonment compared to 5.2 per cent of non-Indigenous convictions. Conversely, non-Indigenous people were much more likely to receive a fine (73.7 per cent compared to 60.2 per cent) (Loh et al 2007: 83). In the Western Australian Children's Court some 22.2 per cent of Indigenous children received a penalty of detention, compared to 8.6 per cent of non-Indigenous children. Non-Indigenous children were much more likely to be fined as a penalty (35.2 per cent compared to 15 per cent) (Loh et al 2007: 115).

Table 7.3 shows that in New South Wales adult Magistrates' Courts, some 18.3 per cent of sentences resulted in imprisonment for principal offences when the offender was Indigenous. The comparable non-Indigenous rate was 4.9 per cent. For one in every three convictions (33.3 per cent) in the local Magistrates' Courts in New South Wales in 2005 where the penalty imposed was imprisonment, the offender was an Indigenous person.

Table 7.3 also shows that Indigenous people were less likely to receive home detention, periodic detention, fines and no conviction (with or without a bond) than non-Indigenous people, a point we return to later in this chapter.

Why are Indigenous people more likely to receive a sentence of imprisonment than non-Indigenous people? The most straightforward explanation would be that Indigenous people commit more serious offences or offences that are more likely to attract a custodial penalty. There is some evidence to support this, in that Aboriginal young people have a greater proportion of matters relating to break-and-enter offences than non-Aboriginal youth, and these offences tend to be more likely to result in custodial sentences (Ferrante et al 2005: 113; Office of Crime Statistics and Research 2005: 40). In relation to Indigenous adults, convictions for offences involving violence are more likely to incur custodial sentences (Snowball and Weatherburn 2006: 1).

In addition a major determinant influencing penalty is a person's prior offending record. When differences in criminal record were controlled for, there were no significant differences in the percentage of Aboriginal and non-Aboriginal young people given a detention order in New South Wales Children's Courts (Luke and Cunneen 1995: 27). A report by the New South Wales Judicial Commission confirmed that Indigenous and non-Indigenous youth received the same number and length of detention orders

Table 7.3: Penalty for principal offence for persons found guilty in the New South Wales Local Court, 2005

Penalty	Indigenous Persons		Non-Indigenous Persons		Total Persons		Indigenous Persons per Penalty Type
	No	%	No	%	No	%	%
Imprisonment	2,430	18.4	4,879	4.9	7,309	6.5	33.3
Home detention	29	0.2	346	0.3	375	0.3	7.7
Periodic detention	133	1.0	1,049	1.0	1,182	1.0	11.3
Suspended sentence with supervision	746	5.6	2,249	2.2	2,995	2.6	24.9
Suspended sentence without supervision	451	3.4	2,092	2.1	2,543	2.3	17.7
Community service order	739	5.6	4,353	4.4	5,092	4.5	14.5
Bond with supervision	1,137	8.6	5,076	5.1	6,213	5.5	18.3
Bond without supervision	1,514	11.4	10,346	10.3	11,860	10.5	12.8
Fine	5,184	39.1	51,344	51.3	56,528	49.9	9.2
Nominal sentence	98	0.7	252	0.3	350	0.3	28.0
Bond without conviction	463	3.5	10,773	10.8	11,236	9.9	4.1
No conviction recorded	327	2.5	7,281	7.3	7,608	6.7	4.3
Total	**13,251**	**100.0**	**100,040**	**100.0**	**113,291**	**100.0**	**11.7**

Source: Adapted from New South Wales Bureau of Crime Statistics and Research (2006: 58–73)

when factors including offence, prior record, bail, employment, and family structure were controlled for (Gallagher and Poletti 1998: 17). In relation to Indigenous adults, Snowball and Weatherburn have also shown that re-offending (along with offences involving violence) accounts for greater use of imprisonment as a penalty (2006: 1).

Accumulating a prior record

We have indicated the importance of a prior record in determining sentencing outcomes. A number of factors are important in understanding the accumulation of an offending history. Various studies have shown that intervention occurs earlier with Aboriginal young people and as a result, Aboriginal young people receive a criminal record at an earlier age (Luke and Cunneen 1995: 9; Cunneen and Luke 2006: 89). Given what we have already established in relation to the adverse use of police discretion in the previous chapters, and the figures on early intervention, it is not surprising that Indigenous people develop extensive criminal records. Police decisions made at the time of apprehension have a compounding effect through the system and over a person's life history.

Earlier discrimination in the system results in Indigenous people being less likely to receive diversionary options and being more likely to experience the most punitive processes and sanctions. These factors compound and apparently equitable treatment at the point of sentencing may simply mask earlier systemic biases (for further discussion see Blagg et al 2005; Cunneen 2006a). In addition the current sentencing trend to treat 'repeat offenders' more harshly, either by way of mandatory sentences or through greater reliance on sentencing principles of retribution and incapacitation, will have the greatest negative impact on Indigenous people. They are precisely the group more likely to have longer criminal histories.

DISCUSSION QUESTION

- How would you account for the significant differences in Indigenous imprisonment rates between different states and territories in Australia?

The purposes and principles of sentencing

The purposes of sentencing are traditionally referred to as retribution, deterrence, rehabilitation, incapacitation and denunciation (ALRC 2006: 133–140). Another purpose of sentencing which is gaining prominence is restorative justice. In addition specific sentencing legislation may refer to other purposes. In New South Wales, for example, s 3A of the *Crimes (Sentencing Procedure) Act 1999* establishes the purposes of sentencing as:

(a) to ensure that the offender is adequately punished for the offence;

(b) to prevent crime by deterring the offender and other persons from committing similar offences;

(c) to protect the community from the offender;

(d) to promote the rehabilitation of the offender;

(e) to make the offender accountable for his or her actions;

(f)   to denounce the conduct of the offender; and

(g)   to recognise the harm done to the victim of the crime and the community.

The different purposes of sentencing may conflict, and it is the role of the judicial officer to balance the pursuit of different purposes in the context of specific cases. Furthermore, if the purposes of sentencing were pursued unchecked then instances of grossly unjust sentences could arise. For example, a repeat minor offender might be incarcerated for long periods of time on the basis of a need for rehabilitation or incapacitation. Thus there is a need to pursue sentencing purposes within the boundaries of established principles of sentencing (ALRC 2006: 142).

The key principles of sentencing are proportionality, parsimony, totality, consistency and individualised justice. Penalties are required to be proportionate to the seriousness of the offence, and seriousness is determined by the harm caused and culpability of the offender. Sentences should be no more severe than is required to meet the purpose of sentencing (parsimony), the sum of individual sentences should not be excessive where the offender is being sentenced for multiple offences (totality), and like cases should be treated alike (consistency). Finally, 'the principle of individualised justice requires the court to impose a sentence that is just and appropriate in all the circumstances of the particular case' (ALRC 2006: 155). Judges and magistrates use both objective and subjective tests when determining an appropriate sentence. An objective test determines the nature and seriousness of the offence (such as the use of violence, the use of a weapon, history of prior offending, the vulnerability of the victim, and so on). The subjective factors include relevant characteristics of the offender which may impact on why the offence was committed (New South Wales Law Reform Commission (NSWLRC) 2000: 39).

Aboriginality and sentencing

Discrimination on the basis of race is prohibited by the *Racial Discrimination Act 1975* (Cth), and sentencing principles apply equally irrespective of the race or cultural background of an offender. The High Court in *Walker* held that:

> It is a basic principle that all people should stand equal before the law. A construction which results in different criminal sanctions applying to different persons for the same conduct offends that basic principle (*Walker v The State of New South Wales* (1994) 182 CLR 45 at 49, per Mason CJ).

As the ALRC (2006: 720) has noted, 'Australian courts have consistently held that Aboriginality is not a mitigating factor in sentencing': see *Rogers v The Queen* (1989) 44 A Crim R 301; *R v Daniel* (1997) 94 A Crim R 96; *R v Fernando* (1992) 76 A Crim R 58. However this does mean that the judge or magistrate cannot take into account matters that are related to the person's background when sentencing an offender. As an Indigenous person, that might include matters such as socio-economic disadvantage, health problems, removal from family and so on. Such considerations are consistent with the principle of individualised justice.

As Brennan J stated in *Neal*:

> The same sentencing principles are to be applied, of course, in every case, irrespective of the identity of a particular offender or his membership of an ethnic or other group. But in imposing sentences courts are bound to take into account, in accordance with those principles, all material facts including those facts which exist only by reason of the offender's membership of an ethnic or other group (*Neal v The Queen* (1982) 149 CLR 305 at 326).

In some states, cultural background is explicitly referred to for matters involving juveniles: in South Australia, s 3(3)(e) of the *Young Offenders Act 1993* and in Western Australia, s 46(2)(c) of the *Young Offenders Act 1994* have these provisions for young people. Commonwealth legislation had included the cultural background of an offender as a relevant factor in sentencing in s 16A(2)(m) of the *Crimes Act 1914* (Cth). However, this and other relevant sections were repealed by the *Crimes Amendments (Bail and Sentencing) Act 2006* (Cth) (see discussion below on recognition of customary law).

The *Fernando* principles

Aboriginality as a relevant factor in sentencing was considered extensively by Justice Wood in *R v Fernando* (1992) 76 A Crim R 58 at 62–63.

(a)   The same sentencing principles are to be applied in every case irrespective of the identity of a particular offender or his or her membership of an ethnic or other group, but that does not mean that the sentencing courts should ignore those facts which exist only by reason of membership of such a group.

(b)   The relevance of the Aboriginality of an offender is not necessarily to mitigate punishment but rather to explain or throw light on the particular offence and the circumstances of the offender.

(c)   It is proper for the court to recognise that the problems of alcohol abuse and violence, which to a very significant degree go hand in hand within Aboriginal communities are very real ones, and their cure require more subtle remedies than the criminal law can provide by way of imprisonment.

(d)   Notwithstanding the absence of any real body of evidence demonstrating that the imposition of significant terms of imprisonment provides any effective deterrent in either discouraging the use of alcohol by members of the Aboriginal society or their resort to violence when heavily affected by it, the courts must be very careful in the pursuit of their sentencing policies to not deprive Aboriginals of the protection which it is assumed punishment provides. In short, a belief cannot be allowed to go about that serious violence by drunken persons within their society are treated by the law as occurrences of little moment.

(e)   While drunkenness is not normally an excuse or a mitigating factor, where the abuse of alcohol by the person standing for sentence reflects the socio-economic circumstances and environment in which the offender has grown up, that can and should be taken into account as a mitigating factor. This involves the realistic recognition by the court of the endemic presence of alcohol within Aboriginal communities, and the grave social difficulties faced by those communities where poor self-image, absence of education and work opportunity and other demoralising factors have placed heavy stresses on them, reinforcing their resort to alcohol and compounding its worst effects.

(f)   In sentencing persons of Aboriginal descent the court must avoid any hint of racism, paternalism or collective guilt yet must nevertheless assess realistically the objective seriousness of the crime within its local setting and by reference to the particular subjective circumstances of the offender.

(g)   In sentencing an Aborigine who has come from a deprived background or is otherwise disadvantaged by reason of social or economic factors or who has little experience of European ways, a lengthy term of imprisonment may be particularly, even unduly, harsh when served in an environment which is foreign to him or her and which is dominated by inmates and prison officers of European background with little understanding of his or her culture and society or own personality.

(h)   In every sentencing exercise, while it is important to ensure that the punishment fits the crime and not to lose sight of the objective seriousness of the offence in the midst of what might otherwise be attractive subjective circumstances, full weight must be given to the competing public interest to rehabilitation of the offender and the avoidance of recidivism on his or her part.

The *Fernando* principles have been generally accepted by the courts. However whether the principles will be taken into account or not will be determined in each individual case. In New South Wales the principles have been applied by the court to vary the usual 3:1 ratio of non-parole period to parole which comprises the total custodial sentence. In a number of Court of Criminal Appeal cases, the non-parole period has been reduced (for a discussion of these cases see NSWLRC 2000: 41).

There is concern that the *Fernando* principles have been rolled back by the courts in recent years (Flynn 2005a). The fact that the offender is Indigenous is of itself not a mitigating factor and does not justify any special leniency without evidence that the offender was affected by the social and economic problems of Aboriginal communities, (*R v Carr* [1999] NSWCCA 200; *R v Pitt* [2001] NSWCCA 156). Justice Wood in dismissing an appeal in *Pitt* held that:

There was nothing of an exceptional kind in the Aboriginality or upbringing of the applicant that called for particular mitigation of sentence. As pointed out in *Ceissman* there is a danger of misinterpreting *Fernando* as a decision justifying special leniency on account of an offender's Aboriginality. It is a mistake to rely on *Fernando* as authority for the proposition that Aboriginal heritage of itself is a mitigating circumstance (*R v Pitt* [2001] NSWCCA 156: 1).

Further, the principles may not be applicable if the Indigenous person is not from a rural or remote area and the offences were not alcohol related (*R v Ceissman* [2001] NSWCCA 73; *R v Morgan* [2003] NSWCCA 230; *R v Walter and Thompson* [2004]; NSWCCA 304). According to Flynn (2005a: 15) the more restrictive position enunciated in recent case law 'reveals an impoverished understanding of the facts that are capable of being material to the sentencing of an Indigenous defendant', and is a retreat from principles of substantive equality. It compares unfavourably with the Canadian approach in *Gladue* (see below).

Factors taken into account when sentencing Indigenous offenders

The NSWLRC (2000) has suggested that the circumstances where Aboriginality is relevant to sentencing can be categorised into three broad areas: factors relevant to the background of Indigenous offenders; factors relevant to the communities from where the offender and/or victim came; and factors relevant to traditional law and custom.

On the basis of an analysis of the case law, the factors relating to the background of an Indigenous offender which may be relevant in a particular case are:

- Whether a custodial sentence is unduly harsh given the background and circumstances of the offender (*R v Fernando* (1992) 76 A Crim R 58; *R v Daniel* [1998] 1 Qd R 499; *The Police v Abdulla* [1999] SASC 239; *R v Tjami* [2000] SASC 311).
- The offender's residence in a remote community and problems associated with living on reserves or in remote areas (*Leech v Peters* (1988) 40 Crim R 350; *Neal v The Queen* (1982) 149 CLR 305).
- The unique difficulties faced by Indigenous people adjusting from a remote traditional community to an urban environment (*Haradine v The Queen* (1991) 61 A Crim R 201).
- The endemic nature of hearing loss among Indigenous people and its consequent social and psychological effects (*R v Russell* (1995) 84 A Crim R 386) and other health problems (*R v Daniel* [1998] 1 Qd R 499).

- Discrimination, exclusion and disadvantage in the background and upbringing of an Indigenous offender (*R v Fernando* (1992) 76 A Crim R 58; *R v Cinch* (1994) 72 A Crim R 301; *Re E (A Child)* (1993) 66 A Crim R 14), including harsh treatment, dispossession and separation from families (*R v Fuller-Cust* [2002] VSCA 168).

For further discussion and additional cases, see NSWLRC (2000: 43–44) and Williams (2003: 98–102).

The courts have also taken account of the views of a particular community in relation to matters such as whether the offender should return to the community, the seriousness of the offence, the offender's character and the nature of an appropriate penalty: see *R v Minor* (1992) 59 A Crim R 227; *Munungurr v The Queen* [1994] 4 NTLR 63; *R v Daniel* [1998] 1 Qd R 499. To some extent this process has been extended and institutionalised through the use of Indigenous courts (discussed below). In Queensland s 9 of the *Penalties and Sentences Act 1992* requires in subsection 2(o) that in sentencing an Indigenous offender, a court must have regard to any submissions made by a community justice group in the offender's community that are relevant to sentencing the offender, including the offender's relationship to the offender's community, any cultural considerations, or any considerations relating to programs and services established for offenders in which the community justice group participates.

Indigenous family violence

There has been much debate on the courts' response to Indigenous family violence and whether that response has been too lenient. Certainly Indigenous women in the late 1980s and early 1990s were at the forefront of drawing attention to the way the courts were ignoring the seriousness of homicide, assault and rape in Indigenous communities (see for example Langton 1991; Payne 1992; and also Bolger 1991; Cunneen 1992). There were judicial comments which supported this view, such as those by Gallop J in *Lane* (unreported, NTSC, 29 May 1980) and Millhouse J in *Mungkill, Martin and Mintuma* (unreported, SASC, 20 March 1991) that rape is not considered as seriously in Aboriginal communities as it is in white communities. Even at this time, though, other senior judges were taking a different view, such as Muirhead J in *R v Pat Edwards* (unreported, NTSC, 1981, cited in McCorquodale 1987a: 390), who stated that he was 'not prepared to regard assaults of Aboriginal women as a lesser evil to assaults committed on other Australian women'. Similarly, in *R v Friday* (1985) 14 A Crim R 471, the Queensland Court of Criminal Appeal found that in the past, crimes of violence by Indigenous people in that state had been dealt with more leniently by the courts than similar cases involving non-Indigenous people, and the plight of Indigenous victims had not been recognised. Similar comments in relation to the need for deterrence and protection of victims, even while acknowledging factors relevant to the background of

Indigenous offenders, were made in *Yougie v The Queen* (1987) 33 A Crim R 302 and *R v Fernando* (1992) 76 A Crim R 58.

In surveying more recent cases, Williams (2003: 101–102) has noted that family violence is one area of sentencing 'where the courts have consistently stressed the seriousness of the offending and the consequential diminishing impact of factors associated with an offender's Aboriginality … the courts have become gradually more stronger in their comments in relation to violence by, in particular, Aboriginal men against Aboriginal women and children'. Cases reflecting this position include *R v Woodley, Boonga and Charles* (1994) 76 A Crim R 302; *R v Daniel* [1998] 1 Qd R 499; *Amagula v White* [1998] unreported, NTSC, No JA92/1997 per Kearny J.

The Northern Territory Court of Criminal Appeal stated in *Wurramurra*:

> The courts have been concerned to send what has been described as 'the correct message' to all concerned, that is that Aboriginal women, children and the weak will be protected against personal violence insofar as it is within the power of the court to do so (*R v Wurramurra* (1999) 105 A Crim R 512 at 520).

The current position of courts in relation to offences of violence against Indigenous women and children is that the same level of protection should be enforced as there is in the non-Indigenous community, that normal sentencing principles will apply and that this includes an assessment of the objective seriousness of the offence.

Customary law and sentencing

Courts may take into account customary law when sentencing an offender. They generally do so in two ways. The first is when the person has been or will be subject to traditional punishment. The second is through recognition that customary law may explain the reason for the commission of a particular offence (see NSWLRC 2000: 85–106 and LRCWA 2006: 178–184).

Traditional punishment

Two principles apply when the courts take into account traditional punishment. The first is that enunciated in *Neal v The Queen* (1982) 149 CLR 305 that courts are required to consider all material facts including those that only arise as a result of a person's membership of a particular group. In matters of traditional punishment, the punishment only exists by reason of the offender's Aboriginality. The second principle is double jeopardy: the person should not be punished twice for the same offence. While the court may not condone traditional sanctions which are unlawful, it may acknowledge the inevitability of the punishment taking place (*R v Minor* (1992) 59

A Crim R 227; *R v Wilson Jagamara Walker* [1994] Supreme Court of Northern Territory Martin CJ, unreported).

The purpose of traditional punishment is usually seen as a form of community healing—either within or between different communities (see Williams 2003: 21). The nature of traditional punishment includes spearing, physical beating, banishment, public acknowledgment and agreement, the application of punishments to other family members, and reprimand (see Williams 2003: 17–20 for further discussion and relevant cases). There are several cases where traditional punishment has been structured into the court's order—usually as a condition of a bond that the offender return to his or her community where some form of punishment will take place (*Munugurr v The Queen* [1994] 4 NTLR 63; *R v Wilson Jagamara Walker* [1994] Supreme Court of Northern Territory Martin CJ, unreported).

Customary law as a reason for offending behaviour

In general the courts have been reluctant to take customary law into account to explain and mitigate an offence. However, in a number of cases of arson the courts have accepted that cultural beliefs were at the basis of the actions (*R v Shannon* (1991) 57 SASR 14; *R v Goldsmith* (1995) 65 SASR 373). For example, in *R v Goldsmith* the court took into account that the offender had set fire to his deceased friend's house in the belief that it would allow his friend's spirit to rest.

Despite adverse publicity over 'customary law defences' in matters of violence against Indigenous women, the reality appears that, although defence counsel may raise customary law in proceedings, the courts generally put significantly more weight on the need for community safety, deterrence and retribution. In *Hales v Jamilmira* [2003] NTCA 9 the court dealt with an offence of sexual intercourse with a child under 16 years of age. The defendant claimed that the victim was his promised wife and he was entitled to have sexual intercourse with her. The court accepted that these were mitigating factors, but the weight to be attributed to them was not such as to warrant significant leniency. Riley J noted:

> Whilst proper recognition of claims to mitigation of sentence must be accorded, and such claims will include relevant aspects of customary law, the court must be influenced by the need to protect women and children, from behaviour which the wider community regards as inappropriate (*Hales v Jamilmira* [2003] NTCA 9 at 88).

In *R v GJ* [2005] NTCCA 20 the court dealt with offences of unlawful assault and sexual intercourse with a child under 16 years of age. The defendant claimed that the victim was his promised wife and he was entitled to have sexual intercourse with her once she had turned 14 years of age. The original sentence imposed by the court was 24 months' imprisonment to be suspended after serving one month. The Director of

Public Prosecutions appealed the case on the ground that the sentence was manifestly inadequate, and the judge gave excessive weight to factors going to the respondent's culpability (customary law and traditional beliefs) and failed to give sufficient weight to the objective seriousness of the crime. The court found that:

> There is no doubt that an Aboriginal person who commits a crime because he is acting in accordance with traditional Aboriginal law is less morally culpable because of that fact … What is contended is that in this case the respondent, although he was entitled to act as he had done according to traditional law, was not obliged to do so, and was not under any pressure to do so … In those circumstances, I consider that less weight should be afforded to this factor (*R v GJ* [2005] NTCCA 20 at 30).

The court found that the objective seriousness of the offences warranted an increased penalty and the total sentence of imprisonment was increased to three years 11 months with a minimum term to be served of 18 months. 'The [original] sentences imposed failed to punish the respondent adequately for the crimes he committed and failed to act as a deterrent to others who might feel inclined to follow their traditional laws': *R v GJ* [2005] NTCCA 20 at 38.

The principles in these cases are first, that there is a distinction between the court taking into account customary law which is likely to lead to the offender being punished, and the court taking into account customary law as a reason for the commission of an offence. 'The latter circumstance does not permit mitigation to the same degree as may be available in the former': *Hales v Jamilmira* [2003] NTCA 9 at 28, per Martin CJ. Second, for customary law to be taken into account as a mitigating factor in sentencing, it is not enough that the behaviour is simply *permissible* under customary law. There needs to be a customary law obligation with significant consequences if the behaviour is not carried out (Williams 2003: 23–24).

Defences

The criminal law relies on the principle that a person can be held responsible or liable for their actions because they are rational actors making choices between right and wrong. Some groups, such as children or those with a mental impairment, may be excused from criminal responsibility because of their incapacity to reason. Even if a person can be held criminally responsible, there may be other reasons for excusing or justifying the behaviour. McRae et al (2003: 532) have noted that 'the fact that an Indigenous defendant is acting in accordance with Indigenous law provides no defence as such'. However, the courts will take into account aspects of Indigenous law as they would any other factors that are relevant to criminal liability.

Consent

The consent of a victim may be an issue in crimes of assault, particularly in situations involving punishment arising from Indigenous law. As a general proposition at common law consent is not a defence to assault occasioning bodily harm, although there are exceptions such as medical treatment (such as surgery), sport (such as football) or other activities (such as tattooing). Generally these exceptions will be based on public interest or general social approval. However it is clear there is some confusion and inconsistency in the law of consent (Brown et al 2006: 688–701).

In *R v Judson* (unreported, District Court of Western Australia, No POR 26/1995, cited in Williams 2003: 64), a number of defendants had been charged with assault occasioning bodily harm arising from the traditional punishment of an Aboriginal girl. The defence relied on evidence that the assault was consistent with traditional punishment and the victim's consent. However in cases where grievous bodily harm might arise from the infliction of traditional punishment, the courts have not accepted that a person may consent to such harm: *Barnes v The Queen* (1997) 96 A Crim R 593. A similar distinction was made in *R v Minor* (1992) 59 A Crim R 227, where the court held that a victim can authorise assault as long as there is no intention to kill or cause grievous bodily harm (Williams 2003: 34).

Provocation

The defence of provocation is a partial defence to murder. It reduces murder to manslaughter. In law the test as to whether someone has been provoked is a subjective and objective test. The subjective test is focused on the subjective state of mind of the individual being prosecuted. The type of question that needs to be considered is whether the conduct actually led to the person losing control. This may allow some consideration of the person's characteristics such as race or ethnicity. The second, objective test involves considering whether an ordinary person in the defendant's circumstances would have lost control. The courts have found that the ethnic or cultural background of the accused is not relevant to whether an ordinary person in the situation of the accused would lose control: *Stingel v The Queen* (1990) 171 CLR 312; *Masciantonio v The Queen* (1995) 183 CLR 58.

The Northern Territory has developed its own jurisprudence in relation to provocation which dates back to Kriewaldt J's decisions in the 1950s. The decision in *R v Muddarubba* [1956] NTJ 317, 322, states:

> In my opinion, in any discussion of provocation, the general principle of law is to create a standard which would be observed by the average person in the community in which the accused person lives. It is clear from the cases decided by the courts

whose decisions bind me that in white communities matters regarded as sufficient provocation a century ago would not be regarded as sufficient today. This suggests that the standard is not a fixed and unchanging standard; it leaves open, and I think properly so, to regard the Pitjintjatjara tribe as a separate community for the purpose of considering the reaction of the average man (cited in ALRC 1986: 302).

The Northern Territory Criminal Code refers in s 34(2)(d) to 'an ordinary person similarly circumstanced'. The Northern Territory Court of Criminal Appeal has held that the ordinary person test for Indigenous people should be understood in the context of an Indigenous person's environment and culture, including that of particular communities: *Jabarula v Poole* (1989) 42 A Crim R 479; *R v Mungatopi* (1991) 57 A Crim R 341.

Honest claim of right and native title

If a person honestly believes they have a lawful entitlement to particular property, then they will not be held criminally responsible for theft. The person must have an honest belief or claim that they were entitled to do or take what they did. Similarly, native title might give rise to a defence to a criminal charge if it can be established that what the defendant was doing was pursuant to exercising a native title right and that the right had not been extinguished by legislation. For further discussion see Williams (2003: 62–63), McRae et al (2003: 533–534), and LRCWA (2006: 137–158).

DISCUSSION QUESTION

- In what ways is Aboriginality relevant in sentencing? Should it be a relevant consideration?

The recognition of customary law

The first major inquiry into Indigenous customary law and issues of recognition was undertaken by the Australian Law Reform Commission (1986). Its recommendations in relation to sentencing included that legislation should provide for the consideration, where relevant, of the customary law of the Indigenous offender's community, and that of the victim's community where relevant.

Both the ALRC's *Sentencing Report* (ALRC 1988) and *Multiculturalism and the Law Report* (ALRC 1992) recommended that an offender's cultural background be included as a factor to be taken into account in sentencing. The ALRC's *Same Crime, Same*

Time: Sentencing of Federal Offenders Report (ALRC 2006) recommended that cultural background be retained as a sentencing factor under s 16(1), (2)(m) of the *Crimes Act 1914* (Cth).

The report of the NSWLRC (2000) recommended that evidence concerning customary laws of both the offender and the victim be taken into account in sentencing. In the most recent discussion on the recognition of customary law, the Law Reform Commission of Western Australia (LRCWA) has recommended recognition within the existing framework of the Western Australia legal system and 'did not support the establishment of a separate formal legal system for Aboriginal people to the exclusion of Australian law' (LRCWA 2006: 13). However, the Commission found that recognition was required to satisfy principles of fairness and justice and to achieve substantive equality for Indigenous people.

The Howard Government introduced the Commonwealth *Crimes Amendments (Bail and Sentencing) Act* in 2006 ostensibly as a response to family violence in Indigenous communities. The legislation had the effect of preventing the courts from taking into account 'any form of customary law or cultural practice' in relation to bail applications, or as a relevant matter in sentencing, or as a consideration in discharging an offender without proceeding to conviction. The HREOC (2006) noted that the legislation does not address family violence in Indigenous communities, is not based on evidenced research, does not promote equality before the law, and undermines initiatives involving customary law such as Indigenous courts.

DISCUSSION QUESTIONS

In considering customary law, there is a range of conceptual questions which need to be addressed. For example:

- What is customary law and how is it distinguished from 'law' and by whom?
- Is the idea of customary law an 'imperialist' concept and part of the discourse of conquest that constructs the laws of Indigenous people as inferior to the imposed laws of the coloniser?
- Does customary law require continuous practice from colonisation to be recognised as valid?
- How does customary law relate to Indigenous self-determination rights and to other human rights?

For further discussion, see Cunneen and Schwartz (2005), Davis and McGlade (2005) and Jackson (1995).

Sentencing options: imprisonment as a sanction of last resort?

It is an accepted common law principle that imprisonment is a sanction of last resort. The principle is recognised in legislation by the Commonwealth and in New South Wales, Victoria, Western Australia, Queensland and the ACT (see NSWLRC 2000: 30 for the relevant legislation). Given the over-representation of Indigenous people in prison, this principle is of particular relevance. International conventions and sentencing legislation in other countries provide some guidance on the consideration of this principle specifically in relation to Indigenous people.

Article 10(2) of the International Labour Organisation (ILO) Convention No 169 states that when sentencing Indigenous and tribal peoples, preference should be given to methods of punishment other than imprisonment. Section 718.2(*e*) of the Canadian Criminal Code requires that all available sanctions other than imprisonment that are reasonable in the circumstances should be considered for all offenders, with particular attention to the circumstances of Aboriginal offenders (McNamara 2000).

The Canadian Supreme Court in *R v Gladue* (1999) 1 SCR 688 at 689 confirmed that the unique circumstances of Aboriginal people needed to be considered in sentencing.

> The provision [s 718.2(*e*)] is not simply a codification of existing jurisprudence. It is remedial in nature and is designed to ameliorate the serious problem of overrepresentation of aboriginal people in prisons, and to encourage sentencing judges to have recourse to a restorative approach to sentencing.
>
> The effect of s 718.2(*e*), however, is to alter the method of analysis which sentencing judges must use in determining a fit sentence for aboriginal offenders ... In sentencing an aboriginal offender, the judge must consider: (a) the unique systemic or background factors which may have played a part in bringing the particular aboriginal offender before the courts; and (b) the types of sentencing procedures and sanctions which may be appropriate in the circumstances for the offender because of his or her particular aboriginal heritage or connection.
>
> Section 718.2(*e*) applies to all aboriginal persons wherever they reside ... In defining the relevant aboriginal community ... the term 'community' must be defined broadly so as to include any network of support and interaction that might be available, including one in an urban centre. At the same time, the residence of the aboriginal offender in an urban centre that lacks any network of support does not relieve the sentencing judge of the obligation to try to find an alternative to imprisonment.

The LRCWA (2006: 374) has recommended a similar provision be introduced into legislation in Western Australia:

> When considering whether a term of imprisonment (or a term of detention) is appropriate the court is to have regard to the particular circumstances of Aboriginal people (Recommendation 37).

Short-term imprisonment

Indigenous people are among those more likely to be sentenced to short-term imprisonment. The reasons for this appear complex. Research in the Northern Territory suggests that the sentence of imprisonment occurs earlier in the offending career of Aboriginal people than non-Aboriginal people (Luke and Cunneen 1998). In New South Wales Indigenous people comprise 16 per cent of the total prison population, however they comprise 20 per cent of short-term sentenced prisoners (Lind and Eyland 2002). In 2004 some 72.4 per cent of custodial sentences for Indigenous people in the lower courts in Queensland involved sentences of six months or less (Cunneen 2005a). Any change to the use of short prison sentences could have a significant impact on Indigenous prisoner numbers entering the system. Research has indicated that if Aboriginal adults given prison sentences of six months or less in New South Wales were given non-custodial sanctions instead, then the number of Aboriginal people sentenced to prison would be reduced by 54 per cent over a 12-month period (Baker 2001: 8).

In Western Australia the abolition of six-month sentences was part of the *Sentencing Legislation Amendment and Repeal Act 2002*. The amended s 86 of the legislation prohibiting prison sentences of six months and less was proclaimed in mid-2004. However, data for 2005 shows only a slight decline in prison receptions by 3.3 per cent, perhaps suggesting a 'bracket creep' among sentences over six months (Loh et al 2007: 146).

Parole

Parole provides the opportunity for an offender to be released to the community after having completed their non-parole period and prior to the expiration of their sentence of imprisonment. The decision to release a prisoner on parole is made by an independent parole board in each state and territory. In interviews with Indigenous prisoners, Cunneen and McDonald (1997: 145) found that:

> Programs run in prison were seen as often superficial, lacking in Aboriginal control and unable to communicate with Aboriginal people effectively. Rehabilitation and eligibility for release on parole was often measured through 'participation' in these programs. Some Aboriginal prisoners saw 'rehabilitation' as simply a measure of conformity to the prison regime. It was widely noted that there are generally no Aboriginal people on the parole boards and there is a lack of experience in assessing Aboriginal people who come up for parole.
>
> There was seen to be a lack of support on release from prison, and the failure to provide external support services increased the likelihood of breaching parole and returning to prison. It was perceived that Aboriginal people faced double discrimination on release from prison: they were black and they were ex-prisoners.

There has been a long-recognised problem with Indigenous offenders accessing parole and breaching parole conditions: see for example recommendation 119 from the RCADIC and the more recent discussion by the NSWLRC (2000: 141–145).

Imprisonment and mandatory sentencing

During the 1990s, the Northern Territory and Western Australia introduced mandatory sentences of imprisonment for specified offences. In the Northern Territory legislation was in place from 1996 until the end of 2001 which imposed mandatory imprisonment for certain property crimes. In 2000–2001 some 79 per cent of prisoners sentenced for property offences were Indigenous—some three times the Indigenous proportion of the general population (ATSISJC nd: 3).

In Western Australia mandatory sentences were introduced for home burglary with the *Criminal Code Amendment Act (No 2) 1996*. They have had a particularly discriminatory effect on Aboriginal young people. Research indicates that between 2000 and 2005 some 87 per cent of all children dealt with under the legislation were Aboriginal children. Aboriginal children from regional areas sentenced to detention are 'taken from their families, communities and culture and must spend at least six months in a detention centre in Perth' (LRCWA 2006: 86). The Law Reform Commission recommended the abolition of mandatory sentences (LRCWA 2006: 86).

Governments argued that the laws were not discriminatory because they applied equally to Indigenous and non-Indigenous offenders. However, the ATSISJC has pointed out that racial discrimination includes 'in purpose or effect'. Governments are required to take different impacts on particular racial groups into account. Factors relating to the laws that can lead to disproportionate impacts on Indigenous people include: selection of offences subject to mandatory detention which target offences overwhelmingly committed by Indigenous people; the exercise of police discretion which fails to divert Indigenous juveniles; and socio-economic disadvantage including educational disadvantage and lack of employment opportunities, which play a large role in determining rates of offending (ATSISJC nd: 4).

Mandatory sentencing and human rights

It has been argued that mandatory sentences of imprisonment and detention breach a number of key articles in the Convention on the Rights of the Child (CROC), the International Covenant on Civil and Political Rights (ICCPR) and the Convention for the Elimination of All Forms of Racial Discrimination (CERD). In summary these include the following.

- *The best interests of the child:* Mandatory sentencing fails to allow consideration of the best interests of the individual child when formulating a sentence.

- *The primacy of rehabilitation for young offenders*: The prospects of rehabilitation through integration into the community are ignored with mandatory sentences of detention.
- *Proportionality and the need for a wide range of sentencing options for young offenders*: Mandatory sentencing ignores the requirement of a variety of dispositions and alternatives to institutionalisation to ensure that children are dealt with in a manner appropriate to their well-being and proportionate to both their circumstances and the offence.
- *Participation in decisions*: Mandatory sentencing makes irrelevant the requirement that children participate and be given a voice in any decisions which affect them.
- *Imprisonment as a sanction of last resort*: The requirement that children and adults be deprived of their liberty only as a last resort and for the shortest appropriate time is ignored by mandatory sentencing.
- *Prohibition on arbitrary detention*: Mandatory sentences of detention may breach the prohibition on arbitrary detention because arbitrariness can incorporate elements of inappropriateness or injustice. Injustice arises because of gross disproportionality.
- *Prohibition on inhuman and degrading punishment*: Mandatory sentencing can give rise to inhuman treatment through the use of incarceration for trivial offences. In these cases, gross disproportionality of sentence can give rise to cruel, inhuman or degrading punishment.
- *Requirement that sentences be reviewable by a higher or appellate court*: Mandatory sentences by their nature are not reviewable in terms of their severity.
- *Prohibition on racial discrimination*: Mandatory sentences disproportionately impact on Indigenous young people and adults (Cunneen 2002).

DISCUSSION QUESTIONS

- Why do mandatory sentencing laws negatively impact on Indigenous people?
- If there is a foreseeable negative impact, does this make the laws racially discriminatory?

The lack of sentencing alternatives, programs and services for Indigenous people

It has been widely noted that Indigenous people, as both offenders and victims, lack the same access as non-Indigenous people to the programs and services offered by the criminal justice system (see, for example, Cunneen 2005a; Mahoney 2005; Morgan and Motteram 2004; LRCWA 2006). These include the absence of or highly restricted availability of:

- non-custodial sentencing options;
- services for Aboriginal victims, particularly of family violence and sexual abuse
- interpreter services;
- offender programs for sex offenders, violent offenders;
- programs and counselling for substance abuse; and
- programs for young offenders.

The Mahoney Inquiry in Western Australia (Mahoney 2005) found that there was a serious deficiency in Aboriginal-specific programs to reduce offending behaviour, and that the lack of appropriate programs for Indigenous offenders may partly explain higher recidivism rates. Lack of appropriate services meant fewer opportunities for rehabilitation and more re-offending (LRCWA 2006: 85).

The ALRC recently noted that existing rehabilitation programs are not appropriately tailored to meet the needs of Indigenous offenders.

> It was said that effective rehabilitation programs for ATSI offenders should be adequately resourced, incorporate principles of Aboriginal healing, and provide ongoing assistance to participants to enable them to avoid engaging in behaviour that may contribute to further offending (ALRC 2006: 723).

Similarly a review of the Aboriginal and Torres Strait Islander Justice Agreement in Queensland found Indigenous offenders are less represented on community corrections than they are in the prison population. One reason for this is the widely acknowledged difficulty of providing effective supervision for community corrections in remote communities. There was widespread concern among Indigenous legal services and magistrates about the lack of sentencing alternatives in remote areas (Cunneen 2005a). In New South Wales a recent parliamentary report also found that many sentencing options were not available in rural areas. In particular supervised bonds, community service orders, periodic detention and home detention were not available in many parts of the state (Legislation Council Standing Committee 2006: xii). Interviews with judicial officers found that more than 70 per cent of judges and 53 per cent of magistrates stated they were prevented from using periodic detention when sentencing Indigenous offenders because of the lack of facilities (NSWLRC 2000: 154).

In New South Wales home detention is only available in the metropolitan areas of Sydney, Wollongong and Newcastle. The NSWLRC (2000: 152) has identified the need for taking a more flexible approach to what qualifies as a 'home' for home detention so as not to exclude Indigenous offenders. Broader interpretations appear to have been utilised in the Northern Territory and Queensland where in remote communities the 'home' may be defined as the community or an outstation.

Indigenous women offenders

There are a number of reasons for a separate consideration of Indigenous women offenders in a discussion on sentencing and punishment. Women in general have been neglected as group in the criminal justice system, and this is even more pronounced with Indigenous women. There appears to be little recognition of the disruption to family, community and cultural life with the incarceration of Indigenous women. Visits from family and friends are more problematic for Indigenous women from remote and rural areas, partly because there are few women's prisons and they tend to be in major cities.

There has been a large increase in imprisonment of Indigenous women over recent years. Between 1993 and 2003 the general female prison population increased by 110 per cent. However the Indigenous female prison population increase over the same period was 343 per cent. In addition research shows that Indigenous women are more likely to have been previously imprisoned than non-Indigenous women (85 per cent compared to 71 per cent in New South Wales) (ATSISJC 2004: 17–19).

The type of offences committed by Indigenous women are relatively specific. Indigenous women are more likely to be imprisoned for violence-related offences than non-Indigenous women. There is evidence to suggest that some of this violence is in response to domestic violence and other forms of abuse (see *Kina* Case study in Chapter 6, and also Cunneen and Kerley 1995b). There has been an increase in imprisonment for robbery offences for Indigenous women, and some suggestion that these offences are related to long-term drug use (Brenner 2002: 13). Many Indigenous women in prison have been sexually abused as either children or adults. Interviews with Indigenous women prisoners revealed that 78 per cent had been victims of violence while adults, and 44 per cent had been sexually assaulted as adults (Lawrie 2002: 41).

Most Indigenous women inmates are not a threat to society and are classified as minimum security. Indigenous women in prison also have specific characteristics compared to other imprisoned women. They tend to be younger than non-Indigenous female prisoners. From surveys in Western Australia, New South Wales and Victoria, about 80 per cent of Indigenous women are mothers, most with young children—yet few seem to access Mothers and Children Units where these are available (Lawrie 2002: 46). The majority have serious psychiatric issues, and are over-represented in prison among those classified at risk, including those engaging in self-harm behaviour while in prison (ATSISJC 2002: 148–149). Research has shown that on release from prison Indigenous women have difficulty accessing post-release support programs (ATSISJC 2004: 12).

When sentencing Indigenous women there are specific factors which need to be taken into account, including their roles in the family and community and a range of historical and contemporary factors. Historical factors include changes in gender roles as a result of colonial intervention and the effects of policies of removing children from their families and the impact this had on women. Contemporary factors include experiences of violence, physical and emotional abuse, substance abuse and financial hardship.

Indigenous women experience potential discrimination on the basis of race and gender. This intersectional discrimination arises because their needs are considered as being met either through services designed for Indigenous men, or non-culturally specific services designed for women. The only Indigenous-run post-release support program for Indigenous women is Yulawirri Nurai in New South Wales.

For further discussion of the issues relating to Indigenous women offenders, see in particular ATSISJC (2002: 135–177), ATSISJC (2004: 11–66) and NSWLRC (2000: 175–220).

Thinking about alternative types of custody and alternatives to custody

There is a need to think about alternative types of custody and alternatives to custody for Indigenous male and female offenders which have the potential to reduce recidivism and increase community capacity building in dealing with offending behaviour.

Canadian corrections and Aboriginal offenders

In Canada the law that governs the way federal corrections is managed makes some very specific provisions to involve Aboriginal communities in the correctional process. Two sections of the *Corrections and Conditional Release Act 1992* (CCRA) provide communities with the opportunity to be active partners in the care and custody of offenders. Section 81 of the CCRA allows for Correctional Services Canada (CSC) to enter into an agreement with an Aboriginal community for the provision of correctional services to Aboriginal offenders and for payment by the CSC for the provision of those services. The CSC may transfer an Aboriginal offender to the care and custody of an Aboriginal community, with the consent of the Aboriginal offender and of the Aboriginal community. An offender can be transferred at any time in his or her sentence to either a community-based custodial facility or non-custodial supervision.

Section 84 of the CCRA encourages the participation of Aboriginal communities in the release planning process by requiring the CSC to consult with the community and seek their input. If the offender agrees, Aboriginal communities may be

CASE STUDY

approached very early in the sentence to determine if there is interest in proposing a release plan (Wilson 1999).

There are many Canadian examples of successful 'healing lodge'-type facilities operated by both the CSC and Aboriginal communities. In particular the Canadian models have emphasised the necessity of a holistic approach which strengthens native culture and responsibility. Some lodges such as the Okimmaw Ohci Healing Lodge are specifically for Indigenous women.

By contrast there are few services for Indigenous prisoners exiting prison that focus on healing processes in Australia. In South Australia there is the Sacred Site Within Healing Centre, and in New South Wales the Yula Panaal Cultural and Spiritual Healing Program for Indigenous women and post-release programs for Indigenous men such as 'Rekindling the Sprit' (see Cunneen 2001a for further examples). Baldry (1997) has recommended the development of small residential centres in regional and urban areas which are run by Indigenous women and have a strong focus on drug rehabilitation, living skills, health programs and personal support.

Indigenous-specific custodial facilities

In New South Wales there has been the development of low-security Indigenous correctional centres: Yetta Dhinnakkal near Brewarrina houses up to 70 minimum-security inmates and Warakirri at Ivanhoe caters for 50 minimum-security inmates. These facilities are designed for Indigenous male prisoners (although non-Indigenous inmates may be considered for inclusion) who have a low-security rating and are moving towards the end of their sentence. The facilities are staffed predominately by Indigenous people. Programs are specifically designed for Indigenous inmates, including cultural programs, health, anger management, domestic violence, alcohol and other drug counselling, education and employment. The programs target first-time young Aboriginal offenders through culturally relevant intensive case management. Community, inmate families and Aboriginal elders are involved in the rehabilitation process by having input into case management.

Indigenous community supervision

There is a great and largely unrealised potential for Aboriginal community-operated supervision of offenders. In Western Australia many Aboriginal communities in the Kimberley and Eastern Goldfields have contractual arrangements so that communities can supervise adult offenders on community-based orders. The Community Supervision Agreement provides the framework for the supervision of offenders in participating communities. It also sets out rates of payment to the community for undertaking the supervision. The scheme has had a number of important effects including a dramatic improvement in the rate at which Aboriginal people successfully

complete some orders. In the Kimberley region of Western Australia, where the largest single number of Community Supervision Agreements operate, the home detention program has a success rate exceeding 80 per cent (Cunneen 2001b).

Indigenous courts and circle sentencing

Indigenous courts (Koori Courts, Murri Courts and Nunga Courts) and circle sentencing have been established for Indigenous offenders in Victoria, Queensland, South Australia, the ACT and New South Wales over the last decade. More recently there have been similar developments in the Northern Territory (Daly and Marchetti 2007) and recommendations for similar processes in Western Australia (LRCWA 2006).

Circle sentencing

Circle sentencing developed in Canada in 1992 from a decision by the Supreme Court of the Yukon in the case of *R v Moses* [1992] 3 CNLR 116 (Yukon Territory Court). The circle is said to be premised on three principles that are part of the culture of the Aboriginal people of the Yukon.

> Firstly, a criminal offence represents a breach of the relationship between the offender and the victim as well as the offender and the community; secondly, the stability of the community is dependent on healing these breaches; and thirdly, the community is well positioned to address the causes of crime (Lilles 2001: 162).

Circle sentencing is part of the court process and it results in convictions and criminal records for offenders (Lilles 2001: 163). Discretion as to whether a sentencing circle is appropriate remains with the judge. The ultimate sentencing decision lies with the judge who is free to ignore the sentencing circle recommendations and is obliged to impose a 'fit' sentence which is still subject to appellate court sentencing guidelines (Green 1998). Not surprisingly, there may be tensions between community involvement in the circle and the power which the judge retains. While at one level there is an appeal to 'equality' within the circle, the circle itself is partly constrained by the wider power of the criminal justice system.

Canadian case law sets out the criteria for involvement in a sentencing circle. These include that the accused has roots in the community and agrees to participate in the sentencing circle; that there are elders or respected non-political community leaders willing to participate; that the victim is willing to participate and has not been subjected to coercion or pressure to agree; and that disputed facts have been resolved in advance.

See *R v Joseyounen* [1996] 1 CNLR 182 for further criteria, and also Green (1998: 76). Although not 'etched in stone' by the court, the criteria have been widely quoted and applied across Canada (albeit with variations such as whether the victim must attend).

Starting at Nowra in 2002, circle sentencing is operating for Indigenous offenders in a number of areas in New South Wales. Circle sentencing guidelines, procedures and criteria are established through the *Criminal Procedure Regulation 2000* [2000–435]. The objectives of the circle sentencing court are to:

(a) include members of Aboriginal communities in the sentencing process;
(b) increase the confidence of Aboriginal communities in the sentencing process;
(c) reduce barriers between Aboriginal communities and the courts;
(d) provide more appropriate sentencing options for Aboriginal offenders;
(e) provide effective support to victims of offences by Aboriginal offenders;
(f) provide for the greater participation of Aboriginal offenders and their victims in the sentencing process;
(g) increase the awareness of Aboriginal offenders of the consequences of their offences on their victims and the Aboriginal communities to which they belong; and
(h) reduce recidivism in Aboriginal communities (Potas et al 2003: 4).

The fundamental premise underlying circle sentencing is that the community holds the key to changing attitudes and providing solutions. The court's deliberations have been typified as power-sharing arrangements. 'It is recognised that if the community does not have confidence that the power-sharing arrangements will be honoured, the prospect that circle sentencing will be successfully implemented is likely to be diminished' (Potas et al 2003: 4).

Although the procedures for circle courts may differ in limited ways from community to community, the usual process is that participants are welcomed to the circle by community elders and the judicial officer, with each person then introducing themselves and explaining why they are there. The facts of the case are presented to the circle by the prosecutor, and the defence is then allowed to comment. Following a period of discussion, participants develop a sentence plan, which the judge uses to sentence the offender.

The Nowra circle sentencing trial was subsequently evaluated by the New South Wales AJAC and the New South Wales Judicial Commission (Potas et al 2003). The evaluation found, inter alia, that circle sentencing helped to break the cycle of recidivism; introduced more relevant and meaningful sentencing options for Aboriginal offenders; reduced the barriers that existed between the courts and Aboriginal people; led to improvements in the level of support for Aboriginal offenders; helped in support for victims, and promoted healing and reconciliation; and generally promoted the empowerment of Aboriginal persons in the community (Potas et al 2003: iv).

Indigenous courts

Indigenous courts are established through legislation in Victoria by the *Magistrates' Court (Koori Court) Act 2002* and in South Australia by the *Statutes Amendment (Intervention Programs and Sentencing Procedures) Act 2003*. Indigenous courts typically involve an Aboriginal elder or justice officer sitting on the bench with a magistrate. The elder can provide advice to the magistrate on the offender to be sentenced and about cultural and community issues. Offenders might receive customary punishments or community service orders as an alternative to prison. Aboriginal courts may sit on a specific day designated to sentence Aboriginal offenders who have pleaded guilty to an offence. The court setting may be different to the traditional sittings. The offender may have a relative present at the sitting, with the offender, his or her relative and the offender's lawyer sitting at the bar table. The magistrate may ask questions of the offender, the victim (if present) and members of the family and community in assisting with sentencing options (see Harris 2004; Marchetti and Daly 2004; and Cunneen 2005a).

As an example, the Brisbane Youth Murri Court sits once a month. Eligibility for the Youth Murri Court is that the offence is one within the jurisdiction of the Children's Court, and that the young person requests the matter be determined by the Murri Court. There are usually two (and sometimes three) elders who sit with the magistrate. The young person's family also has the opportunity to speak to the magistrate and the elders. The Murri Court appears to have a positive impact on the young people who appear before it. Tony Pascoe, the magistrate at the Brisbane Children's Court, has stated:

> The [Youth] Murri Court sessions are intense, emotional occasions with a greater involvement of all parties. I can say that since the Youth Murri Court has been held that there has been a reduction in the number of serious offences committed by young Indigenous persons. There may be a number of reasons for this but I like to think that the Youth Murri Court, by involving the wider community in the concern for the futures of young Aboriginal and Torres Strait Islander people, has in some way contributed to this result (Pascoe 2005: 7).

The conditions placed on court orders may involve meeting with elders or a community justice group on a regular basis and undertaking courses, programs or counselling relevant to their particular needs. A non-indigenous Murri Court magistrate noted the following:

> Orders, particularly probation orders and intensive correction orders, often include conditions requiring attendance on the Justice Group and/or Elders, attendance at counselling and/or programs to address specific issues (for example domestic violence and family violence, alcohol or drug abuse), attendance at Indigenous Men's Groups or

other support groups … The extent of compliance required represents what might be considered to be significant punishment and deterrence whilst offering rehabilitation opportunities (Hennessy 2005: 5).

Harris (2006) has evaluated the Koori Court in Victoria. He found that there were reduced levels of recidivism among participants, and reductions in breach rates for community corrections orders. In addition there was increased participation and ownership of the program by the local koori community.

Indigenous courts and circle sentencing summary

Some Indigenous courts and circle sentencing have a legislative base, while others operate informally.

The aims of the courts include providing better sentencing outcomes for Indigenous offenders, empowering Indigenous communities, reducing recidivism, achieving restorative justice outcomes between the offender and victim and reducing barriers between the courts and Indigenous people.

A significant difference between circle sentencing and Indigenous courts is the greater role for the victim in circle sentencing.

The selection process for offenders differs among jurisdictions, however the criteria tends to be broad. Offenders have to admit guilt to be eligible and participation is voluntary. Indigenous community members usually have a say in the suitability of offenders for participation. Some offences are excluded.

Overall, very few Indigenous offenders appear before these specialist courts. Evaluations of Indigenous courts and circle sentencing have been positive. See generally, Harris (2006); Cunneen (2005a); Daly and Marchetti (2007).

DISCUSSION QUESTIONS

- What are the advantages and disadvantages of providing a legislative base for Indigenous courts?
- Should victims and the community have a role in the sentencing process?

Conclusion

Indigenous people remain dramatically over-represented among the prison population. As a group they do not receive non-custodial sentencing options to the same extent as non-Indigenous people. The reasons for this vary, but represent a need to overcome what Blagg (2005: 320) has described as the 'stubbornly eurocentric' focus of the justice system.

Aboriginality is taken into account in sentencing usually as a factor relevant to the background of the offender. In general though, Australian courts have lagged behind counterparts in Canada, for example, where there is a much more comprehensive view of the importance of Aboriginality in sentencing. Indigenous customary law is relevant in sentencing, however this is usually through the consideration of traditional punishment. Despite a concerted attack on Indigenous customary law in relation to violence against women (for example Kimm 2004; Nowra 2007), the courts have generally held that sentencing objectives of deterrence and community protection will outweigh any mitigation arising from traditional law.

There is much that could be done to develop sentencing alternatives that are consistent with and extend Indigenous control over offending behaviour. At present the major areas of development have been circle sentencing and Indigenous courts. However few Indigenous offenders actually appear before these courts; it was estimated in Queensland that perhaps as little as 0.2 per cent of Indigenous matters went before a Murri Court (Cunneen 2005a: 200). There is also a need to think more openly about how Indigenous communities can exercise greater responsibility in dealing with offenders, through, for example, the development of healing centres or local forms of offender supervision. There is much that could be done to enhance respect for Indigenous human rights, as well as providing systems of intervention that are more likely to have positive outcomes in rehabilitating offenders.

PART 3
Law, Land and Culture

CHAPTER 8

Land Rights

> If we had the means ourselves, or if it was made available we are sure the great expense
> would be the greatest and the progress would be possible by the profits of the venture.
> We claim the native has a right to live in the 'Land of His Father'.
>
> William Cooper (1937)

The struggle for land rights has always been a central part of the platform for Aboriginal people (Behrendt and Watson 2007). Dispossession and theft of traditional land has been a hallmark of the colonisation process, so it is little wonder that the focus for political movements by Aboriginal people would be on reclaiming that land. The claim for land has always been more than just a desire to reclaim soil. There was always the desire to be able to exercise traditional obligations to lands that Aboriginal people have a cultural and spiritual attachment with. But there has also been an understanding that land is the source of life and of sustainability (Kelly and Behrendt 2007).

Many Aboriginal and Torres Strait Islander leaders have understood the connection between the claim to land and its capacity to provide the basis for both economic self-sufficiency and greater independence. When Indigenous people seek to reclaim land either through native title or land rights regimes, it is for the furtherance of the goals of self-sustainability and self-determination as well as to reclaim land for cultural significance.

The meaning of land for Aboriginal people

> We bond with the universe and the land and everything that exists on the land. Everyone is bonded to everything … Ownership for the white people is something on a piece of paper. We have a different system. You can no more sell our land than sell the sky.
>
> Paul Behrendt (Behrendt 1995: 12)

> Our affinity with the land is like the bonding between a parent and a child. You have responsibilities and obligations to look after and care for a child. You can speak for a child. But you don't own a child.
>
> Paul Behrendt (Behrendt 1995: 12)

The relationship to the land is similar in all Aboriginal communities on mainland Australia. People had affiliations with tracts of country and had the right to hunt and feed in certain areas and to perform religious ceremonies in certain places. These custodians were also responsible for ensuring that the resources of a certain area were maintained. Indigenous people knew their relationship to others and the universe through totemic and kinship systems.

The attachment of Aboriginal people to their traditional land and the importance of land in Aboriginal life cannot be overemphasised. Ancestral beings live in the tribal area in spiritual form, generating life. Boundaries of tribal areas are fixed by the stories that ancestors told. People inherited stories and songs and then become the keepers of those stories and that is how the law passed down. This is the way ancestral land was passed on to younger generations for them to care for. This knowledge created an obligation to care for the land, protect the land, respect the past, to not exploit the land's resources, to take the responsibility of passing the country on to future generations and to maintain the religious ceremonies that needed to be performed there.

These ceremonies symbolise the attachment to the land and the commitment to protect it. Special religious significance is attached to the resting places of great ancestors and the landscape was richly symbolic. It is important to note that disputes were never over land. In this way, ancestral land became personal so one was obliged to look after it. Other people's land had no meaning to someone who was a stranger to it (Behrendt 1995).

Historical struggle for land rights

Every Aboriginal group has its own story to tell of resistance and the fight for their land. In the face of continuing resistance, and justifying their actions by a belief in the superiority of their civilisation, the colonisers pushed Aboriginal people off the fertile lands into controlled settlements.

Early advocates in the 1930s who sought citizenship rights for Aboriginal people understood that land was the key to providing Aboriginal people with the capacity to be self-sustaining and to make decisions about their lives for themselves. William Cooper was one of the most vocal advocates for Aboriginal rights, including the return of Aboriginal land, during that time. Throughout his life, Cooper and his peers had borne the infringement of human rights that few other Australians have had to suffer, including being unable to earn equal wages or apply for the same level of financial support when they were unable to find employment, and needing to apply for permission to move from reserves and to marry. Cooper's vision was an Australia where these rights and freedoms were not denied to Aboriginal people and he believed that if the barriers to accessing the benefits and opportunities within Australian society—such as land, employment and education—were removed that Aboriginal people were well equipped, through their own hard work and initiative, to alter their own socio-economic circumstances.

Cooper, like many of his peers, had laboured on the pastoral properties that were once the traditional lands of his family and he saw the wealth that was generated by the production on those lands. Cooper wondered why it was that white people were able to engage in activities that could provide opportunities for their families but he could not do the same. His constant petitions and letters were aimed at making the argument that if he and his peers could be given the same opportunity to work the land, they would break away from the position of being reliant on the state and welfare dependant (Attwood and Marckus 2004).

In 1963, provoked by a unilateral government decision to excise a part of their land for a bauxite mine, the Yolngu people at Yirrkala in north-east Arnhem Land sent a petition written on bark to the House of Representatives demanding that their land rights be respected.

The English version of the petition reads:

The Humble Petition of the Undersigned aboriginal people of Yirrkala, being members of the Balamumu, Narrkala, Gapiny, Miliwurrwurr people and Djapu, Mangalili, Madarrpa, Magarrwanalmirri, Djambarrpuynu, Gumaitj, Marrakulu, Galpu, Dhaluangu, Wangurri, Warramirri, Naymil, Riritjingu, tribes respectfully showeth.

1   That nearly 500 people of the above tribes are residents of the land excised from the Aboriginal Reserve in Arnhem Land.

2   That the procedures of the excision of this land and the fate of the people on it were never explained to them beforehand, and were kept secret from them.

3   That when Welfare Officers and Government officials came to inform them of decisions taken without them and against them, they did not undertake to convey to the Government in Canberra the views and feelings of the Yirrkala aboriginal people.

4   That the land in question has been hunting and food gathering land for the Yirrkala tribes from time immemorial: we were all born here.

5   That places sacred to the Yirrkala people, as well as vital to their livelihood are in the excised land, especially Melville Bay.

6   That the people of this area fear that their needs and interests will be completely ignored as they have been ignored in the past, and they fear that the fate which has overtaken the Larrakeah tribe will overtake them.

7   And they humbly pray that the Honourable the House of Representatives will appoint a Committee, accompanied by competent interpreters, to hear the views of the people of Yirrkala before permitting the excision of this land.

8   They humbly pray that no arrangements be entered into with any company which will destroy the livelihood and independence of the Yirrkala people.

And your petitioners as in duty bound will ever pray God to help you and us.

The bark petition provoked a government inquiry and later the Yolngu launched litigation, but the mine went ahead.

DISCUSSION QUESTIONS

- Why were land rights such a focus for the Aboriginal political movement?
- What did Aboriginal people hope to achieve for their communities and families through land rights?

In August 1966 Gurindji people went on strike demanding wages and a return of some of their traditional lands. The strikers were employed on the Wave Hill Station in the Northern Territory, owned by the British consortium, Vesteys. Two hundred Aboriginal cattle workers and their families walked off Wave Hill Station, striking for better pay and conditions. Like other Indigenous employees of the pastoral industry, the Gurindji people were excluded from the Cattle Station Industry (Northern Territory) Award 1951 (Deane 1996). Gurindji leader, Vincent Lingiari, demanded a wage of $25 per week (Deane 1996). When Vesteys' manager refused his request, the Gurindji declared an immediate strike. Although the strike was sparked by an industrial dispute, its primary goal was repatriation of traditional lands.

For over nine years, the strike brought the issue of dispossession and land rights into the public consciousness. While this was not the first or the only demand by Aborigines for the return of their lands, it attracted widespread recognition and enjoyed wide public support. In 1975, Prime Minister Gough Whitlam handed leasehold title to 3,238 square kilometres of Wave Hill Station back to the Gurindji people.

Throughout the period of the Gurinji strike, there were movements around the country that heightened the awareness of Australians to the socio-economic position of Aboriginal people and of their political aspirations. For example, in 1965 Aboriginal people, including Charles Perkins, led a group of supporters on a 'freedom ride' through western New South Wales protesting discrimination against Aboriginal people.

The tide of public opinion was turning and, in 1967, 90.77 per cent of the Australian population turned out to vote 'yes' in the referendum to count Aboriginal people in the census and give the Commonwealth the power to make laws for Aboriginal people.

On 26 January 1971, Aboriginal activists and their supporters set up the Tent Embassy on the lawns of Federal Parliament House. They called for national land rights and an end to discrimination. In the same year, the Yolngu peoples' fight for land rights led to a Federal Court case, the *Gove Land Rights* case (*Milirrpum v Nabako Pty Ltd* (1971) 17 FLR 141 (NTSC)), where Justice Blackburn found that Yolngu could not prevent mining on their lands because Australia had adopted the legal fiction of terra nullius.

DISCUSSION QUESTION

- Why did the land rights movement become reinvigorated after the 1967 referendum?

Primarily as a result of that case and the increasing pressure from Aboriginal communities for some form of land justice, when the Whitlam Labor Government came into power with a policy of national Aboriginal land rights in 1972, it commissioned the Woodward Inquiry into Aboriginal land rights (Woodward 1973, 1974). The Whitlam Government also established Aboriginal Affairs as a separate ministry served by a separate Department of Aboriginal Affairs (DAA) and introduced a policy of self-determination. During this period, the outstation/homeland movement gained momentum as thousands of Aboriginal people moved out of missions and settlements and back onto traditional lands.

When launching his party's election campaign, Labor leader Gough Whitlam said that, if elected, he would legislate to give Aboriginal people land rights because he believed that all Australians were diminished while Aboriginal people were denied their rightful place in this nation.

But rather than pursue a national land rights law, Prime Minister Gough Whitlam chose to establish a precedent in the Commonwealth-controlled Northern Territory. In February 1973 he appointed Mr Justice Edward Woodward to inquire into appropriate ways to recognise Aboriginal land rights in the Northern Territory. In April of the following year, the final report of the (Woodward) Aboriginal Commission Report proposed Aboriginal legislation for the Northern Territory.

Justice Woodward reported that the aims of land rights were:

- the doing of simple justice to a people who have been deprived of their land without their consent and without compensation;
- the promotion of social harmony and stability within the wider Australian community by removing, as far as possible, the legitimate causes of complaint of an important minority group within that community;
- the provision of land holdings as a first essential for people who are economically depressed and who have at present no real opportunity of achieving a normal Australian standard of living;
- the preservation, where possible, of the spiritual link with their own land which gives each Aboriginal their sense of identity and which lies at the heart of their spiritual beliefs;
- the maintenance and, perhaps, improvement of Australia's standing among the nations of the world by demonstrably fair treatment of an ethnic minority.

Justice Woodward recommended that these aims could be best achieved by:

- preserving and strengthening all Aboriginal interests in land and rights over land which exist today, particularly all those having spiritual importance;
- ensuring that none of these interests or rights are further whittled away without consent, except in those cases where the national interest positively demands it— and then only on terms of just compensation;
- the provision of some basic compensation in the form of land for those Aborigines who have been irrevocably deprived of the rights and interests which they would otherwise have inherited from their ancestors, and who have obtained no sufficient compensating benefits from white society;
- the further provision of land, to the limit which the wider community can afford, in those places where it will do most good, particularly in economic terms, to the largest number of Aborigines.

Woodward said that in reaching his conclusions he had taken full account of the arguments put forward by various vested interests which opposed the granting of land rights, including the mining and resources industry. Woodward insisted that mining and other development on Aboriginal land should proceed only with the consent of the Aboriginal landowners and that the right to withhold consent should only be over-ridden if the government of the day decided that the national interest required it.

He also proposed procedures for claiming land and conditions of tenure. Aboriginal land should be granted as inalienable freehold title—meaning it could not be acquired, sold, mortgaged or disposed of in any way—and title should be communal. He envisaged the transfer to Aboriginal ownership of the government reserve lands and the hearing by an Aboriginal Land Commissioner of claims to unalienated Crown land and Aboriginal-owned pastoral leases based on traditional affiliation.

Although national land rights legislation would never become a reality, the Inquiry did result in the *Aboriginal Land Rights (Northern Territory) Act 1976* (Cth).

Land rights legislation around Australia

- The *Pitjantjatjara Land Rights Act 1981* and *Maralinga Tjarutja Land Rights Act 1984* were passed in South Australia and vested land in traditional owners. Prior to that, the *Aboriginal Lands Trust Act 1966* turned reserves into perpetual leases but did not vest the land in Aboriginal communities.
- Victoria has used legislation to vest specific land in Aboriginal communities such as Framlingham, Lake Condah and Robinvale: *Aboriginal Lands Act 1970, Aboriginal Land (Lake Condah and Framlingham Forest) Act 1987 (Commonwealth), Aboriginal Lands Act 1991, Aboriginal Land (Manatunga Land) Act 1992, Aboriginal Lands (Aborigines' Advancement League) (Watt Street, Northcote) Act 1982* and *Aboriginal Land (Northcote Land) Act 1989*.
- Queensland vested former reserves under a special form of freehold, held in trust by community councils for their residents, by various amendments 1982–1988 to the *Land Act 1962*, and introduced a limited land rights scheme on the basis of traditional/customary affiliation: *Aboriginal Land Act 1991* and *Torres Strait Islander Land Act 1991*.
- Tasmania vested 12 areas in the ownership of a land council in trust for Aboriginal people: *Aboriginal Lands Act 1995*.
- The Commonwealth passed the *Aboriginal Land Rights (Northern Territory) Act 1976* (Cth) and it vested 'scheduled' areas of land in Aboriginal Land Trusts. The *Pastoral Land Act 1992* (NT) enabled parts of pastoral leasehold areas known as 'Community Living Areas' to be claimed on the basis of 'need' and held by Aboriginal corporations. The Commonwealth also passed the *Aboriginal Land Grant (Jervis Bay Territory) Act 1986* that allowed for areas of land to be vested in the ownership of the Wreck Bay Aboriginal Community Council.
- Western Australia has not passed land rights legislation.

The recommendations of Mr Justice Woodward formed the basis of the *Aboriginal Land Rights (Northern Territory) Act 1976*. It passed both houses of the federal parliament with historic bipartisan support on 9 December 1976 under the Fraser Government and came into force on 26 January 1977, one-and-a-half years before the Northern Territory was granted self-government. The Commonwealth *Aboriginal Councils and Associations Act 1976* allowed for the establishment of Local Land Councils in a bid to encourage a degree of Aboriginal self-management.

The Northern Territory

The *Aboriginal Land Rights (Northern Territory) Act 1976* was the first attempt by an Australian government to recognise legally the Aboriginal system of land ownership and put into law the concept of inalienable freehold title. This has allowed Aboriginal people to retain, and in some cases re-establish, their cultural identity, while at the same time contributing to the peaceful and responsible development of the Northern Territory.

When the Act was passed, the former 'reserves' became Aboriginal land. The land was granted without the need for a land claim. It is referred to as Schedule One land. The only land able to be claimed is unalienated Crown land—land that no one else is using or has an interest in—or land which is wholly owned by Aboriginal people. A successful land claim requires the Aboriginal landowners to prove their traditional relationship to the land under claim. This involves extensive research by anthropologists, and the claimants providing evidence before the Aboriginal Land Commissioner who is a judge of the Federal Court or the Supreme Court of the Northern Territory.

The Commissioner must be satisfied that the claimants are the right traditional owners according to Aboriginal law. The Land Commissioner makes his or her recommendation to the Minister for Aboriginal Affairs. He or she must also comment on any detriment to others that may occur should the land be granted and the effect a grant may have on existing or proposed patterns of land usage in the region. The Minister for Aboriginal Affairs decides whether to recommend to the Governor-General to grant all or part of the land under claim.

Land successfully claimed is granted under inalienable freehold title. It cannot be bought, acquired or mortgaged. Communal title is formally vested in Aboriginal Land Trusts comprised of Aboriginal people who hold the title for the benefit of all the traditional landowners.

The Land Councils are representative bodies of elected Aboriginal people. They determine policy and employ expert legal, anthropological and land management staff to assist Aboriginal people in the claiming and management of their land, the protection of their sacred sites and the financial management of income received under the Act.

The functions and responsibilities of the Land Councils are set out in s 23 of the *Aboriginal Land Rights (Northern Territory) Act 1976*. It says the functions of Land Councils are to:

- find out and express the wishes of Aboriginal people about the management of their land and legislation about their land;
- protect the interests of traditional Aboriginal owners of, and other Aborigines interested in, Aboriginal land;
- assist Aboriginal people to protect sacred sites, whether or not on Aboriginal land;

- consult traditional Aboriginal landowners and other Aborigines interested in Aboriginal land about proposals for the use of their land;
- negotiate on behalf of traditional landowners with people interested in using Aboriginal land and land under claim;
- assist Aboriginal people claiming land and, in particular, arrange and pay for legal assistance for them;
- keep a register of Land Council members and members of Aboriginal Land Trusts and descriptions of Aboriginal land; and
- supervise and assist Aboriginal Land Trusts.

In carrying out their functions, the Land Councils must consult with traditional landowners and other Aborigines with an interest in the land. Landowners must give their consent before the Land Council enters into an agreement, or takes any action affecting their land.

The Land Councils also have statutory responsibilities and duties to:

- attempt to conciliate a dispute between Aborigines regarding land matters;
- hold in trust, and distribute to Aboriginal associations, statutory payments from the Aboriginal Benefits Account to communities affected by mining operations and income received on behalf of landowners under negotiated agreements; and
- process applications for permits to enter Aboriginal land.

While seen as in need of improvement, the Northern Territory legislation has enabled Aboriginal people to maintain, and in some cases to re-establish, their cultural identity. It gives some security to those who have moved back to set up outstations on their traditional country. By providing legal title and a measure of control over some traditional lands, it has allowed Aboriginal people to determine the pace and extent of their involvement in the broader Australian society and economy.

When the *Aboriginal Land Rights (Northern Territory) Act 1976* (Cth) was passed it was done with bipartisan support but was strongly resisted by the Northern Territory Government and mining interests. Since then, 44 per cent of the territory has been returned to Aboriginal hands (Norberry and Gardiner-Garden 2006), much of it of importance to the Aboriginal people but not needed by anyone else. The potential for Aboriginal people to retain control over their lands was eroded by the changes to that Act in 2006 (*Aboriginal Land Rights (Northern Territory) Amendment Act 2006* (Cth), passed into law on 17 August 2006). Among the reforms is provision for the grant of 99-year head leases over Aboriginal townships to a new entity that will be responsible for granting sub-leases (*Aboriginal Land Rights (Northern Territory) Act 1976* (Cth) s 19A.

The recent changes to the *Aboriginal Land Rights (Northern Territory) Act 1976* (Cth) also highlight the fact that these systems are often more focused on opening opportunities for non-Aboriginal interests on land than for protecting the capacity for Aboriginal people to use their land as they would like.

DISCUSSION QUESTIONS

- Why do Aboriginal people want to retain control over their lands?
- Why does the government continue to seek to claw back rights to control land under regimes like the *Aboriginal Land Rights (Northern Territory) Act 1976*?

The Howard Government sought to claw back many of the rights given to Aboriginal people in the Northern Territory, particularly with reforms it introduced in 2006 and in the Northern Territory intervention legislation in 2007. As a backdrop to these changes, in 2005 the National Indigenous Council, the Howard Government's appointed Indigenous advisory body, had raised the possibility of compulsory acquisition of townships.

The 2006 changes were to provide for arrangements for 99-year head leases to a Commonwealth or Northern Territory government entity that would take responsibility for sub-leases within an Aboriginal community. The head lease was voluntary and subject to informed consent by the traditional owners. If a head lease was signed, the permit system was relaxed for a sub-lease holder or anyone with a legitimate business relation to a sub-lease. There was limited take-up of the scheme and communities became concerned that they were being drawn into the scheme in order to gain access to essential services and infrastructure. For example, in November 2006, the Thamurrur Council of Wadeye alleged that the Commonwealth was withholding $10 million for desperately needed housing until the community agreed to grant a 99-year lease (Altman 2007). In such circumstances, the issue of whether consent to such arrangements is 'informed consent' was raised.

These changes related to changes as to how the Aboriginal Benefits Account (ABA) was used. Formerly, when distribution of the funds was based on the advice of the ABA Advisory Committee, the minister had more control over how the money was to be distributed.

When the Howard Government enacted the legislation to support its 'intervention' into the Northern Territory in 2007, it included further changes to the *Aboriginal Land Rights (Northern Territory) Act 1976*. It partially repealed the permit system and imposed compulsory acquisition of five-year leases over prescribed communities.

Most concerning of all, however, were the undemocratic methods employed by the Howard Government in developing the changes to the *Aboriginal Land Rights (Northern Territory) Act*. There was no consultation program to ascertain the opinions of Aboriginal people in the Northern Territory. The submission by the Laynhapuy Homelands Association to the Senate Inquiry captures what is wrong with the federal government's approach:

> The changes that the federal government are making to Indigenous affairs generally, and to Land Rights in particular, are happening much too fast for Aboriginal people

to understand, let alone respond to. … Changes are needed and new ways forward need to be carefully developed in partnership with government and business, but the change must be led by us, and implemented in consultation—not imposed (Laynhapuy Homelands Association Inc. 2006).

The New South Wales *Aboriginal Land Rights Act*

New South Wales has Australia's largest Indigenous population, estimated at more than 100,000. Its Aboriginal communities are diverse, ranging from urban to rural and remote, and from modern to traditional in their beliefs and practices.

In 1979, New South Wales legislated to establish an Aboriginal Lands Trust comprising members of the Aborigines Advisory Council. The Trust was given freehold title to most former reserves and the power to sell and acquire land.

A year later, the New South Wales Select Committee of the Legislative Assembly on Aborigines tabled its first report dealing with land rights and sacred and significant sites. The report recognised that in New South Wales, the destruction and fragmentation of Aboriginal society has been so severe that the normal definition of traditional lands does not apply. Land rights are recommended on the basis of need and as compensation for land lost, as well as prior ownership and tradition.

All lobby groups were involved in consultations for the Inquiry. In August 1980, the Final Report was tabled in the New South Wales Parliament and was accompanied by a large demonstration outside Parliament House. The report outlined the urgent need for land rights and emphasised the long wait Aborigines have endured.

The New South Wales *Aboriginal Land Rights Act* was passed in 1983. The Act recognises dispossession and dislocation of New South Wales Aboriginal people. It originally set up a three-tiered New South Wales Aboriginal Land Council (NSWALC) (the Regional Councils would subsequently be abolished) with a 15-year period of funding from non-residential land tax as compensation for lost lands and for Aboriginal people to establish an economic base.

The beneficial intention of the New South Wales land rights regime is stated clearly in the preamble of the Act:

Land in the State of New South Wales was traditionally owned and occupied by Aborigines. Land is of spiritual, social, cultural and economic importance to Aborigines. It is fitting to acknowledge the importance which land has for Aborigines and the need of Aborigines for land. It is accepted that as a result of past Government decisions the amount of land set aside for Aborigines has been progressively reduced without compensation.

In 1988, the Greiner Coalition Government was elected with a policy of abolishing New South Wales Aboriginal Land Rights legislation. It produced two discussion papers recommending mainstreaming of all Aboriginal special services and creation of a Commission to replace the NSWALC and the three-tiered system of Land Councils.

The papers provoked outrage from the Aboriginal community and sectors of the broader community. When the Greiner Government attempted to take over the NSWALC's financial assets, the move was challenged in and rejected by the Supreme Court.

As the state's peak—and in the post-ATSIC era the largest elected—representative body in Aboriginal Affairs, the NSWALC had, at the beginning of 2008, an asset base of over $2 billion in land holdings and over $650 million in cash assets. With this asset base, it aims to protect the interests and further the aspirations of its members and the broader Aboriginal community through social housing, scholarship schemes and community project. It is a self-funding statutory authority responsible for promoting and protecting the rights of the Aboriginal people of New South Wales.

DISCUSSION QUESTIONS

The NSWALC has to balance the need to preserve the assets it has for future generations, but also needs to provide assistance to Aboriginal people who need them today.
*   What principles should guide the balancing of these two goals?
*   What benefits should the Land Council system focus on providing to Aboriginal people in New South Wales?

The state's Land Council network operates as a two-tiered structure, comprising the peak body, NSWALC, a small number of zone offices around the state, and 121 Local Aboriginal Land Councils (LALCs), which are governed by elected boards.

Under the *Land Rights Act*, the NSWALC is empowered to:

*   administer the NSWALC Account and Mining Royalties Account;
*   grant funds for payment of the administrative costs and expenses of LALCs;
*   acquire land on its own behalf or on behalf of, or to be vested in, LALCs;
*   determine and approve/reject the terms and conditions of agreements proposed by LALCs to allow mining or mineral exploration on Aboriginal land;
*   make claims on Crown lands, either on its own behalf or at the request of LALCs;
*   with the agreement of the particular LALCs, manage any of the affairs of that Council;
*   conciliate disputes between Aboriginal Land Councils or between Councils and individuals or between individual members of those Councils;
*   make grants, lend money or invest money on behalf of Aborigines;

- hold, dispose of or otherwise deal with land vested in or acquired by the NSWALC;
- ensure LALCs comply with the Act in respect of the establishment and keeping of accounts and the preparation and submission of budgets and financial reports;
- advise the minister on matters relating to Aboriginal land rights;
- exercise such other functions as conferred or imposed on it by or under the *Aboriginal Land Rights Act 1983* (ALRA) or any other Act.

The preamble of the ALRA states that it is the intention of the legislation to provide a compensatory regime aimed at redressing the impact of dispossession on Aboriginal people in New South Wales:

> WHEREAS:
>
> 1   Land in the State of New South Wales was traditionally owned and occupied by Aborigines:
> 2   Land is of spiritual, social, cultural and economic importance to Aborigines:
> 3   It is fitting to acknowledge the importance which land has for Aborigines and the need of Aborigines for land:
> 4   It is accepted that as a result of past Government decisions the amount of land set aside for Aborigines has been progressively reduced without compensation:

The courts have said that the preamble shows an intention that the Act be compensatory and should be interpreted in a way that is consistent with the beneficial intentions that underpin it.

Under the regime, land can be claimed by the NSWALC or a LALC. The Act establishes a regime for the claiming of land as a mechanism to achieve the aims of the legislation in s 36. Section 36(1) contains the definition of 'claimable Crown lands' and includes:

- land vested in the Crown which can be sold, leased or reserved or dedicated for any purpose under the *Crowns Lands Consolidation Act 1913* (NSW) or the *Western Lands Act 1901* (NSW);
- land which is not lawfully used or occupied;
- land which, in the opinion of the Crown lands minister, is not needed or likely to be needed as a residential land or for an essential purpose; and
- land that is not covered by a registered native title determination application by a claimant or by an approved native title determination that native title exists.

Claims for land rights start with the relevant Land Council lodging its claim with the Aboriginal Land Rights Registrar and the claim is then forwarded to the minister responsible for the New South Wales *Crown Lands Act* for his or her consideration.

The minister then must grant the claim if, at the date of lodgment, the land is:

- Crown land;
- not lawfully used or occupied;
- not needed for an essential public purpose; and
- not needed as residential land.

Land that is acquired under land rights regimes may be used for a number of reasons; it may be used for any community purpose including such things as commercial enterprises and community housing. A right of appeal against a minister's decision to refuse a land claim lies with an appeal to the Land and Environment Court.

The New South Wales *Aboriginal Land Rights Act* is currently going through major reviews. These changes have been targeted at improving the governance practices of the NSWALC and the LALCs and at ensuring a balance between protecting the asset base for the long-term benefit of Aboriginal people and providing immediate benefits to Aboriginal people. In particular, the changes to the legislation in 2006 and 2007 were concerned with matters such as election of members of the NSWALC board and LALC boards, the provision of governance training to all elected members of the NSWALC and LALC boards, improved planning processes, improved membership rules, increased powers of the Minister for Aboriginal Affairs to intervene if a LALC needs to be dissolved due to inappropriate or improper behaviour, and changes to the functions and powers of the registrar to investigate and report on complaints relating to misbehaviour.

Land rights and native title

The *Mabo* case and its promise of native title in 1992 was something that invoked great hope in many Aboriginal people and their communities across the country. In *Mabo*, native title was to be defined by the laws and customs of Aboriginal people. However, this definition, which gave the power to Aboriginal people to define native title, was transformed under legislation (the *Native Title Act 1993* (Cth) s 223) and subsequent case law.

Over more than a decade of native title cases, an increasingly conservative court has narrowed the definition of native title and it is judges, not Aboriginal people, who have the largest role in recognising the existence and defining the content of native title.

Perhaps most famously through the decision in the *Yorta Yorta* case (*Members of the Yorta Yorta Aboriginal Community v Victoria* (2002) 214 CLR 422; [2002] HCA 58) where the court found that the culture of the claimants had been eroded by the history of colonisation and taken with it the native title interests of the Yorta Yorta nation,

Aboriginal people across Australia came to realise the extent to which Australian courts and parliaments can recognise an Aboriginal right or interest but seek to override it through narrow interpretations of facts and with a Eurocentric gaze on Aboriginal history, experience, culture and life.

In 1995, the Indigenous Land Corporation was established as the second part of the Keating Government's response to the *Mabo* decision. The corporation was set up to administer a fund to buy land on behalf of Indigenous people in recognition of the fact that many Aboriginal people would, due to the impact and processes of colonisation, be unable to prove that they maintained a native title interest over their traditional land in the way the law described and defined it.

Native title has long been subjected to the political motivations of governments that have valued certainty for non-Aboriginal property interests over the interests of Aboriginal people. The federal parliament was happy to extinguish the Aboriginal interests when there was a conflict between the two and it was comfortable in repealing the application of the *Racial Discrimination Act 1975* (Cth) from applying to what was clearly a racist valuing of white land interests over black (*Native Title Amendment Act 1998* (Cth)).

In fact, a large feature of the native title regime can be characterised as focused on ensuring the certainty of non-Aboriginal interests. While one of the positives of the system has been the increased role of negotiated agreements between traditional owners and other interests, it is also true to say that the system has been loaded against Aboriginal people because of the weakness of their title and the fact that native title interests are primarily about providing protection of cultural practices; they are not about creating commercial interests.

Although native title and land rights both relate to the recognition of Indigenous people's rights to land, they are very different from both a socio-political and a legal perspective. Land rights legislation and native title legislation were enacted with quite dissimilar political motivations. Land rights legislation, in the various Australian jurisdictions, was enacted in response to a broad social and political movement, which evolved from the 1960s to the 1980s to include people from a broad spectrum of society, both Indigenous and non-Indigenous people—the politically conservative and the radical.

Native title legislation, on the other hand, began in the courts with the judicial recognition of native title in *Mabo (No 2)* in 1992. That decision gave new impetus to the ongoing campaign to have land rights recognised on a *national* basis. It provided the justification to the wavering Labor federal government (although both Labor and Coalition governments had toyed with the idea since the early 1970s) to provide a legislative basis for recognising Indigenous rights to land across the nation. But this was by no means 'land rights', in the sense that we know it in New South Wales. It was not a *political* recognition of Aboriginal rights to land; it was *judicial* recognition.

In other words, land rights legislation stemmed from a broad-based socio-political movement, while native title legislation was enacted in order to provide an administrative structure to channel the native title claims that would inevitably result from *Mabo*.

- What are the advantages of using native title as a basis for claiming land compared to using a land rights claim process such as the one in New South Wales?
- Why is it that the land rights regime has delivered substantially more land to Aboriginal people in New South Wales than the native title regime?
- Why is it that native title has delivered substantially more interests in land to Aboriginal people in Western Australia than a land rights regime?

The fight for land justice continues

Until Aboriginal people are given opportunities to change the economic circumstances of their community—access to education, proper housing, adequate health care and employment opportunities—they are left without the proper capacity to provide for their families. This is especially frustrating when we see non-Aboriginal people and companies making large fortunes off Aboriginal traditional lands without giving very much back to the Aboriginal community.

There has been much rhetoric about improving the economic prospects of Aboriginal communities by opening up opportunities for home ownership and economic development on their lands. In the face of the extreme poverty that many Aboriginal communities live in, this promise of wealth accumulation through home ownership and joint venture development is seductive rhetoric. However, there is a concern that Aboriginal people are now being encouraged to use their major land assets—that they have fought hard to regain either through the stringent land rights regimes where they exist or the even more stringent native title system—to deal with socio-economic issues like health, housing and education that are the responsibility of governments.

It is important that Aboriginal people be given opportunities to engage in the economy but care needs to be taken that the promises of inter-generational wealth do not lead to inter-generational poverty. We also have to make sure that governments take responsibility for the services that they are supposed to provide to Indigenous communities without expecting the shortfall to be paid for with future generations' legacy. In other countries, the privatisation of Indigenous land has meant that large reserves were divided up and parts sold off to non-Indigenous people. This did not alleviate the poverty of those communities; in fact, it worsened it. Those communities were sold the same dream that the capacity to sell off land would lead to riches, and we have to make sure that the same mistakes are not repeated.

Land justice is part of the multi-faceted approach needed to end Indigenous disadvantage. It needs to be a land justice that seeks to benefit Indigenous people rather than secure non-Indigenous interests. And it needs to be accompanied by a commitment to ending the under-funding of Indigenous health, education, housing and community infrastructure. It is this holistic approach that offers the most promise for an improved future for Indigenous people.

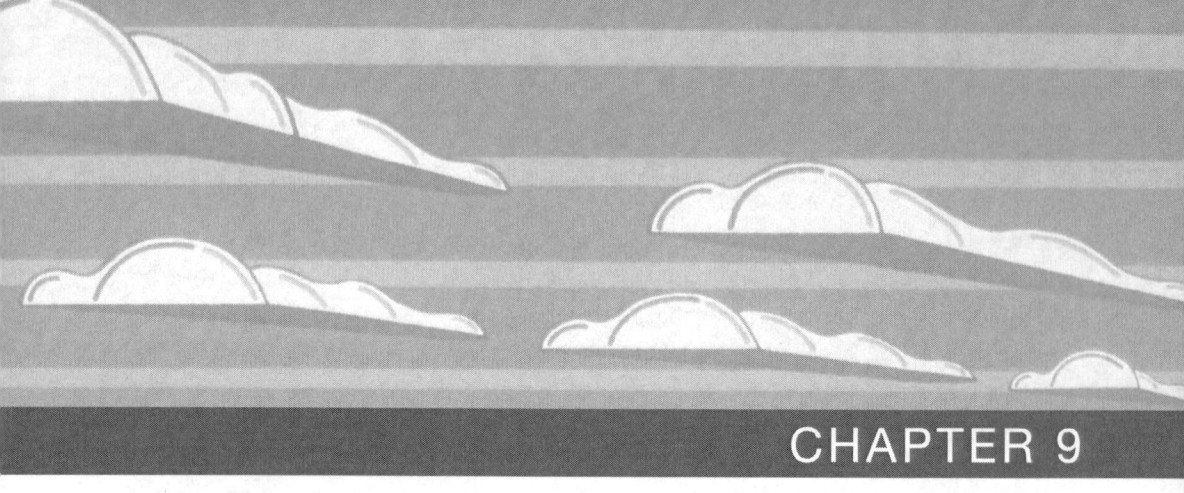

CHAPTER 9

Native Title

Introduction

In 1992 the High Court of Australia belatedly recognised in *Mabo v Queensland (No 2)* (1992) 107 ALR 1 (hereafter referred to as *Mabo (No 2)*) that the Miriam people, of the Mer Islands in the Torres Strait, at the time of colonisation had rights in their lands which they have retained. The court thereby overturned the racist doctrine of terra nullius which literally means empty land in Latin. In the words of Chief Justice Brennan at [63]: 'The common law of this country would perpetuate injustice if it were to continue to embrace the enlarged notion of terra nullius and persist in characterising the indigenous inhabitants of Australian colonies as people too low in the scale of social organisation to be acknowledged as possessing rights and interests in land.' This doctrine was part of a colonial world view which classified peoples in terms of a hierarchy of races with Indigenous peoples at the bottom of the hierarchy. This racist classification laid the foundations for expropriating Indigenous peoples' lands, denigrating their culture, exploiting their labour and in many circumstances treating Indigenous peoples in cruel and inhumane ways.

The High Court recognised native title in the form of a declaration. This acknowledged at common law two things: the first is that the Miriam people had rights to their lands in accordance with their own laws, customs and traditions, while the second is that the common law of Australia recognises these rights. This form of recognition however left many questions open for resolution. If claimants' land is recognised in terms of their own laws and customs, how are these laws and customs proven and recognised within the Australian legal system? Do they need to be translated into doctrine already understood by the common law or can they be understood on their own terms? How, if at all, is this law and custom recognised in other spheres of social, legal and political life? These questions have proven complex and form the core of later common law doctrine with respect to native title. They have practical and symbolic significance. In practical terms they determine the scope and nature of the rights and interests recognised as native title. In symbolic terms they play a role in defining the extent of non-Indigenous recognition of Indigenous peoples' ongoing collective identity and how relations between Indigenous and non-Indigenous Australians are mediated in a contemporary context. This chapter will provide an overview of the statutory responses to *Mabo* and subsequent major High Court decisions. Native title law is complex and dense and space constraints preclude detailed coverage of Federal Court decisions, mediation and arbitration or the *Native Title Act 1993* (Cth) and analogous state and territory native title legislation (see Bartlett 2004; Strelein 2006; Perry and Lloyd 2003).

Mabo (No 2): The findings and its impact

Up until 1992, what had become established historical, political and anthropological knowledge, that is that there are highly developed systems of laws within Aboriginal and Torres Strait Islander cultures, was not recognised on a legal level. This was partially rectified in 1992 with *Mabo (No 2)* which offered the High Court its first opportunity to recognise native title. The plaintiffs in *Mabo (No 2)* claimed that they had occupied and used the Murray islands and surrounding islands, seas, seabeds and reefs since time immemorial and that under their law, individuals, family groups and the community as a whole have rights which have not been extinguished by Australia's or Queensland's sovereignty. The High Court, by a majority of six, with one dissenting judge, held that the plaintiffs owned their land. Their title, native title, was and continues to be based on their own laws and customs. The High Court held that the Crown's ownership is subject to native title and is not absolute. However the Crown as sovereign could extinguish native title. The Crown must show a plain and clear intention to extinguish native title and it can only be extinguished in a way that is lawful under the Constitution and in accordance with state and federal legislation.

Two core ideas about the legal basis of land ownership in Australia were overthrown by *Mabo*. The first idea was that the Crown owned absolute title to the land and that all property rights were granted by the Crown. The court found that what was taken on colonisation was sovereignty and radical title to the land. However this title was burdened with pre-existing native title. As such the established feudal system of land tenure which was imported from England was retained but modified to incorporate native title. The misfit between English feudal tenures and the unique land usage in Australia required consideration and modification in *Wik Peoples v Queensland* (1996) 187 CLR 1, which addressed the relationship between pastoral leases and native title (see discussion below). The second idea about land ownership which was rejected in *Mabo (No 2)* is an idea which was not founded in legal doctrine but rather in political and social practice, this being that the land was legally uninhabited at the time of colonisation.

In *Mabo (No 2)* the High Court found that native title is recognised and protected by the common law but does not originate from the common law. Native title arises from the customs and traditions of the Indigenous people whose rights are recognised. Native title is sui generis, that is, unique. Chief Justice Brennan noted at [64]: 'Native title has its origins in and is given its content by the traditional customs observed by the Indigenous inhabitants of a territory. The nature and incidents of native title must be ascertained as a matter of fact by reference to those laws and customs.' To establish the content of native title, the customs and traditions of the claimants need to be proven. Native title may be large and approximate the fullest title known to English law or it may encompass rights which are more akin in English property law to personal rights of usage rather than land rights. Claimants need to demonstrate that their current customs and traditions give rise to an interest in the land which has, albeit not in a static form, existed continuously from the time of the colonial acquisition of sovereignty. This continuous connection does not necessarily need to include continuous physical presence on the land but may be demonstrated in other ways, for example through ongoing spiritual connections. Native title cannot be sold or dealt with except in compliance with traditional law or to the Crown.

Mabo (No 2) also unveils questions with respect to the impacts of historical injustices and how to address contemporary extinguishment of native title. What recognition should be given to peoples whose native title has been extinguished or who have lost their capacity to prove native title through what *Mabo (No 2)* acknowledges to be a racist and dishonourable expropriation? *Mabo (No 2)* has had a significant impact on relations between Indigenous and non-Indigenous Australians and more broadly on understandings of the colonial process and the status of Aboriginal and Torres Strait Islanders in Australian society (see for example Attwood 1996; Stephenson and Ratnapala 1993; Webber 1995; Patton 1995; Ritter 1998; Strelein 2005; Langton et al 2004; Pearson 2003; Reilly and Genovese 2004; Howitt 2006). While the decision recognised that Indigenous Australians had and continue to have an organised society, it explicitly declined to recognise the sovereign status of Indigenous Australians either at the time of colonisation or currently. Chief Justice Brennan stated that this would challenge Australia's sovereignty and any recognition would undermine the legitimacy of the High Court which gained its authority from the Australian Parliament whose sovereignty would be challenged. This left an unresolved recognition of both the ongoing foundation for native title and more broadly the constitutional status of Indigenous Australians. The decision also left native title vulnerable to the whim of Parliament. In accordance with the majority in *Mabo (No 2)*, native title can be extinguished by a clear Act of Parliament which directly or indirectly intends extinguishment (for a critical assessment of this doctrine see McNeil 1996, 1997). This leaves native title holders extremely vulnerable with the limited protection of the *Racial Discrimination Act 1975* (Cth) which can be repealed or partially repealed by the federal parliament. As will be discussed below this has occurred in both the original *Native Title Act 1993* (Cth) and to a far greater extent with the amendments by the Howard Government to the Act in 1998. Only Justice Toohey in *Mabo (No 2)* considered the possibility of the federal government owing a fiduciary duty to native title holders because of the vulnerability of their title. This is because the Crown has the power to act in a way that adversely impacts on native title holders' property, and fiduciary responsibilities would protect them against abuse of this power (for a discussion of fiduciary duties in the context of native title see Behrendt 2000; Bartlett 2004). While fiduciary duties on the part of governments are recognised in other comparable jurisdictions such as Canada, the Australian High Court has declined to follow Justice Toohey's reasoning in this respect (for a discussion of fiduciary relationships in the Canadian context see Rotman 1996).

In addition to the impact of *Mabo (No 2)* on doctrine and jurisprudence, the decision has had a major, and to some extent polarising, impact on popular and academic understandings of race relations in Australia. Responses have varied from perceptions of opportunity to disdain and fear. The Keating Labor Government responded to the *Mabo (No 2)* decision as a legal recognition which required negotiation and compromise. They promised in addition to honouring native title to develop a social justice package. However, they were voted out of office before this was developed. The Howard Liberal Government, which held office for just over 10 years from 1996 to 2007, unlike its predecessor, failed to embrace the opportunities which *Mabo (No 2)* offered. As will be discussed below, the Howard Government amended the native title legislation to enact in the words of then Deputy Prime Minister, Tim Fisher, 'bucket loads' of extinguishment (Brough 1997). These amendments breached international law and were criticised by the Committee on the Elimination of All Forms of Racial Discrimination. They will have an enduring adverse impact on Indigenous peoples and more broadly on the trajectory of race relations in Australia.

DISCUSSION QUESTIONS

- Can the acknowledgment of the practical existence of Aboriginal and Torres Strait Islander peoples' ongoing laws and customs, without recognition of these laws and customs except for the purpose of proving native title, be legally or morally reconciled?
- Is the common law implicated in the ongoing dispossession of Aboriginal and Torres Strait Islander peoples, which is critiqued in *Mabo (No 2)*, through a failure to protect native title from capricious extinguishment?

The *Native Title Act*

The Keating federal government responded to the *Mabo (No 2)* decision with an attempt to quell the concern about uncertainty from some quarters, primarily mining and agricultural and pastoral interests, by passing native title legislation. This was meant to provide certainty for all parties. The negotiation of the *Native Title Act 1993* (Cth) was fraught with conflict. It was rushed and represented an unrefined compromise between competing interests, which in many respects failed the spirit of equality that was referred to in *Mabo*. This is because it abrogates from the equality required under the *Racial Discrimination Act 1975* (Cth) and for the most part prioritises non-Indigenous rights and interests over native title. The discriminatory aspects of the legislation were significantly exacerbated with the 1998 amendments to the *Native Title Act*. Compared with the USA, Canada and New Zealand, Australia not only belatedly recognised native title but it is also the only jurisdiction which has passed native title legislation and in this way inhibited the development of the common law with respect to native title. Richard Bartlett observed that, 'The result in Australia has been legislation, particularly after amendment in 1998, entailing great complexity and cost, extremely wasteful of time and resources, and productive of combative and litigious approaches. There have been few if any commensurate benefits' (2004: 39).

The *Native Title Act 1993* (Cth) received the Royal Assent on 24 December 1993 and its substantive provisions were proclaimed on 1 January 1994. As discussed above the *Mabo (No 2)* decision, while strongly condemning the role of the common law in dispossessing Indigenous peoples unjustly—in particular the taking of Indigenous peoples' land with no compensation or justification—provided no protection against the legislature continuing the process which in the words of Chief Justice Brennan in *Mabo (No 2)* at [28]:

> ... took from indigenous inhabitants any right to occupy their traditional land, exposed them to deprivation of religious, cultural and economic sustenance which the land provides, vested the land effectively in the control of the Imperial authorities without any right of compensation and made the indigenous inhabitants intruders in their own homes and mendicants for a place to live. Judged by any civilised standard, such a law is unjust and its claim to be part of the common law to be applied in contemporary Australia must be questioned ...

The *Native Title Act* continues this dispossession with a validation of all Crown grants made up until January 1994 and validation of all legislation passed up until 1 July 1993. This not only partially repeals the *Racial Discrimination Act 1975* (Cth), which accords equality to all property interests from its date of operation, but also validates grants and legislation after the well-publicised *Mabo (No 2)* decision was handed down in 1992. However the *Native Title Act* does provide for compensation for this extinguishment. The Act establishes the National Native Title Tribunal (NNTT) to determine native title by agreement and the Federal Court to adjudicate contested determinations. With respect to extinguishment or diminution of native title rights after January 1994, under the Future Acts regime, the Act offers native title holders the same protection as if they held freehold title. With respect to mining grants which override freehold title, the Act provides registered native title claimants with a right to negotiate. This places an onus on parties to negotiate in good faith with the native title claimants. However off-shore grants and those which do not directly interfere with community life, or with areas or sites of particular significance or which do not involve major disturbance to land or waters, are exempted from the negotiation requirements. The time frames for negotiation are restricted to between four and six months depending on the grant, and if agreement cannot be reached a determination is made by the NNTT, which if in favour of native title claimants could be overruled by the minister in the national, state or territory interest. States and territories could establish compatible bodies to perform the functions provided for under the Act. All states and territories have passed complementary legislation, but this was also a prolonged process with attempts, the most notorious being in Western Australia, to pass legislation which substantially undermined native title rights. The initial Western Australian legislation, the *Land (Titles and Traditional Usage) Act 1993* which was found to be incompatible with the *Racial Discrimination Act 1975* (Cth) and was struck down in *Western Australia v Commonwealth* (1995) 183 CLR 373 by the High Court, stands as a vestige of contemporary shame, with its provisions which among other matters purported to extinguish all native title in Western Australia and to replace it with 'rights of traditional usage' which would have been subject to all other titles.

The 1998 amendments to the *Native Title Act*

When the Howard Liberal/National Government was elected into office in 1996 it adopted a hostile stance towards Indigenous rights. This hostility materialised into a derogation of Indigenous rights in many spheres including with respect to native title. The government immediately proposed to amend the *Native Title Act* to make registration of claims more difficult and to increase the interests of miners and pastoralists (Office of Indigenous Affairs 1996). However, it was after the High Court held in *Wik* that the granting of pastoral leases did not in all circumstances extinguish native title, that racially discriminatory legislation, which plundered native title interests, was developed and enacted (see discussion of *Wik* below). As discussed above, the original *Native Title Act 1993* prioritised non-Indigenous grants up until 1993 but provided for equality of treatment with respect to future dealings with native title. The 10-point plan developed by the Howard Liberal Government, and subsequent legislation in 1998, abandoned this commitment to equality for native title holders with respect to future dealings. The amendments added a further 346 pages to the legislation, which was initially 127 pages in length, ensuring that any claim to either racial equality or a simple and user-friendly system for determining native title had been abandoned. The detailed specificity in the amendments was responding to the High Court decision in *Western Australia v Commonwealth* (1995) 183 CLR 373 which provided that any ambiguity in the *Native Title Act* should be interpreted in favour of respecting the *Racial Discrimination Act 1975*. The amendments, among other matters:

- validated grants made by state governments after the enactment of the *Native Title Act* up until the *Wik* decision (December 1996);
- confirmed permanent extinguishment in relation to leasehold, freehold and other tenures;
- expanded the rights of pastoralists;
- made the registration of native title claims more difficult for claimants with no corresponding onerous provisions for non-claimant applications, that is, applications that native title does not exist;
- reduced the right of native title holders to negotiate with respect to mining interests and limited native title claimants' rights to information and comment with respect to other dealings related to their claims; and
- suspended the *Racial Discrimination Act 1975* for the purpose of effecting these amendments.

These amendments received criticism from the United Nations Committee on the Elimination of All Forms of Racial Discrimination which found that they breached the International Convention on the Elimination of All Forms of Racial Discrimination in a number of respects. The Committee in particular found that the provisions with respect to the validation of non-Indigenous interests, deemed extinguishment of native title, the expansion of pastoral interests and the abolition and diminution of the right to negotiate breached the Convention (Australia, Decision of the Committee on the Elimination of Racial Discrimination, 54th session, CERD/C/54/Misc40/Rev 2 and CERD/C/55 Misc Rev 3, 16 August 1999). (For discussion of the findings see Marks 2004).

DISCUSSION QUESTION

- In what ways could Aboriginal and Torres Strait Islander peoples' native title, and rights more broadly, be afforded more secure protection?

Common law developments post-*Mabo (No 2)*

While the *Native Title Act 1993* (Cth) and the subsequent 1998 amendments claimed to codify native title, many aspects of native title are either not addressed or are ambiguous in the Act. This has left a role for the courts to flesh out the meaning and particularities of native title. Issues which were left unresolved or ambiguous by *Mabo (No 2)* and the subsequent native title legislation include:

- the nature and extent of rights recognised within the rubric of native title;
- whether native title is a bundle of rights which can be recognised and extinguished bit by bit or if it encompasses an underlying title;
- how native title is extinguished and in what circumstances extinguishment is permanent; and
- how and in what circumstances native title can coexist with other titles and interests in land.

Some of these questions are addressed in the cases discussed below.

Pastoral leases

In *Wik Peoples v Queensland* (1996) 187 CLR 1, one of the issues with the greatest practical significance with respect to the coexistence of native title and other non-Indigenous titles was raised. Could native title coexist with pastoral leases? A considerable body of Australian land is held under pastoral lease. Pastoral leases are created by statute which means that there is variation between leases across the country, however they have in common a tendency to cover large tracts of land. The Wik and Thayorre peoples brought a claim for land and seas in the Cape York Peninsula of Queensland. They also claimed for damages for the extinguishment of some of their native title rights and interests. Their claim included large pastoral lease holdings. The central question in *Wik* was whether a pastoral lease conferred exclusive possession upon the lessee. If the leases did confer exclusive possession, were the native title interests extinguished or could these rights coexist or in the alternate could they be suspended for the duration of the lease? This entailed the High Court looking at the *Land Act 1919* (Qld) and the *Land Act 1962* (Qld) which conferred the pastoral leases. The High Court examined the history of the leases and found that they were particular to the Australian context and were not intended to exclude Indigenous peoples or their interests. They found that pastoral leases under this legislation were significantly different from common law leases which do confer exclusive possession. The High Court found that these pastoral leases do not confer the broad bundle of rights which a lease usually confers. The leases cover vast tracks of land and the legislation plainly intended that a range of parties could be granted rights to enter onto and benefit from this land. In addition the legislation did not differentiate between licensee (lesser interests at common law) and lessee interests. The majority interpreted the legislation from a 'strong beneficial' approach finding that if there was nothing in the legislation which necessarily made the leases inconsistent with native title interests, then the native title interests survived to the extent that they could coexist. If there was inconsistency then the native title rights had to yield to the extent of the inconsistency. The nature and extent of inconsistencies were matters to be determined on the facts at trial. They were to be determined by comparing the legal rights conferred under the leases with the native title rights claimed and the native title rights would be diminished to the extent of any incompatible inconsistency.

The *Wik* decision catalysed the Howard Government's 10-point plan and subsequent 1998 amendments to the *Native Title Act* which are discussed above. The extent to which the amendments impacted on the *Wik* finding of coexistence was tested in *Wilson v Anderson* (2002) 190 ALR 313. Wilson, a lessee of a lease under the *Western Lands Act 1901* (NSW), which fell within a claim made by Michael Anderson on behalf of the Euahlay-i Dixon clan, sought clarification with respect to whether his lease conferred exclusive possession and if any native title rights or interests which existed in his lease were either extinguished or suspended. The High Court looked to the extinguishment provisions of the *Native Title Act* which were enacted in 1998. If the lease fell within one of the eight categories scheduled in s 23B(2)(c) of the *Native Title Act* then native title would be extinguished. The schedule does include pastoral leases in the Western Lands Division (WLA) but it does not include leases which are exclusively for grazing purposes. Leases under the WLA can be granted in perpetuity or for a term. The Full Federal Court found that leases in perpetuity could coexist with other interests such as native title and therefore do not necessarily extinguish native title. However the High Court considered the perpetual term of the lease as a quality which made it like a freehold and consistent with aspects of exclusive possession, which under the analogous New South Wales *Native Title Act* extinguishes native title completely. This decision will have a severe impact on the capacity for coexistence recognised in *Wik* and is reflective of a High Court which systematically prioritises non-Indigenous rights and interests over Indigenous interests when interpreting the *Native Title Act* (Cth) and analogous state and territory legislation.

DISCUSSION QUESTION

- Discuss the moral and legal basis for prioritising leaseholders' interests where there is inconsistency between native title and lessees' rights.

Freehold title

In *Fejo on behalf of the Larrakia People v Northern Territory* (1998) 195 CLR 96 the question of whether there was any scope for recognition of native title where freehold title had been granted—in particular where the land had been resumed and was therefore at the time of the claim vacant Crown land—was addressed. The Larrakia people brought an action with respect to leases that had been granted over land which they claimed they retained native title rights over, in and around Darwin, Palmerston and Litchfield in the Northern Territory. The land had been granted in 1882 as a freehold but it had been resumed in 1927 by the Commonwealth to use as a quarantine station and then as a leprosarium. These public purposes were revoked in 1980 making the land vacant Crown land again. The action was catalysed by the Northern Territory Government granting leaseholds with the option to acquire freehold over the Larrakia peoples' country. The High Court in *Fejo* reiterated Chief Justice Brennan's opinion from *Mabo (No 2)* that freehold grants permanently extinguished all native title interests. The court noted that freehold title is the largest title known to Australian property law and that it encompasses every act of ownership, thereby precluding the coexistence of native title interests. Lisa Strelein commented:

> This prioritisation of physical access and control did not reflect the unique nature of the relationship to an interest in the land held by Indigenous peoples. Moreover, it went against those aspects of the decision in *Mabo* that embraced the spiritual and non-physical elements of Indigenous peoples' traditions, customs and laws relating to lands. Instead, the High Court superimposed non-Indigenous understandings of relations with land and the rights and interests that could attach to land over the concept of native title … The Court in *Fejo* adopted a vision of law based on power that comes from the capacity to dominate (Strelein 2006: 41, 43 and 44).

A particularly disappointing aspect of *Fejo* is the categorical finding that extinguishment is permanent and even where Indigenous laws and customs prevail, and the land in question is vacant Crown land, extinguishment is final with no opportunity for a concept of suspension or restitution of the original limitation on absolute Crown ownership which forms the essence of recognition in *Mabo (No 2)*. This appears to be a sad and harsh loss of an opportunity to recognise native title interests in a context which is consistent with the basis of native title, a burden on the absolute ownership by the Crown, and could have provided a balance of coexistence between native title and subsequent interests granted by the Crown, without in fact impacting on any non-Indigenous interests. This is because the land is vacant Crown land. The refusal on the part of the High Court to categorise native title as suspended rather than permanently extinguished, where no non-Indigenous interests exist to be prioritised, seems to be a choice to contemporarily perpetuate injustice. *Fejo* confirms the fragility of the common law's claim in *Mabo (No 2)* to be retreating from the injustice of dispossession.

Sea rights

In *Commonwealth v Yarmirr* (2001) 184 ALR 113 the High Court considered recognition of the native title rights of the Mandilarrildugij, Mangalara, Muran, Gadura, Minaga, Ngayndjagar and Mayorram peoples' sea country in the Croker Island region of the Northern Territory. The claimants sought recognition of their rights to exclusive possession, ownership, occupation, use and enjoyment of the sea and seabed and its resources. Mary Yarmirr, one of the claimants, described sea country in the following terms:

> When I use the word 'country', I am talking about dry land, fresh water and the sea. And when I talk about sea country, I am not talking only about the waters of the sea. I am talking about the seabed and the reefs, and the fish and animals in the sea, and our fishing and hunting grounds, and the air and clouds above the sea, and about our sacred sites and ancestral beings who created all the country (cited in Morris 2002).

On appeal to the High Court, the claimants acknowledged that their claim to exclusivity was qualified by the public right to navigate, the international right of innocent passage and the rights of holders of fishing licences. The High Court considered whether the assertion of sovereignty over the territorial waters in the claim area was consistent with native title rights. They held that the assertion of sovereignty was not an assertion of ownership but rather the right to legislate, which does not of itself extinguish native title. They also found that the common law was not inconsistent with native title rights and interests in the sea and seabed, and that s 223 of the

Native Title Act, which provides that native title 'rights and interests are recognised by the common law of Australia', did not prevent recognition of rights beyond the low water mark, which is the territorial limit of the Northern Territory. However the majority held that the public rights of navigation and fishing and the international right of innocent passage are inconsistent with the claimants' assertion of qualified exclusive possession. The majority was not willing to look at the particulars of the inconsistency which could have enabled them to recognise the qualified exclusivity asserted by the claimants. Instead they held that the inconsistency was fundamental. Lisa Strelein noted that this decision blurs the line between the recognition of native title and its extinguishment which has consequences both for how native title is conceptualised and in terms of compensation which may be claimed for extinguishment under the Future Act provisions of the *Native Title Act*. She commented:

> Until this decision, the question of recognition was assumed to be of a different order, which gave much greater respect to Indigenous rights than the extinguishment doctrine. Recognition as opposed to extinguishment, was a contest between normative values of the two legal systems at the point of first contact, hence the only elements of the system of law in relation to land and sea country that would not be recognised were those that are fractious or repugnant to the incoming sovereign. All other rights and interests remain in force until exclusive extinguishment by clear and plain intent by the new sovereign (Strelein 2006: 56).

On the basis of fundamental inconsistency the majority held that the claimants' native title rights to the sea could not be exclusive. While the High Court recognised non-exclusive sea rights they did not clarify what these rights include and so the particulars of non-exclusive sea rights will need to be fleshed out by negotiation or in further litigation.

The nature of native title and extinguishment

All of the native title decisions discussed above address aspects of the nature of native title and extinguishment. However in *Western Australia v Ward* (2002) 191 ALR 1 the High Court provided a more detailed elaboration of these issues. In *Ward* the High Court considered the claim by the Mriuwung and Gajerrong peoples to an area of approximately 8,000 square kilometres in the east Kimberly and Northern Territory. Two highly contested issues with respect to the nature of native title—and related to this the question of whether native title can be partially extinguished—were considered in *Ward*. The court was asked by the claimants to conceptualise native title as an underlying and coherent interest in the land. The court had to determine if the system of laws and traditions, which according to *Mabo (No 2)* and the *Native Title Act* gives rise to the rights claimed, was to be recognised or if native title was to be defined as a 'bundle of rights'. The bundle of rights approach characterises native title in terms of incidents of association and use which correlate with common law property rights and are disassociated from the underlying meaning of the laws and traditions which give rise to them. The *Ward* decision addressed questions about the nature of equality and the depth of the rejection of a hierarchy of races which the High Court purported to embrace in *Mabo (No 2)*.

Justice Lee, at first instance, recognised native title as an underlying interest in the land with lesser interests such as the right to hunt or control access deriving from the broader relationships which are bound to the land. This led to an understanding that inconsistent grants if not absolute, such as a licence for a limited period of time, resulted in a reversion of the native title interest after expiry and if the grant was absolutely inconsistent with the exercise of some native title rights then it resulted in partial extinguishment of the claimants' native title. This acknowledgment of the normative foundation of native title was not upheld on appeal in the Full Federal Court or embraced by the High Court. Both the characterisation of native title as a recognition of a normative relationship grounded in land and the correlating concept of partial extinguishment of inconsistent interests were addressed ambivalently by the majority in the High Court.

Extinguishment

The majority in the High Court held that recognition of native title is withdrawn when:

- the laws and customs which give rise to native title 'clash with the general objective of the common law of the preservation and protection of society as a whole';
- there is no legal or equitable remedy to protect the rights claimed; or
- the rights have been extinguished either under the *Native Title Act* or other valid legislation in a manner that demonstrates the legislature's plain and clear intention to extinguish native title rights or interests.

Native title is extinguished wherever the Crown has granted inconsistent interests, to the extent of the inconsistency, unless otherwise provided for by legislation. This the court held required that incidents of native title be identified to determine if inconsistent grants had been made which would extinguish the native title claimed. The court described native title as 'inherently fragile' because it is subject to the sovereign's right to deal with the land in a manner which extinguishes it. The High Court engaged in the complex task of differentiating grants and interest made under the Past Acts and Intermediate Past Acts sections of the amended *Native Title Act*. This required a technical and detailed consideration of the partial and complete extinguishment of rights within the claim area in accordance with the *Native Title Act*. (For a more detailed discussion of extinguishment under the *Native Title Act* see Wright 2002.)

Nature of title

The High Court affirmed that in accordance with *Mabo (No 2)* and s 223 of the *Native Title Act* native title is defined in terms of the traditional laws and customs of the claimants. These laws and customs must have continuity, but need not be frozen in time, from the time of sovereignty. Native title is recognised where the claims made intersect with rights recognised under the *Native Title Act* and by the common law. The court described the identification of native title as the translation of identified interests in land under the traditional laws and customs into recognised property rights under the *Native Title Act*. The court acknowledged that this fragments the interests being recognised and separates what is recognised from what is granted. They stated at [14]: 'The spiritual or religious is translated into the legal. This requires the fragmentation of an integrated view of the ordering of affairs into rights and interests which are considered apart from the duties and obligations which go with them.' While the majority judgment recognised that native title interests could be inclusive of all property rights known to the common law, including exclusive possession which encompasses freehold title, their reasoning also forayed into attempts to isolate incidents of title, in particular a right to minerals, and to require proof of this incident of usage. The majority affirmed that the ongoing traditional law and customs connecting the claimants to the land or waters under claim need not be a physical connection. Where there has been no extinguishment the majority held that a right to speak for country encompassed a complex relationship with that area which included exclusive possession, occupation, use and enjoyment of that country. It is not clear in areas of non-exclusive rights, where some aspects of extinguishment have taken place, how the exercise of native title rights against parties who have no property rights with respect to the area will be defined. The majority has suggested that non-exclusive native title rights may be defined in terms of activities but it has left open the possibility of other, perhaps more holistic, definitions.

DISCUSSION QUESTION

- What impact do you think the High Court's conceptualisation of the nature of native title will have on common law understandings of Aboriginal and Torres Strait Islander peoples' cultural rights and identity?

Proof of traditional law and customs

In *Members of the Yorta Yorta Aboriginal Community v Victoria* (2002) 194 ALR 538 the limited ability of the High Court to engage with the Yorta Yorta people's understandings of their own culture and traditions highlighted the domination and ethnocentricity of the native title process. The Yorta Yorta Aboriginal community was claiming lands and waters in northern Victoria and southern New South Wales along the Murray River. Justice Olney, the judge at first instance in the Federal Court, found that the 'tide of history had washed away any real acknowledgment of their traditional laws and any real observation of their traditional customs: *Members of the Yorta Yorta Aboriginal Community v Victoria* [1998] FCA 1606 at 129. Justice Olney came to this conclusion by placing great weight on the writings of Edward Curr, a settler, and expressing reservations about the oral evidence presented by the claimants. Justice Olney found at 106 that:

> The most credible source of information concerning traditional laws and customs of the area from which Edward Walker's and Kittu Atkinson/Cooper's early forebears came is to be found in Curr's writings. He at least observed an Aboriginal society that had not yet disintegrated and he obviously established a degree of rapport with the Aboriginals with whom he came into contact. His record of his observations should be accorded considerable weight. The oral testimony of the witnesses from the claimant group is a further source of evidence but being based on oral tradition being passed down through many generations extending over a period in excess of two hundred years, less weight should be accorded to it than the information recorded by Curr ...

Justice Olney looked to the evidence to find a traditional society at the time of colonisation and a contemporary society with the same or a connected kind of presence in the claimed area. Although the claimants were able to demonstrate a continuous physical presence on their land and a continuous connection as a group with their land, Justice Olney found that the laws and customs practised by the claimants were not the same as those practised by the 'original' Yorta Yorta peoples. He found for example the practice of conservation in fishing 'commendable but not one in accordance with Curr's observations' at 123, and likewise he found the practice of the reburial of skeletal remains removed by European colonisers of importance but 'not associated with traditional laws and customs handed down from the original inhabitants' at 124. These conclusions appear to be based on preconceptions about what 'real' Aboriginal laws and customs are and which sort of Aboriginal community could be described as traditional. The claimants appealed to the Full Federal Court claiming that Justice Olney had adopted a 'frozen in time approach' to traditional laws and customs. While the majority in the Federal Court were not certain if Justice Olney had taken this approach, and held that it was wrong if he had done so, they refused to overturn his finding of fact, noting the long and complex hearing and the quantity of evidence presented at trial: *Members of the Yorta Yorta Aboriginal Community v Victoria* (2001) 110 FCR 244.

Unlike the Canadian case of *Delgamuukw v British Columbia* [1998] 1 CNLR 14, where the Supreme Court of Canada at 107 rejected the trial judge's refusal to give independent weight to the claimants' oral histories and held that oral history must be 'accommodated and placed on an equal footing with the types of evidence that the courts are familiar with, which largely consist of historical documents', the majority in the Australian High Court did not question the factual findings of Justice Olney. They also failed to provide guidance with respect to how oral evidence or continuity of traditions could be interpreted by trial judges in a manner which accords some respect to the normative understandings of Indigenous communities in future cases. The plaintiffs in *Delgamuukw* told the British Columbia Court of Appeal in their opening address: 'The challenge for this court in listening to the Indian evidence is to understand the framework within which it is given and the nature of the worldview from which it emanates': *Delagamuukw v British Columbia*, Plaintiff's Opening Address, 11 May 1987 [1988] CNLR 14 at 24. The Australian High Court failed to meet this challenge in *Yorta Yorta* which leaves findings with respect to traditional laws and culture dependant on the individual judge's capacity to listen to and appreciate the claimant's evidence. The High Court reaffirmed the extremely high burden of proof which falls on the claimants to demonstrate continuous acknowledgment and observance of customs from the time of the acquisition of sovereignty to the present. Despite this difficult burden of proof, the High Court failed to establish guidelines which take into account the onerous requirements placed on claimants. The High Court did however confirm that laws and customs change and adapt over time, and that if the changes over time are consistent with the retention of an ongoing society then the laws and customs can be categorised as traditional. However the majority refused to question the trial judge's assessment of the evidence finding that is was 'not shown to have been flawed' at 63. The difficulty which this burden of proof places on claimants is evident in later Federal Court decisions such as *De Rose v South Australia* [2002] FCA 1342.

DISCUSSION QUESTION

- Discuss the manner in which the common law has addressed proof of native title with reference to concepts of equality and pluralism.

Conclusion

Native title litigation, through the paradoxical requirement to demonstrate an ongoing system of traditional laws and customs to prove native title and the concurrent refusal to recognise these laws and customs other than for the purpose of proof of native title, both responds to and magnifies the injustice of the pre-*Mabo* denial of Aboriginal society. This paradox is exacerbated by the requirement to demonstrate an ongoing traditional society in the language of and within the institutional context of a non-Indigenous system of laws which will then only recognise native title if it translates into interests defined by the *Native Title Act*. While the native title process may transform some judicial understanding, through the presentation of evidence in the trial and mediation processes, it also reinforces colonial dominance. The blatant preference for non-Indigenous understandings over Indigenous understandings, and the power of non-Indigenous courts to determine for legal purposes if the claimants' identity will be validated, institutionalises a contemporary hierarchy of races in the judicial system. Native title poses an ongoing challenge to the judicial system: can it recognise the equality and validity of Indigenous society in native title litigation? To do this would require recognition that the post-*Mabo (No 2)* legal framework needs to be reconsidered. Native title has transformed the political landscape in Australia, however the opportunities which *Mabo (No 2)* offered for equality and integrity have yet to be met.

Native title chronology up to *Mabo (No 2)* and High Court cases since *Mabo (No 2)*

1971   In *Miliripum v Nabalco Pty Ltd and the Commonwealth* (1971) FLR 141 (the *Gove Land Rights* case) Justice Blackburn, a single judge of the Northern Territory Supreme Court, decided that Australian common law did not recognise native title and that the plaintiffs did not have rights which could be recognised as property rights in Australian law.

1982   Torres Strait Islanders from the Murray Islands began proceedings in the High Court to challenge the *Gove Land Rights* case. They asked the court for a declaration stating that their traditional rights to land, sea, seabeds and reefs had not been extinguished.

1985   The Queensland Government passed the *Queensland Coast Islands Declaratory Act 1985* which purported to extinguish any traditional land rights which may have existed.

1988   The High Court found that the *Queensland Coast Islands Declaratory Act 1985* (Qld) was invalid as it was inconsistent with the *Racial Discrimination Act 1975* (Cth) which as a Commonwealth Act takes precedence over the state legislation: *Mabo v Queensland (No 1)* (1988) 83 ALR 14 (known as *Mabo (No 1)*).

1992   The High Court delivered its judgment which by a majority of 6 to 1 found that the Murray Islanders hold native title to their islands. They found that Australia was not unoccupied on settlement and that the Indigenous inhabitants had, and continue to have, unless validly extinguished, legal rights to their traditional lands: *Mabo v Queensland (No 2)* (1992) 107 ALR 1.

1993   The *Native Title Act 1993* (Cth) was enacted. This Act validated all Crown grants prior to 1994 and provided that with respect to any future actions native title would be treated with the same respect as 'ordinary', that is, freehold title. It established the National Native Title Tribunal for determining claims which are mediated or conciliated and provided that the Federal Court would determine litigated claims. It also provided for analogous state and territory legislation which was subsequently passed.

1995   In *Western Australia v Commonwealth* (1995) 183 CLR 373 the High Court held that Western Australian legislation, the *Land (Titles and Traditional Usage) Act 1993*, which among other matters purported to extinguish all native title in Western Australia and to replace it with inferior 'rights of traditional usage' was invalid because it was incompatible with the *Racial Discrimination Act 1975* (Cth) and the *Native title Act 1993* (Cth).

1996   The High Court delivered its judgment in *Wik Peoples v Queensland* (1996) 187 CLR 1. The majority held that the pastoral leases which were granted under Queensland legislation did not confer exclusive possession to the grantee and that they were a form of tenure different from common law leases. Each pastoral lease needed to be examined to determine what has been granted and native title would have to yield to the extent that it was inconsistent with the grant.

1998   The *Native Title Act 1993* (Cth) was amended by the Howard Liberal Government to deliver 'bucket loads' of extinguishment.

1998   In *Fejo on behalf of the Larrakia People v Northern Territory* (1998) the High Court held that a grant of freehold by the Crown, even if the grant had been revoked with a result of vacant Crown land, permanently extinguished native title.

1999   In *Yanner v Eaton* (1999) 166 ALR, the High Court held that the *Queensland Fauna Conservation Act 1974* (Qld), which made taking crocodiles and other fauna without a licence an offence, did not extinguish native title. Mr Marandoo Yanner, who had been convicted under the Act for taking crocodiles without a licence, was found to be exercising his native title rights, and the quashing of his conviction by the Queensland Court of Appeal was upheld.

2001   In *Commonwealth v Yarmirr* (2001) 184 ALR 113 The High Court recognised non-exclusive native title rights to the sea and seabed up to and beyond the low water mark, which is the territorial limit of the Northern Territory. The content of this non-exclusive native title was not detailed in the decision.

2002   In *Western Australia v Ward* (2002) 191 ALR 1 the High Court made determinations with respect to the extinguishment of native title under the amended *Native Title Act*. Native title would not be suspended but rather partially extinguished where there is inconsistency between non-Indigenous interests and native title. This entails identifying incidents of native title and incidents of competing title and matching them to determine the extent of the inconsistency. The court also made findings with respect to the nature of native title.

2002 In *Yorta Yorta Aboriginal Community v Victoria* (2002) the High Court held that the traditional laws and customs which give rise to native title rights and interests must be dated to pre-colonial sovereignty. They also held that the current laws and traditions must be part of a continuous normative society from sovereignty to the date of the claim. However, it was accepted that societies change over time and that the laws and traditions do not need to be frozen in time. The extent of transformation over time which the court would recognise was not elaborated upon. The court also held that where traditional laws and customs are proven they need to be recognised in terms of doctrine understood by the common law to confer native title. The High Court upheld Justice Olney's findings of fact at first instance, which gave little weight to the oral evidence of the claimants and relied heavily on a colonialist's contemporaneous account of the Yorta Yorta peoples' traditional laws and customs.

2002 In *Wilson v Anderson* (2002) 190 ALR 313, the High Court held that grazing leases granted under the *Western Lands Act 1901* (NSW), which are not included on the schedule for extinguishment in the amended *Native Title Act*, when granted in perpetuity, extinguish native title.

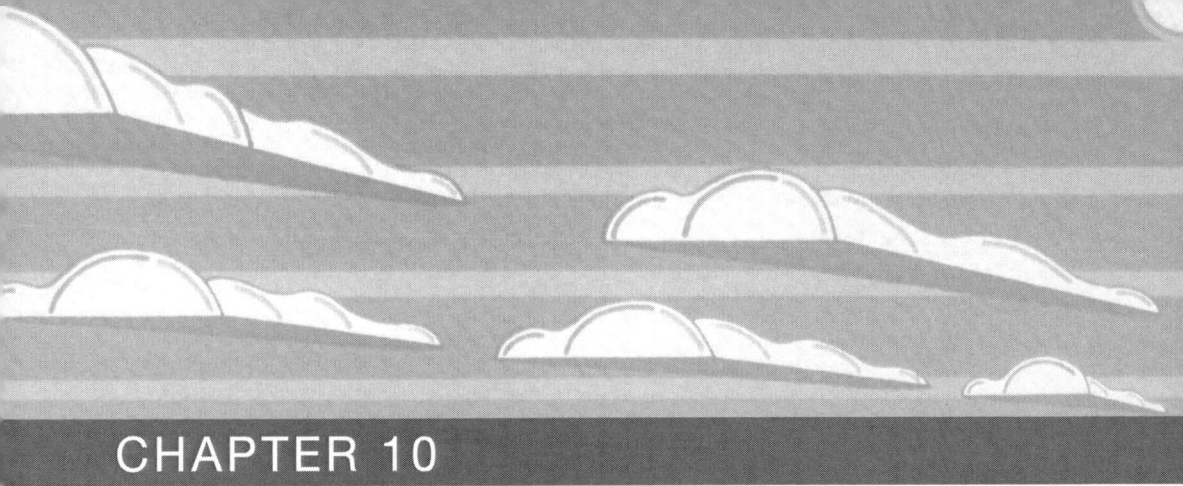

CHAPTER 10

Protecting Culture

Robynne Quiggin

Introduction

In this chapter we will consider the legal issues for Aboriginal and Torres Strait Islander people in relation to their culture.

In order to consider these issues we begin by looking at the special nature of Indigenous culture, and a number of the mechanisms available to maintain, support, promote and protect it. Some of these mechanisms are based in legislation and case law,

---

1   The author would like to thank Toomelah-Bogabilla Local Aboriginal Land Council, Peter Thompson, Julie Macken and Lyndon Ormond-Parker for their assistance.

and some are not legally enforceable. There are usually three factors that will determine the use of the different mechanisms. First it will depend on the nature of the cultural heritage; second, the ways in which it is created; and, third, the identity of those who seek to utilise it.

A significant feature of Australia's laws is that they are drafted and enforced by a system premised on a world view and value system which are often substantially different to that of the value systems common to many Indigenous Australians. This has mattered to varying degrees in different circumstances. Critiques of these legal measures include that the laws are premised on a reductionist view of Indigenous culture in which the complex relationships between people, ancestors, law and custom, creation, land, water, knowledge, ceremony, objects, plants and animals are categorised into interests capable of recognition by the Australian legal system. In that way, aspects of Indigenous culture are often recast into interests capable of some protection, generally from the intrusion of competing interests. For example, complex relationships of custodianship and responsibility for places, knowledge or objects may be recast as exclusive 'ownership' by one group or another in order to achieve recognition from Australian law. Conversely, in other cases, significant cultural responsibilities and obligations are mistakenly devalued and recast as deserving only of the right to 'notification', or 'consultation' rather than the rights belonging to property owners.

Kerwin and Leon note:

> There is a propensity to ignore Aboriginal definitions when developing cultural heritage legislation, providing the basis for a cultural terra nullius. For example, the way cultural heritage protection laws were redesigned after the Hindmarsh Island Bridge fiasco. These laws focus on 'bones and stones', rather than taking a holistic humanist view of culture and provide far weaker protection and ownership rights for Aboriginal cultural heritage (Kerwin and Leon 2002).

The *Hindmarsh Island Bridge* case is an example of the application of particular principles of the Australian legal system including statutory interpretation and procedural fairness which resulted in benefit to some interests and detriment to the Indigenous people seeking to assert customary law requirements, including restrictions based on clan, family, age and gender (see Chapter 12).

As well as domestic laws, in this chapter some of the international declarations, covenants, treaties, and policies will be reviewed. These are important in part as a source of domestic laws and in part because those which are not enforceable remain an important source of standards for adoption in Australian law and policy.

There are many Commonwealth, state and territory laws which are deserving of attention in a chapter such as this. However, in order to provide some flesh on the bones of discussion of this broad area, we will limit discussion to Commonwealth laws.

What is Indigenous cultural heritage?

When we refer to Indigenous people, we refer to a group of people with many similarities, but also great cultural diversity in relation to languages, cultural practices, beliefs, culturally important knowledge, objects, places and relationships. There are many Aboriginal and Torres Strait Islander people who prefer to be referred to with reference to their clan, language group or location, rather than the term 'Indigenous'.

What do we mean by the cultural heritage of Indigenous Australians? A number of terms have been developed in the task of definition, including 'heritage' and 'Indigenous cultural and intellectual property' and its abbreviation 'ICIP', 'traditional knowledge', 'Indigenous knowledge', and 'traditional ecological knowledge' referring either to the whole or to some component parts.

Definitions must encompass a broad range of materials including the full range of the tangible and intangible material created by Indigenous people, and archival records created by non-Indigenous people. At the same time, definitions must capture a sense of the weight and depth of the transmission of Indigenous culture, now in the context of colonisation, without which a list of objects is meaningless.

Essential to all the work on definitions is the notion that Indigenous culture is what the relevant Indigenous people say it is, and it should be treated in the manner the relevant Indigenous people say it should. Expressed more formally, the notions of self-determination and free prior informed consent are central in any regime of respect and protection for Indigenous culture.

In her 1998 study for the Australian Institute of Aboriginal and Torres Strait Islander Studies and the Aboriginal and Torres Strait Islander Commission, *Our Culture: Our Future*, Terri Janke developed the following definition (Janke 1998), adapted by the study's Indigenous Australian working group from United Nations Special Rapporteur Professor Daes's 1995 report *Principles and Guidelines for the Protection of the Heritage of Indigenous People* (Daes 1995).

In this chapter we will use the term Indigenous cultural heritage, but the following definition, excerpted from *Our Culture: Our Future*, provides a succinct and comprehensive list of the kinds of knowledge, objects, materials and places we will be referring to.

> Heritage consists of the intangible and tangible aspects of the whole body of cultural practices, resources and knowledge systems that have been developed, nurtured and refined (and continue to be developed, nurtured and refined) by Indigenous people and passed on by Indigenous people as part of expressing their cultural identity, including:
>
> • literary, performing and artistic works (including music, dance, song, ceremonies, symbols and designs, narratives and poetry);

- languages;
- scientific, agricultural, technical and ecological knowledge (including cultigens, medicines and sustainable use of flora and fauna);
- spiritual knowledge;
- all items of moveable cultural property including burial artefacts;
- Indigenous ancestral remains;
- Indigenous human genetic material (including DNA and tissues);
- cultural environment resources (including minerals and species);
- immovable cultural property (including Indigenous sites of significance, sacred sites and burials);
- documentation of Indigenous people's heritage in all forms of media (including scientific, ethnographic research reports, papers and books, films, sound recordings).

The heritage of an Indigenous people is a living one and includes items which may be created in the future based on that heritage.

Any definition of Indigenous cultural and intellectual property should be flexible to reflect the notions of the particular Indigenous group and the fact that this may differ from group to group and may change over time (Janke 1998:11–12).

The transmission of Indigenous cultural heritage is an essential feature of it. There will often be rules about passing culture on, setting out who can know and practise aspects of culture. These rules remind us that much Indigenous culture is linked both to the dreaming, and to the ancestors who have carried it on to the present day.

This link between past and present, the identity of the custodians and creators of Indigenous culture, the capacity of culture to adapt and change and the means of transmission are central to understanding Indigenous cultural heritage.

The discourse about definition brings into sharp relief the issues that arise when trying to develop useful terms which describe Indigenous cultural heritage in its entirety, maintain the integrity of its cultural distinctiveness, capture its ongoing relevance and dynamism and convey the characteristics which Western legal systems value and regard as triggers for safeguard mechanisms. It remains a significant challenge to accurately represent Indigenous culture while maximising access to the currently available legal mechanisms. For example, Australian copyright laws have provided extremely useful remedies for Indigenous artists whose works, embodying important cultural knowledge, were used without their authority. Successful copyright infringement actions have provided a means for Indigenous people to assert their rights to control the use of their works, raised the profile of Indigenous artists as copyright owners and increased the knowledge of Indigenous artists about their rights. But there are some Indigenous people who feel that definitions which characterise Indigenous cultural heritage as 'intellectual property' encourage a perception that Indigenous people's cultural heritage is only valuable if it can be translated into property or a commodity for the marketplace.

Indigenous cultural and intellectual property is not the only term to have come in for debate. Terms such as 'heritage' and 'traditional knowledge' are thought by some to connote a narrow concept of Indigenous people's culture and associated knowledge, characterising them as something from a bygone era, rather than as vibrant, relevant and capable of significant adaptation and development. For this reason some people prefer the term 'Indigenous knowledge' for this aspect of Indigenous cultural heritage.

These criticisms are important, and remind us to avoid a reductionist or contracted view of Indigenous cultural heritage. But it is an inescapable fact that in the absence of reforms such as a National Indigenous Cultural Authority (Janke 1998: 226, Janke 2008: 18) or a *sui generis* law, that adopts and applies accurate definitions and effective mechanisms which represent the true nature of Indigenous cultural heritage, it remains essential to maximise the use of existing laws.

The impact of colonisation on Indigenous culture has been both disruptive and transformative—to say the least. While colonisation has disrupted many Indigenous authority structures, it remains vital that Indigenous people retain the rights to speak for their culture. The rights of self-determination, free prior informed consent and respect for customary practice are fundamental to any legal or policy regimes of recognition and protection of cultural rights.

Indigenous Australians have expressed the need to the following rights in relation to cultural heritage (referred to here as 'Indigenous cultural and intellectual property' or ICIP):

- the right to own and control ICIP;
- the right to control the commercial use of ICIP in accordance with traditional customary laws;
- the right to benefit commercially from the authorised use of ICIP;
- the right to full and proper attribution;
- the right to protect sacred and significant sites;
- the right to own, use, control and manage lands, territories and natural resources including biological materials such as minerals and species (Daes 2004: 13);
- the right to prevent derogatory, offensive and fallacious uses of ICIP;
- the right to have a say in the preservation and care, protection, management and control of cultural artefacts, human remains, archaeological and significant traditional sites, traditional food resources, and traditional and contemporary cultural expressions such as rituals, legends, and the designs used in, for instance, art, weaving, dances, songs and stories;
- the right to control use of traditional knowledge of medicinal plants, agricultural biodiversity, environmental management, and the recording of cultural customs and expressions;

- the right to control use of the particular language, which may be intrinsic to cultural identity, knowledge, the skill and teaching of culture (Janke and Quiggin 2005: 10, 11).

In addition the United Nations Special Rapporteur on Indigenous peoples includes:
- The right of permanent sovereignty over natural resources (Daes 2004: 13).

Regulation of cultural heritage

Some of the most significant mechanisms which support the participation of Indigenous people in caring for their cultural heritage are the more recently developed laws and policies which engage Indigenous people in land, water and species management. Generally focused on partnership with state government land and resource management agencies, jurisdictions and programs vary in the extent to which government agencies provide for Indigenous control, respect customary practices, and appropriately recognise Indigenous people's knowledge. However, they are an essential aspect of cultural heritage protection, and can provide a means of asserting a more extensive approach to Indigenous people's control over their cultural heritage.

Peter Thompson recalls the processes undertaken by Aboriginal people (Wiimpatja) of western New South Wales for recognition of 'local ownership and control, and regional organisation and support' which were part of the campaign for the area known as Mutawintji National Park:

> Having held a number of meetings to clarify the important issues, in 1983 the local Aboriginal people … put up signs saying 'Mootawingee, Closed by the Owners' and turned the tourist buses back to town, but not before talking with the passengers about why they were undertaking the blockade. For Wiimpatja, the National Park wasn't just a tourist attraction: it is a place of sacred water holes, creation stories, ceremonies, ancient art sites and spiritual strength for them and the broader community of western NSW.
>
> One of the interesting things about the Mutawintji experience was that it did involve shifting a paradigm. That paradigm was that the National Parks Service manages National *Parks*—and they will only talk to Aboriginal people about how to manage the Aboriginal *sites* inside the parks. But here you had a group of people who were saying 'Look, we're not talking to you about managing *sites*, we're talking to you about managing the *country*' (Thompson and Goodall 2008: 325–6).

In September 2008 Wiimpatja joined with friends to celebrate the ten year anniversary of the hand back of their land and the establishment of a joint management arrangement with the government. Chair of the current Board, Wiimpatja academic Kim O'Donnell honoured the work of previous Board members and looked forward to ongoing activities by Wiimpatja owners, working with government to care for their country (O'Donnell 2008).

Protection of Movable Cultural Heritage Act 1986

From 1986, the *Protection of Movable Cultural Heritage Act 1986* has regulated the movement of objects of cultural significance both into and out of Australia. The Act implements Australia's obligations under the 1970 UNESCO Convention on the Means of Prohibiting and Preventing the Illicit Import, Export and Transfer of Ownership of Cultural Property. It sets out a system for categorising and controlling the movement of particular sorts of objects, from the very old, to more recently created culturally significant objects.

The subjects of the Act are classes of 'objects that are of importance to Australia, or to a particular part of Australia, for ethnological, archaeological, historical, literary, artistic, scientific or technological reasons, being objects falling within one or more of the following categories' including objects recovered from Australian soil or waters, objects relating to members of the Aboriginal race of Australia and descendants of the Indigenous inhabitants of the Torres Strait Islands, objects of ethnographic art or ethnography, objects of decorative or fine art, objects of scientific or technological interest, books, records, documents or photographs, graphic, film or television material or sound recordings and any other prescribed categories (s 7).

To qualify as an object of Australian Aboriginal and Torres Strait Islander heritage the object must meet certain criteria, including: it must be an object of cultural significance to Aboriginal or Torres Strait Islander people; or be made by Aboriginal or Torres Strait Islander people; and not created specifically for sale, and be at least 30 years old, and not be adequately represented in Aboriginal or Torres Strait Islander community collections, or public collections in Australia (*Protection of Moveable Cultural Property Regulations 1987* Part 1.2, Part 1, Schedule 1).

The Act provides for the establishment of a National Cultural Heritage Control List, and then divides the objects which qualify to be listed into two categories, Class A and Class B. Class A objects include sacred and secret ritual objects, bark and log coffins used as traditional burial objects, human remains, rock art and dendroglyphs (carvings on trees).

Class A objects cannot be exported out of Australia, but Class A objects can be temporarily imported into Australia from museums, art galleries or private collections in other countries for instance, subject to the granting of a certificate by the minister authorising the subsequent export of the object (*Protection of Moveable Cultural Property Regulations* Note, Part 1.3, Part 1, Schedule 1). Class B objects can be exported if they have a permit or certificate (Note 1, 1.4, Part 1, Schedule 1).

Included in Class B are recently created objects including those relating to famous and important Aborigines or Torres Strait Islanders, or to other persons significant in Aboriginal or Torres Strait Islander history, objects made on missions or reserves, objects relating to the development of Aboriginal or Torres Strait Islander protest and self-help movements and original documents, photographs, drawings, sound recordings, film and video recordings and any similar records relating to objects included in this category (1.4, Part 1, Schedule 1).

The Act also regulates the movement of Indigenous and non-Indigenous archaeological objects if they are of significance to Australia and were recovered after being in the place from which they were removed for at least 50 years, and if the objects of equivalent quality are not represented in at least two public collections in Australia (*Protection of Moveable Cultural Property Regulations* 2.2(b), Part 2, Schedule 1). Works of fine art or decorative art are also regulated if they were made in the Indigenous tradition by an Aboriginal or Torres Strait Islander person, purchased for over $10,000 and are more than 20 years old. In these cases a permit or certificate is required before they can be exported from Australia (Part 5, Schedule 1 and Mellor and Janke 2003).

The Act also prescribes rules for the movement of certain specimens, requiring that a permit be acquired before any type of specimen of present-day flora or fauna, a palaeontological object or a mineral under certain circumstances may be moved (*Protection of Moveable Cultural Property Regulations* 3.4(h), Part 3, Schedule 1). This kind of regulation has significance for Indigenous people who wish to monitor the activities of bioprospectors on land and waters. The operations of the biotechnology industry in Australia and the world has seen an intense interest in Australia's biodiversity and particularly the properties of different plants. The knowledge held by Indigenous people can be enormously valuable for guiding research and development into potential products. It gains some limited recognition and protection under the *Environment Protection Biodiversity Conservations Regulations*, and similar state and territory legislation.

The *Protection of Movable Cultural Heritage Act 1986* seeks to create a balance between allowing the movement of objects to and from Australia, and maintaining government control over collections and records of objects of significance. For example, the Act provides that if people export objects without permits, they are liable to forfeiture of the object, and in some cases criminal sanctions can apply (*Protection of Movable Cultural Heritage Act* s 9).

In addition to laws monitoring the movement of cultural material, the states, territories and the Commonwealth have legislation for the protection and preservation of Indigenous people's cultural heritage.

Aboriginal and Torres Strait Islander Heritage Protection Act 1984

One of these laws is the Commonwealth's *Aboriginal and Torres Strait Islander Heritage Protection Act 1984* which was drafted as an interim measure in 1984. It was extensively reviewed in 1996 by her Hon Elizabeth Evatt (Evatt 1996). Substantial changes were recommended to increase the capacity for Indigenous people to protect their heritage.

The recommendations included: minimum standards across all jurisdictions; provision for greater Indigenous involvement with cultural heritage protection and management including establishment of Aboriginal heritage bodies; and early engagement in all planning processes. Unfortunately, many of these recommendations remain unimplemented by parliament. However, Indigenous people have frequently sought, with different levels of success, to utilise the Act for the protection of their heritage.

That Act's purposes are:

> The preservation and protection from injury or desecration of areas and objects in Australia and in Australian waters, being areas and objects that are of particular significance to Aboriginals in accordance with Aboriginal tradition (*Aboriginal and Torres Strait Islander Heritage Protection Act 1984* s 4).

The Act provides for the minister to make declarations on behalf of Aboriginal people seeking the preservation or protection of a specified area from injury or desecration if he or she is satisfied that the area is significant to Aboriginal people and that it is under serious threat of injury or desecration (s 10). If the minister is convinced that an area is *in immediate* threat of injury or desecration he or she may make an emergency declaration under s 9 of the Act, which can have effect for 30 days, and may be extended for a further 60 days. The minister can receive applications for preservation or protection of a specified object or class of objects from injury or desecration (s 12). The minister can also authorise a person to make an emergency declaration in relation to an area or object(s) under serious and immediate threat of injury or desecration (s 18).

The Act has been utilised by Indigenous people on a number of occasions, including the long campaign for the protection of Boobera Lagoon, located about 16 kilometres south-west of Goondawindi in northern inland New South Wales. The Toomelah–Boggabilla Local Aboriginal Land Council and its members have conducted a 30-year campaign to have the Lagoon protected, and 'for proper recognition of their traditional knowledge and skills. Proper recognition includes effective participation in land and water management including stock access, camping and vehicle access and control over any future irrigation proposals' (Quiggin 2001: 7).

One of their most strenuously pursued strategies was a declaration by the minister under the *Aboriginal and Torres Strait Islander Heritage Protection Act 1984* to prevent damage to the integrity of the Lagoon by water-skiing and the use of powerboats. The activities were opposed by the Toomelah–Boggabilla Local Aboriginal Land Council for two reasons which were set out by John Basten QC's comments in the report to the minister by Hon Hal Wootten QC AC by and on behalf of the Toomelah–Boggabilla Aboriginal Land Council in 1995. First and most importantly, it is offensive to the cultural and spiritual importance of the Lagoon. Second, powerboats and water-skiing contribute to environmental damage to the area. The 1993 environmental impact study of the area implicated water-skiing in the damage to flora and fauna, citing adverse effects of the wave action and vehicle access; fish numbers and water quality were diminished as a result of turbidity; and the soil erosion was the result of wave action (Quiggin 2001).

In addition to the problems arising from water-skiing, in 2000, the surrounding land and water also suffered degradation as a result of stock movement and general tourist activities.

After a lengthy application and consideration process, in 2000, the declaration was finally granted, only to be subsequently delayed for two years by the minister. The minister explained the delay by the need to find an alternative to meet the needs of recreational water users (Hill 2000). Finally the declaration was made effective from May 2002 to 30 April 2004 prohibiting the use of powerboats and water-skiing on the lagoon, but not before work was commenced on an alternative water-skiing site at the Goondiwindi Serpentine Water Park, funded largely from Environment Australia's 'Protecting and conserving Australia's heritage places' budget (Department of Environment and Heritage 2002–2003; Thompson 2008 pers comm).

The dedication, resilience and determination of the generations of Aboriginal people and their supporters who fought to protect Boobera Lagoon were ultimately successful, and must be recognised both as an important victory and a great lesson in the use of the Act. But it is difficult to escape the conclusion that the value placed by government on the interests of the Aboriginal cultural custodians is less than robust, and dependent not only on meeting the needs of other stakeholders, but finding a way to fund them.

In 2000, as the Toomelah–Boggabilla Local Aboriginal Land Council continued its campaign for protection, Australia's compliance with its obligations to protect Indigenous cultural heritage under the International Covenant on Civil and Political Rights (ICCPR) came under scrutiny by the committee which monitors the Convention, the Human Rights Committee.

Article 27 of the ICCPR provides:

> In those States in which ethnic, religious or linguistic minorities exist, persons belonging to such minorities shall not be denied the right, in community with the other members of their group, to enjoy their own culture, to profess and practise their own religion, or to use their own language.

The committee member from Mauritius, Mr Lallah took the case of Boobera Lagoon as an example of the importance of entrenching the Covenant's human rights in domestic law to both ensure that Indigenous people have a effective means to protect their cultural and spiritual heritage, and to ensure that those rights were not treated as inferior to the rights of other stakeholders. He said:

> If the right under article 27 had legislative authority, had been legislatively ordained, then people affected in those minorities could have gone to court, could have asked

for a remedy and that remedy would have entitled them to have a direct and primary say in what constitutes their culture and traditions and would have enabled the court to make a judgment about the priority, for example, of water skiing over cultural and religious rights (Human Rights Committee 2000).

While the operation of the Act played a critical part in the protection of Aboriginal people's cultural heritage, this was not achieved without the enormously determined efforts of successive generations and their supporters who continued to assert their rights and obligations to their country in the face of opposition.

The Boobera Lagoon area is now managed by the Boobera Lagoon Reserve Trust Board. The majority of board members are Aboriginal people; other local stakeholders are also represented. At its inaugural meeting the Board's first decision was to ban water-skiing on Boobera Lagoon (Thompson 2008, pers comm). Since then it has also overseen other measures like restrictions on stock access to the water and investigation of the declining water levels including research into the associated water table (Reynolds 2008, pers comm).

In addition to protection of land and waters, the *Aboriginal and Torres Strait Islander Heritage Protection Act* has been used on many occasions to prevent damage to objects where there is a threat of injury or desecration (s 12). This has generally occurred when important objects or collections, including objects from the Thompson or Strehlow collections, were about to be sold. The Act has been used to delay the sale, to provide Aboriginal people an opportunity to investigate the nature of the objects and, on a number of occasions, to purchase the objects for the purpose of returning them to their home community or to a collection institution within Australia (Ormond-Parker 2008, pers comm).

Recently, the *Aboriginal and Torres Strait Islander Heritage Protection Act* has undergone further direct amendment as a result of the assertion of rights to objects of cultural significance to the Dja Dja Wurring Native Title Group.

As part of its 2004 exhibition entitled *Etched on Bark 1854*, at Museum Victoria, bark etchings which had been loaned by the British Museum and the Royal Botanic Gardens Kew were displayed. The conditions of the loan were set out in a contract between the cultural institutions and the loan was subject to the requirements of s 12 of the *Protection of Movable Cultural Heritage Act 1986*. This section allows Class A or Class B objects to be temporarily imported and subsequently exported if the minister provides a certificate allowing this movement of the objects.

The bark etchings were described by Museum Victoria as: 'The earliest surviving Aboriginal bark etchings in Australia, they are the only remaining examples of artistic work done by Kulin men from the Loddon and Murray Rivers during the nineteenth century. Two bark etchings have also been borrowed from the British Museum and the Royal Botanic Gardens, Kew' (Australian Parliament House 2005–2006).

The Dja Dja Wurrung Native Title Group sought and obtained a declaration under the *Aboriginal and Torres Strait Islander Heritage Protection Act 1984* which stated in part:

The declaration is intended to protect and preserve the three cultural heritage objects from further threats of injury and desecration by their removal from Museum Victoria to the British Museum without the written consent of the Traditional Owners, and is made subject to the following terms and conditions:

a   That the three cultural objects will continue to be displayed and/or secured at Museum Victoria under the direction of the Inspector in consultation with the relevant Traditional Owners by the Manager Bunjilaka Aboriginal Centre.

b   That the State of Victoria and Museum Victoria will negotiate with Traditional Owners the Dja Dja Wurrung and Jupagalk Native Title Groups as to the future location of the three cultural heritage objects.

c   That the British and Australian Governments negotiate the final repatriation of all Indigenous Australian Ancestral Human Remains and Grave Goods held without consent by various British institutions and privately for recovery, return and reburial by Australian Traditional Owners' (*Museum Boards of Victoria v Carter* [2005] FCA 645 par 2).

The Dja Dja Wurrung Native Title Group was able to use the Commonwealth law because previous attempts to pass Aboriginal cultural heritage protection laws by the Victorian State Parliament had been unsuccessful and the Commonwealth Act specifically provided for application processes in Victoria. In order to return the loaned objects in accordance with the contract, Museum Victoria sought to have the declarations set aside by the Federal Court.

The Dja Dja Wurrung Native Title Group had been successful in delaying the return of the objects, and raising the issues, both with the cultural institutions, state and federal parliaments and the media; nevertheless the objects were eventually returned to Britain.

In response to this case, the federal government substantially amended the *Aboriginal and Torres Strait Islander Heritage Protection Act 1984* by inserting s 12(3A) to ensure that no declaration made by the minister under the Act can prevent the movement of objects where there is a certificate acquired pursuant to the *Protection of Moveable Cultural Property Act 1986* in place.

The *Aboriginal and Torres Strait Islander Heritage Protection Act 1984* was amended in a less direct manner nearly 10 years previously when the federal government of the day passed the *Hindmarsh Island Bridge Act 1997*, an Act to facilitate the construction of the Hindmarsh Island bridge, and for related purposes. Section 4 of this Act exempted the Hindmarsh Island area from the operation of the *Aboriginal and Torres Strait Islander Heritage Protection Act 1984* and, once the High Court agreed that the law was not an invalid exercise of the race power (s 51(xxvi) of the Australian Constitution), put an end to the Ngandjerri people's attempt to use the *Aboriginal and Torres Strait Islander Heritage Protection Act 1984* to protect their heritage from desecration as a result of development.

Other Commonwealth laws

The *Environmental Protection and Biodiversity Conservation Act 1999* implements Australia's obligations under the Convention on Biological Diversity to which it is a signatory. The Convention imposes a number of obligations on state parties. The best known are the obligations under Article 8(j) which states:

> Each Contracting Party shall, as far as possible and as appropriate:
>
> (j)   Subject to its national legislation, respect, preserve and maintain knowledge, innovations and practices of indigenous and local communities embodying traditional lifestyles relevant for the conservation and sustainable use of biological diversity and promote their wider application with the approval and involvement of the holders of such knowledge, innovations and practices and encourage the equitable sharing of the benefits arising from the utilization of such knowledge, innovations and practices;

The parties to the Convention established an Ad Hoc Open-ended Inter-Sessional Working Group on Article 8(j) and Related Provisions, at the Conference of the Parties in 1998, and the Working Group adopted a program of work for the state parties 'to implement the commitments of article 8 (j) of the Convention and to enhance the role and involvement of indigenous and local communities in the achievement of the objectives of the Convention' (COP 5 Decision V/16, 2005).

The Ad Hoc Open-ended Inter-Sessional Working Group on Article 8(j) and Related Provisions is also called on to collaborate with other working groups pursuing goals of the Convention including the Ad Hoc Open-ended Working Group on Access and Benefit-sharing, at present charged with negotiating an international regime for the fair and equitable sharing of benefits arising out of the utilisation of genetic resources, and the Ad Hoc Open-ended Working Group on Protected Areas. These collaborative requirements, together with the active participation of Indigenous volunteers (International Indigenous Forum on Biodiversity), ensure that Indigenous people's interests have a voice in this forum.

Within Australia, the *Environmental Protection and Biodiversity Conservation Act 1999* establishes the National Heritage List and the Commonwealth Heritage List, both of which include natural, Indigenous and historic places which are identified as having heritage values.

The *Environmental Protection and Biodiversity Conservation Act 1999* also establishes the Australian Heritage Council. The Council includes Indigenous members and one of its tasks is to identify the Indigenous people with rights and interests in a place that is considered for listing. The Council must then invite the views of the relevant Indigenous people on the question of listing, and their views are considered by the minister in his or her decision-making process. In addition to the Australian

Heritage Council, an Indigenous Advisory Committee advises the minister on the operation of the *Environmental Protection and Biodiversity Conservation Act 1999*. The Indigenous Advisory Committee meets to contribute their knowledge and skills to advise the minister.

Repatriation

An important aspect of the management and protection of Indigenous cultural heritage in the context of colonisation is the extensive work undertaken by Indigenous people and organisations such as the Tasmanian Aboriginal Centre, the Foundation for Aboriginal and Islander Research Action (FAIRA) and non-Indigenous people to repatriate human remains and objects of significance including sacred objects, gender-restricted objects and objects which can only be seen by initiated people taken from their place of origin and stored in research institutions and museums, both in Australia and overseas.

The documentary records of the removal of human remains and objects show practices including the raiding of graves, the mutilation of deceased people's remains and other forms of theft and brutality that tell us how the material came to be so far from home. Museums often became the recipients of privately collected human remains and significant objects, sometimes exhibiting them, sometimes using them for experiments and data collection, and frequently storing them with varying levels of record-keeping and curatorial practices.

Two obstacles to the repatriation of human remains and objects have been firstly, the reluctance of institutions to see the material as anything other than part of their own research collection; and, secondly, poor curatorial and record-keeping practices creating difficulties with identifying source communities and ensuring that complete collections of human remains are returned. Both of these issues have complicated the return of materials to their places of origin. As a result of enormous advocacy work by Indigenous Australians, it is now more common for the return of remains to be permitted as Lyndon Ormond-Parker and Cressida Fforde explain:

> Since the 1970s, continued requests by communities to museums, and intensive lobbying of government, have resulted in the return of a significant number of collections and instigated the development of museum policy and state legislation. Significant steps in this process include the return of Truganini's remains (1976), the Crowther Collection (1985) and other Tasmanian remains (1988) from the Tasmanian Museum and Art Gallery; the campaign for the return of the Murray Black Collection from the Department of Anatomy of the University of Melbourne in the mid 1980s; the return of the Kow Swamp fossils in 1990 and the return of Mungo Woman in 1992 (Fforde and Ormond-Parker 2001: 9: see also Ryan 1981, 1974; Cove 1995; Clark 1983; Meehan 1984; Weatherall 1989).

In 2000, the prime ministers of Britain and Australia signed a Joint Statement committing Britain to the return of Aboriginal remains held in their museums which stated in part:

> The Australian and British governments agree to increase efforts to repatriate human remains to Australian indigenous communities. ...
>
> We agree that the way ahead in this area is a cooperative approach between our governments. ...
>
> More research is required to identify indigenous human remains held in British collections. Extensive consultation must also be undertaken to determine the relevant traditional custodians, their aspirations regarding treatment of the remains and a means for addressing these. ...
>
> The governments agree to encourage the development of protocols for the sharing of information between British and Australian institutions and indigenous people. In this respect we welcome the initiative of the British Natural History Museum which has catalogued 450 indigenous human remains (Fforde and Ormond-Parker 2001: 12).

Indigenous people continue to lobby for repatriation, and for better systems to allow Indigenous communities to locate, fund and lead the repatriation processes. Many Australian museums have adopted protocols for their dealings with Indigenous material.

Bob Weatherall, leading Gomilaroi expert and advocate for repatriation, recommends greater control for Indigenous people in the repatriation process, particularly advocating for 'one-stop shop' Aboriginal-controlled clearing houses, which recognise that Indigenous people are best placed to manage and resolve the complex provenance and protocol issues (Weatherall 2004). This more unified and Indigenous-controlled approach to repatriation, with proper support to Indigenous communities receiving the material, is also recommended by Franchesca Cubillo, a Larrakia, Bardi, Wardaman and Yanuwa curator expert in repatriation and cultural institutions (Cubillo 2006:16–17).

The repatriation of Indigenous people's ancestral remains and objects is a solemn and often deeply moving subject, and so it is appropriate to conclude our discussion of it with the words of former ATSIC Commissioner Rodney Dillon. Commissioner Dillon, as he then was, made the following remarks in 2003 when the Royal College of Surgeons in London officially handed over 60 Aboriginal human remains to a delegation including FAIRA representative Bob Weatherall, and two traditional custodians, Major Sumner (Ngarrindjeri) and Henry Atkinson (Yorta Yorta) who had travelled to Britain to collect the remains. Referring to the ancestors Mr Dillon said:

> They have been absent for a century or more, the remains are not complete, but now at least their spirits have returned ... The trade in our remains was once vigorous

and prolonged—it happened within the memory of people still alive. There were those who made a living from taking our remains. Our graves were robbed. Some of us were murdered to order. Imagine how the spirits of those returned must now feel, their graves violated, their people dispersed and dispossessed over the period of their absence.

And what would they think of the country they're returning to, where their descendants are still second class citizens and their traditional lands continue to be degraded and desecrated? Today is a happy occasion, but repatriations such as this also stir up powerful emotions. They remind us of the profound sadness underlying many Indigenous lives (Ormond-Parker 2003: 4).

Knowledge, language and expressions of Indigenous cultural heritage

Much of the cultural heritage of Indigenous Australians is in the form of knowledge, for example languages, knowledge about the environment, customary laws, food production, medicines, orally transmitted stories and songs just to name a few. It is often not in physical form and is therefore described as intangible. Much Indigenous cultural heritage which is in physical form also embodies knowledge, stories, laws or information and so has an intangible and tangible component. Definitions of Indigenous knowledge encounter the same problems as definitions of Indigenous cultural heritage, as Nakata et al explain:

> Indigenous knowledge defies simple definition. Indigenous knowledge is commonly understood as traditional knowledge, although there is debate about whether the term Indigenous knowledge should be used interchangeably with the term traditional knowledge or whether it is more accurately a subset of the traditional knowledge category (WIPO 2001). Despite contentious terminology, Indigenous knowledge is understood to be the traditional knowledge of Indigenous peoples. In Australia, a common misunderstanding is that this equates Indigenous knowledge to 'past' knowledge, when in fact Indigenous people view their knowledge as continuing (Nakata et al 2005: 7).
>
> Whilst Indigenous knowledge systems are now recognised as dynamic and changing, orally transmitted from generation to generation and produced in the context of Indigenous peoples' close and continuing relationships with their environment, definitions, nevertheless, tend to reflect or include the particular focus of those who define it (Nakata et al 2005: 7–8).

Nakata et al note that the tendency to define Indigenous knowledge by Western values results in simplification and misrepresentation. 'For example, there is a tendency to view Indigenous knowledge as an unevaluated or untested data set for the scientific community to extract, validate and incorporate into scientific frameworks' (Nakata et al 2005: 8).

Nakata et al recommend the urgent and careful documentation of Indigenous knowledge because of its historical destruction, current fragile existence, and threatened future (Nakata et al 2005: 9). There are a number of Indigenous Knowledge projects being undertaken by Aboriginal and Torres Strait Islander people across Australia in which Indigenous people are creating, collecting and holding databases of recordings of their cultural knowledge. These projects, such as the Traditional Knowledge Revival Pathways (www.tkrp.com.au) by the Kuku Thaypan People, are community driven and follow specific local protocols with a focus on teaching the next generations while recording knowledge and expressions of culture such as dance, story and song. These innovative projects encapsulate both the aspects of transmission and content essential to Indigenous culture.

Language

Some of the most vibrant cultural heritage work is occurring with Indigenous languages, in encouraging language speakers, language teaching, revitalising endangered languages and recording language. Language is an integral part of Indigenous Australians' cultural heritage. Language embodies ways of thinking, words for place-specific things, culturally distinct concepts and knowledge and important grammatical structures. The singing, storytelling and teaching of language are an extremely important way of practising culture and passing on Indigenous knowledge. There is extensive language work going on across the country today.

It is widely agreed there were at least 250 distinct languages spoken in Australia at the time of colonisation. In addition there would have been many dialects spoken by different clan groups. At present there is important work going on across the nation including recording language speakers, accessing old recordings, teaching languages, developing teaching resources and generally including language more widely in daily life, arts and entertainment, to strengthen language and culture.

In many of these projects, increasing attention is being given to the legal relationship between the project managers and linguists, and the language speakers. This is because recordings made in the past have often remained the property of the linguist or anthropologist making the recording, or the cultural institutions for which they were working at the time. Indigenous people seeking to revitalise language today can feel frustrated at the requirements to negotiate access to recordings of their forebears, especially for such important work as revitalising culture and teaching Indigenous young people.

The Federation of Aboriginal and Torres Strait Islander Languages (FATSIL) and the Artists in the Black Legal Service of the Arts Law Centre of Australia have developed protocols and sample agreements for communities and linguists or other consultants working on language projects. These protocols are intended to encourage ownership by the Indigenous community of any outcomes of joint projects.

The legal framework whereby Australian law recognises proprietary interests in the intangible is called intellectual property law. Intellectual property law can be thought of as a group of laws which are primarily drafted to recognise and protect the rights of people to their creative effort. And, importantly for our discussion here, the focus of intellectual property law is recognition of *economic* rights in creative effort.

The World Intellectual Property Organisation (WIPO) describes intellectual property as 'creations of the mind: inventions, literary and artistic works, and symbols, names, images, and designs used in commerce' (http://www.wipo.int/about-ip/en/).

The law of intellectual property is very much a product of the social and economic forces which have shaped recent modes of production. So intellectual property is divided by WIPO into two categories (http://www.wipo.int/about-ip/en/). These are copyright and industrial property.

1   Copyright includes the following subject matter: literary works such as novels, poems and plays, films, sound recordings, musical works, artistic works such as drawings, paintings, photographs and sculptures, architectural designs, television and sound broadcasts and published editions.

2   Industrial property which includes inventions (patents), trademarks, industrial designs, and geographic indications of the source of products and services.

In addition to these two categories is the law relating to confidentiality, often applied to protect the trade secrets of businesses.

The restricted nature of Indigenous knowledge — breach of confidence

The law of confidentiality gives legal effect to the idea that if someone is given information which they know has the quality of confidentiality, they have an obligation to respect the confidence. Megarry J set out the three elements required to be proved if breach of confidence is to succeed in the case of *Coco v A N Clark (Engineers) Ltd* [1969] RPC 41. First, the information itself must have the necessary quality of confidence about it. Second, the information must have been given in circumstances which included an obligation of confidence. And third, there must have been an unauthorised use of the information which caused detriment to the party which communicated the information.

The law has been used a number of times to protect Indigenous cultural material, most notably in the case of *Foster v Mountford* (1976) 29 FLR 233. In this case Justice Muirhead agreed to restrain publication of a book called *Nomads of the Australian Desert* which included important cultural information which had been given to the author by members of the Pitantjatjara language group, on the basis of a possible breach of confidence if the material were published. Justice Muirhead stated that 'revelation of the secrets to their women, children and uninitiated men may undermine the social and religious stability of their hard-pressed community' (at 236).

There are no protection measures specifically for Indigenous people's intangible cultural heritage in Australia. But with their usual commitment to protecting culture, Indigenous people and the people who work with them have creatively utilised existing legal protections. As we discussed in the early part of this chapter, achieving legal protections for Indigenous cultural material has sometimes required a kind of re-contextualising of the issues in order to gain access to legal remedies. This is probably no more true than in the case of intellectual property laws when they are utilised as a mechanism for protection.

Copyright

'The basic principle behind copyright protection is the concept that an author (or artist, musician, playwright or film-maker) should have the right to exploit their work, through reproduction and/or public dissemination, without others being allowed to copy that creative work' (McKeogh et al 2004: 133). In Australia, the law in relation to copyright in works is set out in the *Copyright Act 1968* (Cth). Categories of subject matter, known in the Act as 'works', include artistic, literary, dramatic and musical works. The Act also sets out the law in relation to 'subject matter other than works' including films, sound recordings, television and sound broadcasts, and published editions of works.

The owner of copyright in a work or other subject matter has a number of rights. Depending on the nature of the work or subject matter, these include the exclusive rights to:

- reproduce the work in material form;
- publish the work;
- communicate the work to the public (this refers to the right to transmit works online, or by broadcast);
- make an adaptation of the work; and
- enter into a commercial rental arrangement (*Copyright Act 1968* (Cth) ss 31, 85, 86 and 87).

An author of an artistic, literary, musical, dramatic work and of a cinematographic film may also hold moral rights in the work or film. Moral rights include:

- the right to be attributed;
- the right not to be falsely attributed; and
- the right of integrity (*Copyright Act 1968* (Cth), ss 193, 195AC, 195AI; in addition the Act also provides performers with moral rights in live performances or recordings).

For custodians of Indigenous culture, moral rights may provide some relief in instances where a creator is not properly acknowledged or where their cultural material is altered in a way that is detrimental to their reputation. Although this has not yet been tested in the courts, it may hold the promise of an effective remedy for Indigenous people in the future. This is especially so if we see repeated instances of misappropriation of cultural material in culturally inappropriate contexts such as the unauthorised reproduction of cultural works on souvenirs, dress fabric and carpets. As these instances of misappropriation generally do not attribute the artist, they may well infringe artists' copyright, moral right of attribution and moral right of integrity.

Using copyright law to protect Indigenous heritage

The exclusive rights of a copyright owner are acquired at the time of the creation of the material, *but only if* the creator meets certain conditions including the following.

No copyright protection for ideas or information

The general rule is that copyright protection subsists in the *expression* of the cultural material. There is no copyright in an idea or information—it must be expressed in the form of one of the subject matter categories listed above (literary, musical, dramatic, artistic works, published editions, sound recordings, broadcasts, films). This means that the underlying knowledge component of the cultural heritage in an artistic work for example, may not be protected by copyright, even though there is copyright in the actual expression, that is, the imagery. Further, there is no copyright protection for a style, such as dot painting or cross-hatching.

Material form

Associated with the proposition that copyright does not subsist in an idea or information is the requirement of 'material form'. This requirement has created difficulties for Indigenous cultural custodians seeking copyright protection, because orally transmitted knowledge, stories, songs, dances, techniques and methods cannot generally be protected by copyright laws unless they have been committed to some permanent form like writing, sound recording, film or photography. And, to complicate matters further, the general position of the law is that the maker of the permanent form is the copyright owner. So for example the copyright owners in a recorded interview may be the interviewee, and/or the person who made the recording or their employer: this is a general example and would change according to the factual matrix.

Originality

In addition to the requirement of material form, the material must be original (*Copyright Act 1968* (Cth) s 32). This issue was dealt with in the now well-known *Carpets case*

(*Milpurrurru v Indofurn* (1994) 54 FCR 240). The case involved a group of artists whose paintings were reproduced in an art portfolio by the National Aboriginal Gallery with their permission, but which were subsequently reproduced on carpets overseas which were then imported into Australia for sale. The designs depicted in the paintings were works associated with cultural stories which had been handed down to the artists as part of their cultural heritage and subject to customary rules. In considering the issue of the originality of the paintings, von Doussa J in *Milpurrurru v Indofurn* stated that 'although the artworks follow traditional Aboriginal form and are based on dreaming themes, each artwork is one of intricate detail and complexity reflecting great skill and originality' (at 216).

Identifiable author

There must be an identifiable author of the cultural material for copyright to subsist (*Copyright Act 1968* (Cth) s 32 sets out the requirements). This has posed difficulties for Indigenous people trying to protect very old cultural heritage such as designs on carved trees, or rock art because, although Indigenous people may still be conducting their inherited responsibilities for maintaining the cultural heritage today, the actual creator of the work may not be identifiable because of the lapse of time.

In addition, copyright recognises ownership by individual authors and corporations (ss 10, 32). This can be incompatible with communal or collective ownership and obligations of custodianship as opposed to ownership.

Duration

The duration of the term of copyright protection differs depending on the nature of the material. For example, the copyright term for a song, or play, or painting lasts until 70 years after the death of the author (*Copyright Act* s 33) or 70 years after publication (s 33). If copyright in the cultural material has expired, the material has, as far as the law is concerned, entered the public domain and the copyright or moral rights protections no longer attach to the material. So, artworks such as rock art or bark etchings for example cannot be protected using copyright laws although associated works such as more recently taken photos of the rock art or bark etchings may be subject to copyright. Nevertheless, the absence of copyright protection is not a reason to forget the protocols associated with respectful use of Indigenous cultural materials.

Employment and Crown copyright

The general position of copyright ownership is that the creator is the owner, but the Act provides a number of important exceptions to this general principle. While the precise legal position will vary according to the circumstances, two of the exceptions can be stated as follows.

First, where the creator makes the work as part of their employment, unless there is a contract to the contrary, the employer will generally be the copyright owner (*Copyright Act 1968* (Cth) s 35(4)). The second exception relates to works, films and sound recordings made under the direction and control of the Crown. In these cases, unless there is a contract to the contrary, the Crown will be the copyright owner (ss 176–179).

Infringing copyright

Infringing copyright is unlawful, and civil penalties apply. Copyright is infringed if a substantial part of copyright material is used without the owner's permission. It is in this area of infringement that Indigenous creators have brought many successful actions for the unauthorised use of their works, and while the Act does not specifically provide penalties for misappropriation of the underlying knowledge, by taking the infringement actions the Indigenous custodians have enforced these rights.

The question of the obligations of artists who work with the knowledge of Indigenous people was the subject of the case *John Bulun Bulun v R & T Textiles Pty Ltd* (unreported, FCA, 3 September 1998). In that case von Doussa J found that there was a fiduciary relationship between the artist Mr Bulun Bulun, the creator and copyright owner of the artistic work, and the Ganalbingu people, whose knowledge had been embodied in the artistic work in accordance with the laws and custom of the Ganalbingu people. Von Doussa J stated:

> Having regard to the evidence of the law and customs of the Ganalbingu people under which Mr Bulun Bulun was permitted to create the artistic work, I consider that equity imposes on him obligations as a fiduciary not to exploit the artistic work in a way that is contrary to the laws and custom of the Ganalbingu people, and, in the event of infringement by a third party, to take reasonable and appropriate action to restrain and remedy infringement of the copyright in the artistic work.

While the nature of the relationship between Mr Bulun Bulun and the Ganalbingu people is such that Mr Bulun Bulun falls under fiduciary obligations to protect the ritual knowledge which he has been permitted to use, the existence of those obligations does not, without more, vest an equitable interest in the ownership of the copyright in the Ganalbingu people. Their primary right, in the event of a breach of obligation by the fiduciary, is a right in personam to bring action against the fiduciary to enforce the obligation: *John Bulun Bulun v R & T Textiles Pty Ltd* (unreported, FCA, von Doussa J, 3 September 1998 at 18).

Cultural harm damages

In the *Carpets* case, von Doussa J considered the way in which the treatment of the paintings had impacted on the artists. He believed that it had caused great upset and cultural harm to the artists. 'The court noted that the standing of the artist within the community can be affected where the artworks are reproduced without the consent of the group and in a culturally offensive manner. This was because, regardless of whether the artists authorised the reproduction of their artworks on carpets, they were responsible under Indigenous law for the transgression that had occurred and were liable to be punished for such a breach' (Janke and Quiggin 2005: 23).

How does copyright law assist in the protection of Indigenous cultural heritage?

Indigenous authors have made excellent use of the *Copyright Act 1968* (Cth) for two purposes: first, protecting the right to control and manage cultural material; and, second, protecting their economic rights as the creators of cultural material. Some examples include the following.

Recording projects

Many Indigenous communities are working on creating recordings of their languages, oral histories and cultural practices themselves. When the copyright vests in the Indigenous knowledge holder, or the community organisation making the recordings on behalf of the community, the Indigenous owners and custodians of the cultural heritage can use their recordings for purposes they agree to, prevent uses they are not in agreement with, and ensure that the recordings of their cultural heritage are used in accordance with their cultural rules and protocols.

Indigenous publishing houses

Indigenous publishing houses such as Magabala Books, IAD Press and Aboriginal Studies Press provide an important source of, and outlet for, Indigenous cultural print material. Indigenous authors, illustrators and keepers of Indigenous language and Indigenous knowledge are published by these organisations. Examples of best practice in publishing include books like *Anmatyerr Plant Stories* by the women of Laramba (Napperby) (2003), compiled by Jenny Green, and *Arrente Traditional Healing* by Veronica Perrurle Dobson (2007), where the Aboriginal people who contribute their knowledge are the copyright owners of the material.

Using notices

Even though copyright might not specifically protect the underlying knowledge in a work, it is valuable to utilise notices on Indigenous cultural heritage material, which puts the world on notice that rights are asserted, even if they are not necessarily backed up by the force of Australian law (yet). The following notice, developed originally by Sally McCausland, provides a good template:

> The images in this artwork embody traditional ritual knowledge of the (name) community. It was created with the consent of the custodians of the community. Dealing with any part of the images for any purpose that has not been authorised by

the custodians is a serious breach of the customary law of the (name) community, and may also breach the *Copyright Act 1968* (McCausland 1999: 4).

Patents

The law of patents has produced some very controversial outcomes for Indigenous people around the world, and is rarely regarded as a suitable mechanism for the protection of Indigenous people's cultural heritage. Indigenous people's knowledge about flora has often been misappropriated and become the source of substantial research and development which in some instances has resulted in the development of a new product or invention for which a patent may then be sought. These developments have rarely acknowledged or remunerated the contribution of Indigenous people.

Unlike copyright, patents are only granted if there is a successful application phase, and the patent meets all the requirements for registration. The *Patents Act 1990* (Cth) s 18 sets out the rules for patents in Australia and requires that to be patentable, an invention:

    (a)   is a 'manner of manufacture'
    (b)   (i)   is novel; and
            (ii)   involves inventive step
    (c)   is useful; and
    (d)   must not have been the subject of secret use.

Like copyright though, a patent gives the owner monopoly rights over the patented material or process for the term of the patent. After that time, the details of the invention are disclosed to the public and other people may use the information to make money from it. Many Indigenous people oppose the characterisation of their cultural heritage in this way and believe that it is incompatible with customary ways of managing knowledge, plants and country.

Over the years there have been some famous—or rather infamous—cases of patents over uses of Indigenous people's knowledge and resources. One famous example is the case of the patent over turmeric, which had been used for centuries by Indians for medicinal and other purposes.

In 1995, the United States Patent Office (USPTO) granted US Patent No 5,401,504, to the patent applicant, the University of Mississippi Medical Centre, for the use of turmeric in wound healing. The patent was challenged by the Indian Council for Scientific and Industrial Research (CSIR) in the USA. The CSIR claimed that the patent did not meet the required standard of novelty, because the previous uses had been published in India (Prakash 1998; Radding 2003).

Indigenous peoples of the Pacific region have developed a particularly strong analysis of these issues, partly in response to problems such as the attempt to patent a cell line of the Hagahai people of Papua New Guinea (Mead and Ratura 2007), but also in the positive work of drafting Model Laws for the Protection of Expressions of Culture for the Pacific Island Developing States.

Indigenous Australians have been working to prevent unauthorised use of their knowledge and plants, and to encourage more respectful treatment of their cultural heritage. At the local level, some of this work has focused on developing protocols and research agreements for engagement with research institutions. At the state and federal level Indigenous people have advocated for more effective programs, policies and measures, such as the regulations made pursuant to the *Environment Protection Biodiversity and Conservation Act 1999* (Cth), and state and territory laws. At the international level Indigenous Australians lobby members of the working groups of the parties to the Convention on Biological Diversity, and the Intergovernmental Committee on Intellectual Property and Genetic Resources, Traditional Knowledge and Folklore (the IGC) for proper recognition of Indigenous people's voices and interests.

Apart from lobbying for policy and law reform, many Indigenous Australians are also undertaking recording and collection of their own knowledge for privately controlled knowledge databases and teaching purposes.

Authenticity—using intellectual property and trade practices laws

Intellectual property and trade-related mechanisms are used by Indigenous people to discourage and prevent trade in unauthentic artworks and cultural objects. These mechanisms focus on strengthening recognition of the value of Indigenous-produced works and protecting the rights of Indigenous creators and producers of goods and services.

Trade marks and geographic indicators are a useful way to alert consumers to the qualities or origins of a product or service, and to build the reputation of Indigenous producers and service providers. A trade mark is:

> ... a sign used, or intended to be used, to distinguish goods or services dealt with or provided in the course of trade by a person from goods or services so dealt with or provided by another person (*Trade Marks Act 1995* (Cth) s 17).

A sign may include a letter, a word, name, signature, numeral, device, brand, heading, label, ticket, an aspect of packaging, shape, colour, sound or scent, or a combination of any of those things (*Trade Marks Act* s 6).

Trade marks must be registered. An application must be made for registration and certain criteria must be met. A number of arts traders use trade marks and logos to distinguish their brand.

Commonwealth, state and territory law prohibits misleading or deceptive conduct. The *Trade Practices Act 1974* (Cth) has been used by the Australian Competition and Consumer Commission to prosecute traders engaging in misleading or deceptive conduct, when they falsely marketed and sold their products as authentic, Aboriginal-made products. The matters were settled by consent (*ACCC v Australian Icon Products Pty Ltd, Federal Court proceedings Q33 of 2003* and *ACCC v Australian Aboriginal Art Pty Ltd; Henry Peter De Jonge; Bruce Leslie Read, Federal Court proceedings Q131 of 2003*). By prosecuting companies which pretend to consumers that they are selling authentic Indigenous products, the misappropriation of Indigenous people's cultural heritage in the market is discouraged.

Protocols

Although we have focused on the law as a method of recognition and protection for Indigenous cultural heritage, the development of protocols should not be underestimated as a source of guidance for those people trying to work collaboratively and ethically with Indigenous people and their cultural heritage. Protocols can take a number of forms including guiding principles, standards, suggestions or a checklist of questions which can encourage respectful best practice.

Protocols are not intended to provide definitive answers to all questions which arise out of the many complexities of working with Indigenous people, their cultural material and knowledge. Instead they give some suggested principles, standards and questions which might be of concern to Indigenous people during collaborative projects or processes. Protocols often focus on particular projects, work or situations. In some instances, protocols are developed by Indigenous communities, and may include quite specific directions on how to engage with that specific community. A list of protocols is included at the end of this chapter.

International work

A number of different international forums have been working on measures which provide recognition and protections for Indigenous people's rights to their cultural heritage. Some of these measures can be found in international human rights conventions and the commentary of committees which monitor and interpret the provisions of the conventions.

When states become signatories to international human rights conventions they voluntarily agree to abide by the provisions of the treaty, and to report at regular intervals to the monitoring committees. Many conventions also have a procedure called an Optional Protocol, which provides individuals the opportunity to report allegations of violations of provisions of the conventions by their nation state.

Each of the main United Nations human rights conventions includes articles of relevance to the cultural heritage of Indigenous peoples, and the jurisprudence of the monitoring committees is also an important source of guidance on appropriate standards for state parties.

Declarations, principles and guidelines which might be adopted as part of international law by nations do not have the same binding obligations of national implementation or reporting mechanisms. Nevertheless they inform the international community of appropriate standards and contribute to the international community's understanding, implementation and development of human rights principles. Of great moment, in 2007, was the adoption by the General Assembly of the Declaration of the Rights of Indigenous People.

The Declaration was originally drafted in the early stages of the commencement of the Decade for Indigenous Peoples in 1993. The Declaration includes a number of articles which propose important standards for respectful engagement with Indigenous cultural heritage. Special Rapporteur on Traditional Knowledge at the United Nations Permanent Forum on Indigenous Issues, Professor Mick Dodson, notes that arguably the most explicit provision for the protection of Indigenous traditional knowledge is contained in Article 31 of the Declaration.

Paragraph 1 of the Article states:

> Indigenous peoples have the right to maintain, control, protect and develop their cultural heritage, traditional knowledge and traditional cultural expressions, as well as the manifestations of their sciences, technologies and cultures, including human and genetic resources, seeds, medicines, knowledge of the properties of fauna and flora, oral traditions, literatures, designs, sports and traditional games and visual and performing arts. They also have the right to maintain, control, protect and develop their intellectual property over such cultural heritage, traditional knowledge, and traditional cultural expressions.

Other important statements of Indigenous people's aspirations and rights include: the Julayinbul Declaration; the Mataatua Declaration on Cultural and Intellectual Property Rights of Indigenous Peoples; the Cusco Declaration on Access to Genetic Resources, Traditional Knowledge and Intellectual Property Rights of Like-minded Megadiverse Countries; and the Muscat Declaration on Intellectual Property and Traditional Knowledge.

A significant source of international policy development is the United Nations Permanent Forum on Indigenous Issues (UNPFII). The UNPFII 'is an advisory body to the Economic and Social Council, with a mandate to discuss Indigenous issues related to economic and social development, culture, the environment, education, health and human rights' (UNPFII 2008). It provides an important forum for Indigenous people to network and discuss many issues of importance, including cultural heritage.

The World Intellectual Property Organisation (WIPO) has also undertaken a number of programs of work relating to Indigenous people's intangible cultural material. As part of its work, WIPO established in 2000 a committee which undertakes work on traditional knowledge. This committee is called the WIPO Intergovernmental

Committee on Intellectual Property and Genetic Resources, Traditional Knowledge and Folklore (IGC). Participants in IGC meetings include members of WIPO and the European Union; accredited inter-governmental organisations and international and regional non-governmental organisations (NGOs) also participate as observers. The IGC has developed Policy Objectives and Core Principles for the Protection of Traditional Cultural Expression and Expressions of Folklore. It is also working on a major project on the digitisation of cultural heritage, including a database of 'codes, guides, policies, protocols and standard agreements relating to the recording, digitisation and dissemination of intangible cultural heritage, with an emphasis on intellectual property issues' (WIPO 2008).

And finally, our brief review of international work would not be compete without mentioning again the work of the parties to the Convention on Biological Diversity and the Indigenous people who attend the meetings and advocate for the rights of Indigenous people, including rights in relation to cultural heritage discussed previously in this chapter.

Conclusion

Indigenous Australians continue to assert their rights and obligations to their cultural heritage in local, state, territory, national and international arenas. The nature of Indigenous cultural heritage often requires Indigenous people to think outside the square, to stretch laws, policies and programs designed to regulate commodities and economic relationships in order to assert rights to culture and customary practice.

For the moment, there is a fairly mixed patchwork of laws from which advocates weave the most effective solutions. However, at the local level, cultural practices continue, are revived, taught to the young, treasured, celebrated and strengthened. Indigenous cultural heritage is being advanced both at the grassroots level, and in the national and international arenas. The bigger vision of the one-stop shop (Weatherall 2004), or national Indigenous cultural institution (Janke 1998; Commonwealth of Australia 2008: 240), administered by Indigenous people with expertise in negotiating both Indigenous cultural protocols and bureaucracy, backed by the laws specifically designed to effectively recognise and protect Indigenous cultural heritage and the rights of those responsible for it, is alive and well. It continues to be honed in the hearts and minds of many Indigenous people, and those who support them.

Appendix

Protocols for Research and Cultural Institutions

- Australian Institute of Aboriginal and Torres Strait Islander Studies Guidelines for Ethical Research in Indigenous Studies
- Central Land Council General Research Protocol
- Code of Ethics and Standards of Practice of the International Society of Ethnobiologists
- Aboriginal and Torres Strait Islander Protocols for Libraries, Archives and Information Services, endorsed by Aboriginal and Torres Strait Islander Library and Information Resources Network: Alex Byrne, Alana Garwood, Heather Moorcroft and Alan Barnes
- Taking the Time—Museums and Galleries, Cultural Protocols and Communities, A Resource Guide: Museums Australia Inc. (Qld)
- Previous Possessions, New Obligations: Museums Australia, (1994)

Protocols for the Arts and Media

- The Greater Perspective: Protocol and Guidelines for the Production of Film and Television on Aboriginal and Torres Strait Islander Communities: Lester Bostock
- Indigenous Protocol, written for Special Broadcasting Services: Darlene Johnson
- Valuing Art, Respecting Culture: Protocols for Working with the Australian Indigenous Visual Arts and Craft Sector: Doreen Mellor with a legal section by Terri Janke
- Towards a Protocol for Filmmakers Working with Indigenous Content and Indigenous Communities, Issues Paper: Terri Janke under commission for the Australian Film Commission
- Australia Council Protocols for Various Indigenous Artforms, written for the Aboriginal and Torres Strait Islander Board of the Australia Council, including:
  - Visual Arts: Protocols for Producing Indigenous Australian Visual Art and Craft: Terri Janke
  - Writing: Protocols for Producing Indigenous Australian Literature: Terri Janke,
  - Media Art: Protocols for Producing Indigenous Australian New Media: Terri Janke
  - Music: Protocols for Producing Indigenous Australian Music: Robynne Quiggin
  - Performing Arts: Protocols for Producing Indigenous Australian Performing Arts: Robynne Quiggin
- Some locally developed protocols including Community Cultural Development NSW Respect, Acknowledge, Listen: Practical Protocols for Working with the Indigenous Community of Western Sydney: Angela Hurley

Protocols for Native Title and Development

- Development and Indigenous Land: A Human Rights Approach: Human Rights and Equal Opportunity Commission and Griffith University, (2002)

Protocols for Biodiversity and Heritage

- Akwe: Kon Guidelines, Secretariat of the Convention on Biological Diversity, Montreal, (2004)
- Bonn Guidelines Secretariat of the Convention on Biological Diversity, Montreal, (2002).

PART 4

Law, Rights and Governance

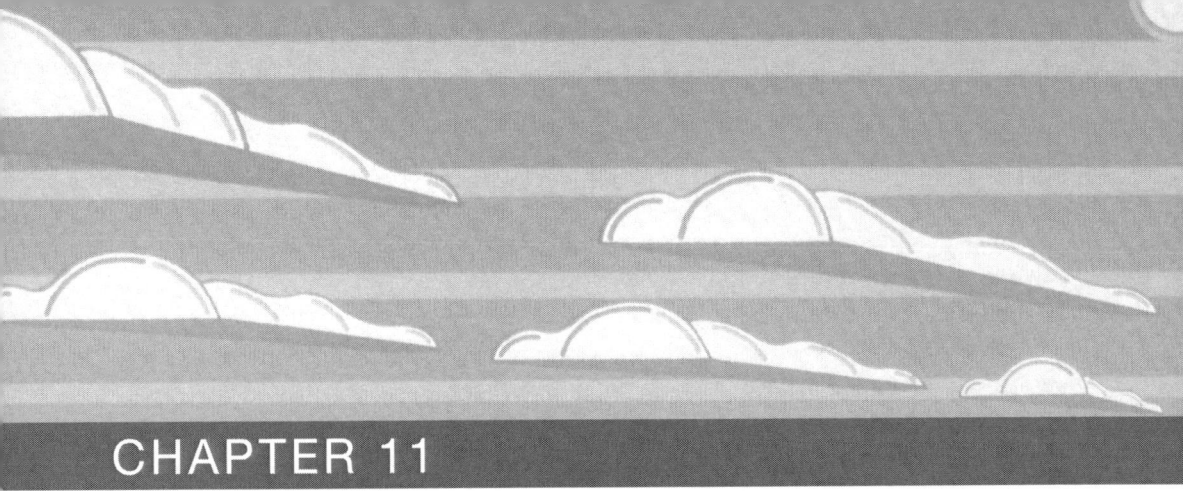

CHAPTER 11

Racial Discrimination and the Law

In March 2008 articles appeared in the news nationally about Aboriginal women from Yeundumu who were refused accommodation at a hostel in Alice Springs on the basis of their Aboriginality. The *National Brisbane Times* reported:

> The youth leaders had travelled 300 kilometres to Alice Springs last weekend to be trained by the Royal Life Saving Society before the opening of their local pool. After booking into the hostel on Saturday, the manager, Englishwoman Shelly Ball, asked them to leave … 'The manager told us to leave the hotel because there were Asian backpackers complaining about us just because we were black. Because they are afraid of Aboriginal people,' said Sharelle Young, 16, who was in the group (Smiles 2008).

While overt incidents like this are less common than more covert or inadvertent racist behaviour, they are not uncommon. Mr Tom Calma, the Aboriginal and Torres Strait Islander Social Justice Commissioner, reported hearing many anecdotal accounts of Indigenous Australians being refused accommodation or being asked to pay higher rates for rooms. He has expressed concern about the incident being indicative of more widespread and systemic problems in the provision of accommodation and services to Aboriginal and Torres Strait Islander People (*Sydney Morning Herald* 12 March 2008). This ugly incident is a stark reminder of the importance of anti-discrimination legislation despite its limitations and shortfalls. While anti-discrimination legislation primarily targets individual acts of prejudice, the broader edifice of colonialism and its pervasive impact on Indigenous communities, families and individuals requires a much deeper and more complex response. Such a response should characterise equality at a collective group level and encompass understandings of cultural and political rights which recognise Indigenous people's history, identity and aspirations at an individual as well as a collective level. These broader conceptions of equality and Indigenous rights are discussed across this book but see Chapters 14 and 15 in particular. Anti-discrimination legislation is grounded in liberal ideas of equality that presume a common canvas of individual rights which are protected against either direct or indirect discrimination. This chapter will discuss the origins of the *Racial Discrimination Act 1975* (Cth) (RDA) in the Convention on the Elimination of all forms of Racial Discrimination; the scope of the RDA; and the opportunities and limitations which this legislation affords.

Race and ideas about race thinking

The causes of racial discrimination are embedded in historical, social and political relationships. These are clearly beyond the scope of racial discrimination legislation. However anti-discrimination legislation can serve a limited constructive purpose and can contribute to the broader changes in understanding which are required to bring about more fundamental change. It can do this in a number of ways. One is by educating communities about discrimination and its underlying causes and a related way is the focus which claims can bring to discriminatory practices and experiences. However this focus can be limited or even counter-productive where the legislation and framework for interpreting claims of racial discrimination are embedded in dominant perspectives which could perpetuate rather than address racism. This is evident with the very limited success which claimants have had in bringing racial discrimination claims under the RDA (Gaze 2005).

Race is a social construct which has categorised peoples in accordance with genetic, ethnic, cultural, national and physical criteria. Racism refers to prejudices which lead to adverse attitudes towards and treatment of people on the basis of these criteria. For example, adverse presumptions may be made about peoples' abilities, intelligence, hygiene and character on the basis of 'race'. Some of these presumptions have been embedded in laws. For example the idea of a hierarchy of races with whites being at the top of the hierarchy and Aboriginal and Torres Strait Islander people at the bottom was given legitimacy in *Cooper v Stuart* (1889) 14 App Cas 286 which allowed the British to disregard Indigenous Australians' rights, including their ownership of land. Institutional racism operates where the institutions and social standards are defined by and predominantly benefit dominant groups and exclude and marginalise others on the basis of race. From as early as 1839 up until the late 1950s Aboriginal and Torres Strait Islander people's lives were closely regulated through legal definitions of race, based on proportions of blood, according to the political and administrative objectives of Aboriginal protection authorities and other bureaucracies (McCorquodale 1986). Blood-quotums were used to regulate who people could associate with, where they could live, where they could go and more broadly what rights and benefits they could obtain or more frequently be excluded from (Dodson 1994; HEREOC 1997). The construct of race has been used to justify grossly unfair policies including the dispossession of Aboriginal and Torres Strait Islander peoples from their lands (see Chapters 8 and 9) and the forced and unjustified removal of children from their families (see Chapter 2). The statistical and systemic disadvantage which Indigenous peoples face in contemporary Australia is closely tied to these historical processes of control, definition and dispossession. While laws which explicitly discriminate on the basis of race are less common, and require explicit suspension of the RDA or at least a plain and clear intention to override it, the impacts of past discrimination permeate all aspects of Australian society.

CERD

The International Convention on the Elimination of All Forms of Racial Discrimination (CERD) was adopted by the United Nations General Assembly on 21 December 1965 and entered into force on 4 January 1969. CERD developed out of international concern with racial discrimination, particularly in the context of apartheid laws and policies in South Africa. However CERD addresses racial discrimination more broadly and provides an ongoing mechanism for interpreting the Articles of CERD and establishing normative standards to combat racial discrimination. State parties which have ratified the CERD are required to submit periodic reports on their compliance with it. These are reviewed by the CERD Committee which is made up of independent experts. It then makes recommendations with respect to measures which need to be taken to comply with CERD. The Committee also makes General Recommendations which provide guidance on the meaning of Articles and requirements for compliance. There is also provision in CERD for individuals to make complaints where they have exhausted all avenues of domestic redress (Pritchard 1999). The dynamic nature of the CERD interpretation process, in the context of the experience gained through the participation of all signatory states, provides guidance with respect to how CERD can be translated into practice.

Article 1 of CERD defines the term 'racial discrimination' broadly as:

> ... any distinction, exclusion, restriction or preference based on race, colour, descent, or national or ethnic origin which has the purpose or effect of nullifying or impairing the recognition, enjoyment or exercise, on an equal footing, of human rights and fundamental freedoms in the political, economic, social, cultural or any other field of public life.

Australia ratified CERD in September 1975. In signing CERD Australia has undertaken to implement policies to eliminate racial discrimination and promote understanding between races. One of the first measures that Australia took to implement CERD was the passing of the *Racial Discrimination Act 1975* (Cth). While its provisions adopt many of the Articles of CERD, its interpretation and implementation have failed to develop in the dynamic manner in which CERD has. The narrow focus of the RDA, which is discussed below, can be compared with the breadth of recommendations with respect to State Periodic Reports and the General Recommendations of CERD, also referred to below. The application of CERD to Indigenous peoples is part of a broader framework of international human rights law with respect to Indigenous peoples which has been developing over the past 30 years. The RDA, while an important symbol of the reprehension which the community has for racism, has failed to establish a normative understanding of equality and non-discrimination which substantially addresses the discrimination which Aboriginal and Torres Strait Islander peoples face or to affirm the cultural and collective rights of Aboriginal and Torres Strait Islander peoples.

Article 5 of CERD provides a broad prohibition on racial discrimination including with respect to civil, political, economic, social and cultural rights. In 1997 the CERD Committee adopted a General Recommendation concerning Indigenous peoples, General Recommendation XXIII (51) Concerning Indigenous Peoples UN Doc CERD/C/51/Misc 13/Re 4 (1997). The CERD Committee called upon all state parties to:

- recognise and respect Indigenous peoples' distinct culture, history, language and way of life as an enrichment of the state's cultural identity and to promote their preservation;
- ensure that members of Indigenous peoples are free and equal in dignity and rights and free from any discrimination, in particular that based on Indigenous origin or identity;
- provide Indigenous peoples with conditions allowing for a sustainable economic and social development compatible with their cultural characteristics;

- ensure that members of Indigenous peoples have equal rights in respect of effective participation in public life, and that no decisions directly relating to their rights and interests are taken without their informed consent;
- ensure that Indigenous communities can exercise their rights to practise and revitalise their cultural traditions and customs, to preserve and practise their languages.

The CERD Committee also called on parties to CERD to recognise and protect the rights of Indigenous peoples to own, develop, control and use their communal lands, territories and resources and, where they have been deprived of their lands and territories traditionally owned, to return these. Where this is not possible they should be justly compensated and this should wherever possible be in the form of land and territories.

This General Recommendation clearly reflects the CERD Committee's recognition that to combat discrimination, measures need to be implemented which give effect to Aboriginal and Torres Strait Islander peoples' collective cultural rights as well as their right to substantive equality in the economic, social, cultural and political spheres of life. These rights are closely aligned with claims which Indigenous peoples have made in the international and domestic arena to self-determination (see Chapter 14).

The CERD Committee had a good working relationship with Australia from the time Australia ratified the Treaty in 1975 until the conservative Howard Government was elected into office in 1996. The Howard Government embarked on a number of legislative and policy projects which attracted the attention of the CERD Committee (Marks 2004, 2006). The amendments to the *Native Title Act 1993* (Cth) in 1998 attracted particular concern. In August 1998, the CERD Committee took the extraordinary measure of using its early warning and urgent actions procedures to request information from the Australian Government about the proposed changes to the *Native Title Act*. The Committee found that '… provisions that extinguish or impair the exercise of indigenous title rights and interests pervade the amended Act' (CERD Committee, Decision 2 (54) on Australia: Australia. 18 March 1999. UN Doc CERD/C/53/Misc.17/Rev.2.) The CERD Committee requested that Australia suspend the amendments and engage in discussion with Aboriginal and Torres Strait Islander peoples to find solutions which comply with CERD. The Australian Government rejected CERD's findings. The CERD Committee reiterated its concerns about Australia's compliance with respect to the amendments to the *Native Title Act* in their concluding observations of Australia's periodic report in 2000 and again in 2005. (See Chapter 9 for a discussion of the amendments to the *Native Title Act* and subsequent case law. For a discussion of interaction between the *Native Title Act 1993* and the RDA see Donaldson and Park 2003.)

The CERD Committee in their response to Australia's Periodic Report in 2002 also expressed concern and made recommendations with respect to a number of matters including the following.

- The Committee noted the lack of an entrenched guarantee against racial discrimination in Australian law (for discussion of related constitutional issues see Chapter 12).
- The Committee noted the extraordinary harm inflicted by racially discriminatory policies of forced separations of Aboriginal and Torres Strait Islander children from their families and expressed concern about the government's lack of support for an apology or monetary compensation for those affected by these policies. (As discussed in Chapter 3, with a change of government in 2007 there has been a formal apology by Prime Minister Rudd, but as of April 2008 the government refuses to compensate members of the Stolen Generations.)
- The Committee expressed grave concern about the rate of incarceration of Indigenous people. It recommended an increase in efforts to seek effective measures to address socio-economic marginalisation, the discriminatory approach to law enforcement and lack of sufficient diversionary programs. (See Chapters 5, 6 and 7 for a discussion of criminal justice issues.)
- The Committee recommended a review of all minimum mandatory sentencing schemes with respect to minor property offences which impact disproportionately on Indigenous Australians. (See Chapter 7 for a discussion on mandatory sentencing.)
- Serious concern was expressed about the extent of continuing discrimination faced by Indigenous Australians in the enjoyment of their economic, social and cultural rights. The Committee recommended that sufficient resources be allocated to eradicate these disparities within the shortest time possible.

By 2005, when Australia submitted its next periodic report to CERD, the Indigenous NGOs—which play a crucial role in providing the treaty-monitoring committees such as CERD with information which is not forthcoming from the government—had lost most of their funding and thereby their capacity to present information to the Committee. Further, the Human Rights and Equal Opportunity Commission (HREOC) had also had its funding reduced and it did not send a representative. The Aboriginal and Torres Strait Islander Commission (ATSIC) which did send a representative was about to be dismantled. Despite this, the CERD Committee made extensive and similar comments and recommendations to those made in 2002 with respect to Australia's failure to comply with CERD (CERD 2005). With a new Labor Government elected in late 2007, the tide may turn towards greater concern for and compliance with Australia's international human rights obligations.

Racial discrimination legislation

In Australia, there is Commonwealth and state and territory legislation which prohibits discrimination on a number of bases including race. There is also legislation which prohibits racial vilification. This chapter focuses on the Commonwealth legislation. The RDA was passed in 1975 in response to Australia's ratification of CERD. It adopts many of the provisions of CERD.

Section 9 defines direct and indirect race discrimination in broad terms. Section 9(1) provides:

> It is unlawful for a person to do any act involving a distinction, exclusion, restriction or preference based on race, colour, descent or national or ethnic origin which has the purpose or effect of nullifying or impairing the recognition, enjoyment or exercise, on an equal footing, of any human right or fundamental freedom in the political, economic, social, cultural or any field of public life.

In 1990, the Act was amended to include s 9(1A) which explicitly prohibits indirect discrimination. While s 9(1) already prohibited acts which both have the purpose or effect of discriminating, this provision clarified any ambiguity with respect to indirect discrimination. In addition to this general prohibition the Act also specifically prohibits discrimination in access to places and facilitates, land, housing and accommodation, goods and services, employment and the right to join a trade union (ss 11–15). Section 10 of the Act provides for equality before the law. Therefore if a federal, state or territory law fails to include people in a racially discriminatory way, s 10 extends the benefit of the law to these people. Likewise if a federal, state or territory law denies people, in a racially discriminatory way, rights or freedoms, the operation of these laws will be invalid for inconsistency with the RDA. However federal legislation can and has been passed which has the clear and plain intention to override the RDA.

Human rights and fundamental freedoms

The meaning of human rights and fundamental freedoms in ss 9 and 10 of the RDA have been interpreted broadly to encompass the human rights as proclaimed in the Universal Declaration of Human Rights (per Brennan J in *Gerhardy v Brown* (1985) 159 CLR 70); as described in CERD (per Deane J *Mabo v Queensland (No 1)* (1988) 166 CLR 70); and in accordance with 'the claim of each and every person to the enjoyment of rights and freedoms generally acknowledged as fundamental to his or her existence as a human being and a free individual in society' (per Mason J in *Gerhardy v Brown* (1985) 159 CLR 70). The preamble to the RDA provides that it is enacted to prohibit racial and certain other forms of discrimination and to give effect to CERD. The human rights referred to in Article 5 of CERD include the right to personal security, economic, cultural and social rights, the right to housing, public health, education and training and other civil rights. While the affirmation and acknowledgment of these rights is noble, the attainment of the rights expressed in ss 9 and 10 is compromised by both the inadequate means to bring actions for breach of these rights, the individual nature of remedies available for redress, and the failure to connect the protection of these individual rights with collective rights and systemic racism. However, Martin Flynn suggests that s 9 of the RDA could be used to find that indirect acts of discrimination preclude Aboriginal people from access to the services and goods supplied by governments which are available to other low-income and disadvantaged sections of the community (2005c). Such a finding could indirectly challenge systemic discrimination in areas such as health and education.

Racist motivation

While race, ethnic or national origin have not been defined in the RDA they have been interpreted as broad social constructs (*Williams v Tandanya Cultural Centre* (2001) 163 FLR 203). In accordance with s 9, race, colour, national or ethnic descent needs to be a reason for the behaviour which a complainant alleges is discriminatory. However race does not need to be the only or even a dominant reason for an act to be found to be discriminatory (s 18 of the RDA). Proving a racist basis for complaints has proven to be very difficult. This is because racist reasons are not usually given for racist decisions or actions. Complainants typically have to draw inferences from the circumstances to demonstrate their case. The existence of systemic racism is not sufficient to demonstrate racial discrimination. In *Murray v Forward* the complainant asked HREOC to draw the inference that he had been discriminated against on the basis of his Aboriginality. He claimed that presumptions about his literacy had been made which he alleged could only be explained with regard to stereotypes about Aboriginal peoples' inadequate literacy. Sir Ronald Wilson stated:

> I have not found the resolution of this issue an easy one. Counsel acknowledges that to accept his submission on behalf of the complainant I must exclude all other inferences that might reasonably be open. I am sensitive to the possible presence of systemic racism, when persons in a bureaucratic context can unconsciously be guided by racist assumptions that may underlie the system. But in such a case there must be some evidence of the system and the latent or patent racist attitudes that infect it. Here there is no such evidence. Consequently there is no evidence to establish the weight to be accorded to the alleged stereotype (unreported, HREOC, 10 September 1993 at 4, cited in HREOC 2005).

This plainly places a high burden on the complainant. Frequently those who allege discrimination are in a more vulnerable position than the parties discriminating against them. This vulnerability is part of complex power imbalances which pervade Australian society. Indigenous complainants are less likely than respondents to have the financial resources or access to the documentation to conduct the research to enable them to adduce evidence of the systemic discrimination or racist attitudes which pervade the institution which they are making a complaint against. Would it not be fairer to require the respondent, once the complainant has demonstrated racial discrimination by inference, to bear an evidentiary burden to show they were not making decisions on the basis of racist stereotypes? Not only does the complainant have to bring evidence to prove the systemic racism on which their inferences are based but they are also often required to meet a higher than usual standard of proof. This is called the *Briginshaw* standard (*Briginshaw v Briginshaw* (1938) 60 CLR 336). The rationale for this standard being required in discrimination matters is that the allegations are serious and a finding of discrimination would have a significant impact on the respondent (see for example *Sharma v Legal Aid Queensland* [2002] FCAFC 196 cited in HREOC 2005: chapter 3, 11–13). Applying the more onerous *Briginshaw* standard to the scrutiny of complainant's evidence in racial discrimination matters means that discrimination, which is already difficult to prove because it is rarely overt, becomes even more difficult. The process of bringing a complaint is more technical and costly and the chances of succeeding more remote. There can also be adverse consequences for complainants whose vulnerability may be reinforced, rather than their rights vindicated, through a process which appears to make proof of discrimination elusive. While the *Briginshaw* standard is premised on the significance of a finding of racial discrimination, a longer term impact of this standard may be a capacity for respondents to feel invincible in this sphere because successful claims are unlikely. The difficulty for plaintiffs in demonstrating that race was the motivation for the respondent's conduct has been addressed in legislation in the UK. The *Race Relations Act 1976* (UK) provides that the onus falls on the respondent to prove that race was not the ground for their conduct once the complainant has adduced evidence from which race discrimination could be inferred in the absence of other explanations (s 54A(2)).

DISCUSSION QUESTION

- Does the *Briginshaw* standard in discrimination matters reinforce the privilege of the powerful or does it provide necessary protection for respondents against findings which have great stigma attached to them and which could have permanent adverse impacts on them?

Underpayment and non-payment of wages to Indigenous Australians

In *Baird v State of Queensland* [2006] FCAFC 162 the plaintiffs claimed that their payment of wages under the award was less than others performing similar work and that this was in breach of s 9 of the RDA. The case was a claim with respect to wages between 1975 (when the RDA was enacted) and 1986 when the claimants received award wages. The claimants were Aboriginal people living in the Hope Vale and Wujal Wujal communities in northern Queensland. These communities were managed at the time of the claims by the Lutheran Church which was funded by the Queensland Government. The church was not a respondent in the case and the case failed at first instance because of this. However the applicants were successful on appeal. Allsop J, with Spender and Edmonds JJ in agreement, found that the calculation and payment of grants by the Queensland Government involved the setting of a sum for payment of wages below the award rate, that the distinction in rates used was based on race and that this had the effect of impairing the applicants' human rights in accordance with s 9(1) of the Act. The parties agreed to orders which included the payment of damages of between $17,000 and $85,000 plus interest to individual appellants and an apology from the Minister for Communities, Disability Services, Seniors and Youth. As this case illustrates, discretionary acts in public life must comply with the RDA.

Equality before the law

Section 10 of the RDA provides a right to equality before the law. It is intended to give effect to Article 2 of CERD which requires state parties to 'rescind or nullify any laws and regulations which have the effect of creating or perpetuating racial discrimination'. This section of the RDA has been important for protecting Indigenous peoples' rights. Attempts by both the Queensland Government and the Western Australian Government to extinguish native title have been found to be in breach s 10 and therefore invalid. The *Queensland Coast Islands Declaratory Act 1985* (Qld) was passed while *Mabo (No 2)* was being litigated. It was an attempt to pre-empt any finding of native title by deeming complete and beneficial ownership of all of Queensland by the Crown. The High Court found this Act to be invalid because its operation deprived Aboriginal and Torres Strait Islander people of their property rights (*Mabo (No 1)*). Following the passage of the *Native Title Act 1993* (Cth) the Western Australian Government passed the *Land (Titles and Traditional Usage) Act 1993*. This Act purported to extinguish all native title in Western Australia and to replace it with statutory rights to access certain land for traditional usage. The High Court found that this legislation was invalid for inconsistency with s 10 of the RDA (*Western Australia v Commonwealth (The Native Title Act case)* (1995) 183 CLR 373). However the limitation of legislative rather than constitutional protection of basic human rights, such as equality before the law and the prohibition of racial discrimination, is evident in cases such as *Western Australia v Ward* (2002) 213 CLR 1 where amendments which expressly override the protection provided by the RDA have been held to be valid. If more robust protection for these rights is to be attained it needs to be constitutionally entrenched (see Chapter 12). The possibility of s 10 of the RDA providing broader protection against discriminatory state and territory laws remains to be tested. For example could legislation such as child protection legislation, which provides in all Australian jurisdictions for foster care payments but does not provide this allowance for kin care payments to Indigenous carers, be in be in breach of s 10 of the RDA? Likewise could criminal law provisions such as mandatory sentencing laws in Western Australia, which have a disproportionate impact on Aboriginal and Torres Strait Islander people, and perhaps have the implicit object of targeting Aboriginal people, be in breach of s 10 of the RDA?

DISCUSSION QUESTIONS

- Is or should the requirement of equality before the law in s 10 of the RDA be directed to whether there is discrimination on the face of the law or in its operation?
- What difficulties do you think Indigenous complainants could encounter when bringing actions for indirect discrimination with respect to s 10?

Special measures

The RDA provides limited circumstances when it is legitimate to discriminate on the basis of race. This is provided for in s 8 which is based on Article 1(4) of CERD. Section 8 allows special measures for the sole purpose of the advancement of certain racial or ethnic groups or individuals where this is necessary for them to enjoy or exercise their human rights. These special measures must be discontinued once the objective for which they were taken has been achieved.

Gerhardy v Brown

CASE

In *Gerhardy v Brown* (1985) 159 CLR 70 s 19 of the *Pitjantjatjara Land Rights Act 1981* (SA), which requires people who are not Pitjantjatjara to obtain a permit to enter Pitjantjatjara land, was challenged. Robert Brown, an Aboriginal man who was not

Pitjantjatjara, was charged with entering the lands without a permit. He claimed that the permit requirement was in breach of the RDA and therefore invalid. The High Court found the permit to be a special measure under s 8(1) of the RDA. The requirements of s 8(1) include that the provision is for the sole purpose of securing the adequate advancement of the Pitjantjatjara so that they can enjoy and exercise their human rights equally with others and that this special measure had not yet achieved its objective. These requirements imply that the special measure is a temporary benefit which is necessary for a period of time until circumstances improve and the barrier to equality which the measure is addressing has been overcome. This interpretation of the permit provisions under the *Land Rights Act* misses a fundamental aspect of cultural control which the permits protect. It highlights a limitation with the High Court's conceptualisation of equality in the RDA and its failure to address recognition of cultural difference which is not founded in disadvantage but rather in more permanent difference. A more nuanced interpretation of equality in *Gerhardy v Brown* could have facilitated a definition of discrimination which could distinguish between legitimate distinctions based on cultural difference and those which are offensive. Such distinctions do not victimise either those who are excluded from, or those who are subject to, the distinction but rather recognise substantive and legitimate difference (Sadurski 1986).

DISCUSSION QUESTIONS

- What are the dangers and what are the benefits of recognising different laws on the basis of ongoing relevance for Aboriginal and Torres Strait Islander or other minority cultural or ethnic groups?
- Do Indigenous Australians have a different claim to legal recognition of their interests, such as permits controlling entrance to large tracks of land as provided for under the *Pitjantjatjara Land Rights Act*, compared with other minorities?

Racial vilification

In 1995 amendments were made to the RDA which prohibit offensive behaviour on the basis of race, colour, national or ethnic origin. Section 18C provides that it is illegal to do an act in public which is reasonably likely to offend, insult, humiliate or intimidate another person or group of people and the act is done because of the race, colour, or national or ethnic origin of the other person or group. This section requires race to be a motivation in the behaviour. The Act provides exemptions for conduct which is said or done:

- reasonably and in good faith in the performance, exhibition or distribution of artistic work; or
- in the context of academic, artistic, scientific or other work in the public interest; or
- in publishing reports which are fair and accurate and in the public interest; or
- fair comment of genuinely held beliefs on a matter of public interest (s 18D).

This is the most extensively litigated section of the RDA.

DISCUSSION QUESTION

- How do new modes of communication through the internet pose particular problems with respect to racial vilification?

Creek v Cairns Post Pty Ltd

The *Cairns Post* published a story about the removal of a two-year-old Aboriginal girl from her white foster parents and her placement with Ms Creek. Ms Creek was an Aboriginal relative of the child's deceased mother and the guardian of her two brothers. The main issue which the article explored was whether the Queensland Department of Family Services, Youth and Community Care had based their decision on a reaction to the Stolen Generations report which had been published earlier that year.

The complaint related to the photos which were published to accompany the article. There was a photo of the child, a photo of the white foster parents, Mr and Mrs Macdonald, and a photo of the applicant Ms Creek. The photo of Mr and Mrs Macdonald showed them in their living room with comfortable furniture and books and photographs in the frame. The photo of Ms Creek showed her in a bush camp with a shed behind her and young children in the shed. Ms Creek complained that the photograph misrepresented her usual living circumstances and implied that the child would be living in a bush camp. Ms Creek in fact lived in a comfortable four-bedroom house and the bush camp was a recreation area about four hours from her home which she and her family visited. The photograph of Ms Creek at the camp had been taken on an earlier occasion, with her consent, in relation to an unrelated story about assistance which she had rendered in locating some New Zealand backpackers who had become lost in a remote area.

CASE STUDY

The first question which the court considered in *Creek v Cairns Post Pty Ltd* (2001) 112 FCR was whether the photograph was reasonably likely to offend or humiliate a person in Ms Creek's position. The court considered whether an Aboriginal mother, or one who cares for children, who lived in the township of Coen would feel offended, insulted or humiliated if they were portrayed as living in rough bush conditions in the context of a report about a child's welfare. Justice Kiefel noted at para 13, 'In that context it is implied that person would be taking the child into less desirable conditions. The offence comes not just from the fact that it is wrong, but from the comparison which is invited by the photographs ...'

Despite finding that the photos were objectively, reasonably likely to offend someone in Ms Creek's position, her claim against the *Cairns Post* failed. Section 18C(1)(b) of the RDA provides that:

> ... the act is done because of the race, colour or national or ethnic origin of the other person or of some or all of the people in the group.

In assessing the above provision Justice Kiefel noted at para 28, 'In the present case the question is whether anything suggests race as a factor in the respondent's decision to publish the photograph. The context of the story is of course race, but merely to publish a photograph of a person involved in the story could not mean that considerations of race can be taken to have actuated the publication. It is something which commonly occurs in media reports. Rather, the enquiry is whether the publication of a photograph, showing the applicant's apparent living circumstances, was motivated by considerations of race.' Justice Kiefel found that there was no evidence suggesting that the publication was motivated by race and therefore Ms Creek's claim failed.

DISCUSSION QUESTIONS

- What message do you think the Federal Court finding is giving Ms Creek and the *Cairns Post*?
- Does the finding in this case reflect the court's perception of what a reasonable publisher would understand by juxtaposing the two photos in the news article?
- Should the motivation of the respondent be a necessary requirement in finding behaviour which a respondent has engaged in unlawful under s 18?
- Do you think historical definitions and representations of Aboriginality are relevant to the meaning and motivation for photos such as those in the *Cairns Post* described above?

The effectiveness of the RDA for Indigenous peoples

As discussed above the RDA has a limited purpose to educate and set a normative standard for public conduct and to provide an avenue for complaint and redress where individuals have experienced discrimination. There are many reasons why the RDA has only limited success in achieving these objectives. These are found in both the conceptual framework of the legislation and in its procedure and operation. At a conceptual level the legislation fails to conceptualise discrimination as a systemic problem. This is evident in the individual focus of complaints and in particular the limitation which the *HREOC Act (1986)* (Cth) sets for the Federal Court to make orders which go beyond the complainant's individual situation (s 46PO(4)). The remedies seek to address the particular matter before the court as if the individual's situation is experienced in isolation rather than as part of a structural situation. The RDA therefore lacks the capacity to identify, let alone address, cultural and structural barriers which pervade formal and informal institutions which impact on and perhaps even determine the distribution of rights and interests which are ostensibly protected by anti-discrimination legislation. Martin Flynn suggests that the RDA could be used to address what he describes as an aspect of statistical equality. The RDA has been interpreted as protecting the right to an equal opportunity to partake in the human rights protected by it: *Gerhardy v Brown* (1985) 159 CLR 70. Flynn suggests that indirect discrimination could be argued where Aboriginal and Torres Strait Islander people are denied, through attributes specific to them, equal access to services which the rest of community can partake in. For example an inability to access government support because of a composite of factors including inadequate numeracy, literacy, inadequate personal records, inability to communicate for the purpose in English and other attributes (Flynn 2005c). However, we have seen that direct discrimination has been difficult to prove and although indirect discrimination has not been claimed frequently, it is likely to be even more difficult to prove than direct discrimination.

DISCUSSION QUESTION

- What are some of the hurdles which a complainant would need to overcome to bring an action for racial discrimination on the basis of a denial of equal access to government services?

The second conceptual problem with the Act is its failure to conceptualise equality in a manner which facilitates recognition of Indigenous peoples' collective cultural and political identity. This is highlighted with the Special Measures provision in the

RDA, which the High Court has interpreted as only legitimating differential treatment as a temporary measure to overcome disadvantage. This understanding of equality fails to recognise relevant cultural differences in an affirmative and ongoing way. As discussed with respect to *Gerhardy v Brown* above, the recognition of provisions in the *Pitjantjatjara Land Rights* Act 1981 (SA) to control entry onto Pitjantjatjara land was upheld by the High Court in a strained and less than satisfactory manner. The High Court's interpretation implies that permits are an interim measure until the Pitjantjatjara people have overcome their disadvantage. Plainly the permits are part of a legislative framework designed to permanently accord the Pitjantjatjara people control over their land. The RDA embodies an outmoded understanding of the exercise of human rights. International human rights law has through General Comments and Country Reports, with respect to CERD and other treaties which Australia is signatory to, recognised the relationship between recognition of Indigenous peoples' collective rights and their capacity to exercise their human rights (see Chapter 14). As discussed above, the CERD Committee has made recommendations with respect to state parties' obligations to recognise Indigenous peoples' distinct rights to their culture, language, history and way of life including rights to control their communal lands and participate in political processes. In particular the Committee has noted that no decision relating to Indigenous peoples' rights and interests should be taken without their informed consent: *General Recommendation XXIII (51) Concerning Indigenous Peoples* UN Doc CERD/C/51/Misc 13/Re 4 (1997).

At an operational level the RDA has had limited success for Indigenous peoples. There are a number of reasons for this, the first being that not many Indigenous people lodge complaints and of those who do only a small percentage are successful. Beth Gaze has assessed claims brought under the RDA between 2000 and 2004 and she found that complainants had limited success. She found that in 2003–2004 only 15 per cent of discrimination complaints made to HREOC were with respect to race and only 5 per cent of these were brought by Aboriginal and Torres Strait Islander people. The proportion of racial discrimination complaints settled at conciliation in 2003–2004 was 24 per cent. There is no information available on what percentage of the 76 per cent of complaints which could not be conciliated were lodged in the Federal Court. However between April 2000 and September 2004 only 35 racial discrimination matters were heard in the Federal Court and only six of these were successful. The cases that were successful were with respect to racial vilification and breach of the rights under s 10 to enjoy equality before the law. No racial discrimination claims with respect to s 9 were successful (Gaze 2005).

There are numerous reasons for the limited number and success of Indigenous complaints. These include information barriers, lack of geographic access to anti-discrimination tribunals, the cost of bringing complaints and language and cultural barriers which Indigenous people face. As discussed above with respect to the requirement that complainants demonstrate the racist motivation for discrimination, it is very difficult to adduce evidence which meets the stringent *Briginshaw* standard of proof. If a complainant fails, they usually have costs awarded against them which can be considerable if the respondent is a powerful person or institution with the resources to hire expensive legal counsel.

Inconsistency of s 9 of the RDA with state and territory laws which operate to discriminate makes them potentially invalid. This is because s 109 of the Constitution provides that federal laws override state laws where there is inconsistency between otherwise valid laws. However later Commonwealth legislation can override the RDA. This highlights the need for constitutional entrenchment of basic democratic, civil and human rights such as the prohibition of discrimination and equality before the law. The Commonwealth has on a number of occasions suspended or exempted the operation of the RDA from legislation with the specific purpose of passing discriminatory legislation. For examples, see amendments to the *Native Title Act* discussed in Chapter 9 and the intervention into Aboriginal communities in the Northern Territory discussed in Chapter 4.

One of the most successful elements of the RDA was the establishment of a Race Discrimination Commissioner and an Aboriginal and Torres Strait Islander Social Justice Commissioner. Both these officers have researched and provided information on the prevalence of racism and its impacts. They have researched and recommended social policy to redress discrimination at a more fundamental level than provided for by the RDA.

Conclusion

The pervasive nature of prejudice in the social institutions of Australian society including schools, police services, health services, shops and consumer services impacts in a spectrum of ways from subtle presumptions and norms within these institutions to more overt forms of discrimination against Aboriginal and Torres Strait Islander individuals and groups. It is impossible to address these systemic and entrenched forms of discrimination through individual complaints. Focusing on individual complaints can serve to detract from the inequality which is experienced at a community and group level. This is because individual complaints can shift the focus away from the systemic nature of the problem to problematic individuals. Equality which recognises substantial difference requires incorporation of Indigenous understandings in the institutions of society, which in turn requires community development and self-determination models to redress exclusion and disadvantage.

Racist attitudes and racial discrimination have their foundations in historical and contemporary individual and institutional experiences. Anti-discrimination laws can, however, play a role in redressing the systemic and personal experiences which underlie racist attitudes and in this way reduce the impact of racial discrimination and disadvantage on Aboriginal and Torres Strait Islander individuals and communities. If the RDA is to be more effective in playing this role it should be reformed to embody a conceptual understanding which recognises the participatory and cultural rights of Indigenous Australians. It should also not only recognise special measures which facilitate affirmative action in response to disadvantage but require that discriminatory disadvantage be addressed in areas enumerated in CERD such as health, employment, education and housing.

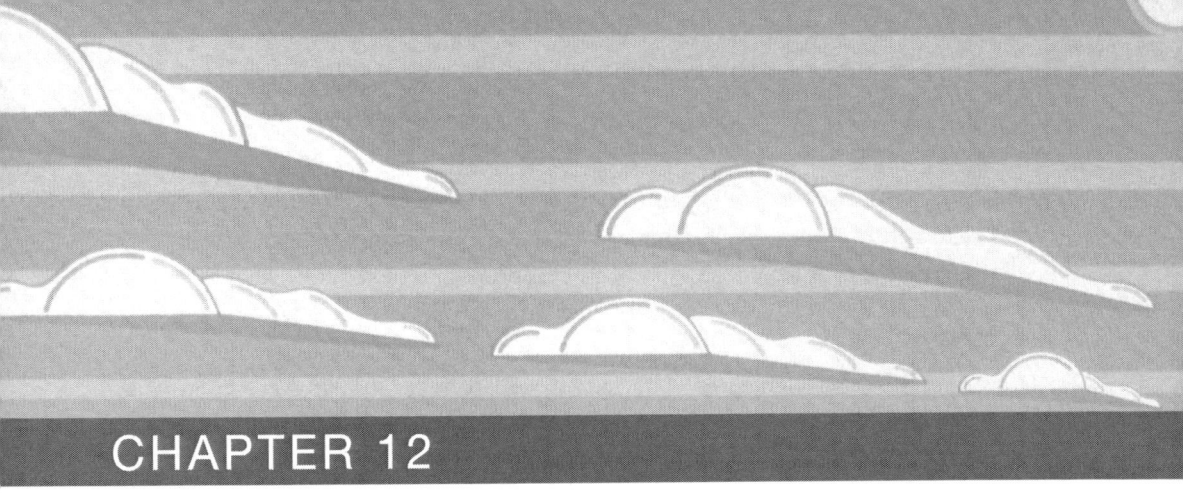

CHAPTER 12

Constitutional Change: Strengthening Rights Protection

The Australian Constitution sets out our system of government, defining the powers and relationships between our three arms of government—the executive, the judiciary and the legislature—and it also defines the way that power is distributed between the federal and state and territory governments.

Our Constitution does its work in a mechanical and practical way and does not make for inspiring reading, but our foundational document does contain many of the values that the drafters of the original document wanted to instil into it. It reveals a lot about the kind of Australia our founding fathers wanted for us and a lot about our community today. In particular, it reveals a lot about our relationship with Aboriginal people.

The values of our founding fathers

At the time Constitution was drafted, Aboriginal people were excluded from participating in the process, reflecting the way in which they were excluded from participating in the main institutions in Australia at that time. Along with entrenched beliefs about the inferiority of women, beliefs of white racial superiority were rife at the time the Constitution came into force in 1901. Also prevalent was a paternalistic belief that Aboriginal people were so inferior to Europeans and their culture that they would eventually die out as a race. While these views do not appear expressly in the text of the Constitution, they have left a legacy.

Alongside the ideologies of racial superiority that existed at the time of the Constitution, other key decisions by the drafters reflected their values and also helped shape the kind of system of government we have today. David Marr, in his *Quarterly Essay* 'His Masters Voice' makes an observation about the Australian ethos that also influenced our Constitution. In an essay that looks at the way in which many Australians did not complain about or protest against the continual way in which federal governments have wound back many basic civil rights and government accountabilities he makes the following observation:

> We've known what's going on. If we cared, we didn't care enough to stop it. Boredom, indifference and fear have played a part in this. So does something about ourselves we rarely face: Australians trust authority. Not love, perhaps, but trust. It's bred in the bone. We call ourselves larrikins, but we leave our leaders to get on with it. Even the leaders we mock (Marr 2007: 5).

The trust in government of which Marr writes is not just a characterisation of our general attitude today but was an aspect of the Australian attitude that was evident at the time that the modern Australian nation was founded.

The framers of our Constitution believed that the decision-making about the protection of rights—which ones we recognise and the extent to which we protect them—were matters for the parliament. They discussed the inclusion of rights within the Constitution itself and rejected this option, preferring instead to leave our founding document mostly silent on these matters. They had looked at the United States Constitution, a model that entrenched rights and had the judiciary as the body which was given the job of interpreting rights, and preferred a model that left this job to the legislature.

The framers did have a discussion about the inclusion of rights within the Constitution itself. A non-discrimination clause was proposed by Andrew Inglis Clark through the Tasmanian Parliament (Williams 1999: 37) that, in part, stated:

> ... nor shall a state deprive any person of life, liberty, or property without due process of law, or deny to any person within its jurisdiction the equal protection of its laws.

This clause that would have entrenched some rights in the Australian Constitution was rejected for two reasons. First, it was believed that entrenched rights provisions were unnecessary, and, second, it was considered desirable to ensure that the Australian states would have the power to continue to enact laws that discriminated against people on the basis of their race.

The power to make laws that were discriminatory was not just considered necessary to enable state parliaments to continue to make laws that would specifically discriminate against Aboriginal people, but were also believed necessary in order to implement legislation that would discriminate against other races. There were special rules that regulated the movement of Chinese Australians that had become general practice during the gold rushes. And there was a desire to be able to strictly control who came to our country. The first laws passed by the new Australian parliament were immigration laws that passed the White Australia Policy into law.

DISCUSSION QUESTIONS

- What were some of the prevailing ideological assumptions that would have been prevalent at the time the Constitution was drafted?
- In what ways did those ideological assumptions influence the drafting of the Constitution?

For Indigenous people, the Australian Constitution, as it was originally drafted, symbolised three things:

- It highlighted the way in which the modern Australian state was founded without any involvement of Indigenous people in the process and therefore represented the way in which they were marginalised within Australian society.
- Not only were Indigenous people excluded from the nation-building process of drafting the Constitution, there was no recognition within the document of their unique place as the traditional owners of the country.
- By leaving the Constitution silent about rights, Australians were content to rely on governments to protect them. For Indigenous Australians, this trust in the benevolence of government would leave them vulnerable to exploitation and the breach of their human rights.

It is not surprising then that in the broader political agenda that Aboriginal and Torres Strait Islander people have engaged in to achieve social justice that reform of the Constitution has been a continuing aspiration.

1967 referendum

On Australia Day in 1938, a group of Aboriginal people protested in front of Australia Hall after they were moved off the Town Hall steps. This small protest was the culmination of decades of activism by Indigenous communities and their leaders in the south-east of Australia such as William Cooper, William Ferguson and Fred Maynard who had sought the same rights as all other Australians, especially in relation to their ability to own land, to access jobs and to access education and health services.

The protest was also a beginning. It was the beginning of the Indigenous rights movement and the long road to the search for equality under the legal system. Inclusion through equal access to education, employment and the economy were seen as key ways of improving the situation of Aboriginal people. Men like Cooper and Maynard had worked on pastoral stations that they were prevented from owning. They were self-taught men and they believed that if Aboriginal people were given the same opportunities as other Australians and could make the key decision about their communities, their families and their lives, they would be able to find their own solutions to their problems. This notion of access and opportunity underpinned the desire for 'citizenship rights' and with the claim for land and the desire for self-determination created the key platforms in the Indigenous political agenda.

The focus on citizenship rights as an important part of the campaign for Indigenous equality was a key platform in the activism of advocates like Cooper, Ferguson and Maynard and it influenced future generations.

The Federal Council for Aboriginal Advancement (FCAA) emerged in the 1950s as the first national representative body for Aboriginal people. It later became the Federal Council for the Advancement of Aborigines and Torres Strait Islanders (FCAATSI). It was the dominant voice on Aboriginal rights until the late 1960s. Its agenda focused on 'citizenship rights' but it also called for special rights for Aboriginal people as well.

It became a driving force in the call for an amendment to the Constitution that would provide protection to Indigenous people. Momentum for change was propelled by the influence of the civil rights movement in the USA and the increasing attention that Aboriginal activists like Charles Perkins were able to draw to the plight of Indigenous people who were living in third world conditions. Perkins had headed the Freedom Rides throughout north-west New South Wales. On his bus was a group of university students that included future New South Wales Chief Justice Jim Spiegelman and historian Ann Curthoys. They brought to the attention of people in the cities the crude and racist conditions that existed in places like Walgett and Brewarrina, garnering public sympathy for Indigenous issues (Goodall 1996).

The involvement of prominent non-Aboriginal people like Jessie Street in these campaigns saw non-Aboriginal people work alongside emerging Aboriginal leaders such as Doug Nicholls, Joe McGuiness and Kath Walker to work for a referendum that would include Indigenous people in the Constitution with the intention that it would improve their living conditions and give them access to the same opportunities and services that other Australians unquestioningly enjoyed.

Australia has been extremely reluctant to alter its Constitution, seemingly suspicious of many of the proposed changes. The Constitution can only be amended by a referendum and requires a Bill to be first passed by the Commonwealth parliament. A referendum is then put to the Australian people and to pass, it must attract an overall national majority and by a majority in a majority of states.

When voting 'yes' in the 1967 referendum, Australians voted to make two changes to the Constitution:

- to allow for Indigenous people to be included in the census; and
- to give the federal parliament the power to make laws in relation to Indigenous people.

The referendum in 1967 became one of only eight changes but with the most resounding endorsement, winning over 90 per cent of voters and carrying all six states. At a time when many parts of Australia were actively practising segregation, this was an extraordinary result. This support reflected a moment in Australian history that was a high-water mark for the relationship between Aboriginal and non-Aboriginal people.

The referendum also enjoyed bi-partisan support for a 'yes' vote, a prerequisite to ensuring its success. Political leadership was shown across the spectrum to support the constitutional change that would grant more power to the federal parliament. It can be inferred that the relatively uncontentious nature of the changes—including Indigenous people in the census and increasing federal government power over them—assisted in obtaining this bi-partisan support. A more radical change, one that more directly called for the entrenchment of Indigenous rights, would not have enjoyed this popular support.

Perhaps because of the focus on 'citizenship rights' in the decades leading up to the referendum, and because the rhetoric of achieving equality for Aboriginal people that was used in 'yes' campaigns, it was inevitable that there would be a mistaken perception that the constitutional change allowed Aboriginal people to become citizens or attain the right to vote. In fact, the 1967 referendum achieved neither of those things.

Inclusion in the census

Marilyn Lake, in her biography of Faith Bandler, goes some way towards explaining why those who advocated so hard for the constitutional change thought it went further than it did (Lake 2002). The notion of including Indigenous people in the census was, for those who advocated a 'yes' vote, more than just a body-counting exercise. It was thought that the inclusion of Indigenous people in this way would create an imagined community and as such it would be a nation-building exercise, a symbolic coming together that would go some way to make up for their exclusion from the process in 1901. It was hoped that this inclusive nation-building would overcome an 'us' and 'them' mentality that made many Australians see themselves as being different—and superior—to Aboriginal and Torres Strait Islander people.

Sadly, this anticipated consequence did not eventuate. The inclusion of Indigenous people in the census did not create a psychological shift in the way that they were seen by other Australians and in the end, the constitutional amendment did only result in a body-counting exercise. Despite the best of intentions, inclusion in the census was not an effective way to initiate a belated act of inclusive nation-building.

The power to make laws in relation to Indigenous people

It was thought by those who advocated for a 'yes' vote that the changes to s 51(xxvi) (the 'races power') of the Constitution to allow the federal government to make laws for Indigenous people was going to herald in an era of non-discrimination for Indigenous people. There was an expectation that the granting of additional powers to the federal government to make laws for Indigenous people would see that power used benevolently and mean an end to the discriminatory way that they had been treated by state governments.

However, the faith in federal governments only using that additional power for the benefit of Indigenous people was to prove to be misplaced. One example of the way in which federal governments have failed to use the power benevolently was in the passing of the *Native Title Amendment Act 1998* (Cth), legislation that prevented the *Racial Discrimination Act 1975* (Cth) from applying to certain sections of the *Native Title Act 1993* (Cth). Similarly, the legislation that implemented the Northern Territory intervention in 2007 suspended the operation of the *Racial Discrimination Act 1975* (Cth) so that it did not protect Aboriginal people who were at risk of losing their land or being discriminated against in relation to their welfare payments.

Consideration as to whether the races power can be used only for the benefit of Aboriginal people, as the proponents of the 'yes' vote had intended, was given some residual attention by the High Court in *Kartinyeri v Commonwealth (the Hindmarsh Island Bridge case)* (1998) 195 CLR 337. This case arose when, in order to resolve a dispute between Aboriginal people and developers over the construction of a bridge, the federal government passed legislation that stopped heritage protection legislation from applying to the contested area. That is, the government simply repealed the protections contained in the heritage protection legislation so that the Aboriginal people who claimed the contested area was sacred to them had no ability to attempt to protect it from being destroyed by the construction of the bridge.

It was argued by the legal representatives of the Aboriginal people as part of the case that, when the 1967 referendum was passed, it was with the clear intention that the federal government should only use the power to protect Aboriginal people. Therefore, they reasoned, the federal government was not given the power to act in a way that would disadvantage Aboriginal people.

Only Justice Kirby argued that the races power did not extend to legislation that was detrimental to or discriminated against Aboriginal people. Justice Gaudron said that while there was much to recommend the idea that the races power could only be used beneficially, the proposition in those terms could not be sustained. Justices Gummow and Hayne held that the power could be used to withdraw a benefit previously granted to Aboriginal people and thus to impose a disadvantage.

When analysing the failure of the amendment of the races power to ensure benevolent and protective legislation as its proponents envisaged, one is reminded of the original intent of the framers to leave decisions about the rights to the legislature. They trusted that parliament would be the best arbiter of how to protect rights. Those who campaigned so hard to change the constitution in 1967 made the same assumption. In both cases we can see the evidence of the observation made by David Marr that Australians, despite their love of making fun of authority, place a lot of trust in it as well.

DISCUSSION QUESTION

• In what ways has the decision to trust governments to make the key decisions about rights protection impacted on Aboriginal people?

The unintended consequences of the 1967 referendum

While the 1967 referendum did not produce a new era of equality for Aboriginal people as its proponents had hoped, its most enduring, though perhaps unintended, consequence was the new relationship it created between federal and state and territory governments. By granting the power to the federal government to make laws in relation to Indigenous people, key areas of Indigenous policy such as housing, health, education and employment became responsibilities that were shared with state and territory government. And rather than being a relationship of cooperation, it is one that has seen governments of both levels try to blame the other for the failure of Indigenous policy and to shift the responsibility and the cost away from themselves. This 'cost-shifting' and 'blame game' goes some way towards explaining one of the structural barriers to achieving social justice for Aboriginal and Torres Strait Islander people in Australia today.

A recent example of this 'cost-shifting' was the response prompted by negative media coverage of findings of high incidence of sexual assault in some communities in the Northern Territory and gang violence in others in early 2006. Many other factors contribute to the cyclical poverty and despondency within some Aboriginal communities that create, over decades, the environment in which the social fabric unravels and violence, sexual abuse, substance abuse and other anti-social behaviour is rife. The then Federal Minister for Aboriginal Affairs, Mal Brough, blamed the situation on the Northern Territory Government saying that it had not put enough police into communities where violence was endemic. While he was correct that any community of several thousand people with no police force would have law and order issues, it was a simplistic response that focused the blame on a single factor—policing—that was the sole responsibility of the Northern Territory Government. In response, the then Northern Territory Chief Minister Claire Martin asserted that the problem was the federal government's failure to provide adequate housing and health and education services. She was also correct that the lack of adequate funding created underlying factors that led to dysfunction.

The consequence of this type of cost-shifting that has been a characteristic of the Indigenous affairs portfolio since 1967 is that governments of all levels continue to under-fund the most basic Aboriginal community needs like health services, educational facilities and adequate housing services.

The flaws in the assumption that the 1967 referendum was going to herald in a new era of non-discrimination for Indigenous people became apparent very quickly. Aboriginal and Torres Strait Islander people woke up the morning after the Australian public endorsed the referendum with no change to the poor conditions that they were living in and still facing the same discrimination in their everyday life in relation to their access to goods and services (Goodall 2006).

Aboriginal people quickly became disillusioned by the lack of changes that followed from the referendum and the continuing discrimination facing Indigenous people and the poor socio-economic conditions of their communities. They rejected the notion of assimilation but embraced the idea of equal rights and equal opportunities for Aboriginal people.

In this environment, a new generation of activists was created whose protests culminated in the establishment of the Aboriginal Tent Embassy on the lawns of what is now Old Parliament House and from here, the modern land rights movement was formed.

The legacy of the silences in the Constitution

The new momentum in the political activism of Aboriginal people who continued to campaign for changes to the legal system that would create equality for Aboriginal people and recognise and protect their rights highlighted how the 1967 referendum had failed to change the way in which the Constitution, as it was originally drafted, failed to recognise the unique status and place of Indigenous people in Australia and continued to leave the recognition and protection of their rights to the benevolence of government. This continuing reliance on the benevolence of government left many Aboriginal and Torres Strait Islanders vulnerable to the whims of government policy.

An instructive example of this vulnerability can be seen in the High Court case of *Kruger v Commonwealth* (1997) 190 CLR 1. This was the first case to be heard in the High Court that considered the legality of the formal government assimilation-based policy of removing Indigenous children from their families.

In *Kruger*, the plaintiffs had brought their case on the grounds of the violation of various rights by the effects of the Northern Territory Ordinance that allowed for the removal of Indigenous children from their families. The plaintiffs had claimed a series of human rights violations including the implied right to due process before the law, equality before the law, freedom of movement and the express right to freedom of religion contained in s 116 of the Constitution. They were unsuccessful on each count, a result that highlighted the general lack of rights protection in the Australian system of governance and the ways in which, through policies like child removal, there was a disproportionately high impact on Indigenous people as a result of those silences.

The *Kruger* case illustrated the way in which the issue of child removal—seen as a particularly Indigenous experience and a particularly Indigenous legal issue—can be expressed in language that explains what those harms are in terms of rights held by all other people: the right to due process before the law, equality before the law, freedom of movement and freedom of religion.

Kruger also highlights how few of the rights that many Australians would assume are protected by our legal system are in fact protected. It is a reminder of the silences about rights in our Constitution and that these silences were intended. It gives us a practical example of the rights violations that can be the legacy of that silence.

DISCUSSION QUESTION

- What do the combined results in the cases of *Kartinyeri* and *Kruger* say about the Australian legal system? What message do they send to Aboriginal people?

The continuing agenda for constitutional change

Given the way in which the Constitution has failed to provide recognition of Indigenous people and protection of their rights, it is not surprising that the agenda for Constitutional reform remains a key part of the agenda for legal reform that seeks to achieve social justice for Indigenous people.

In *Securing a Bountiful Place for Aborigine and Torres Strait Islanders in a Modern Free and Tolerant Australia* (Brennan 1994), the Constitutional Centenary Foundation raised the following possible options for constitutional change in relation to Indigenous people as it sought to raise discussion about the Constitution in the lead-up to the Centenary of Federation:

- seek to recognise Aboriginal and Torres Strait Islander peoples, their history and their culture in the Constitution;
- enshrine the principle of non-discrimination;
- grant the Commonwealth primacy over Indigenous affairs;
- negotiate an instrument of reconciliation;
- recognise Indigenous people's entitlement to self-determination;
- grant self-government to remote communities; and
- recognise the inherent sovereignty of Indigenous peoples.

The Aboriginal and Torres Strait Islander Commission (ATSIC) undertook extensive consultations with the Aboriginal community about what a social justice package should include. Consideration was given within these consultations about the possible options for constitutional reform. In its publication, *Recognition, Rights and Reform* (ATSIC 1995), it noted that while constitutional change is difficult to achieve, its consultations showed overwhelming support for the reform of the Constitution, especially in relation to the recognition of Indigenous peoples. It recommended regional, zone and state-based conventions to discuss options for constitutional reform and to the principle of negotiating constitutional reform. Further recommendations included:

- that prior to any constitutional referendum, the opinion of the Indigenous community be canvassed;
- that the Commonwealth government commit to a public awareness program to create an environment for change and understanding of Indigenous constitutional perspectives; and,
- that the Commonwealth government ensure that Aboriginal and Torres Strait Islanders are adequately represented in any national constitutional convention which is held as part of broader processes.

The Preamble to the Constitution

Despite the emphasis on including Aboriginal and Torres Strait Islander people in the process, the Howard Government added consideration of a Preamble to the referendum that was being put to the Australian people in 1999 as to whether or not they wanted to become a Republic.

The Preamble was subject to public debate but not the collaborative consultation process that *Recognition, Rights and Reforms* and its associated consultations had advocated. Its final wording read as follows:

With hope in God, the Commonwealth of Australia is constituted as a democracy with federal system of government to serve the common good.

We the Australian people commit ourselves to this Constitution:

proud that our national unity has been forged by Australians from many ancestries;

never forgetting the sacrifices of all who defended our country and our liberty in time of war;

upholding freedom, tolerance, individual dignity and the rule of law;

honouring Aborigines and Torres Strait Islanders, the nation's first people, for their deep kinship with their lands and for their ancient and continuing cultures which enrich the life of our country;

recognising the nation-building contribution of generations of immigrants;

mindful of our responsibility to protect our unique natural environment;

supportive of achievement as well as equality of opportunity for all;

and valuing independence as dearly as the national spirit which bind us together in both adversity and success.

However, the Preamble that Howard intended to take to the Australian people would be accompanied by a clause that would stipulate that, if passed, it would have no legal force and could not be used in constitutional or statutory interpretations. It was a Preamble without any legal weight. This lack of legal force is different to the usual role that a Preamble plays. John Quick and RR Garran describe this usual role as follows:

The proper function of a preamble is to explain and recite certain facts which are necessary to be explained and recited, before the enactments contained in an Act of Parliament can be understood. ... It usually states or professes to state, the general object and meaning of the Legislature in passing the measure. Hence it may be legitimately consulted for the purpose of solving an ambiguity or fixing the connotation of words which may possibly have more than one meaning, or determining the scope or limiting the effect of the Act, whenever the enacting parts are, in any of these respects, open to doubt (Quick and Garran 1976).

The Preamble was rejected at the referendum held on 6 November 1999. It also failed to capture the imagination of most Aboriginal and Torres Strait Islanders who felt that the words 'honouring Aborigines and Torres Strait Islanders, the nation's first people, for their deep kinship with their lands and for their ancient and continuing cultures which enrich the life of our country' did not go far enough in recognising their unique status as the traditional owners of the country. Ultimately, there was little support from the Indigenous community who felt little ownership for this form of words.

Howard sought to resurrect the issue of the Preamble and the role that it could play in recognising Indigenous people in the lead-up to the 2007 election. Again, this was without the consultation with Indigenous people that had been highlighted as being essential to ensure that the constitutional change gained a broad consensus and acceptance and thus acted as a form of nation-building, a process of bringing black and white people together. Howard had pledged that, should he be re-elected, he would take a draft preamble that recognised Aboriginal people as the first people to the Australian public within 100 days of election.

While Rudd gave in-principle support at the time of Howard's announcement, he later said he would not stick to the 100-day time frame that Howard had suggested. It remains to be seen whether Rudd will address this constitutional reform agenda during his time as prime minister.

DISCUSSION QUESTIONS

- What values should a Preamble to the Australian Constitution contain?
- What recognition should it give to Aboriginal and Torres Strait Islander people?

The Council for Aboriginal Reconciliation

The Council for Aboriginal Reconciliation, in their Final Report, indicated that constitutional reform was a key aspect of the pathway forward and is still part of the unfinished business of reconciliation. One of the key recommendations in the Council for Aboriginal Reconciliation's Final Report (Council for Aboriginal Reconciliation 2000c) was that:

> The Commonwealth Parliament prepare legislation for a referendum which seeks to:
> - recognise Aboriginal and Torres Strait Islander peoples as the first peoples of Australia in a new Preamble to the Constitution; and
> - remove s 25 of the Constitution and introduce a new section making it unlawful to adversely discriminate against any people on the grounds of race.

Section 25 of the Constitution is a relic from the intention of the framers who wanted Australian law to permit legislation that was discriminatory. It reads:

> For the purposes of the last section, if by the law of any State all persons of any race are disqualified from voting at elections for the more numerous House of the Parliament of the State, then, in reckoning the number of the people of the State or of the Commonwealth, persons of the race resident in that State shall not be counted.

The phrase 'if by the law of any State all persons of any races are disqualified from voting at elections' clearly has racist implications. It referred to the fact that at the time the Constitution was passed it was permissible, and conceivable, that states would pass legislation that prevented Australian citizens from voting because of their race.

Today, the clause, though unlikely to be implemented, offends the principle of racial equality. It is considered desirable to remove it so that our Constitution is free from overt expressions of racism.

A bill of rights for Australia

The *Kruger* case highlighted the way in which the absence of a rights framework in general has had a disproportionate impact on Aboriginal and Torres Strait Islander people who have been particularly vulnerable to having their human rights infringed. Australia is the only Commonwealth country that has not modernised its legal system to include human rights standards that became universally accepted with the emergence of the international human rights instruments and institutions after World War II. Even the United Kingdom, whose legal system we adopted, has updated its laws to include the protection of human rights.

There are two types of bills of rights: a constitutional model that entrenches rights and leaves interpretation to the judiciary; and a legislative model that is contained in a parliamentary Act and interpreted by the parliament (see Williams 2007 for discussion). The USA and South Africa have a constitutional bill of rights; New Zealand and the United Kingdom have a bill of rights in legislative form.

The advantage of the legislative model is that it is the parliament, not judges, who decides how to balance rights. It keeps the action of balancing rights in the public domain with judges having more of a monitoring role. This allows for the general population to be much more involved with decision-making either through lobbying or at election time. That is, it can energise the community to participate in debates about what kind of society it should have. It means that, when governments debate the balancing of rights or propose to override aspects of a bill of rights, a discussion takes place in the public realm which allows citizens to become actively involved. The effect of this can be seen in Canada where the experience of a legislative bill of rights, that preceded the constitutional enshrinement of certain rights, led to a more heightened awareness among Canadians that they held certain rights against their government.

The weakness with it, and the strength of the Constitutional model, is that because the bill of rights is an Act of Parliament, it can be overridden if the legislature wants to. If rights are entrenched in the Constitution, politicians cannot override them. Only a constitutional model can stop a government from withdrawing the protection of human rights whenever it wants to.

It is easy to understand why, in the absence of rights protections that have left Indigenous people so vulnerable, there is interest in improving that rights protection through a bill of rights, but there are still conflicting views about whether or not we need one in the Australian legal system. One of the key arguments against a bill of rights is that under our legal system, rights are already well protected through both the common law and legislation such as the anti-discrimination and sex discrimination Acts. From an Indigenous point of view, this argument overlooks the many examples where relying on government benevolence has not been enough. The removal of children is one and heritage protection is another. When Doreen Kartinyeri sought to enforce heritage protection laws that were being repealed to ensure that the Hindmarsh Island Bridge could be built over her traditional and sacred land, the court told her that, if the federal parliament can grant heritage protection, it is free to take it away if and when it so chooses. From the continual extinguishment of native title rights to the abolition of a national representative structure, the experience of Aboriginal people often highlights how dependent we are on the benevolence of governments that too often do not have the best interests of Aboriginal people at heart.

There is an argument that says that it is more appropriate for the elected arm rather than the non-elected arm of government to make decisions about rights. This is part of the reason why many people prefer the legislative bill of rights model. However, the argument that judges are not capable of making decisions about human rights is a curious one. Every day the judiciary is involved with balancing rights—landlord and tenant, shareholder and director, debtor and creditor, custodial and non-custodial parent—and there is no question of their capacity to make important decisions between those competing interests, so it is curious as to why it is perceived that they would lack the capacity to do so in other contexts.

A further argument against a bill of rights would be that it is too inflexible and that rights that might be relevant now may not be so in the future. The right to bear arms, entrenched into the American Constitution, is perhaps the best example of that phenomenon. This again is an argument that really targets a constitutional rather than legislative bill of rights since the latter does allow for rights to be included or excluded as society and its values evolve.

The claim that a bill of rights should be rejected because it is creates 'a lawyer's picnic' seems to value dislike of the legal profession above the rights of people and ignores the unfettering of the power of politicians. The experience in the ACT with its *Human Rights Act 2004* (the ACT and Victoria are the only jurisdictions that have passed legislative bills of rights in Australia) also shows how shallow these claims of increased litigation are. Under that legislative bill of rights, there have been few cases where the rights under the Act have been referred to and the overwhelming impact has not been on the hip pocket of lawyers but on bureaucrats who are now required to think about the rights of the citizens of the ACT when they implement policies and programs. That is, the greatest impact has been to make government more accountable to the people in the way it does business.

Finally, in relation to specific groups such as Indigenous people, there is an argument that, in other jurisdictions that have had a bill of rights, such as the USA, human rights have not been protected. It is also posited that Stalin's Russia and Hitler's Germany supposedly had rights protections in this form. This is an argument that is based on two erroneous assumptions. The first erroneous assumption is that a bill of rights will cure any rights violation. Most advocates of a bill of rights would only go so far as to say that it offers an additional buffer to or fettering of a government's powers over its citizens. The second erroneous assumption is that laws act independently of the society by which they are created. They do not, though they can sometimes, lead to normative change within that community. The impact of anti-discrimination legislation is perhaps a good example of that.

Bills of rights do not have to specifically mention the needs and experiences of minorities to offer them special protection. All rights have a special resonance for Aboriginal and Torres Strait Islander people. The right to freedom from forced work, the right to take part in public life, rights to education and work and rights to a fair trial are fundamental human rights that have not been protected and the failure to do so has impacted on Indigenous people the most. For the members of the Stolen Generations who could not get redress from the High Court for the breaches of their human rights in the *Kruger* case, the protection of freedom of movement, freedom of religion, equality before the law and the protection of the family will have particular resonance and significance.

In fixing the silences of the Constitution left by the framers, it would also be open for Australia to adopt a legislative bill of rights that will provide the necessary flexibility and keep most of the debates about rights within the public realm while at the same time choosing a few key principles and rights to enshrine into the Constitution for greater protection. For example, freedom from racial discrimination, the right to due process before the law or the right to equality before the law may be the kinds of rights that could be singled out for protection in the Constitution if we were to change the Constitution so that it was no longer predicated on the assumption that the Australian legal system should tolerate racially discriminatory laws.

DISCUSSION QUESTIONS

- What are the arguments for and against a bill of rights?
- What are the differences between a statutory bill of rights and a constitutional bill of rights?
- Should Australia have a bill of rights at the national level?

Unfinished constitutional business

The three key areas that continually arise as underlying reasons to look at constitutional reform as a way of achieving social justice for Aboriginal and Torres Strait Islander people are:

- the appropriateness of acknowledging the unique place and role of Aboriginal and Torres Strait Islander people in Australia in our founding document;
- the need to modernised or update the Constitution so that it provides stronger protection of human rights, fixing the silences that were deliberately left in the Constitution by the original drafters; and
- providing an opportunity, by working in an inclusive way, to achieve constitutional change and engage in a nation-building process that was not undertaken when the Constitution was first drafted.

The constitutional reform agenda

The key mechanisms most often put forward as ways of achieving the goals of improved rights protection for Aboriginal and Torres Strait Islander people are:

- **A new Preamble to the Constitution that recognises the unique place of Aboriginal and Torres Strait Islanders:** A Preamble is important because it sets the tone for the rest of the document. In our Constitution, a new Preamble will offer an opportunity to articulate our shared goals, principles and ideals as a nation. If recognition of prior sovereignty and prior ownership were contained in a constitutional Preamble, courts may be able to read the Constitution as clearly promoting Indigenous rights protection.
- **A bill of rights:** As the *Kruger case* showed, very few rights are protected by our Constitution. Those that appear in the text have been interpreted in a minimal manner. Although members of the High Court have implied some rights, this is a precarious approach to rights protection. A bill of rights that granted rights and freedoms to everyone would be a non-contentious way in which to ensure some Indigenous rights protection. Public discussion needs to be focused on whether we should have a constitutional or a legislative bill of rights and, indeed, a legislative bill of rights could be viewed as an interim step towards a constitutionally entrenched bill of rights.

CASE STUDY

- **The inclusion of a non-discrimination clause in the body of the Constitution:** Such a clause could enshrine the notion of non-discrimination in the Constitution. Such a clause must also adhere to the principle that affirmative action mechanisms aid in the achievement of non-discrimination, consistent with international human rights norms.
- **Specific constitutional protection:** An amendment could be made to include a specific provision about Indigenous rights. In Canada, a comparable jurisdiction with a comparable history and comparable relationship with its Indigenous communities, the *Constitutional Act 1982* added the following provision to the Constitution:

  > Section 35(1): the existing aboriginal and treaty rights of the aboriginal peoples of Canada are hereby recognized and affirmed.

- **Repeal of s 25 that permits discriminatory laws in relation to voting:** The reminders in the Constitution that the original document was drafted by people who believed in theories of white supremacy and endorsed racially discriminatory practices should be removed.

Some of these steps to improve the Australian rights framework for Indigenous people—a constitutional Preamble, a bill of rights—would have benefits for all Australians. This reinforces the point that emerges from the litigation in the *Kruger* case, namely, that many of the rights of Indigenous people that are infringed are not 'special rights' but rights held by all people. Furthermore, measures that protect the rights of all Australians will have particular relevance and utility for Indigenous people.

The issue of the kind of Constitution and system of governance we have is not just a legal one. Just as the framers of the Constitution were unable to keep the document they drafted devoid of the values and prejudices that they had, our modern Constitution and the legal system it creates will inevitably be a reflection of our values as a country and for this reason, the question of constitutional reform is also a philosophical one.

It is easy to look back critically at the drafters of the Constitution and decry their values and beliefs but the more important question to be asked is how the Constitution protects the values that we would seek in Australian society today. This necessarily involves us asking what kind of Australia do we want to live in. Do we want a society that is guarded, fearful, backward looking, insular and intolerant? Or do we want a society that is forward looking, inclusive and generous? Do we want to live in a community where difference is looked upon suspiciously or one in which it is celebrated? Do we want a system of laws that are considered fair because they look neutral on their face or do we want a legal system that is considered equitable because it has no hidden prejudices and biased outcomes?

DISCUSSION QUESTIONS

- What would a reconciled Australia look like?
- What role can the options for constitutional change that have been raised play in achieving that?

CHAPTER 13

Indigenous Governance: Amending the Mainstream

The history of the colonisation of Indigenous Australia is a story of disempowerment. Aboriginal and Torres Strait Islander people have been subjected to the forced removal from their lands, the forced removal of their children, and regulations that dictated where they could live, where they could work and whether they could marry or not. It is little surprise that, given this history of having had rules made for them, being able to make decisions for themselves is a key aspiration of Indigenous people and their communities. This is especially so since the periods where they had the least say in important aspects of their lives coincided with the imposition of flawed policy approaches such as assimilation.

Indigenous Australians identify as sovereign peoples who never ceded their land and continue to feel that they are a distinct peoples with a distinct identity and a distinct history (Behrendt 2003a: 95). This sense of distinct political identity finds validation and support in the international human rights regime that recognises the right to self-determination of peoples, an internationally recognised right of all peoples to freely determine their political status and pursue their economic, social and cultural development, but in practice is usually discussed in terms of self-governance or governance (see Article 1, International Covenant on Civil and Political Rights and International Covenant on Economic, Cultural and Social Rights and Article 3 of the Draft Declaration on the Rights of Indigenous Peoples). This means a key role in the shaping of policy, greater autonomy and control in the provision of appropriate services in the areas of health, housing and education, and recognition of Aboriginal law, jurisdiction and self-government.

The combination of the belief that sovereignty was never ceded, the belief that Indigenous people have the right to self-determination and a history of disempowerment explain why the issue of governance has been a key aspiration of Indigenous people and a key part of the social justice and political agenda.

Aboriginal and Torres Strait Islander people have long advocated for greater participation in the decision-making institutions of the state and for more autonomy in the form of devolved authority across a wide range of jurisdictions, including land ownership and management, health, welfare, economic development, law and education (Smith 2002: 6). This is an aspiration for greater control over decision-making that affects peoples' day-to-day lives.

Charles Perkins observed that the paternalism of the past in decision-making about Indigenous people needed to be broken:

> From an Aboriginal viewpoint, I believe that our mistake over the years has been to look towards the white people, in positions of influence, to solve our problems. This has been our fundamental error. Recent history tells us that we should have known for the past 200 years. It is amazing to me, that we, the Aboriginal people, have not yet absorbed that white people in responsible positions are no better than us (in fact they are worse, given their educational background), at managing or solving difficult individual or community problems) (Perkins 1994).

DISCUSSION QUESTION

- Why is the desire to have control over the decisions that affect their lives a central part of the aspirations of Aboriginal and Torres Strait Islander people?

The attempt to give governance an institutional form

The wish for greater autonomy and independence is a universal desire among Indigenous communities expressed by those living in geographically integrated urban communities, those living in rural areas and those living in discrete remote communities. This aspiration for increased autonomy and control over policy and service delivery needs to find some kind of institutional form. Sometimes, these are institutions that are formed by Indigenous people and in other instances they are institutions that are designed by the government to facilitate a way to include Indigenous people in decision-making around policy and service delivery.

Before the 1967 referendum, which gave powers to the federal government to make laws for Aboriginal and Torres Strait Islander people, the main responsibility for policy-making with respect to Indigenous people's welfare was with the states. The Commonwealth's only involvement with Indigenous affairs was in relation to the Indigenous populations that lived in the Northern Territory and the ACT and the agency with this responsibility was the Department of the Interior. The key ideology that drove the government approach was the philosophy of assimilating Indigenous people into non-Indigenous society, and participation by Aboriginal and Torres Strait Islander people into the policies and laws that governed their life was extremely limited, consisting only of informal advice which governments could easily choose to ignore. In effect, Indigenous affairs prior to 1967 were entirely 'mainstreamed'.

After the 1967 referendum, the Commonwealth began to take a limited role in Indigenous affairs policy-making and service delivery with the states maintaining the principal policy-making role. The Coalition Government established the Council for Aboriginal Affairs (CAA), which was comprised of three non-Indigenous men appointed by the government and also set up a small Office of Aboriginal Affairs (OAA), initially within the Prime Minister's Department. Its role was to implement policy, liaise between the Commonwealth and the states, and administer legislation within the Indigenous affairs portfolio. Indigenous people had no formal role within the structures to shape or influence the advice given to government.

When the Whitlam Government came to power in December 1972, the Commonwealth government began to play a more significant role in policy-making and service delivery in Indigenous affairs. Whitlam established the Department of Aboriginal Affairs (DAA) in 1973. It took over the functions of both the CAA and the OAA. Its role was to provide advice to the government on Indigenous affairs policy as well as to implement and administer Indigenous affairs policy. It was the central Commonwealth Indigenous affairs agency until the Aboriginal and Torres Strait Islander Commission (ATSIC) commenced operations in March 1990.

In the same year that DAA was established, the first national body elected by Indigenous people themselves was also established. The National Aboriginal Consultative Committee (NACC) was an advisory body and its main role was to advise the Commonwealth on Indigenous affairs policy. Its relationships with the Whitlam Government and the DAA were strained from the beginning as the NACC demanded a more influential role, including control over the Indigenous affairs budget. There was also criticism of the NACC from Indigenous people that the electorates were too large and that the election process was not fair (Pratt and Bennett 2004).

When the Fraser Government came to power in 1975, it commissioned a review of the NACC which concluded that it had not been an effective mechanism for providing advice or consulting with Indigenous people (Department of Aboriginal Affairs 1976). It was disbanded in 1977 and replaced with the National Aboriginal Conference (NAC).

The NAC was also an elected body and it was to have the role of giving advice to the federal minister and being a channel of communication between Indigenous communities and the Commonwealth government (Encyclopedia of Aboriginal Australia CD-Rom 1994). Like the NACC, its relationship with the federal government was strained. And, also like the NACC, criticism from Indigenous communities focused on the quality of the representation by NAC members (Bennett 1989). A review of the body was commissioned under the Hawke Government and, at the same time, an audit of its operations revealed problems with the NAC's financial management. As a result, the NAC was abolished in April 1985.

In 1980, the Aboriginal Development Commission (ADC) was established. It was a statutory authority run by a board of 10 Indigenous commissioners appointed by the government. It had a limited role in service delivery up until the time that ATSIC came into being in 1990.

At about the same time, the Aboriginal Provisional Government (APG) was created. It was a political organisation that reflected a view that true representation of Aboriginal and Torres Strait Islander people had to be done through institutions that were independent of the federal government. Chairman Bob Weatherall (1990) described the APG as representing 'the reality that only we, as Aboriginal people, can forge a proper place for ourselves and those generations of Aborigines to come'. While it ran out of political momentum as ATSIC began to dominate the landscape of Indigenous affairs, it represented the fact that Aboriginal and Torres Strait Islander people are constantly exploring alternative institutional models to create a mechanism for greater autonomy.

DISCUSSION QUESTION

- What are the differences between bodies like the National Aboriginal Conference and a body like the Aboriginal Provisional Government in terms of how they advocate on behalf of Aboriginal people?

The establishment of ATSIC

Two years after the NAC had been disbanded, the Hawke Government announced that it would establish ATSIC, a body that would combine both representative and executive roles, through an organisation of regional councils and a national board elected by Indigenous people, which would assume the program administration roles of both the DAA and the ADC.

Following an extensive consultation process on its ATSIC proposal, the ATSIC legislation was originally introduced into parliament in August 1988. The original Bill was withdrawn and revised legislation—featuring considerably stronger public accountability mechanisms—brought into parliament in May 1989.

The Howard-led Opposition was vehemently opposed to the concept of ATSIC, because of an objection to any body that Howard perceived gave Indigenous people 'separate' status. Howard expressed his opposition to ATSIC:

> I take the opportunity of saying again that if the Government wants to divide Australian against Australian, if it wants to create a black nation within the Australian nation, it should go ahead with its Aboriginal and Torres Strait Islander Commission (ATSIC) legislation … The ATSIC legislation strikes at the heart of the unity of the Australian people. In the name of righting the wrongs done against Aboriginal people, the legislation adopts the misguided notion of believing that if one creates a parliament within the Australian community for Aboriginal people, one will solve and meet all of those problems (Howard 1989).

Over 90 amendments were made to the legislation, making it the second-most amended piece of legislation to have passed through parliament since Federation (the native title legislation being the most amended). The *Aboriginal and Torres Strait Islander Commission Act 1989* was eventually passed by parliament in early November 1989. ATSIC began operating in March 1990.

The legislative objectives of ATSIC combining both representative and executive roles, set out in the *ATSIC Act*, were:

- to ensure maximum participation of Aboriginal and Torres Strait Islander people in government policy formulation and implementation;
- to promote Indigenous self-management and self-sufficiency;
- to further Indigenous economic, social and cultural development; and
- to ensure coordination of Commonwealth, state, territory and local government policy affecting Indigenous people.

The functions given to ATSIC in the Act set out a range of legislative mandates to meet these objectives, namely to:

- formulate and implement programs;
- monitor the effectiveness of programs conducted by all bodies and agencies;
- develop policy proposals, to assist, advise and cooperate with all and sundry;
- advise the minister on all matters;
- provide advice to the minister when requested;

- protect cultural material and information; and
- collect and publish statistical material (if the Australian Bureau of Statistics approved).

The objects and function, when read together, established a framework of responsibilities that conferred on ATSIC the primary role of advising the federal government on any matters relating to Aboriginal and Torres Strait Islander peoples and for the oversight of all government effort in policy development and the provision of services to Aboriginal and Torres Strait Islander peoples. ATSIC was asked to:

- maximise the participation of Aboriginal and Torres Strait Islander peoples in the formulation and implementation of programs; and
- provide an effective voice within the government.

This legislative mandate appeared to give genuine power to Aboriginal and Torres Strait Islander people over the management of, and decision-making in, Indigenous affairs.

However, the combination of these roles had an inherent source of tension. ATSIC was to be accountable to the federal government in its service delivery and monitoring role and at the same time its elected arm was to be accountable to its Indigenous constituency.

ATSIC's original structure consisted of two parts: a representative arm, and an administrative arm. The representative structure was comprised of 35 elected ATSIC Regional Councils. They were clustered into 16 zones, each of which elected a full-time Commissioner to sit on the ATSIC Board. Another Commissioner was elected from the Torres Strait, which comprised its own zone. Up until 1999, the federal government appointed the Chair of ATSIC. After that, the Commissioners elected the Chair.

ATSIC's administrative arm consisted of several hundred Commonwealth public servants, engaged by ATSIC under the *Public Service Act 1999* (Cth), and headed by a Chief Executive Officer (CEO) appointed by the minister. The role of the administrative arm was to support ATSIC's elected representatives and administer the various programs for which ATSIC had responsibility. In April 2003, the then Minister for Indigenous Affairs, Philip Ruddock, announced the establishment of a new agency, Aboriginal and Torres Strait Islander Services (ATSIS), to administer ATSIC's programs and make decisions about grants and other funding to Indigenous organisations from 1 July 2003. While Ruddock emphasised at the time that the establishment of ATSIS did not represent a move towards 'mainstreaming' ATSIC's programs, it effectively removed direct control of ATSIC's budget and its programs away from ATSIC's elected representatives.

A large amount (up to 85 per cent) ATSIC's budget was quarantined for its main programs—the Community Development Employment Project (CDEP) scheme and the Community Housing and Infrastructure Program (CHIP). The remaining money was spent on a range of programs including those geared towards the preservation and promotion of Indigenous culture and heritage, and the advancement of Indigenous rights and equity.

ATSIC never had responsibility for Indigenous education and for most of its life had no fiscal responsibility for Indigenous health. In other words, a large part of the responsibility for policy development and service delivery remained with federal and state governments. But this did not stop most of the blame for poor socio-economic statistics and failure of policy and program falling at ATSIC's feet, even for matters for which it had no responsibility. However, because it was never clearly able to articulate its successes, it gave ammunition to its critics who claimed that it was a failed experiment.

ATSIC also, like all previous representative bodies, attracted criticism from Aboriginal people themselves who complained that the process for the selection of the representatives was flawed. This was not helped by the media attention given to allegations of impropriety by members of the ATSIC Board that drew attention away from the work that ATSIC was actually doing.

DISCUSSION QUESTIONS

- Why do Aboriginal and Torres Strait Islander people feel a need to have a national representative voice?
- Is the establishment of a national representative body divisive?

The demise of ATSIC

In November 2002, the federal government announced a review that would 'examine and make recommendations to government on how Aboriginal and Torres Strait Islander people can in the future be best represented in the process of the development of Commonwealth policies and programmes to assist them. In doing so the reassessment will consider the current roles and functions of ATSIC' (Ruddock 2002).

The review delivered its report, *In the Hands of the Region—A New ATSIC* (Hannaford et al 2003), to the federal government. It recommended against abolishing ATSIC but recommended some fundamental structural changes. These included:

- an overhaul of ATSIC's representative structure, in order to overcome the sense of detachment between local Indigenous communities and the national board;

- •   a strengthening of, and increased emphasis on, regional planning processes; and
- •   a permanent delineation of the roles of ATSIC's elected representatives and its administrative arm, but achieved by amending the *Aboriginal and Torres Strait Islander Commission Act 1989* rather than by the existence of a separate agency such as ATSIS.

Despite the recommendation that the body be reformed, the Prime Minister, Mr Howard, and the Minister for Indigenous Affairs, Senator Amanda Vanstone, announced the government's intention to abolish ATSIC on 15 April 2004. This followed the Australian Labor Party's announcement a few weeks earlier that it would do likewise if elected to government later that year. The national body was to be abolished immediately legislation could be passed and with the regional councils being abolished in the following year.

> We believe very strongly that the experiment in separate representation, elected representation, for indigenous people has been a failure. We will not replace ATSIC with an alternative body (Hannaford et al 2003).

Howard and Vanstone also announced that the government would appoint a group of Indigenous people to advise it.

The 'bold experiment' had failed but language of the announcement of ATSIC's abolition was reminiscent of Howard's original ideological objection to a representative body. Many observers believed it was inevitable that Howard would eventually move to abolish a body whose creation he had so opposed. Opposition Leader Mark Latham's pre-election posturing made it easier for the trigger to be pulled.

The tragedy was that ATSIC, for all its flaws, was in many ways quite innovative. It sought to accommodate an elected body into a federal government agency and this was always going to be difficult. Less complicated institutional structures have taken more than 12 years to find their feet. Other strengths included its ability to give a national Indigenous perspective of a range of key issues from native title to human rights, positions that often challenged those of the government. It also had an interface with the federal bureaucracy that previous elected bodies did not have and it had a large budget that allowed it to exert more influence than a body that simply had an advisory role. Its regional representative structure and the planning processes the representatives engaged in were able to identify the specific needs of diverse Aboriginal and Torres Strait Islander communities in consultation with the people who lived there.

There were also glaring weaknesses within the structure. There was no articulation of the relationship between the Board and the Regional Councils and little clarity about the relationships between the CEO and the minister, and the CEO of ATSIC and the Chair of ATSIC. There was a failure to provide ATSIC with an interface with state governments, which have responsibility for so much of the Indigenous portfolio. ATSIC spent most of its time administering its CDEP and CHIP programs at the expense of developing policy in other areas. And some of the key functions of the body, such as monitoring the effectiveness of programs for Aboriginal persons and Torres Strait Islanders, had been under-utilised.

But perhaps the biggest weakness ATSIC had was the perception that the public held of it. ATSIC was too often portrayed as being responsible for every Indigenous issue. It is not widely appreciated that it did not have fiscal responsibility for the areas of health and education and was only a supplementary funding provider on issues such as domestic violence, languages, heritage protection and housing. In addition to this, there was also a failure to appreciate that a large percentage of the ATSIC budget was quarantined for programs such as CDEP and CHIP. These misconceptions directed attention away from government departments (federal and state and territory) with responsibility for Indigenous policy and service delivery.

The ability to treat ATSIC as a source of inadequate policy and ineffective service delivery stemmed from media coverage of serious criminal allegations against senior ATSIC board members. There was no doubt that the continued presence of board members who were subject to continuing allegations and questioning undermined the credibility of the institution and made it vulnerable to attack. This was exacerbated by the misinformation about ATSIC and its responsibilities that were prevalent in comments within the media and by politicians. These attacks not only accused ATSIC of ineptitude in relation to policy-making and program delivery, but also criticised its governance processes.

Not only was this misinformation unfair to ATSIC, which was not in some cases responsible for the policy areas it was accused of failing in, it deflected criticism from the governments and agencies that were responsible for those shortcomings.

The post-ATSIC environment

New government arrangements

With the abolition of ATSIC, the responsibility for programs formerly managed by ATSIC and ATSIS were transferred to mainstream Commonwealth departments and agencies from July 2004. The Office of Indigenous Policy Coordination (OIPC) was created within the Department of Immigration and Multicultural and Indigenous Affairs to coordinate services and programs to take over the responsibilities of ATSIS. A network of 22 Indigenous Coordination Centres (ICCs), coordinated by the Office of Indigenous Policy Coordination and staffed by mainstream government agencies, replaced existing ATSIC–ATSIS regional offices. The fundamental impact of this was to mainstream Indigenous policy-making and service delivery.

Ironically, the decision to abolish the national and regional representative bodies coincided with a new approach to Indigenous affairs by the government that sought to negotiate more with Indigenous communities. At the same time as it was developing policies such as Shared Responsibility Agreements and Regional Agreements, it had abolished the existing interface through which governments could consult with Indigenous people and it had nothing to replace it with.

It was argued that the strength of the new administrative arrangements was their attempt to seek to better coordinate agencies who had responsibility for service provision and policy development for Indigenous peoples and their communities.

However, there are several major problems with the new administrative arrangements that were immediately identified (Pratt and Bennett 2004):

- The changes to the administration of Indigenous affairs at the national level have been done swiftly, without vision, planning or consultation.
- The development of the new regime has been ad hoc, reactionary, and without solid evidentiary foundation.
- There is no evidence that the assumptions underpinning the new arrangements are workable.
- The removal of Regional Councils has taken away a key level of representative Indigenous governance.
- The new arrangements focus more on service delivery than policy development.
- There was little consultation with Indigenous peoples about the new arrangements.
- The transfer of staff from ATSIS to other agencies has resulted in a loss of corporate knowledge that will not be replaced. The public service lost most of its senior Indigenous bureaucrats as part of the transfer. The five senior members of staff at OIPC are non-Indigenous.

The changes to the administrative arrangements that sought to abolish ATSIC were driven by two ideologies:

- the elimination of Indigenous representation from effective participation in government policy and program delivery; and
- the transfer of Indigenous specific programs to mainstream agencies.

The National Indigenous Council

The government also established the National Indigenous Council to replace the ATSIC Board of Commissioners, and to provide advice on Indigenous affairs matters to it. The Council consists of 14 appointed members. While the federal government has claimed that this new body is not designed to replace ATSIC, it was to become the primary Indigenous advisory body to the federal government.

Its creation raises several issues about the principles of representation. Appointed bodies are nothing new in the Indigenous arenas; most Indigenous bodies have them, including the Indigenous Land Corporation (ILC), Indigenous Business Australia (IBA) and Aboriginal Hostels.

The replacement of elected representatives at the national level by a group of hand-picked appointees has fundamentally changed the nature of the advice given. They are not in positions where they have the legitimacy of being able to put forward views on behalf of Indigenous peoples and are not accountable back to them in the way that elected representatives are.

Appointed representatives have no responsibility to represent broader Indigenous interests. They are appointed as individuals and act in that capacity. Unlike elected representatives, appointees acting in an individual capacity are not accountable to the community whose interests their decisions will affect.

And the new body is advisory only. It has no capacity to ensure that its advice is followed. In particular, the appointed body has no leverage with the bureaucracy.

The desire for regional representation

Aboriginal and Torres Strait Islander communities are diverse in culture and circumstance and therefore their needs are very different. Communities that are enclaves within urban areas, finding themselves a sub-group of a larger, non-Indigenous political unit, have different needs and strategies to those of Indigenous communities living in remote and distinct geographical areas where they may already be engaged in initiatives that can be categorised as decentralised self-governing actions (Behrendt 2003a: 87).

Some Indigenous communities in Australia are formed around connections to traditional lands, others to areas where governments forcibly moved Indigenous families; some communities have emerged alongside regional or urban centres, others to sites of political or cultural significance.

It is not surprising then that a key level of governance for Aboriginal and Torres Strait Islanders develops at a local level and, as represented in the ATSIC structure, the regional level. Smaller units allow more effective representation of an interest or perspective. This is especially so for geographically remote communities which may take control of issues such as policing matters and the development of local councils with ordinance-making powers.

Community-based programs were recommended by the Royal Commission into Aboriginal Deaths in Custody. This led to the establishment of several community-based programs that allowed the community to deal with problems such as intoxicated persons who would have been arrested and placed in police holding cells but were allowed to stay in safe houses where they were looked after by members of the community. Similar programs have been designed to allow Aboriginal communities to deal with problems of juvenile crime, such as vandalism.

The Pitjantjantjara have been able to establish an area of land claimed back through legislative provisions on which they have introduced their own rules at a local government level. The area now held by the community covers a large area of land in South Australia, towards the border of the Northern Territory. Courts have affirmed the right of the Pitjantjantjara to legislate at this level.[1]

Many Indigenous people are of the view that their needs and aspirations may be most effectively negotiated and managed on a regional level (Behrendt, McCausland et al 2007). Indigenous communities have been exploring possible options for developing institutions that would allow for representation and governance at the regional area, often relying on entities created under various legislative instruments, such as the native title representative bodies and prescribed bodies corporate that could be created under the *Native Title Act 1993* (Cth), to deliver a mechanism through which aspirations for greater autonomy could be pursued. In particular, much thought is often given to ways in which the interests and perspectives of traditional owners can be represented alongside those of resident Indigenous populations.

For example, in north-west New South Wales, the Murdi Paaki Regional Assembly, a group established by a network of community working parties, has expressed the desire to develop a regional governance capacity to improve access to resources and opportunities through the region they represent in western New South Wales (Murdi Paaki Regional Council 2002: 2).

The Murdi Paaki Regional Assembly proposes that a regional authority would represent and advocate for the interests of Aboriginal and Torres Strait Islander communities and people in the region; provide regional coordination to ensure the equitable distribution of funding to communities; negotiate funding arrangements and agreements with government agencies to meet the needs of communities; enter into service contracts with Aboriginal organisations; and formulate a regional development plan (Murdi Paaki Regional Council 2002: 12–13).

The Central Land Council (CLC) in the Northern Territory has also proposed a 'new and innovative model' of regional governance for Aboriginal communities in Central Australia that would deal directly with the federal government for funding, and in turn, deal directly with individual communities (Central Land Council 2004: 67). The CLC has outlined certain key principles to guide the development of an Aboriginal regional governance structure, including that it must be 'based in, or compatible with, Aboriginal law'; have control over areas such as 'funding allocations, economic development, service delivery'; have the 'power to enter into agreements with all tiers

---

1   *Gerhardy v Brown* (1985) 159 CLR 70.

of government, and third parties'; have the capacity for 'monitoring, control and coordination of service delivery'; and ideally, 'be provided for by a Commonwealth statutory regime' (Central Land Council 2004: 67).

The Northern Territory *Building Effective Governance Conference* recommended that Regional Authority structures and processes should be driven by Indigenous people; recognise and build upon customary law and values; build upon existing community strengths and capacities; and build upon the foundations of both Indigenous culture and contemporary best practice in order to achieve the most legitimate and effective forms of Indigenous governance (Final Recommendations 2003). Peter Yu has argued that regional governance is central to Indigenous participation in the nation's society and economy:

> Regional empowerment is ... the key ingredient to a reconciled Australia. When I raise
> the concept of regional governance I am not advocating some form of separatism, but
> quite the opposite. It is a mechanism that will empower Aboriginal people to negotiate
> our inclusion and participation in the society and economies we share with our non-
> Indigenous neighbours (Yu 2001: 251).

The Aboriginal and Torres Strait Islander Social Justice Commissioner's *Social Justice Report 2000* identified the development of governance structures and regional autonomy as having the potential to bring together the goals of promoting recognition of Indigenous rights and the related goal of overcoming disadvantage and achieving economic independence (Aboriginal and Torres Strait Islander Social Justice Commissioner 2001).

A regional approach to governance for Aboriginal and Torres Strait Islander communities has been associated with effective policy measures such as achieving a critical mass of competent professional personnel; economies of scale in costs, infrastructure and service delivery; the facilitation of cost-sharing and more streamlined financial management systems; transference of best practice; and avoidance of duplication of services and structures.

However, alongside those benefits are some key challenges: building governing capacity and internal accountability; finding experienced professional staff; overcoming disruptive factionalism; promoting competent leadership; and achieving productive relationships with traditional owners and governments.

Much of the difficulty associated with past policies affecting Indigenous people and their rights has been the result of onerous legislation imposed from above involving protracted, expensive litigation with little outcome for Indigenous communities, or top-down approaches that do not take into account the priorities and aspirations of those communities. Support of regional governance structures in Aboriginal and Torres Strait Islander communities can assist in overcoming that 'one-size-fits-all' approach to policy and program delivery.

Self-governance and corporate governance

Increasingly, Aboriginal and Torres Strait Islanders are required to form themselves into incorporated entities in order to access funding and undertake certain activities. The key benefit of incorporation is that it creates a legal personality for a community through which it can enter legal arrangements with others. The corporate structure created takes on the benefits and liabilities of any legal agreements protecting the individuals involved. The corporate structure also protects individuals in the community from personal liability.

The downside of the corporate structure is that it is administratively complex, and takes a particular, culturally specific form. Indigenous groups form corporations for a variety of reasons, including the establishment of land councils, business entities and service provision organisations. Often incorporation is a requirement to gain the benefits of other government schemes such as under the *Native Title Act 1993*.

In 1974, the Woodward Aboriginal Land Rights Commission proposed the idea that Indigenous specific legislation be enacted for Indigenous organisations. Woodward argued for a regime based on the following principles:

(i)   the legislation must be simple, so that those who are working under it can readily understand it;

(ii)   it must be flexible, so as to cover as wide a range of situations and requirements as possible;

(iii) it should, so far as possible, make provision for Aboriginal methods of decision-making by achieving consensus rather than by majority vote;

(iv)   it must contain simple provisions for control of the situation if things go wrong within an organisation through corruption, inefficiency, outside influences or for other reasons, and

(v)   it should be so framed as to avoid taxation of any income which has to be devoted to community purposes (Australian Institute of Aboriginal and Torres Strait Islander Studies 1996: 2).

The result was the *Aboriginal Councils and Associations Act 1976* (Cth) (the ACA Act) and many Aboriginal organisations choose to incorporate under it. The Act was designed to create a simpler and more flexible process for the incorporation of Aboriginal corporations than existed under existing state-based corporations law and to provide corporate structures that were more suited to the needs of Aboriginal communities.

The ACA Act has three substantive sections. Chapter II creates the position of Registrar of Aboriginal Corporations whose functions include, among other things, maintaining public registers of Aboriginal councils and of incorporated

Aboriginal associations; advising Indigenous communities on the procedures for the constitution of councils and the incorporation of associations under the Act, and arbitrating disputes.

Chapter III provides a framework for the creation of Aboriginal councils, and council areas. It provides for the establishment of a much more substantial Indigenous governance structure in the form of Aboriginal councils. Under the Act, Aboriginal councils have a potentially wide range of functions including, among others, the delivery of housing, health, education and training, communication, roads, and welfare services and the power to make by-laws and to impose minor penalties for their breach. Given the hostility of state governments in the late 1970s to the establishment of Aboriginal councils under Commonwealth legislation at the time, it is perhaps not surprising that few applications for establishing a council were made, and no councils have ever been established.

Chapter IV provides a framework for the incorporation of Aboriginal incorporated associations. For many Indigenous communities, incorporation under the ACA Act is a prerequisite to accessing various forms of government assistance. It contains detailed rules on the creation of Indigenous incorporated associations, the rights and duties of members and directors, and the powers and responsibilities of the Registrar in relation to Indigenous associations. The requirements for incorporation are modelled on mainstream models of incorporation.

A review of the ACA Act in 1996 found that many of the prescriptive requirements in the Act were not culturally appropriate. For example, the rules for the holding of meetings, including general meetings, do not reflect the decision-making structures in communities; and the extensive (and apparently growing) powers of the Registrar have worked against culturally appropriate incorporations because of the concern of the Registrar to ensure statutory compliance. The underlying issue is that corporations law is ill-equipped to cater for the particular needs of Aboriginal communities, and has difficulty remaining simple and flexible. The 1996 review of the ACA Act concluded that in its present form, Indigenous peoples were better off using mainstream state or Commonwealth statutes of incorporation.

In June 2005 the former Minister for Indigenous Affairs, Amanda Vanstone, announced that the *Corporations (Aboriginal and Torres Strait Islander) Bill 2005* (Cth) (CASTIB) would replace the ACA Act. Senator Vanstone described the CATSIB as a response to Indigenous demands for greater scrutiny of community organisations:

> Indigenous people expect their corporations to provide the best possible services and they are sick and tired of being the victims of unscrupulous or incompetent administrators. This Bill is an important part of the Government's reforms and will ensure that Aboriginal people get a better deal and better value for money (Vanstone 2005).

At the time of the 2005 Bill, 2,800 associations were incorporated under the ACA Act (Explanatory Memorandum, *Corporations (Aboriginal and Torres Strait Islander) Bill 2005* (Cth): 6). The majority were established in order to provide community services. Only 1 per cent of those incorporated were formed for commercial purposes (Corrs Chambers Westgarth Lawyers et al 2002).

Part 2–4 of the CATSIB removed the 'one-size-fits-all' approach of the ACA Act and replaced it with a division of corporations into small, medium and large. The Registrar is empowered to exempt individual and classes of corporation from the requirements of Chapter Seven pertaining to record keeping and reporting (CATSIB Part 7–4 Division 353). In making a determination the Registrar must have regard to factors including the appropriateness of the reporting obligations and whether they would constitute an unreasonable burden (CATSIB s 358–5). The Explanatory Memorandum foreshadows that small corporations will be the beneficiaries of exemptions, in particular those whose sole purpose is to hold title to communal land (Explanatory Memorandum, CATSIB: [5.384]).

However, the CATSIB still restricts the ability of communities to design their corporations to suit local circumstances. For example, s 243–5(a) provides that a corporation must not have more than 12 directors. This provision may conflict with a desire to strive for broad community representation. For example, in recent years some native title representative bodies increased the size of their boards in order to be representative of their constituencies. Some were forced to take this step as a part of the re-recognition process required by the 1998 amendments to the *Native Title Act 1993* (North Queensland Land Council 2005).

The CATSIB also allows non-Indigenous people to become directors of Indigenous corporations (CATSIB s 246–1(3)(b)). The Explanatory Memorandum claims that the reform:

> ... improves flexibility for corporations to permit non-Indigenous membership which is often important to ensure that services can be provided to non-Indigenous people or adopted children. As some corporations are the only providers of essential services in some communities it also ensures that non-Indigenous members of such communities are not disadvantaged (Explanatory Memorandum, CATSIB: [3.27]).

On the other hand, most of those representing Indigenous organisations who gave evidence at the Senate hearings argued that in spite of provisions requiring an Indigenous majority, the appointment of non-Indigenous directors would usurp Indigenous control.

As stated by Michael Prowse of the Central Land Council:

> Quite often people are not comfortable using the kind of processes that other people with corporations in other parts of Australia might use. Voting is quite often not used but a process of consensus decision-making is used. We would suggest that to permit

non-Indigenous membership of Indigenous corporations would quite often lead to a chaotic situation with Aboriginal people being overwhelmed by non-Aboriginal people, who may have better capacities to read and write and to use techniques and instruments of non-Aboriginal law. We suggest that the provision is one that should be struck out of the bill (Legal and Constitutional Legislation Committee 2005: 12).

The reforms will apply to all Indigenous corporations, including those holding title to land. Hypothetically, non-Indigenous developers and mining companies will be able to seek appointment as directors. While one result could be successful partnerships between Indigenous communities and industry, the reforms may also lead to exploitation.

Aboriginal legal academic, Nicole Watson, has observed that the ACA Act proves that the blunt instrument of external accountability is not an appropriate means to achieve that end and that a better response would be to not overwhelm community organisations with a regime mirroring legislation designed to regulate corporations driven by the profit motive. Instead, the question to be asked is whether the corporation is really a culturally appropriate vehicle for the delivery of essential services to Indigenous people (Watson 2006a).

Indigenous people have been forced to form incorporated bodies to facilitate the provision of services and to meet other shared, community-based aims. The involuntary nature of the creation of many organisations means that communities have been required to establish entities even though they may lack the expertise or desire to understand the consequences or technical requirements of incorporation.

For this reason, there has been a large emphasis on the issue of corporate governance and capacity building within Indigenous communities so that more people have the skills required to ensure that the statutory requirements involved in running an incorporated body are met.

There has been research undertaken to identify the factors that are consistently present in successful Indigenous community organisations (Australian Collaboration 2007). The factors include:

- the use of planning tools such as strategic plans and marketing plans;
- mechanisms for internal accountability such as good communication with staff, occupational health and safety policies, time keeping, set hours of work;
- mechanisms for external accountability such as grant acquittal, timely production of annual reports, compliance with regulators, regular reports to clients and corporation members;
- a preparedness to constantly and consistently monitor, review and adjust operations for improved performance and results, and an appreciation that funding bodies rely on performance data and outcomes to continue funding programs;

- provision of flexibility in employment options for staff; this must be underpinned by a commitment to professionalism in the conduct and performance of work;
- understanding that a service to the Indigenous community occurs in a wider socio-economic and political context and seeing ways to bed the service into a framework of community development;
- in rural and remote sectors, successful community organisations often require lateral thinking and problem solving; the limitations of their location and the lack of social infrastructure provide the need to think outside the square when problem solving;
- successful organisations know what business they are in and what they do well; they do not expand simply for the sake of it;
- successful organisations survive change; they also survive changes of leadership.

There is an increasing focus on 'governance issues' that refer to the need to strengthen corporate governance practices rather than on developing mechanisms and institutions through which the community can exercise more autonomy or have a platform from which to advocate for their particular view or perspective.

DISCUSSION QUESTIONS

- Why are local institutions so important to Aboriginal communities?
- Is the use of corporations the right way to structure Aboriginal community organisations? In what other ways might this be done?

A new representative body?

When the Rudd Government was elected in 2007, it had a policy to establish a new representative body for Indigenous people. In December 2007 the terms of the appointees to the National Indigenous Council came to an end and the new Minister for Indigenous Affairs, Jenny Macklin, did not renew their appointments.

The Rudd Government has indicated that such a body will not be another ATSIC and its approach in the first instance is to consult with Aboriginal and Torres Strait Islanders about what such a body should look like. If they are to consult in a way that will make the majority of Indigenous people feel that they have been included in the process and have some ownership of the new model, the process will take many months, even years.

Building a new representative body

In building a new body, the Rudd Government might want to consider two lessons that can be learned from the history of continuous attempts to establish a representative structure since 1967.

The first lesson is that it will never be satisfactory to hand pick advisors to represent the interests of Aborigines and Torres Strait Islanders. Aborigines and Torres Strait Islanders want a say in who represents them and they want their representatives to be accountable to them.

The second lesson that the ALP can use immediately in the development of a new representative model is to avoid the right-wing rhetoric that barks ignorantly that ATSIC was a failure. ATSIC was flawed, no doubt, but the smartest thing that the Rudd Government can do is to take a more sophisticated approach and learn from what did and did not work about the ATSIC model. Even with a cursory look, some of the key lessons would include:

- The need to have an interface with the state and territory governments. Some of the key decisions about Indigenous policy—including health, housing, education and employment—are shared between the federal and state/territory governments. ATSIC did not have a formal way of providing representation at the state level, though some states provided an informal one.
- The body should focus on policy and monitoring, not service delivery. ATSIC became overwhelmed with its administration of CDEP and CHIP, which meant that it did not devote the time that it should have to developing policy and monitoring the way in which government was performing on the areas it still retained responsibility for, most notably health and education.
- The need for accountabilities and strict codes of conduct that, if breached, remove people from elected office. This would be assisted if Indigenous leaders, when faced with accusations of impropriety, were able to be more astute at judging how any attack on the integrity of the representative body makes it vulnerable and has longer term consequences.
- A natural level of governance for many communities is at the regional level. This makes sense given the diversity of needs and diversity of cultures across the country. It allows for a level of government where people at the community level can feel involved with the dynamics of government. Regional Councils were a clear part of the ATSIC model and the ATSIC legislation provided for planning processes to occur at that level so Aborigines and Torres Strait Islanders could be included in the procedure for identifying the priorities within

CASE STUDY

their areas. They, after all, are best placed to advise what it is that they need most. So whatever model it is that the Rudd Government finally proposes, it must make sure that it accommodates the need to have a parallel system of representation at the regional level that can then feed in to a national voice. In this way, the diverse views and needs of communities around the country can be canvassed but brought together to combine for a single voice on issues of national importance.

DISCUSSION QUESTIONS

- What should a national representative structure for Aboriginal people look like?
- Should it be elected or appointed? How should it be structured? What roles and functions should such a body take on?

Conclusion

Aborigines and Torres Strait Islanders feel the absence of a national representative voice. No national structure currently exists to provide critique of the abolition of CDEP, the quarantining of welfare payments, the failure to support the Declaration on the Rights of Indigenous Peoples, the flaws in shared responsibility agreements and the continual underspending on Indigenous health. The vacuum left no other voice on the national stage other than the handful of Indigenous commentators who were given a platform in the national mainstream media.

Finally, Indigenous people have learned that when a body is created by the government and funded by the government, it can abolish it at its whim. This explains why there continues to be attempts by Indigenous people to establish bodies and organisations which are independent of government.

A tension will continue to exist between the institutions that are created by government for Indigenous communities in an attempt to enable them to exercise more control over their own affairs (corporations, ATSIC, and so on) and the limitations of those institutions in delivering to Aboriginal and Torres Strait Islander communities the level of self-governance that they desire.

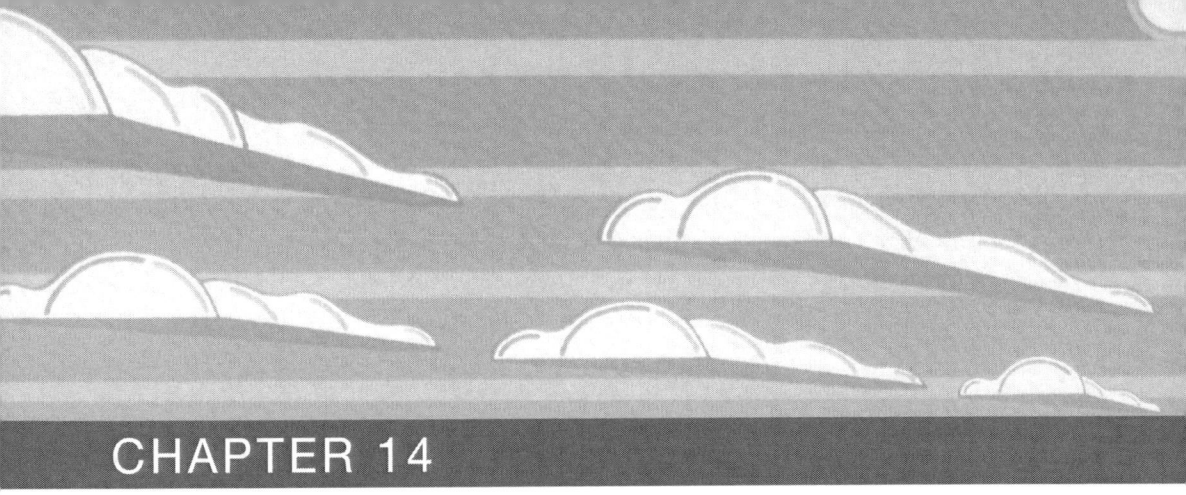

CHAPTER 14

A New Order: Self-Determination

During the conservative era of the Howard Government, it became acceptable and prevalent to refer to 'self-determination' as a 'failed experiment'. This rhetoric always confused the inherent right to self-determination that is recognised under international law and the failure of government policy that the government itself had labelled as 'self-determination'. The latter bore no resemblance to the former but the end result has been that there is an erroneous presumption that self-determination in its proper form has been implemented and proved to be unsuccessful.

It was the Whitlam Government that introduced a policy described as 'self-determination' which included the direct funding of incorporated Indigenous organisations and communities and the establishment of an elected Indigenous advisory body. This remained the policy approach to Indigenous affairs by all governments (though the Fraser Government preferred the term 'self-management') until the Howard Government was elected in 1996. The Howard Government indicated that it would no longer support the principle of self-determination and it also announced that it would actively oppose the recognition of Indigenous peoples' entitlement to the right to self-determination in international negotiations (Dodson and Pritchard 1998), actively opposed the recognition of self-determination extending to Indigenous peoples and voted against the Declaration on the Rights of Indigenous Peoples.

The focus on international arenas to complement the rejection of the principle in the Australian domestic realm highlights the relationship between the developments in international law on the recognition of the rights of Indigenous people and the legitimacy of the political aspirations for Indigenous people in Australia.

Indigenous people and international law

When European powers began their colonial expansion there was a view among scholars that certain rights were held by Indigenous peoples under international law. For example, Francisco de Vitoria believed the Indians to be rational human beings and as such they enjoyed certain fundamental rights. For this reason, he rejected the view that papal donation to the Spanish provided a sufficient and legitimate basis for Spanish rule over Indian lands (Munoz 1946: 92). He maintained that discovery of the Indians' land alone could not confer title to the Spaniards any more than if the Indians had discovered Spain. Vitoria believed that colonisation could be justified if there was no sovereign over a territory. If Indians were unfit to be sovereign, the Spanish could legitimate a claim of sovereignty. In such a case, the coloniser could administer the territory (Grotius 1950). Vitoria put two provisos on this claim to sovereignty. First, the claim to sovereignty was temporary and had to be relinquished once the Indigenous peoples were capable of governing themselves; second, sovereignty claimed by the Spaniards had to be administered in the interests of the Indigenous peoples, not for the profit of the colonisers.

Indigenous peoples were believed to have rights essential to humanity but could lose those rights following a 'just war'. Grotius endorsed the concept of a just war under three broad categories—defence, recovery of property, and punishment (Grotius 1950: Ch XII). He rejected the Christianising mission as fulfilling any of those criteria. Grotius believed that Indigenous peoples and other non-Christians did not lose their property rights merely because they were non-Christians, whether their lands were discovered or conquered.

Other theorists, such as Locke (1689) and de Vattel (1852), believed that sovereignty could be asserted if there was no use of the land. This interpretation meant that Indigenous peoples whose cultures were more recognisable to Europeans because of parallels with their own—use of farming methods, permanent housing—were more likely to receive protection from recognised rights under international law.

Despite scholastic recognition of their rights, actual protections of the rights of Indigenous peoples were minimal during the period of colonisation. The sovereignty of Indigenous nations was recognised in varying degrees reflecting the absence of an international standard or norm concerning interaction with Indigenous peoples of states being colonised. Sometimes treaties were signed with Indigenous peoples, as they were in New Zealand and in North America; in Australia, no treaty was signed with the Indigenous peoples.

Treaties themselves, though documents signed by two or more sovereigns, lost recognition as internationally binding documents and instead became intentionally unbinding documents (Tomas 1996). This move from treating the document as an agreement between two nations to treating it as an internal matter stripped Indigenous nations of any recognised sovereign capacity.

This erosion of Indigenous rights in the face of colonial agendas continued despite the views of many scholars that they should have been recognised and protected under international law. For example, in 1888 the Institute of International Law adopted a statement on the conditions required for a state to secure an occupied territory which included a duty to watch over Indigenous populations, ensure their education and take responsibility for their moral and material conditions. Though this was a paternalistic interpretation of the duties owed by a colonising nation, it does show an understanding that Indigenous peoples retained certain inherent rights that colonisers were violating.

By creating an international legal system that upheld their exclusive sovereignty, states were presumed independent and equal and guarded from interference in their internal affairs by others. This principle of 'non-interference' allowed states to develop policies, even genocidal ones, in relation to their Indigenous peoples that were shielded from outside scrutiny. As Hurst Hannum noted, international law was made by states, for states, to the virtual exclusion of Indigenous peoples' territorial and sovereign rights (Hannum 1996).

With its agenda up until the First World War of asserting claims of colonisation and negotiating disputes between colonial powers, international law developed as a Eurocentric body of law. This Eurocentrism was compounded by the agenda set by the (primarily European) World Wars that moulded international law through European politics, European stability and European control over the world order.

Given this genesis and climate of development, Indigenous rights, from the colonial period until the end of the First World War did not have a place within the rubric of international law. Any reference to Indigenous people at all was usually to enable colonial powers to justify their actions over their acquired territories. For instance, the Covenant of the League of Nations, adopted in 1919, committed all League members to undertake to secure the just treatment of native inhabitants under their control. But this provision was designed to validate colonial occupation rather than to ensure that Indigenous populations were allowed rights protection.

International law was also held not to apply to wandering tribes, so those Indigenous peoples who could not fit into a European concept of 'society' were also denied protection of their sovereignty and rights.

In Australia, Indigenous people were considered nomadic even though they had a society that recognised distinct property relationships between Indigenous peoples and their land. The lack of fences and houses was seen as further evidence of the British right to invade and steal. Later, the International Court of Justice in an Advisory Opinion declared that the nomadic nature of Indigenous peoples did not deprive them of their sovereignty: see *Advisory Opinion on Western Sahara* [1975] ICJR at 39.

International law may have been a tool to justify colonisation. But colonised people, after the Second World War, adopted the rhetoric of international human rights law and sought to gain access to the institutions of the United Nations to assert claims of sovereignty, autonomy and/or the protection of human rights. Much of the assertions for independence and recognition of Indigenous rights focused on the principle of self-determination.

DISCUSSION QUESTION

- Have treaties assisted in protecting Indigenous people in the countries that entered into them?

The principle of self-determination under international law

Debates within the international arena during the inter-war period and in the early post-Second World War period were concerned with restructuring Europe and dividing up the colonial empires of the defeated nations (see for example Gayim 1993). One major difference in the approach of international community and international law in its framework for developing a stable world order was an increased suspicion of nationalism. Another difference was the reluctance to allow atrocities to be committed behind the mask of state sovereignty.

These two changes led to a human rights framework that was:

- individualistic rather group focused; and,
- allowed greater interference with state sovereignty than previously.

A framework of individual rights was structured on the theory that members of minority groups would be satisfied if individual rights to equality and non-discrimination were respected. This framework, which ignored national minorities and groups, led to the United Nations Charter being seen by some as a step back from the League of Nations framework that had been specifically concerned with protecting minority *groups* (Mazower 1997: 58).

This new human rights framework did not interfere with the sovereignty of member states but sought to make member states accountable to the provisions of international human rights covenants that they had ratified. Customary norms that developed out of these instruments would place pressure on all states, whether they had ratified provisions or not.

The pivotal foundation of the post-Second World War framework was the emergence of the right of self-determination, enshrined in Article 1 of the International Covenant on Civil and Political Rights (ICCPR) and Article 1 of the International Covenant on Economic, Social and Cultural Rights (ICESCR). Both articles adopt the same language:

> All peoples have the right to self-determination. By virtue of that right they freely determine their political status and freely pursue their economic, social and cultural development.

This principle of self-determination was intended to be the foundation stone of a new and stable world order. Self-determination was vested in 'peoples' and was applicable against a state. This formulation was an exception to the new international law framework since it was one of the few areas in which a right was to be vested in a group. It was revolutionary in that, in certain circumstances, it gave 'peoples' a right exercisable against their state. At the time it was envisaged as being applicable to 'peoples' within the territory of defeated European empires. It was not thought to apply to overseas colonies.

General Assembly Resolution 1514 of 1960 confirmed the legitimacy of the aspiration of independent statehood for colonial territories with their colonial boundaries intact, regardless of the arbitrary character of most of such boundaries. This new framework of self-determination that surrounded the United Nations and international human rights instruments was used by various minority groups or colonised nations which harnessed the rhetoric in a movement that started a decolonisation of many African and Pacific nations, always in countries where the colonised population remained a majority. Thus, the principle of self-determination was extended from European minorities to colonial situations. But this decolonisation process was not applied across the board. It was generally deemed inapplicable to colonial situations where the colonised populations constituted a minority. International law developed what became known as the 'blue water thesis' (General Assembly Resolution 1541 in Principles IV and V) that precluded from decolonisation procedures the enclaves of Indigenous peoples living within the external boundaries of independent states, such as in Australia (see Anaya 1996: 43; Ofuatey-Kodjoe 1977: 119; Bennett 1978: 12–13). While state sovereignty over distant or external colonial territories was eroding, it remained over the enclaves of Indigenous groups within states and worked to keep them outside the realm of international law.

This extension of the principle of self-determination in certain colonial situations did not give any relief to claims made by Indigenous nations who had been overrun through population invasions by colonisers, while having their own population levels lessened through the implementation of genocidal practices by the conquering nations. These numerical differences that made Indigenous peoples minority groups in their colonised states reinforced the fact that the colonisers had managed to establish a legitimate self-governing state.

Thus, this development of international law in the decolonisation period, despite the extension of the norm to certain colonised nations, did not help many Indigenous peoples and it certainly did not assist Aboriginal and Torres Strait Islander people in Australia. Not being the recipients of this new interpretation of the principle of self-determination, many Indigenous peoples had to seek other avenues in the international legal framework to assert their rights, autonomy and independence.

Many Indigenous peoples have not been considered as 'peoples' for the purpose of the principle of self-determination. They continue to find it hard to fit their claims into the rubric that requires them to show distinct territorial boundaries since much of their lands were stolen during the colonisation process. They are also unable to justify the violation of the principle of non-intervention since most live in countries that have recognised, legitimate governments. Unable to assert their own sovereignty and unable to undermine the legitimacy of the colonising sovereign, Indigenous peoples remain at the mercy of their colonising state for rights protection and steps towards autonomy.

The denial of the status of 'peoples' to Indigenous nations shows the way that international law can thwart rights through a semiotic blockage. The ICCPR and ICESCR both state that the principle of 'self-determination' applies to all 'peoples'. The exercise of the right is subverted by denying that Indigenous *peoples* fit the description of peoples for that purpose.

With the rejection of the assertion that they should be accorded the same status as other colonised nations, Indigenous peoples did not sit idly by.

DISCUSSION QUESTIONS

- Is the way Australia treats its Indigenous people something other countries notice?
- Is a perception that Australia has a good human rights reputation internationally important?
- What image does Australia project internationally?

Indigenous people within the United Nations framework

Aboriginal people, having been excluded from the principle of self-determination, have developed two strategies within the international legal framework:

- to find alternative ways of being recognised under international law, such as through the Declaration of Indigenous Peoples; and
- to develop and transform the notion of 'self-determination' by broadening its definition and using the word as a political slogan with a more encompassing meaning.

Both of these processes subvert the state-centred nature of international law. First, they attempt to allow a non-state actor (the Indigenous person or group) to act in the international arena; second, they facilitate the development of norms based on pressure from a non-state entity as opposed to allowing international law to be seen as developing as a result of the consensus between states.

Although international mechanisms and norms are not always responsive or effective, the activity of Indigenous advocates within the frameworks of the United Nations and international law highlights the inventiveness of Indigenous peoples in pursuing alternative approaches towards better rights' protections. In addition to providing evidence of energetic agency, this experience shows how small changes within a structured framework can facilitate larger institutional and normative changes.

The International Labour Organization

It was in the International Labour Organization (ILO), not the United Nations, in which the issue of Indigenous rights first came to prominence. ILO Convention No 107 of 1957 (ILO 107) was the first contemporary international human rights document that recognised Indigenous peoples as having distinct issues of international concern. Until this document, policies relating to Indigenous rights were primarily deemed the concern of states and thus an internal matter.

Despite its groundbreaking recognition of Indigenous peoples as entities under international law, ILO 107 was ineffective because its underlying ideology of assimilation caused Indigenous peoples to be wary of the document; and its provisions that recognised the rights of Indigenous peoples to land made governments wary of the document.

Article 2(1) of ILO 107 illustrates the paternalistic nature of the convention. It gives no recognition of a right to self-determination, autonomy or self-government:

> Governments shall have the primary responsibility for developing co-ordinated and systematic action for the protection of the population concerned and their progressive integration into the life of their respective countries.

Although the aim of the document was to promote improved social and economic conditions for Indigenous populations this was done within a framework that does not envisage a place for the long-term politically significant cultural and associational patterns of Indigenous populations.

The provision that concerned governments because of its implications for Indigenous rights movements domestically was Article 11:

> The right of ownership, collective or individual, of the members of the populations concerned over the lands these populations traditionally occupy shall be recognised.

The inclusion of Article 11, which was read as being a basis for the recognition of land rights, ensured that ILO 107 was never ratified by some states with Indigenous populations. Australia never ratified the Convention because of its implications on the issue of land rights. There was no recognition of native title in Australia at the time the Convention was written. This showed the greatest limitation of international covenants and conventions: if states are not interested in the intentions, content and norms of international instruments, they are free to ignore them. These instruments do not tightly bind states, even those that ratify instruments.

Indigenous peoples gained access to the ILO through labour organisations. Their presence in the arena was felt as early as 1930 when the rights of Indigenous people were raised in relation to working conditions and slavery (see *Forced Labour Convention of 1930* (ILO No 29)).

But the conventions are not declarations of the aspirations of Indigenous peoples. The process by which international instruments are negotiated reveal the level to which those instruments are the result of compromises and concessions by the states debating them. Even though there are enforcement mechanisms for some instruments, these are rarely used. States take care with the language of documents they do not intend to ratify because even though a state may not assent to an international instrument, the norms that develop around it by the actions and expectations of other states can lead to the development of customary international laws and norms that are expected to be respected. Concern over the ideology of assimilation underpinning ILO 107 led to revision of the document and the introduction of ILO Convention No 169 of 1989 (ILO 169). Even though ILO 169 moved away from the ideology of assimilation, the convention still refused to recognise the right to self-determination.

The revised Convention did recognise, *inter alia*:

- rights to the protection of social, cultural, religious and spiritual values and practices and the institutions of Indigenous peoples;
- rights to participate freely in the dominant culture of the state;
- rights to non-discrimination and freedom from oppression;
- rights to own land which Indigenous peoples traditionally occupy; and
- rights to have spiritual attachments to land respected.

ILO 169 did use the term 'Indigenous peoples' but with the specific proviso that there was nothing to be implied into the use of the term that meant recognition of the right to self-determination, leaving the change devoid of political substance. Without recognition of this right, there is no recognition of the rights of Indigenous peoples to have decision-making power in decisions on issues that concern them.

Many argued that the ideological framework on which ILO 169 is based, ignoring the basic right to self-determination as it does, should be rejected. If Indigenous peoples are to be governed by the norms of a document that refuses to recognise their entitlement to the aspiration of self-determination—a right available to all peoples—the compromise was too great (Strelein 1996).

Despite the shortcomings and ideological flaws of ILO 107 and ILO 169, these Conventions did create an impetus for Indigenous scholarship and action both in the international arena and domestically. They also produced pressure on the United Nations to further investigate the situation of Indigenous peoples in countries all over the world.

International human rights instruments

Having found the fundamental right to self-determination closed to them through a semantic blockage, one alternative avenue available to Indigenous peoples to protect their rights is through the invocation of protections set out in other provisions of international instruments. The protections set out in international human rights documents are addressed to all individuals. Indigenous peoples are confined to claiming the rights as individuals, rather than as members of groups.

The international instruments are said to be aspirational. As with the ILO, enforcement mechanisms are weak and difficult to enforce against violating states, even when gross breaches have occurred. There are also few mechanisms that allow individuals to complain about breaches of the provisions of human rights covenants.

It should be noted that the international covenants and conventions are designed to make the individual the beneficiary of the right. The exception to this is the right to self-determination in both Article 1 of the ICCPR and Article 1 of the ICESCR, and Article 27 of the ICCPR that is directed at protecting minority groups. It states:

> In those States in which ethnic, religious or linguistic minorities exist, persons belonging to such minorities shall not be denied the right, in community with other members of the group, to enjoy their own culture, to profess and practice their own religion, or to use their own language.

Article 27 recognises the group nature of the right to enjoy cultural and religious practices and language. The Article recognises that to enjoy the rights protected by the Article, there needs to be an appreciation of the group that is needed to ensure substantive protection. The right is still vested in the individual. More broadly, the Convention on the Prevention and Punishment of the Crime of Genocide is designed to protect groups.

Indigenous peoples have several avenues for complaint within the framework of these instruments. Many international covenants have monitoring and reporting procedures. This usually means that a country will present its report to the appropriate commission.

There are also complaint procedures in place to bring complaints in front of the United Nations Commission on Human Rights and its Subcommission. Economic and Social Council (ECOSOC) Resolution 1235 (XLII) of 1967 authorises the Commission and Subcommission to examine violations. Information can come from virtually any source. Responsive action is entirely discretionary. ECOSOC Resolution 1503 (XLVII) of 1970 allows for the consideration of communications from individuals and non-governmental organisations that concern gross patterns of rights violations. This procedure is done in closed sessions and action is usually private communication with the state concerned. The First Optional Protocol of the ICCPR allows individual claims to be brought in front of the Human Rights Committee.

Indigenous peoples can fit their grievances within the framework of these Conventions and Covenants. In some instances they could petition as individuals (through First Optional Protocol of the ICCPR); in other instances they could seek to have an international non-government organisation represent their case in the international arena; and in other instances would need to have another state press their claims for them. Reports can be submitted to the Human Rights Committee and the Committee for the Elimination of All Forms of Racial Discrimination. These reports can counter the reports submitted by states under the reporting requirements. The Committees can then confront states about alleged human rights violations.

Although the provisions of many international instruments are currently not interpreted in a way that ensures strong protection of the rights of Indigenous peoples, Indigenous groups have been actively working within the institutions of the United Nations to ensure their presence is noted and their political agendas are taken into account in policy formation whenever possible.

This is a way of ensuring a change in the longer term as norms develop to make states bound to principles that they would not have consented to. Norms that develop through international human rights frameworks are not just moral obligations for states, they are legal ones. These emerging customary international laws have already been shown on occasion to have been influenced by advocacy on behalf of Indigenous peoples.

There is no doubt that these emerging norms impact on states. Governments are aware of their obligations under international law, whether or not they choose to abide by them. Indigenous peoples themselves understand how the international arena can provide a springboard for substantive changes that will allow the greater respect for the rights of Indigenous peoples within their own states.

And while the major human rights instruments dealt with Indigenous people incidentally, many Indigenous groups worked hard to carve out a space within the United Nations bodies that dealt specifically with the issues of Indigenous peoples.

The Working Group of Indigenous Populations

One area in which Indigenous peoples have changed the process within the United Nations was with the development of the Working Group on Indigenous Populations (WGIP).

In 1994, the Commission on Human Rights Sub-Commission on the Prevention of Discrimination Against Minorities recommended to the ECOSOC that it approve the participation of Indigenous persons and organisations, without regard to consultative status, in meetings of the United Nations, including the Commission itself, during which the draft United Nations declaration was being discussed (E/CN.4/Sub.2/ 1994/L.60, 24 August 1994). This effectively opened up the forum to Indigenous groups and individuals from around the world without requiring them to seek consultative status first. It was one of the first steps towards allowing consultation with and input from groups whose members would be the direct beneficiaries of the resultant international document.

The open access to the United Nations through the WGIP had three consequences:

- It provided a meeting place for Indigenous peoples to discuss issues with other Indigenous peoples. This allowed for an information exchange and network building that has strengthened Indigenous rights movements around the world.
- The ability to raise grievances outside of the rhetoric of election campaigns and vote-winning tactics in the domestic arena, however lowly the forum within the United Nations framework, allowed Indigenous peoples to make claims and accusations against violating states.
- It gave confidence to Indigenous peoples who were claiming that their rights had been violated. Their assertions are reinforced by the existence of human rights instruments that articulate the legitimacy of the claims that they are making. This adds to the veracity with which these claims can be asserted against the state.

These advantages that have emerged from the open forum were countered by the complaints about the WGIP, in particular that it is so far down the United Nations institutional food chain. As a sub-committee of a sub-committee, the WGIP had little impact on the outcomes that will eventually be decided by states, and it did not foster direct Indigenous participation in other relevant areas of the United Nations.

In 1994, the United Nations General Assembly launched the International Decade of the World's Indigenous Peoples (1995–2004) to increase the United Nations' commitment to promoting and protecting the rights of Indigenous peoples worldwide. As part of the decade, several United Nations specialised agencies worked with

Indigenous peoples to design and implement projects on health, education, housing, employment, development and the environment that promote the protection of Indigenous peoples and their traditional customs, values and practices.

A Second International Decade of the World's Indigenous People (2005–2015) was proclaimed by the General Assembly. The goal of the decade is to further strengthen 'international cooperation for the solution of problems faced by indigenous people in such areas as culture, education, health, human rights, the environment and social and economic development, by means of action oriented programmes and specific projects, increased technical assistance and relevant standard setting activities' (http://www.un.org/esa/socdev/unpfii/en/news_internationalday2006.htm).

DISCUSSION QUESTIONS

- Why are Indigenous people so interested in using international law to progress their political aspirations?
- What are the benefits of developing networks with Indigenous people from other countries?

The Permanent Forum

On 28 July 2000, the ECOSOC established the Permanent Forum to serve as an advisory body to the Council (Resolution E/RES/2002/22). On 13–24 May 2002 the first session of the Permanent Forum on Indigenous Issues took place at the United Nations in New York.

The Forum allows Indigenous people to represent their own interests directly to any major body of the United Nations as it will advise and report directly to the ECOSOC, one of the six main bodies of the United Nations. The Forum is made up of 16 independent experts—eight nominated by governments and eight appointed by the President of the Council—following consultations with governments on the basis of consultations with Indigenous organisations.

It provides a formal setting in which Indigenous peoples will be able to participate and communicate directly with governments and civil society. Its mandate is to discuss Indigenous issues relating to economic and social development, culture, the environment, education, health and human rights and specifically to:

- provide expert advice and recommendations on Indigenous issues to the Council, as well as to programs, funds and agencies of the United Nations through the Council;
- raise awareness and promote the integration and coordination of activities relating to Indigenous issues within the United Nations system; and
- prepare and disseminate information on Indigenous issues.

The Declaration on the Rights of Indigenous Peoples

A major achievement of the WGIP was the Declaration on the Rights of Indigenous Peoples. It was adopted by the General Assembly on Thursday 13 September 2007. The Declaration is the most comprehensive statement of the rights of Indigenous peoples ever developed, giving prominence to collective rights to a degree unprecedented in international human rights law. The adoption of this instrument is the clearest indication yet that the international community is committing itself to the protection of the individual and collective rights of Indigenous peoples.

Some of the central principles contained in the Declaration concern:

- non-discrimination and fundamental rights, self-determination (including autonomy and participation rights);
- cultural integrity;
- rights to lands, territories and natural resources; and
- other rights relating to socio-economic welfare.

One of the key principles in the Declaration, for which Indigenous peoples consistently fought, is Article 3 on the collective right to self-determination. Self-determination is found in both of the major international human rights covenants, the ICCPR and the ICESCR, and the Declaration mirrors their language. Article 3 of the Declaration adopts this language and applies it specifically to Indigenous peoples.

There is substantial disagreement at the international level over what self-determination requires in any particular context, and especially over how the right to self-determination interacts with another fundamental principle, state sovereignty, as expressed through the protection of a state's territorial integrity and its political unity.

Article 46(1) now provides that nothing in the Declaration may be:

> construed as authorizing or encouraging any action which would dismember or impair, totally or in part, the territorial integrity or political unity of sovereign and independent States.

On the one hand then, the Declaration as adopted by the General Assembly imposes constraints on self-determination; on the other, this simply replicates existing tensions in international law, leaving potential conflicts between the principle of self-determination and that of state sovereignty to be addressed on a case-by-case basis. It remains to be seen how Article 46 will interact with the main provisions on lands and resources (Article 26) and on existing treaty rights (Article 37), which were left untouched (Global Indigenous Peoples' Caucus Steering Committee 2007: 5).

Article 4 states that Indigenous peoples have 'the right to autonomy or self-government in matters relating to their internal and local affairs, as well as ways and means for financing their autonomous functions'. While Indigenous peoples 'have the right to maintain and strengthen their distinct political, legal, economic, social and cultural institutions' they retain 'their right to participate fully, if they so choose, in the political, economic, social and cultural life of the State'.

With respect to participation, Indigenous peoples have the right to participate in decision-making in matters that would affect their rights, through their chosen representatives (Article 18). More specifically, law and policy-makers are required to engage in good faith consultation with Indigenous peoples with the aim of obtaining their 'free, prior and informed consent before adopting and implementing legislative or administrative measures that may affect them' (Article 19).

In particular, Indigenous peoples are entitled to be 'actively involved in developing and determining health, housing and other economic and social programmes affecting them and, as far as possible, to administer such programmes through their own institutions' (Article 23). Indigenous peoples are entitled to 'determine the structures and to select the membership of their institutions in accordance with their own procedures' (Article 33(2)).

The rights recognised in the Declaration are intended to constitute a minimum standard for the 'survival, dignity and well-being' of Indigenous peoples (Article 43). Further, nothing in the Declaration may be construed as diminishing the rights Indigenous peoples already have now or may acquire in the future (Article 45).

Article 46 provides that the Declaration must be read in accordance with principles of justice, democracy, respect for human rights, equality and non-discrimination, as well as the principles contained in the United Nations Charter. However, any limitations placed on the exercise of Declaration rights as a result must be 'strictly necessary' for securing respect for the rights and freedoms of others and for meeting the 'most compelling requirements of a democratic society'.

States are required, in consultation with Indigenous peoples, to take appropriate measures (including national legislation) to achieve the goals of the Declaration, and to provide Indigenous peoples with access to financial and technical assistance for the enjoyment of the rights contained in it (Articles 38–39).

That Australia voted against the adoption of the Declaration on the Rights of Indigenous Peoples in the United Nations General Assembly came as no surprise to those who had followed Indigenous Affairs closely in this country. Prime Minister John Howard won power in 1996 in part on a platform to claw back the native title rights that had been recognised by the Australian High Court in 1992 and in part on a platform that was xenophobic and anti-immigrant. Howard's government was conservative and so it was no surprise that he was unsympathetic to supporting the recognition of Indigenous rights.

But Howard had a very personal passion for reclaiming the national story to one that celebrated the white settler past and rejected what he called a 'black armband' view of history, one that paid too much attention, in his view, to the atrocities committed against Indigenous people in the past (frontier violence, dispossession of land, forced removal of children from families as part of an assimilation policy). Howard believed strongly that we should not, as a nation, be made to feel ashamed of our past and the best way to do that was to not dwell on the dark parts of Australia's history. He made appointments to many of Australia's key cultural institutions—from the National Museum of Australia to our national broadcaster—of like-minded, right-wing ideologues.

His lack of empathy for Indigenous experience, history and perspectives was matched by his policy failure in Indigenous affairs. Early on in his first term as Prime Minister, John Howard rejected what he called the 'rights agenda' in Indigenous affairs. Instead, he said, his government was going to focus on 'practical reconciliation' and concentrate on the key areas of health, housing, education and employment. Seductive rhetoric, but at the end of his 11 years in power, the difference in life expectancy between Indigenous and non-Indigenous Australians remained one of 17 years and the poorer levels of health, higher levels of illiteracy, lower levels of employment and poorer housing standards that plagued Indigenous communities had not improved in any noticeable way.

With such a strong aversion to the notion of human rights, it was no surprise that the principles in the Declaration on the Rights of Indigenous Peoples were deemed to be antagonistic to the philosophical approach of the Howard Government. And its rejection of the idea of 'Indigenous rights' was representative of a broader ideological approach that was sceptical of the international human rights regime in general.

Howard's broader antagonism towards international human rights instruments and their monitoring body was made clear in his government's response to the report issued in 2000 by the Committee on the Elimination of Racial Discrimination. From its treatment of the members of the Stolen Generations to the extinguishment of native title rights, the Australian government received strong criticism when its policies were compared to the standards set by the Declaration to Eliminate all forms of Racial Discrimination.

The Howard Government's response to the report was to dismiss it with an attitude that said arrogantly that the United Nations had no right to tell us what to do. Why pick on us, the politicians spluttered, when there are human rights abusers far, far worse than us—like China, Afghanistan and North Korea? Reports from international human rights monitoring bodies hardly made a blip on the Australian political radar after that. Attempts to initiate debates about human rights were quickly shouted down by the Howard Government and the right-wing media as an indulgence engaged in by out-of-touch elites.

The newly elected Labor Government, led by Prime Minister Kevin Rudd, has had a clear policy of becoming a signatory of the Declaration: different to Howard's approach and indicative of a different attitude towards Indigenous rights and the United

Nations human rights institutions and instruments. However, while the new policy is to sign on to the Declaration, there has been no indication given by the new Australian government as to *how* they will implement the principles contained within it.

It is expected that the Rudd Government will seek to rebuild the reputation that Australia had developed prior to John Howard's 11-year reign as an active and conscientious participant in United Nations human rights forums. Domestically, Rudd has already clearly distinguished his approach to Indigenous affairs from his predecessor's but the real test of his commitment will come when he finally announces how and to what extent he will implement the rights articulated in the Declaration on the Rights of Indigenous Peoples into Australian law.

The influence of international law on Australian law

Norms established under international norms can filter into the domestic law of Member States (Williams 1999). The experience of Australia can provide two examples of the way that developing international norms permeate state institutions.

First, obligations under international conventions lead to substantive legislative changes and institutional developments within ratifying states. Australia's obligations under the Convention on the Elimination of All Forms of Racial Discrimination provided the basis for the government to pass the *Racial Discrimination Act 1975* (Cth). Under the Australian Constitution, the federal government has the power to make laws in relation to any of the heads of powers set out in s 51. Section 51(xxix) states that the government has the power to 'make laws for the peace, order, and good government of the Commonwealth with respect to "external affairs"'. The High Court has found that an obligation under a treaty falls within that section (*Commonwealth v Tasmania* [1983] HCA 21; *Koowarta v Bjelke-Petersen* [1982] HCA 27; *Richardson v Forestry Commission* [1988] HCA 10; *Commonwealth v Queensland* [1920] HCA 79).

Second, norms which have developed under international law have been used to interpret laws in Australia. One example of this was the case of *Minister for Immigration and Ethnic Affairs v Teoh* [1993] FCA 423 where the High Court found, in that case, that the international customary norm of 'the protection of the child' should be invoked by the court to give guidance on the interpretation of Australia's domestic law. Although the court said that this norm should be taken into account, the case is difficult in that the norm of 'best interest of the child' is already a part of the Australian law in the *Family Law Act 1975* (Cth) so it is unclear to what extent the international norm was used in the case.

Australia is far more dependent on human rights standards as a guide for the protection of human rights domestically. It remains the only Commonwealth country that has not modernised its legal system to include a bill or charter of rights. Without a framework that can provide a mechanism to scrutinise government policy and its impact on the human rights of its citizens, the Australian government has no internal human rights benchmark that makes it accountable for its actions. In the absence of such an internal human rights system, it is more reliant than other countries on the international human rights regime as a standard against which to judge government action.

DISCUSSION QUESTION

- How could the Declaration on the Rights of Indigenous Peoples be incorporated into Australian law?

Indigenous people and the right to self-determination in Australia

The language of international law, particularly the concepts of 'self-determination' and 'sovereignty', have pervaded the expression by Aboriginal and Torres Strait Islander people of their political aspirations. These too are often misunderstood or mis-represented so it is helpful to take a closer look at what Indigenous people actually mean when they talk about exercising their rights to self-determination and sovereignty.

The belief that Aboriginal people remain a sovereign people derives from the fact that Indigenous people have never formally ceded their land and continue to feel a distinct identity and a distinct history. Consider the argument for the basis of a treaty as explained by Aboriginal leader Galarrwuy Yunupingu:

A treaty which is recognised by international convention must state that:

- Aboriginal people are the indigenous sovereign owners of Australia and adjacent islands since before 1770 and as such have rights and treaty rights;
- their sovereignty was never ceded; and
- the doctrine of terra nullius cannot be supported in international law as the legal basis for European occupation of, and acquisition of sovereignty over, their land (Yunupinga 1987).

These aspirations and exercise of the right to self-determination all conceive of ways in which to shape the relationship between Indigenous people and the Australian state. While it has on occasion been mooted that Aboriginal people are seeking to form a separate state and therefore divide Australia, this is a rare view, with the predominant approach being one that has seeks to accommodate Aboriginal and Torres Strait Islanders' political aspirations within the Australian state and its institutions (Behrendt 2003a).

Sovereignty—an Aboriginal perspective

Prominent Aboriginal activist Kevin Gilbert was one of the strongest and most passionate advocates of 'sovereignty'. In a draft treaty written in consultation with Aboriginal Members of the Sovereign Aboriginal Coalition at Alice Springs in 1987 (see Attwood and Marckus 1999: 312–313) Gilbert (1973) wrote the following points about a 'Sovereign Position':

> 1.1.5   We are free to manage our own affairs both internally and externally to the fullest possible extent, in the proper exercise of our Sovereign Right as a Nation
>
> ...
>
> 1.1.7   Our Sovereign Aboriginal Nation, fulfilling the criteria of Statehood, having Inherent Possessory Root Title to Lands, a permanent population and a representative governing body according to our indigenous traditions, having the ability to enter relations with other States, possesses the right to autonomy in self-determination of our political status, to freely pursue our economic, social and cultural development and to retain our rights in religious matters, tradition and traditional practice.
>
> 1.1.8   We, the Sovereign Aboriginal People are to be accorded our right and proper recognition as a People and a Nation State, subjects of international law.

Gilbert and his co-authors envisage a single Aboriginal nation with the same status of other nations but he also concedes that it is not possible for this aspiration to amount to Aboriginal people achieving separate statehood:

> Leaving out all the other considerations that spring to mind it seems to me that defence and security considerations alone will ensure that the separate state ... will remain a dream (Gilbert 1973: 190).

Through language that is as moral as it is political and legal, Indigenous people are attaching a unique interpretation to the term 'sovereignty'. It includes concepts such as representative government and democracy, the recognition of cultural distinctiveness and notions of the freedom of the individual that are embodied in liberalism. These claims take place by seeking a new relationship with the Australian state with increased self-government and autonomy, though not the creation of a new country (Behrendt 2003a).

It is this firm belief that Aboriginal nations remain sovereign entities that then gives rise to the belief that, as a distinct 'peoples', they are entitled to exercise the right to self-determination.

In practice, the exercise of the right to self-determination manifests in many ways. In the First Report 1993 of the Aboriginal and Torres Strait Islander Social Justice Commission, self-determination is spoken about in the following terms:

> Self-determination is intimately related to calls for a treaty and constitutional recognition of indigenous rights. They all flow from an endeavour to regain recognition of our original rights to the freedom and control of our lives which were lost with the invasion of our lands and to gain a recognition of those rights which is secure. On a basis which is not dependant on grace or favour or welfare but in recognition of our original place and our continuing distinct cultural identity which we wish to retain (Aboriginal and Torres Strait Islander Social Justice Commission 1993: 50).
>
> The absence of self-determination is experienced by Aboriginal and Torres Strait Islander people in an intimate, daily way. Confinement to mainstream government services relating to health, housing, education and employment is, to many indigenous peoples, reminiscent of the missionary days (Aboriginal and Torres Strait Islander Social Justice Commission 1993: 56).

Some people have stated that the recognition of sovereignty is the historical and cultural base from which to build self-determination for Indigenous people. This way of conceptualising the relationship between the two concepts embraces 'sovereignty' as a concept that belongs to Indigenous people while seeking to utilise the use of the tools of self-determination identified in the First Report 1993 of the Aboriginal and Torres Strait Islander Social Justice Commission (Behrendt 2003a).

The recurring issues that emerge in discussions about what the exercise of sovereignty and self-determination means in practice covers diverse areas, including:

* **the recognition of past injustices** through processes such as reconciliation, a Preamble to the Constitution and a treaty;
* **increased autonomy and decision-making** through decentralisation of government power, the creation of economic bases for Indigenous communities, the recognition of customary laws and the development of regional framework agreements;
* **the recognition of property rights** including the recognition of land rights and other property rights, compensation for lost property interests and the application of the principle of non-discrimination when it comes to dealings with Aboriginal interests in land, the recognition of hunting and fishing rights and water rights, and a right to negotiate;
* **protection of cultural practice and customary laws** including experimenting with institutions;
* **the equal protection of rights** including entrenched constitutional protection of some rights and a bill of rights.

What becomes clear is that there is a spectrum of rights that are included in the 'recognition of sovereignty' and the 'exercise of self-determination'. The above categorisation is deceptive in that the rights identified are more complexly interrelated than a checklist makes them appear. The recognition of property rights is necessary for the protection of cultural heritage, autonomy and self-government are related to economic self-sufficiency, which is again linked to the recognition of property rights but also an essential prerequisite to the recognition of customary law.

Among those rights, some require fundamental changes to the structure of Australian society, some could be achieved with legislation and others should already be recognised.

DISCUSSION QUESTION

- How could the right to self-determination be incorporated into Australian law?

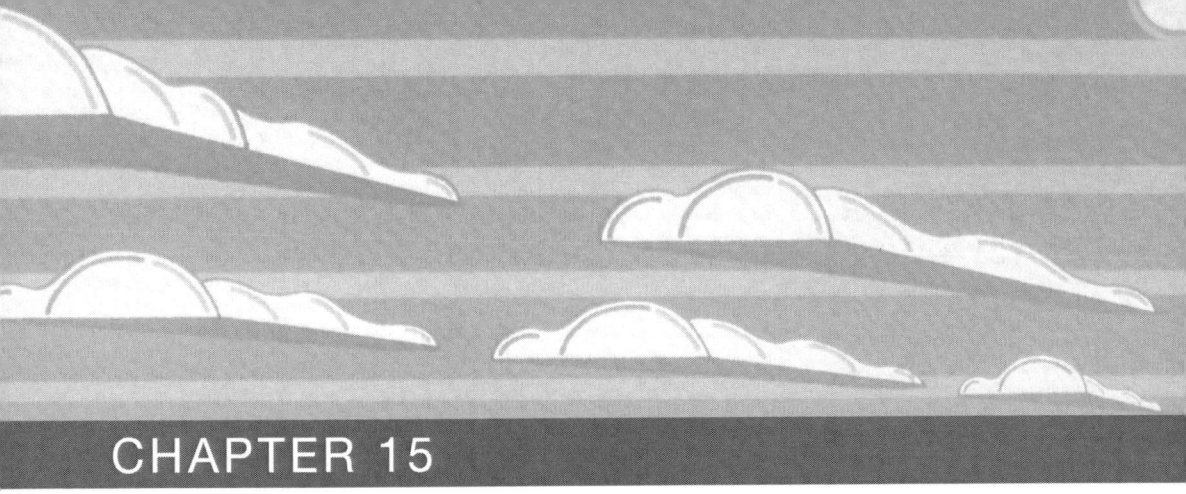

CHAPTER 15

Unfinished Business

The 1992 decision in the *Mabo* case was a high-water mark in the relationship between Indigenous and non-Indigenous Australians. The overturning of the doctrine of terra nullius marked a rejection of a legal fiction that was offensive to Aboriginal and Torres Strait Islanders and the recognition of a form of native title was an admission by the Australian legal system that Indigenous people had inherent rights.

However, the interest in a reconciliation movement that sought to improve the relationship between Aboriginal and non-Aboriginal Australians and to narrow the stark differences in the socio-economic position between the two groups had already begun before the High Court handed down its *Mabo* decision. The Council for Aboriginal Reconciliation had already been established to begin looking at a process of reconciliation that would involve Indigenous and non-Indigenous Australians in a process of creating a better relationship between the two and improving the disparity between the life opportunities of Indigenous people. This process sought to look at a wide range of issues, from symbolic actions to improved legal recognition and protection.

The decade of reconciliation and the Council for Aboriginal Reconciliation

In 1991, the Commonwealth Parliament voted unanimously to establish the Council for Aboriginal Reconciliation (CAR) and a formal nine-year reconciliation process. The long title of the *Council for Aboriginal Reconciliation Act 1991* sets out the rationale behind the establishment of CAR, namely:

(a) Australia was occupied by Aborigines and Torres Strait Islanders who had settled for thousands of years before British settlement at Sydney Cove on 26 January 1788;

(b) many Aborigines and Torres Strait Islanders suffered dispossession and dispersal from their traditional lands by the British Crown;

(c) there has been no formal reconciliation between Aborigines and Torres Strait Islanders and other Australians;

(d) by the year 2001, the centenary of Federation, it is most desirable that there be such a reconciliation; and

(e) as a part of the reconciliation process, the Commonwealth will seek an ongoing national commitment from governments at all levels to cooperate and to coordinate with the Aboriginal and Torres Strait Islander Commission as appropriate to address progressively Aboriginal disadvantage and aspirations in relation to land, housing, law and justice, cultural heritage, education, employment, health, infrastructure, economic development and any other relevant matters in the decade leading to the centenary of Federation, 2001.

The Federal Parliament directed CAR to undertake a range of functions, including to consult Aborigines and Torres Strait Islanders and the wider Australian community on whether reconciliation would be advanced by a formal document or documents of reconciliation. The Council was made up of 25 community leaders drawn from Aboriginal and Torres Strait Islander communities, the industries that had the most impact on Aboriginal people and from business and other sectors.

After extensive consultations, CAR determined that such documents would have to be 'people's documents' which parliaments, organisations, institutions and people in the community could accept and commit to and should:

- express the Australian people's hopes and aspirations for reconciliation;
- share responsibility with Aboriginal and Torres Strait Islander peoples for making progress to overcome disadvantage through negotiated actions;
- recognise that much remained to be done; and
- outline an ongoing process which enables Australians to work together towards a reconciled nation.

CAR set out its key priorities as being:

- **the Documents of Reconciliation**, namely, developing a national document of reconciliation and by acknowledgment within the Constitution of Australia;
- **the Partnerships in Reconciliation**, between Aboriginal and Torres Strait Islander peoples and governments, business, peak organisations and community groups to achieve social and economic equality;
- **the People's Movement For Reconciliation** to achieve justice and equity for all Australians, to embrace the unique place of Indigenous peoples in the life of the nation and to ensure that the work of reconciliation continues beyond the life of CAR.

The Keating Government's commitment to reconciliation in the early days of the life of CAR is perhaps best illustrated by the speech the Prime Minister Paul Keating delivered at Redfern Park in Sydney on 10 December 1992. In this historic speech, he said:

> … we cannot confidently say that we have succeeded as we would like to have succeeded if we have not managed to extend opportunity and care, dignity and hope to the Indigenous people of Australia—the Aboriginal and Torres Strait Island people.
>
> This is a fundamental test of our social goals and our national will: our ability to say to ourselves and the rest of the world that Australia is a first rate social democracy, that we are what we should be—truly the land of the fair go and the better chance.
>
> There is no more basic test of how seriously we mean these things.
>
> It is a test of our self-knowledge. Of how well we know the land we live in. How well we know our history. How well we recognise the fact that, complex as our contemporary identity is, it cannot be separated from Aboriginal Australia. How well we know what Aboriginal Australians know about Australia …
>
> We simply cannot sweep injustice aside. Even if our own conscience allowed us to, I am sure, that in due course, the world and the people of our region would not. There should be no mistake about this—our success in resolving these issues will have a significant bearing on our standing in the world.
>
> However intractable the problems may seem, we cannot resign ourselves to failure—any more than we can hide behind the contemporary version of Social Darwinism which says that to reach back for the poor and dispossessed is to risk being dragged down.
>
> That seems to me not only morally indefensible, but bad history.
>
> We non-Aboriginal Australians should perhaps remind ourselves that Australia once reached out for us. …
>
> I think what we need to do is open our hearts a bit.
>
> All of us.
>
> Perhaps when we recognise what we have in common we will see the things which must be done—the practical things (Keating 1992).

By contrast, the Australian Reconciliation Convention was held in Melbourne in mid-1997 and resulted in an overwhelming response from the Australian public. Prime Minister John Howard addressed the Convention but by that time his antagonism towards the rights focus of reconciliation was apparent and his failure to apologise to the members of the Stolen Generations was seen as a symbol of his disregard for the key elements of the reconciliation process. Delegates at the Convention turned their back on him as a silent protest against his derailing of the reconciliation process.

The Social Justice Commissioner

In December 1992, the federal parliament created the position of the Aboriginal and Torres Strait Islander Social Justice Commissioner within the Human Rights and Equal Opportunity Commission (HREOC). The position was a response to the findings of the Royal Commission into Aboriginal Deaths in Custody and the National Inquiry into Racist Violence and it was also a response to the extreme social and economic disadvantage faced by Indigenous Australians.

The Social Justice Commissioner's roles includes reviewing the impact of laws and policies on Indigenous peoples, reporting on Indigenous social justice and native title issues, and promoting an Indigenous perspective on issues and monitoring the enjoyment and exercise of human rights for Indigenous Australians. This monitoring role includes reviewing legislation, providing policy advice and undertaking research on Indigenous human rights issues and an active involvement with the development of international human rights standards.

The *Human Rights and Equal Opportunity Commission Act 1986* (Cth) and the *Native Title Act 1993* (Cth) both require the Social Justice Commissioner to produce a Social Justice Report and a Native Title Report which are to be tabled in parliament.

The other important role played by the Social Justice Commissioner is an educative one that seeks to promote better understanding and respect for the rights of Aboriginal and Torres Strait Islander people.

During the time that the office has been established, it has provided an important monitoring role, even after the budget of HREOC was drastically cut under the Howard Government. Especially after the abolition of ATSIC, the Social Justice Commissioner was a prominent and respected voice on the national stage providing critique of policy directions and advice on Indigenous issues.

The social justice package

While the *Mabo* decision became the impetus for the Keating Government to negotiate the *Native Title Act 1993* to facilitate the large number of subsequent claims to native title and establish the National Native Title Tribunal, it was also the trigger for the establishment of an Indigenous Land Fund and an Indigenous Land Commission to administer it and it was also supposed to be accompanied by a social justice package.

The Indigenous Land Fund and the Indigenous Land Corporation

Legislation in the form of the *ATSIC Amendment (Indigenous Land Corporation and Land Fund) Bill 1994* established the Indigenous Land Corporation (ILC) which commenced on 1 January 1995. It had responsibility for the Land Fund that was established for the purpose of assisting Aboriginal peoples and Torres Strait Islanders to acquire land and to manage it in a way that provides economic, environmental, social or cultural benefits to the people. The Fund was established in recognition of the fact that most Aboriginal people would not receive a direct benefit from the *Mabo* decision because they had been dispossessed of their land and therefore could not meet the test developed by the High Court to prove their native title.

The ILC acquires and manages land in a way that will provide them with social, cultural and economic benefits. It also prepares national and regional strategies related to the acquisition of land and management and environmental issues relating to Indigenous land. The Land Fund was created from specific amounts drawn from consolidated revenue over a 10-year period. The ILC received amounts from the Fund each year equal to the realised real returns on investments made by the Fund.

The intention to establish a social justice package

The third aspect of the Keating Government's response to the *Mabo* decision was supposed to be the development of further measures to remedy institutional and structural impediments to the full participation of Aborigines and Torres Strait Islanders in Australian economic, social and cultural life. In other words, they wanted to establish a social justice package.

In July 1994, a consultation process was established to develop the social justice package.

DISCUSSION QUESTION

• Why was the social justice package an essential element of the response to the *Mabo* case?

Recognition, Rights and Reform

In 1995, ATSIC published a document, *Recognition, Rights and Reform: A Report to Government on Native Title Social Justice Measures* (ATSIC 1995). It was a response to the inquiry about further measures that the Australian government should consider to address the dispossession of Aboriginal and Torres Strait Islander peoples as part of the social justice package.

In preparing the report, ATSIC had consulted widely. As such, it became, and remains, the most accurate blueprint for reforms that reflect the views of Aborigines and Torres Strait Islanders as to how best to achieve social justice.

Recognition, Rights and Reform responded to the Keating Government's desire for constructive and realistic proposals to increase the participation of Indigenous peoples in Australia's economic life, to safeguard and develop Indigenous cultures, to help develop a positive community consensus and to contribute to a lasting reconciliation.

The report noted that, at the time the social justice package was being considered, there were several other key initiatives that, in addition to the *Native Title Act 1993* and establishment of the Indigenous Land Fund and the Indigenous Land Corporation, were concerned with achieving social justice for Aboriginal and Torres Strait Islander people, namely:

- a federal government access and equity strategy;
- action taken to implement the government's response to the recommendations of the Royal Commission into Aboriginal Deaths in Custody;
- major reviews of policies and programs in the key areas of Aboriginal and Torres Strait Islander employment, education and health;
- the work of the Council for Aboriginal Reconciliation;
- the Centenary of Federation that was to occur in 2001; and
- the International Decade of the World's Indigenous People was commencing with a focus on the international recognition of Indigenous rights.

These activities that coincided with the consultations and proposals for the social justice package highlight the fact that there were several areas of action on Indigenous issues, particularly focused on Indigenous rights, that culminated in creating a feeling that it was possible to achieve a new era of non-discrimination and recognition for Aboriginal and Torres Strait Islander people.

The recognition of fundamental rights and entitlements of Indigenous peoples was a central aspect of the proposals in *Recognition, Rights and Reform*. The report noted that the ability to exercise and enjoy those rights—the normal citizenship or equality rights that Indigenous peoples share with all Australians and the distinctive rights of Indigenous peoples—was critical to the achievement of social justice for Aboriginal and Torres Strait Islander people.

It identified several key areas where rights could be protected and made proposals in relation to each of them, namely:

- **Citizenship and equality rights** with particular issues identified as:
  - the enormous level of unmet need in Aboriginal and Torres Strait Islander communities for basic service delivery such as housing and infrastructure

which results from a failure of governments responsible for delivering those services;

– ensuring access and equity for Aboriginal and Torres Strait Islander people who are largely reliant on mainstream service delivery from all levels of government; and

– ensuring an adequate and equitable range of service delivery in respect of remote and predominantly Aboriginal and Torres Strait Islander communities.

• **Indigenous rights** where, with a view that the recognition of and support for self-determination is fundamental, further work was identified in the form of:

– Autonomy rights, which focus upon the right of Indigenous peoples to determine the way in which they live and control their social, economic and political systems;

– Identity rights, which relate to the right to exist as distinct peoples with distinct cultures; and

– Territory and resource rights, which encompass such things as land entitlements, the right to resources of that land, and the use of those resources.

Recognition, Rights and Reform put forward a broad range of recommendations that covered the following areas:

• The rights of Aboriginal and Torres Strait Islander peoples as citizens, including:

– the reinforcement of access and equity provisions through legislation to ensure Indigenous people can better access their citizenship entitlements;

– an increased commitment to supporting international instruments which reinforce Indigenous rights; and

– support for measures to define, recognise and extend Indigenous rights including new initiatives in areas such as communal title and assertion of coextensive rights

• **The recognition of the special status and rights of Indigenous Australians and the achievement of greater self-determination for Aboriginal and Torres Strait Islander peoples,** namely:

– the promotion and advancement of the constitutional reform agenda;

– Indigenous representation in parliament with interim arrangements for speaking rights by the ATSIC Chairperson;

– the development of processes to start work on compensation issues;

– the promotion of regional agreements as a means of settling social justice issues on a regional basis commencing with pilot studies;

- recognition of a self-government option for indigenous people within the framework of self-determination;
- support for initial work to develop a framework for a treaty and negotiation arrangements;
- legislative recognition of the Aboriginal and Torres Strait Islander flags; and
- increased support for public awareness initiatives.

- **Ensuring that Indigenous Australians are able to exercise their rights and share equitably in the provision of government programs and services.**
- **The protection of the cultural integrity and heritage of Indigenous Australians,** including:
  - legislative reforms to strengthen heritage protection legislation and protect Indigenous rights to cultural property;
  - providing for greater involvement in environmental decision-making;
  - implementing the report of the Law Reform Commission on Aboriginal customary law; and
  - support for extension of language programs and broadcasting initiatives.
- **Measures to increase Aboriginal and Torres Strait Islander participation in Australia's economic life**, including:
  - fostering closer links with industry;
  - accessing the Community Development Employment Projects (CDEP) Scheme as an entitlement and removing anomalies;
  - implementation of business training proposals of Aboriginal Employment Development Policy (AEDP);
  - fostering regional economic development; and
  - further development of strategic business opportunities and resources for a stake in industry.

Other major proposals canvassed by the *Recognition, Rights and Reform* report were: major institutional and structural change, including constitutional reform and recognition; regional self-government and regional agreements; and the negotiation of a treaty or comparable document.

The report had recommended that implementation of the social justice package should be targeted for implementation by 2001, the date at which the Council for Aboriginal Reconciliation was to report on its progress.

However, the election of the Howard Government in 1996 meant that no social justice package was implemented.

DISCUSSION QUESTIONS

- What are effective ways of engaging the broader Australian community in debates about reconciliation?
- Why has reconciliation been so successful at the local community level, even when it stalled as an issue on the national agenda?

The recommendations of the Reconciliation Council

After a very extensive public consultation process, the Council drew up two documents of reconciliation: the Australian Declaration Towards Reconciliation and the Roadmap for Reconciliation. It presented these documents at Corroboree 2000 on 27 May 2000. The following day, over 250,000 people crossed the Sydney Harbour Bridge to show their support for the reconciliation process.

The Australian Declaration Towards Reconciliation stated:

We, the peoples of Australia, of many origins as we are, make a commitment to go on together in a spirit of reconciliation.

We value the unique status of Aboriginal and Torres Strait Islander peoples as the original owners and custodians of lands and waters.

We recognise this land and its waters were settled as colonies without treaty or consent.

Reaffirming the human rights of all Australians, we respect and recognise continuing customary laws, beliefs and traditions.

Through understanding the spiritual relationship between the land and its first peoples, we share our future and live in harmony.

Our nation must have the courage to own the truth, to heal the wounds of its past so that we can move on together at peace with ourselves.

Reconciliation must live in the hearts and minds of all Australians. Many steps have been taken, many steps remain as we learn our shared histories.

As we walk the journey of healing, one part of the nation apologises and expresses its sorrow and sincere regret for the injustices of the past, so the other part accepts the apologies and forgives.

We desire a future where all Australians enjoy their rights, accept their responsibilities, and have the opportunity to achieve their full potential.

And so, we pledge ourselves to stop injustice, overcome disadvantage, and respect that Aboriginal and Torres Strait Islander peoples have the right to self-determination within the life of the nation.

Our hope is for a united Australia that respects this land of ours, values the Aboriginal and Torres Strait Islander heritage, and provides justice and equity for all (http://www.austlii.edu.au/journals/AILR/2001/7.htm).

The Roadmap for Reconciliation included four strategies:

The National Strategy to Sustain the Reconciliation Process focused on engaging all levels of government, the private sector, community and voluntary organisations publicly to support the ongoing reconciliation process, provide resources and increasingly involve Aboriginal people and Torres Strait Islanders in their work. It recommended the establishment of Reconciliation Australia to maintain a national leadership focus for reconciliation, report on progress, provide information and raise funds to promote and support reconciliation activities. It further highlighted the importance of concentrating on education about reconciliation.

The National Strategy to Promote Recognition of Aboriginal and Torres Strait Islander Rights proposed a number of actions, including some constitutional and legislative processes, to assist the progressive resolution of outstanding issues for the recognition and enjoyment of Aboriginal and Torres Strait Islander rights. It included recommending the establishment of legislative processes to deal with the 'unfinished business' of reconciliation, allowing for negotiated outcomes on matters such as Indigenous rights, self-determination within the life of the nation, and constitutional reform.

The National Strategy to Overcome Disadvantage aimed at creating a society where Aboriginal people and Torres Strait Islanders enjoy a similar standard of living to that of other Australians, without losing their cultural identity. It focused on education, employment, health, housing, law and justice.

The National Strategy for Economic Independence focused on the pathways to economic independence. It looked at both the importance of education and skills development and engagement in the economy through access to jobs and resources and effective business practices.

In its final report, CAR (2000c) made the following six key recommendations:

1   The Council of Australian Governments (COAG) agree to implement and monitor a national framework whereby all governments and the Aboriginal and Torres Strait Islander Commission (ATSIC) work to overcome Aboriginal and Torres Strait Islander peoples' disadvantage through setting program performance benchmarks that are measurable (including timelines), are agreed in partnership with Aboriginal and Torres Strait Islander peoples and communities, and are publicly reported.

2   All parliaments and local governments pass formal motions of support for the Australian Declaration Towards Reconciliation and the Roadmap for Reconciliation, enshrine their basic principles in appropriate legislation, and determine how their key recommendations can best be implemented in their jurisdictions.

3   The Commonwealth Parliament prepare legislation for a referendum which seeks to:

–   recognise Aboriginal and Torres Strait Islander peoples as the first peoples of Australia in a new preamble to the Constitution; and

–   remove section 25 of the Constitution and introduce a new section making it unlawful to adversely discriminate against any people on the grounds of race.

4   Recognising that the formal reconciliation process over the last decade has achieved much and has helped bring Australians together, all levels of government, non-government, business, peak bodies, communities and individuals commit themselves to continuing the process and sustaining it by:

–   affirming the Australian Declaration Towards Reconciliation and actioning the Roadmap for Reconciliation;

–   providing resources for reconciliation activities and involving Aboriginal and Torres Strait Islander peoples in their work;

–   undertaking educational and public-awareness activities to help improve understanding and relations between Aboriginal and Torres Strait Islander peoples and the wider community; and

–   supporting Reconciliation Australia, the foundation which has been established to maintain a national leadership focus for reconciliation, report on progress, provide information and raise funds to promote and support reconciliation.

5   Each government and parliament:

–   recognise that this land and its waters were settled as colonies without treaty or consent and that to advance reconciliation it would be most desirable if there were agreements or treaties; and

–   negotiate a process through which this might be achieved that protects the political, legal, cultural and economic position of Aboriginal and Torres Strait Islander peoples.

6   That the Commonwealth Parliament enact legislation (for which the Council has provided a draft in this report) to put in place a process which will unite all Australians by way of an agreement, or treaty, through which unresolved issues of reconciliation can be resolved.

This report included a draft *Reconciliation Bill 2001*. Aboriginal Senator Aden Ridgeway introduced it to parliament as a private member's Bill but it was never passed.

Prime Minister John Howard had already signalled his unwillingness to progress the reconciliation agenda. At the hand-over of the Final Report by CAR he announced that his government rejected the recommendation of a treaty with Indigenous peoples, preferring instead to concentrate on the concept of 'practical reconciliation'.

This 'practical reconciliation' described a policy of government funding in targeted areas that go to the core of socio-economic disadvantage, namely, employment, education, housing and health:

> We are determined to design policy and structure administrative arrangements to address these very real issues and ensure standards in education and employment, health and housing improve to a significant degree. ... That is why we place a great deal of emphasis on practical reconciliation (Howard, cited in Behrendt 2002c: 26).

Despite the popularist rhetoric that he would focus on 'practical' matters, the socio-economic areas that he claimed he would focus on had not improved. In his Menzies Lecture, delivered on 13 December 2000, just a few days after receiving the Final Report from the Council for Aboriginal Reconciliation, Howard stated the following:

> It is true, as was noted recently, that past policies designed to assist have often failed to recognise the significance of indigenous culture and resulted in the further marginalisation of Aboriginal and Torres Strait Islander people from the social, cultural and economic development of mainstream Australian society (Howard 2000).

Under this view, current socio-economic disparity is the result of past cultural conflict and unsympathetic policy-making and it is what has been instrumental in establishing a welfare mentality.

> This led to a culture of dependency and victimhood, which condemned many indigenous Australians to lives of poverty and further devalued their culture in the eyes of their fellow Australians.

The main issues, according to this view, are welfare dependency, victimhood and poverty and they can be redressed according to the proponents of 'practical reconciliation' by a more benevolent legislature. It is absolutely true that past government policies such as child removal practices have contributed to the socio-economic inequalities and systemic racism experienced in Indigenous communities and families today. But this has been compounded by the absence of a rights framework that can protect from unfair and racist policy-making.

For a government that claimed that Indigenous problems should not just have money thrown at them, the focus on funding will confine Indigenous empowerment to the policy-making area. And it does so in a manner that only, at a cursory level, seeks Indigenous input. It fails to delegate responsibility for decision-making about how money for programs should be directed to communities that are receiving funds.

The 'practical reconciliation' approach did not attack the systemic and institutionalised aspects of the impediments to socio-economic development. While claiming that 'more handouts' are not going to make a difference, it failed to address the issues it claimed to be targeting and put strategies in place that go to the heart of historical and institutional racism. The 'practical reconciliation' approach also failed to appreciate that there need to be real outcomes and protection of rights, and that these include economic rights and property rights.

The recognition and protection of these rights would put land under people's feet, allow access to natural and other economic resources and work towards ensuring that Indigenous communities were economically self-sufficient.

Without a rights framework that works, there is no ability to create and protect the rights to economic self-sufficiency and Indigenous peoples, families and communities will be dependent on welfare.

By the time the Howard Government left power, the reconciliation process had stalled and the language of rights in relation to Indigenous issues had become unpopular. The work of CAR and ATSIC to develop blueprints and pathways to move forward were left dormant.

The re-emergence of the issue of a treaty

At the Corroboree event in 2000, as John Howard expressed his unwillingness to progress the reconciliation process in the way that CAR was suggesting, the then Chair of ATSIC, Geoff Clarke, put the idea of a treaty between Indigenous and non-Indigenous Australia clearly on the agenda. The idea of a treaty was part of the key recommendations of CAR which recommended the development of a process by which to start negotiations about a treaty. By this time, the issue of a treaty had been discussed by the Aboriginal leadership for over two decades.

Patrick Dodson saw a treaty as an opportunity to set down broad principles that would facilitate and guide further discussions about unfinished business:

> We have got to have an agreement between the Commonwealth and Aboriginal people. This would probably need a referendum. That agreement would need to negotiate our prior ownership and occupation of this land. Part of the Labor Party platform was to negotiate a treaty with us but the Commonwealth has taken no action. A treaty would contain the broad principles—the points of departure—for discussions about other rights, such as those to land, language and culture. (Berger 1988: 11)

In calling for a referendum, he also believed that there needed to be a change in the way that non-Indigenous Australians see Indigenous people and the way that they conceptualise the relationship that Indigenous people currently have with the dominant culture.

The Senate Standing Committee on Constitutional and Legal Affairs in its report, *Two Hundred Years Later*, also recognised the need for a resolution to the issues left outstanding by the lack of an agreement-making process:

> ... the Committee is of the view that if it is recognized that sovereignty did inhere in the Aboriginal people in a way not comprehended by those who applied terra nullius doctrine at the time of occupation and settlement, then certain consequences flow which are proper to be dealt with in a compact between the descendants of those Aboriginal peoples and other Australians (Senate Standing Committee 1983).

A treaty is a settlement or agreement arrived at by 'treating' or negotiation. A treaty gives rise to binding obligations between the parties who make it. It is an agreement between two parties who seek to have their relationship formalised. The word 'treaty' covers a range of ideas and concepts, including a contract or compact, a covenant, an agreement, a settlement or international arrangements between nation states.

Several arguments have been put forward as to why a treaty should be negotiated between Indigenous and non-Indigenous Australia. In particular, it is argued that a treaty could recognise and protect Indigenous rights and make up for the exclusion of Aboriginal and Torres Strait Islander people from the nation-building process of drafting the Constitution. A treaty is also seen as a way of recognising the unique status of Aboriginal and Torres Strait Islander peoples as first peoples and the distinctive rights and special status based on prior occupation that flow from that.

It is also argued that a treaty will deliver many important benefits as a framework for settling relationships between Indigenous peoples and governments at local, regional, state, territory and federal levels; legal recognition including constitutional recognition that Aboriginal and Torres Strait Islander peoples have inherent rights which must inform all processes of governments in Australia; and improved services such as health, housing, education and employment in accordance with the legitimate aspirations of Indigenous peoples.

A treaty under Australian law could take many forms. It could be an agreement under international law in the form of a treaty, an agreement that is supported by the Constitution, an agreement that is supported by legislation, or a simple agreement that is not legally binding. An agreement under international law would be most difficult to pursue because Indigenous people are not recognised as a separate state under international law. An agreement that had no legal status would by merely symbolic and therefore of little use in terms of substantially changing the relationship between Indigenous and non-Indigenous Australians.

The more likely forms of such an agreement would be as part of the Constitution or as legislation. Inclusion in the Constitution would give a treaty the greatest protection but would need a referendum in order to be implemented. For example, s 35 of the Canadian Constitution provides protection of treaties. It simply states:

> The existing Aboriginal and treaty rights of the Aboriginal peoples of Canada are hereby recognised and affirmed.

A treaty in legislative form could be passed by any federal parliament with the will to do so (which would have the power under the races power: s 51(xxvi)) but would, as a piece of legislation, be vulnerable to being overruled by subsequent legislation.

The parties negotiate the contents of a treaty that can be as broad or narrow as the parties agree upon. In the context of a treaty between Indigenous and non-Indigenous Australians, specific areas that might be covered could include a prohibition of racial discrimination, recognition of the rights of equality and ways in which self-determination could be exercised, access to education and training and employment opportunities, the protection of laws, cultures and languages, control, ownership and management of land, waters and resources, benefits from resource development and economic and social development. A treaty could provide, among other things, a symbolic recognition of sovereignty and prior occupation, a redefinition and restructuring of the relationship that Indigenous peoples have with Australia, the granting of better rights protection and the basis for regional self-government.

It is also possible that a national treaty could be a standard-setting document which allows for local or regional treaties containing fundamental, bottom-line principles and, at the same time, it should provide mechanisms for local and regional decision-making processes.

What might a treaty process look like?

If a treaty process were to be undertaken, it would raise some key challenges for Indigenous people.

Who would have the authority to sign a treaty on behalf of Indigenous people? As the focus of the treaty debate turns to processes and frameworks, the issue of who is going to have the authority to represent, negotiate on behalf of and sign for Indigenous parties is going to become increasingly important.

Who will be counted as 'Indigenous'? The Canadian experience shows that when there are benefits that flow from a treaty, the issue of band membership becomes a contentious one and the difference between 'status' and 'non-status' First Nations peoples a matter of great tension in Indigenous communities. A treaty or a series of treaties will bring the issues of identity and qualification for inclusion to

CASE STUDY

the forefront and Australians will need to be prepared to deal with this. As we have already seen from the native title debates, there is fracturing within the Indigenous community over who are appropriate beneficiaries for identified Indigenous rights. The recognition of rights to land has seen traditional owners pitted against Indigenous people whose families have moved in to or were forced to move in to the claim area three to four generations ago.

Would treaties also be made with state and territory governments? Treaties, as agreements between nations, have been traditionally between the Indigenous people and the federal government of their colonising nation states. However, in the Canadian context, this two-party approach has been changed to a tripartite negotiation. The *Inherent Right to Self-Government Policy* states that treaty negotiations now take place between the provinces, federal government and First Nations people. The inclusion of provinces as third parties to the negotiations was claimed to be as a matter of practicality based on the transfer of natural resources from federal to provincial hands through various agreements and a 1930 constitutional amendment.

How do you make sure that a treaty negotiation is fair when there is a power imbalance between the parties? There is an inherent power imbalance in any negotiation where one party is both the arbiter and a party to the negotiations. Where the treaty negotiation is between Indigenous peoples and the Australian state and directed by the Australian legal system, there is an inherent bias in favour of the government. A more pronounced power imbalance occurs where one of the parties to the negotiations is also the one to interpret the agreement. In the context of treaties, a power imbalance occurs where one arm of government (the judiciary) interprets a treaty entered into by another arm of government (the legislature). Although the doctrine of the separation of powers would treat them as different entities with different functions, both represent the Crown in right of Australia.

DISCUSSION QUESTIONS

- Should there be a treaty between Aboriginal and Torres Strait Islander people and the Australian government?
- If so, what form should it take and what issues should it include?

Treaty-making has been a long-term negotiation process that, if successful, takes decades to conclude. This becomes a trap as Indigenous peoples have to wait a long time for the benefits of negotiations.

There are two ways in which this long-term model of treaty-making could be altered to pass on the benefits of a treaty to Indigenous people and their communities more quickly.

The first is to ensure that agreement-making that is already occurring at a local and regional level—whether under native title legislation or through other mechanisms—is allowed and encouraged to continue while federal negotiations about process and framework take place. This means that agreement-making that can achieve practical outcomes for Indigenous people will not be put on hold while a national process is established, something that may take decades. It also means that those communities that already have the agency and the capacity to negotiate and exercise self-determination can go ahead and do that.

The national framework, when concluded, should have standards against which other agreements can be tested. This could mean that, where appropriate, regional and local agreements concluded before the federal agreement could be negotiated to the extent that standards within those documents are less than the standards set out by the federal framework. This would not be dissimilar to the process being undertaken in Canada where old treaties, whose content is often narrow, are being reinterpreted and renegotiated in light of the more expansive *Inherent Right to Self-Government Policy*.

Another way to ensure a fluid process is to provide for progressive treaty-making. Rather than waiting until the whole content of the treaty is negotiated, it could be that each issue, as it is agreed upon and ratified, becomes part of the treaty but is implemented from that date. This would mean that the easier issues, as they were resolved, would come into effect and allow Indigenous people to enjoy the benefits of those clauses without having to wait for the more difficult issues to be resolved. This approach would also mean that treaty-making could be an on-going process. As new issues arise—biotechnology, genetic engineering, intellectual property, water rights—which earlier negotiators did not anticipate, they could be negotiated and incorporated into the treaty. This more flexible approach to treaty-making will also better reflect the ongoing relationship between Indigenous and non-Indigenous Australians since, like any relationship, it is fluid, flexible and changeable.

A treaty's ability to assist in the development of that relationship will depend on our answers to the following questions:

- Will a treaty be merely symbolic or will it promote substantial change? Could it do both? What will a treaty mean?
- What rights and processes will a treaty protect and enshrine? What will a treaty do?
- How will a treaty allow for flexible approaches to self-government, policies and programs to be built? How will a treaty work?
- How will a treaty assist in making the fundamental link between policy and structural change? How will a treaty stop racism? How will a treaty be effective?

• What other mechanisms, processes and changes do we need to ensure that cost-shifting between state and federal governments and ineffective and under-funded projects do not continue to define approaches to Indigenous issues? Do we need a bill of rights as well as a treaty? How do we ensure that a treaty will be protected?

There has been a tendency to create a false divide between rights issues like a treaty and socio-economic issues like health. Issues of poor health in the Indigenous population that are evident in higher infant mortality and lower life expectancy rates can only be combated with a holistic approach. This involves interventions through policy-making to address problems as they arise and structural and institutional changes to prevent those problems from arising in the first place.

Arguably, the most effective way to develop policy is to ensure that it is linked to an agenda for broader structural and institutional change and that discussions of human rights will seem irrelevant if they do not work with strategies that target socio-economic disadvantage (Behrendt 2003a).

In other words, rather than seeing policy-making and rights as an 'either/or' dichotomy, the relationship should be seen as a trajectory with effective and targeted policy at one end, long-term institutional change at the other and a strong connection developed between the two.

Human rights are not abstract concepts. When young children in Redfern get picked up and driven around in the back of a police wagon for no reason other than that they are black, that is a breach of their human rights. When a woman receives a custodial sentence because the *Bail Act* disproportionately disadvantages Indigenous people, that is a breach of her human rights. When Aboriginal men are turned away from hospitals for being drunk when they are actually suffering an epileptic fit, that is a breach of their human rights.

The challenge is to provide a framework so that people who feel the impact of policies like over-policing, the impact of racism in the provision of services and the impact of racist legislation have more avenues of redress than the members of the Stolen Generations have had.

A new era for reconciliation?

When the Howard Government left government, it signalled an end to an era in which progress on reconciliation had stalled. It closed an era in which Australia had a prime minister who did not believe in saying 'sorry' to the Stolen Generations, dismissed the *Bringing Them Home* report as too emotive and countered that only one in ten children were taken away and that it was for their own good, derailed the reconciliation process, used the decision in the *Wik* case to fuel an anti-Aboriginal election, who termed native title and the right to negotiate as un-Australian and who repealed the application of the *Racial Discrimination Act 1975* (Cth) from applying to Aboriginal people three times: during the Hindmarsh Island dispute, through the *Native Title Amendment Act 1998* (Cth) and in relation to the Northern Territory intervention.

The end of the Howard era and the election of the Rudd Government gave rise to an expectation that the reconciliation process could be renewed. Rudd, in opposition, supported, without any amendment, Howard's intervention in the Northern Territory including the aspects that repealed the *Racial Discrimination Act*, the abolition of the permit system and the compulsory quarantining of all welfare payments.

But in other ways, the approach to Indigenous issues by the Howard and Rudd Governments is starkly different. Prime Minister Rudd's apology to the Stolen Generations was one key illustration of this. Many Australians understood that the importance of saying 'sorry' was that it indicated a willingness to revisit the unfinished business of reconciliation.

However, the willingness to give an apology and the refusal to establish a compensation scheme for members of the Stolen Generations highlight the challenges as Australia enters a new era. While there will be plenty of recommendations that have been identified in the work done on developing frameworks for reconciliation that Prime Minister Rudd can enact that will show more willingness to improve the relationship between Indigenous and non-Indigenous people, there will still be a large gap between what the Rudd Government is willing to deliver and what the hopes and aspirations of the Indigenous community are.

For example, the Rudd Government has agreed to sign the Declaration on the Rights of Indigenous Peoples but has not indicated how and to what extent the government will incorporate the principles into Australian law. The government will face similar challenges with the recommendations from CAR, the *Recognition, Rights and Reforms* report, the Royal Commission into Aboriginal Deaths in Custody and the *Bringing Them Home* report. Similar challenges will be faced by the question of how to create a new national representative body and the desire by Aborigines and Torres Strait Islanders to exercise self-governance in some form at a regional level.

However, that there is more opportunity to progress reconciliation under Rudd than there was under Howard. There is also more opportunity to return to the rights framework that was understood to be an essential part of any strategy to achieve social justice. Recognising Indigenous rights to land, water, fishing, culture, language, health, education, family and self-determination and deciding how they are protected, whether by treaty, constitutional protection or special legislation, could again become part of the conversation with governments about what reconciliation between Indigenous and non-Indigenous people might look like.

Bibliography

Aboriginal Child Sexual Assault Taskforce, (2006) *Breaking the Silence: Creating the Future—Addressing Child Sexual Assault in Aboriginal Communities in NSW*, New South Wales Attorney General's Department, Sydney.

Aboriginal Justice Advisory Council, New South Wales, (1999a) 'Report on the *Children (Protection and Parental Responsibility) Act 1997*', AJAC, Sydney.

Aboriginal Justice Advisory Council, New South Wales, (1999b) *Policing Public Order, Offensive Language and Behaviour. The Impact on Aboriginal People*, AJAC, Sydney.

Aboriginal Justice Advisory Council, New South Wales, (2000) *Aboriginal People and Bail Courts in New South Wales*, AJAC, Sydney.

Aboriginal Justice Implementation Commission, (1999) 'Report of The Aboriginal Justice Inquiry of Manitoba', <http://www.ajic.mb.ca/reports/final_toc.html> accessed 23 May 2008.

Aboriginal Justice Inquiry—Child Welfare Initiative, (2003) 'Report of the MKO 22nd Legislative Government House Annual General Assembly Opaskwayak Cree Nation', 9–11 September 2003.

Aboriginal Legal Service of Western Australia, (1994) *Counting the Cost: Policing in Wiluna 1994*, Aboriginal Legal Service of Western Australia, Perth.

Aboriginal and Torres Strait Islander Social Justice Commissioner, (nd) 'Submission to the United Nations Committee on the Rights of the Child for their Day of General Discussion on the Rights of Indigenous Children', Unpublished, <www.hreoc.gov.au/social_justice/croc/sub3.htm> accessed 25 September 2006.

Aboriginal and Torres Strait Islander Social Justice Commission, (1993) *First Report 1993*, Australian Government Publishing Service, Canberra.

Aboriginal and Torres Strait Islander Social Justice Commissioner, (2001) *Social Justice Report 2000*, HREOC, Sydney.

Aboriginal and Torres Strait Islander Social Justice Commissioner, (2002) *Social Justice Report 2002*, HREOC, Sydney.

Aboriginal and Torres Strait Islander Social Justice Commissioner, (2003) *Social Justice Report 2003*, HREOC, Sydney.

Aboriginal and Torres Strait Islander Social Justice Commissioner, (2004) *Social Justice Report 2004*, HREOC, Sydney.

Aboriginal and Torres Strait Islander Social Justice Commissioner, (2006) *Ending Family Violence and Abuse in Aboriginal and Torres Strait Islander Communities*, HREOC, Sydney.

Altman, J., (1983) *Aborigines and Mining Royalties in the Northern Territory*, Australian Institute of Aboriginal Studies, Canberra.

Altman, J., (1983) 'The Payment of Mining Royalties to Aborigines in the Northern Territory: Compensation or Revenue?', CEPR Discussion Paper no 77, Centre for Economic Policy Research, Research School of Social Sciences, The Australian National University.

Altman, J., (1985) 'Report on the Review of the Aboriginals Benefit Trust Account (and Related Financial Matters) in the Northern Territory Land Rights Legislation', Australian Government Publishing Service, Canberra.

Altman, J., (co-edited with Morphy, F. and Rowse, T.), (1999) *Land Rights at Risk? Evaluations of the Reeves Report*, Research Monograph no 14, Centre for Aboriginal Economic Policy Research, The Australian National University, Canberra.

Altman, J., (with Levitus, R.), (1999) 'The Allocation and Management of Royalties under the *Aboriginal Land Rights (Northern Territory) Act*', Centre for Aboriginal Economic Policy Research (CAEPR) Discussion Paper no 191, CAEPR, The Australian National University, Canberra.

Altman, J., (with Linkhorn, C. and Clarke J., assisted by Fogarty W. and Napier K.), (2005) 'Land Rights and Development Reform in Remote Australia', CAEPR Discussion Paper no 276, Centre for Aboriginal Economic Policy Research, The Australian National University, Canberra.

Altman, J., (2007) '"National Emergency" and Land Rights Reform: Separating Fact from Fiction', Oxfam Australia, 7 August 2007.

Anaya, S. J., (1996) *Indigenous Peoples in International Law*, Oxford University Press, Oxford.

Anaya, S. J., (2004) *Indigenous Peoples in International Law*, Oxford University Press, New York.

Atkinson, J., (2002) *Trauma Trails: Recreating Song Lines*, Spinifex Press, Melbourne.

ATSIC, (1995) *Recognition, Rights and Reforms: Report to Government on Native Title Social Justice Measures*, Australian Government Publishing Service, Canberra.

Attwood, B. (ed), (1996) *In the Age of Mabo: History, Aborigines and Australia*, Allen & Unwin, Sydney.

Attwood, B. and Marckus, A., (1999) *The Struggle for Aboriginal Rights: A Documentary History*, Allen & Unwin, Sydney.

Attwood, B. and Marckus, A., (2004) *Thinking Black: William Cooper and the Australian Aborigines' League*, Aboriginal Studies Press, Canberra.

Australian Bureau of Statistics, (2003) *The Health and Welfare of Australia's Aboriginal and Torres Strait Islander Peoples*, Catalogue no 4704, ABS, Canberra.

Australian Bureau of Statistics, (2004) *National Aboriginal and Torres Strait Islander Social Survey 2002*, Catalogue no 4714, ABS, Canberra.

Australian Bureau of Statistics, (2005) *The Health and Welfare of Australia's Aboriginal and Torres Strait Islander Peoples*, Catalogue no 4704.0, ABS, Canberra.

Australian Bureau of Statistics, (2005a) *Deaths*, Catalogue no 3302, ABS, Canberra.

Australian Bureau of Statistics, (2006) *Prisoners in Australia*, Catalogue no 4517.0 ABS, Canberra.

Australian Collaboration, (2007) *Successful Strategies in Indigenous Organisations*, Australian Institute of Aboriginal and Torres Strait Islander Studies, Canberra, <http://www.australiancollaboration.com.au/research/index.html>.

Australian Institute of Criminology, (2001) *Persons in Juvenile Corrective Institutions 1981–2000— with a Statistical Review of the Year 2000*, Australian Institute of Criminology, Canberra.

Australian Institute of Health and Welfare, (2006a) *Child Protection Australia 2004–05*, cat no CWS 26. AIHW, Canberra (Child Welfare Series no 38).

Australian Institute of Health and Welfare, (2006) *Family Violence Among Aboriginal and Torres Strait Islander Peoples*, AIHW, Canberra.

Australian Institute of Aboriginal and Torres Strait Islander Studies, (1996) *Final Report of the Review of the Aboriginal Councils and Associations Act 1976*, vol 1, 33 ('The Fingleton Review').

Australian Law Reform Commission, (1986) *The Recognition of Aboriginal Customary Laws*, Report no 31, Australian Law Reform Commission, Sydney.

Australian Law Reform Commission, (1988) *Sentencing*, Report no 44, Australian Law Reform Commission, Sydney.

Australian Law Reform Commission, (1992) *Multiculturalism and the Law*, Report no 57, Australian Law Reform Commission, Sydney.

Australian Law Reform Commission, (1994) *Equality Before the Law: Justice for Women*, Report no 69, Australian Law Reform Commission, Sydney.

Australian Law Reform Commission, (2006) *Same Crime, Same Time: Sentencing of Federal Offenders*, Report no 103, Australian Law Reform Commission, Sydney.

Australian Parliament House, Bills Digest no 67 (2005–06), *Aboriginal and Torres Strait Islander Heritage Protection Amendment Bill 2005*, <http://www.aph.gov.au/library/Pubs/bd/2005-06/06bd067.htm> accessed 11 May 2008.

Baker, J., (2001) 'The Scope for Reducing Indigenous Imprisonment Rates', Crime and Justice Bulletin no 55, New South Wales Bureau of Crime Statistics and Research, Sydney.

Baldry, E., (1997) 'Convicted Women: Before and After Prison', *Current Issues in Criminal Justice*, vol 8, no 3, p 275.

Bamblett, M., (2007) 'Ten Years of Truth Telling: What Bringing Them Home Means To Us All', SNAICC, *'Remember Me': Commemorating the Tenth Anniversary of the Bringing Them Home Report*, Melbourne, pp 8–13.

Bargen, J., (1999) 'Youth Justice Conferencing: The Debate Continues', *Indigenous Law Bulletin*, vol 4, no 20, pp 18–19.

Bargen, J., (2000) 'The *Young Offenders Act 1997*: Is the Diversionary Scheme Being Diverted?', *Judicial Officers Bulletin*, vol 12, no 3, pp 17–20.

Bartlett, R., (2004) *Making a Claim Under the Native Title Act 1993, Native Title in Australia*, 2nd edn, LexisNexis Butterworths, Brisbane.

Beaglehole, J. C. (ed), (1955) *The Journals of Captain James Cook on his Voyages of Discovery*, vol 1, Cambridge University Press, Cambridge.

Beckett, J., (1988) 'Aboriginality, Citizenship and Nation State', *Social Analysis*, no 24.

Behrendt, J., (1993) '*Aboriginal Land Rights Act 1983* (NSW): "Lawfully Used and Occupied"—Some Recent Interpretations', *Aboriginal Law Bulletin*, 5.

Behrendt, J., (2006) 'Comment on the National Indigenous Council's Indigenous Land Tenure Principles from a Native Title Perspective', *Journal of Indigenous Policy*, 8.

Behrendt, L., (1995) *Aboriginal Dispute Resolution*, The Federation Press, Annandale.

Behrendt, L., (1999) 'Charting Democracy and Aboriginal Rights in Australia's Psychological Terra Nullius', in Patmore, G. and Glover, D. (eds) *New Voices for Social Democracy: Labor Essays 1999–2000*, Pluto Press, Melbourne.

Behrendt, L., (2000) 'Bargaining on More than Good Will: Recognising a Fiduciary Obligation in Native Title', *Land, Rights, Laws: Issues of Native Title*, vol 2, no 4, Native Title Research Unit, Australian Institute of Aboriginal and Torres Strait Islander Studies, Canberra.

Behrendt, L., (2000) 'The Protection of Indigenous Rights: Contemporary Canadian Comparisons', Issues Paper 1999–2000. Department of the Parliamentary Library, Canberra.

Behrendt, L., (2001a) 'Towards Improved Rights Protections', *Journal of Australian Indigenous Issues*, vol 3, no 4, 3.

Behrendt, L., (2001b) 'Indigenous Self-determination: Rethinking the Relationship between Indigenous Peoples and the State', *University of New South Wales Law Journal*, 24(3), pp 850–861.

Behrendt, L., (2002a) 'Self-determination and Indigenous Policy: The Rights Framework and Practical Outcomes', *Journal of Indigenous Policy*, 1, pp 43–58.

Behrendt, L., (2002b) 'The Link Between Rights and a Treaty', *Balayi: Culture Law and Colonialism*, 4, pp 21–28.

Behrendt, L., (2002c) 'Unfinished Journey–Indigenous Self-determination', *Arena Magazine*, vol 58, p 26.

Behrendt, L., (2003a) *Achieving Social Justice: Indigenous Rights and Australia's Future*, The Federation Press, Annandale.

Behrendt, L., (2003b) 'Practical Steps Towards a Treaty—Structures, Challenges and the Need for Flexibility' in ATSIC & AIATSIS, *Treaty: Let's get it Right*, AIATSIS, Canberra.

Behrendt, L., (2003c) 'Power from the People: A Community-based Approach to Indigenous Self-determination', *The Flinders Journal of Law Reform*, 6(2), pp 135–150.

Behrendt, L., (2003d) 'It's Broke so Fix It: Arguments for a Bill of Rights', *Australian Journal of Human Rights*, 9(1), pp 257–262.

Behrendt, L., (2005a) 'National Representative Structures', *Ngiya Issues*, Paper 1, Sydney.

Behrendt, L., (2005b) 'Our Institutions in a Reconciled Australia', *Journal of Indigenous Policy*, 4, pp 27–37.

Behrendt, L., (2005c) 'Treaty and/or Health', *Balayi*, 7, pp 154–156.

Behrendt, L., (2006a) 'Indigenous Self-determination: Rethinking the Relationship of Rights and Economic Development', in Worby G. and Rigney L.I. (eds), *Sharing Spaces: Indigenous and Non-Indigenous Responses to Story, Country and Rights*, (API-Network).

Behrendt, L., (2006b) 'The Mabo Lecture', *Journal of Indigenous Policy*, 8, p 103.

Behrendt, L., (2007) 'The Long Path to Land Justice: The Mabo Lecture 2007', *Journal of Indigenous Policy*, 8, pp 103–115.

Behrendt, L., Brennan, S., Strelein, L. and Williams, G., (2005) *Treaty*, The Federation Press, Annandale.

Behrendt, L. and Kelly, L., (2006) 'Creating Conflict: Case Studies in the Tension Between Native Title Claims and Land Rights Claims', *Journal of Indigenous Policy*, 8, p 73.

Behrendt, L. and Kelly, L., (2008) *Resolving Aboriginal Disputes: Land Conflict and Beyond*, The Federation Press, Leichhardt, New South Wales.

Behrendt, L., McCausland, R., Williams, G., Reilly, A. and McMillan, M., (2007) 'The Promise of Regional Governance for Aboriginal and Torres Strait Islander Communities', *Ngiya: Talk the Law*, vol 1, no 1.

Behrendt, L. and Watson, N., (2007) 'Shifting Ground: Why Land Rights and Native Title Have Not Delivered Social Justice', *Journal of Indigenous Policy*, issue 8, pp 94–102.

Bennett, G., (1978) *Aboriginal Rights and International Law*, Royal Anthropological Institute of Great Britain and Ireland, London.

Bennett, S., (1989) *Aborigines and Political Power*, Allen & Unwin, Sydney.

Berger, J., (1988) *Aborigines Today: Land and Justice*, Anti-Slavery Society, 11, London.

Bird, G., Martin, G. and Nielson, J. (eds), (1996) *Majah: Indigenous Peoples and the Law*, The Federation Press, Sydney.

Blackstock, C. and Trocme, N., (2004) *Community Based Child Welfare for Aboriginal Children: Supporting Resilience through Structural Change*, Centre of Excellence for Child Welfare, <http://www.cecw-cepb.ca/files/file/en/communityBasedCWAboriginalChildren.pdf> accessed 23 May 2008.

Blackstone, W., (1807) *Commentaries on the Laws of England*, <http://www.lonang.com/exlibris/blackstone/> accessed 30 October 2008.

Blagg, H., (1997) 'A Just Measure of Shame?: Aboriginal Youth and Conferencing in Australia', *British Journal of Criminology*, vol 37, no 4, pp 481–506.

Blagg, H., (1998) 'Restorative Visions and Restorative Justice Practice', *Current Issues in Criminal Justice*, vol 10, no 1, pp 5–14.

Blagg, H., (2000) 'Crisis Intervention in Aboriginal Family Violence', Summary Report, Partnerships Against Domestic Violence, Commonwealth of Australia, Canberra.

Blagg, H., (2005) *A New Way of Doing Justice Business? Community Justice Mechanisms and Sustainable Governance in Western Australia*, Background Paper 8, Law Reform Commission of Western Australia, Perth.

Blagg, H., Morgan, N., Cunneen, C. and Ferrante, A., (2005) 'Systemic Racism as a Factor in the Over-representation of Aboriginal People in the Criminal Justice System', Report to the Equal Opportunity Commission and Aboriginal Justice Forum, Melbourne.

Blagg, H. and Valuri, G., (2004) 'Self-policing and Community Safety: The Work of Aboriginal Community Patrols in Australia', *Current Issues in Criminal Justice*, 15(3), pp 205–219.

Board of Inquiry into the Protection of Aboriginal Children from Sexual Abuse, (2007) *Little Children are Sacred—the Report of the Northern Territory Board of Inquiry into the Protection of Aboriginal Children from Sexual Abuse*, Northern Territory Government, <http://www.nt.gov.au/dcm/inquirysaac/pdf/bipacsa_final_report.pdf> accessed 23 May 2008.

Bolger, A., (1991) *Aboriginal Women and Violence*, Australian National University North Australia
 Research Unit, Casuarina.

Borg, T. and Paul, A., (2004) *Indigenous Parenting Project*, Secretariat of National Aboriginal and
 Islander Child Care (SNAICC), Melbourne.

Borg, T. and Paul, A., (2005) *Indigenous Parenting Project*, Secretariat of National Aboriginal and
 Islander Child Care (SNAICC), Melbourne.

Brennan, F., (1994) *Securing a Bountiful Place for Aborigine and Torres Strait Islanders in a Modern
 Free and Tolerant Australia*, Constitutional Centenary Foundation, Canberra.

Brennan, S., (2006) 'Economic Development and Land Council Power: Modernising the *Land
 Rights Act* or Same Old Same Old?', *Australian Indigenous Law Reporter*, 10(4).

Brennan, S., Bosnjak, V. and Williams, G., (2003) 'Rights-based Reconciliation Needs Renewed
 Action from Canberra', *Alternative Law Journal*, 28(3), p 122.

Brenner, K., (2002) *Indigenous Women in the Victorian Prison System: A Snapshot*, Department of
 Justice, Melbourne.

Brough, J., (1997) 'Wik Draft Threat to Native Title', *The Sydney Morning Herald*, 18 June, p 3.

Brown, D., Farrier, D., Egger, S., McNamara, L. and Steel, A., (2006) *Criminal Laws*, The Federation
 Press, Leichhardt.

Buti, T., (1998) 'Kruger and Bray and the Common Law', *University of the New South Wales Law
 Journal*, 21(1), pp 232–240.

Central Land Council, (2004) *Evidence to Senate Select Committee on the Administration of
 Indigenous Affairs*, Proof Committee Hansard, 24 August 2004.

Chamberlain, C. and MacKenzie, D., (2003) *Australian Census Analytic Program: Counting the
 Homeless*, Australian Bureau of Statistics, Canberra.

Chan, J. (ed), (2005) *Reshaping Juvenile Justice: The New South Wales Young Offenders Act 1997*,
 Sydney Institute of Criminology Monograph Series, Sydney.

Chan, J., Bargen, J., Luke, G. and Clancey, G., (2004) 'Regulating Police Discretion: An Assessment
 of the Impact of the New South Wales *Young Offenders Act 1997*', *Criminal Law Journal*,
 28(2), pp 72–92.

Chan, C. and Cunneen, C., (2000) *Evaluation of the Implementation of the New South Wales Police
 Service Aboriginal Strategic Plan*, Institute of Criminology, Sydney.

Charlesworth, H., (1999) 'Human Rights and Reconciliation in International Perspective'
 Australian Cultural History, 18, pp 9–21.

Charlesworth, H., (2002) *Writing in Rights: Australia and the Protection of Human Rights*,
 University of New South Wales Press, Sydney.

Chesterman, J., (2001) 'Defending Australia's Reputation, How Indigenous Australians Won Civil
 Rights' (Part One), *Australian Historical Studies*, vol 32, no 116, pp 20.

Chesterman, J., (2005) *Civil Rights: How Indigenous Australians Won Formal Equality*, University of
 Queensland Press, St Lucia.

Chesterman, J. and Galligan, B., (1997) *Citizens Without Rights*, Cambridge University Press,
 Melbourne.

Clark, J., (1983) 'Tasmanian Museum and Art Gallery', *COMA Bulletin*, 12, 18.

Clarke, J., (2001) 'Cubillo v Commonwealth: Case Note', Melbourne University Law Review, 25(1), pp 218–294.

Clements, C., (2006) Inquest into the Death of Mulrunji, Office of the State Coroner, Brisbane, <http://www.justice.qld.gov.au/courts/coroner/findings/mulrunji270906.doc>.

Cody, A., (2001) 'Case Note: Williams v The Minister, Aboriginal Land Rights Act 1983', Australian Journal of Human Rights, 7(1), pp 155–168.

Cohen, C. P., (1993) 'The Developing Jurisprudence of the Rights of the Child', St Thomas Law Review, vol 6, pp 1–96.

Cohen, C. P., (1998) 'International Protection of the Rights of Indigenous Children', in Cohen C.P. (ed), The Human Rights of Indigenous Peoples, Transnational Publishers, New York.

Committee on the Rights of the Child (2005), Consideration of Reports submitted by States Parties under Article 44 of the Convention–Concluding Observations: Australia, 40th session, UN Doc CRC/C/15?Add268. Office of the United Nations High Commissioner for Human Rights, Geneva, <http://www.umhchr.ch/tbs/doc.nsf/>

Commonwealth of Australia, (2008) Australian 2020 Final Summit Report, Department of the Prime Minister and Cabinet, One National Circuit, Canberra.

Concluding Observations of the Committee on the Elimination of Racial Discrimination, (2005), Australia, 14/04/2005. CERD/C/AUS/CO/14. (Concluding Observations/Comments) 21 February–11 March 2005.

Cooper, W., Secretary Australian Aborigines' League, to the Minister for the Interior, Thomas Paterson, 16 June 1937, Department of the Interior, Correspondence files, 'Australian Aborigines League', NAA, CRS A659, 1940/1/858, in Attwood, B. and Markus, A. (2004) 'Thinking Black: William Cooper and the Australian Aborigines' League', Aboriginal Studies Press, Canberra.

Cornwall, A., (2002) Restoring Identity, Final Report, Public Interest Advocacy Centre, Sydney.

Council for Aboriginal Reconciliation (CAR), (2000a) 'Achieving Economic Independence', Corroboree 2000, Sydney Opera House, 27 May 2000.

Council for Aboriginal Reconciliation (CAR), (2000b) 'Australian Declaration Towards Reconciliation', Corroboree 2000, Sydney Opera House, 27 May 2000.

Council for Aboriginal Reconciliation (CAR), (2000c) 'Final Report of the Council for Aboriginal Reconciliation to the Prime Minister and the Commonwealth Parliament', Canberra, December 2000.

Council for Aboriginal Reconciliation (CAR), (2000d) 'Overcoming Disadvantage', Corroboree 2000, Sydney Opera House, 27 May 2000.

Council for Aboriginal Reconciliation (CAR), (2000e) 'Recognising Aboriginal and Torres Strait Islander Rights', Corroboree 2000, Sydney Opera House, 27 May 2000.

Council for Aboriginal Reconciliation (CAR), (2000f) 'Roadmap for Reconciliation', Corroboree 2000, Sydney Opera House, 27 May 2000.

Council for Aboriginal Reconciliation (CAR), (2000g) 'Sustaining the Reconciliation Process', Corroboree 2000, Sydney Opera House, 27 May 2000.

COP 5 Decision V/16, 2005, Annex, Objectives.

Corrs Chambers Westgarth Lawyers, Anthropos Consulting, Dodson M., Mantziaris, C. and Rashid, S. B., (2002) *A Modern Statute for Indigenous Corporations: Reforming the Aboriginal Councils and Associations Act 72* ('The Corrs Review').

Cove, J., (1995) *What the Bones Say: Tasmanian Aborigines, Science and Domination*, Carleton University Press, Ottawa.

Cowlishaw, G., (1991) 'Inquiring into Aboriginal Deaths in Custody: The Limits of a Royal Commission', *Journal for Social Justice Studies*, no 4, pp 101–115.

Crime Research Centre, (1995) *Aboriginal Youth and the Juvenile Justice System of Western Australia*, University of Western Australia, Nedlands.

Criminal Justice Commission, (1994) *A Report of the Investigation into the Arrest and Death of Daniel Alfred Yock*, Goprint, Brisbane.

Criminal Justice Commission, (1996) *Aboriginal Witnesses in Queensland Criminal Courts*, Goprint, Brisbane.

Crosthwaite, A., (1999) 'The Diversion and Disposition of Young Aboriginal Offenders in Western Australia: A Human Rights Perspective', *Griffith Law Review*, vol 8, no 1, pp 171–199.

Cubillo, F., (2006) *Churchill Fellow: To Ascertain how Government Legislation, Organisational Policies and Community Strategies have Facilitated the Repatriation of Indigenous Human Remains—New Zealand, United States of America, Canada, United Kingdom, Recommendations*.

Cunneen, C., (1990a) *Aboriginal/Police Relations in Redfern with Special Reference to the Police Raid of 8 February 1990*, Report Commissioned by the National Inquiry into Racist Violence, Human Rights and Equal Opportunity Commission, Sydney.

Cunneen, C., (1990b) *Aboriginal Juveniles and Police Violence*, Report Commissioned by the National Inquiry into Racist Violence, Human Rights and Equal Opportunity Commission, Sydney.

Cunneen, C., (1992) 'Judicial Racism' in McKillop, S. (ed), *Aboriginal Justice Issues*, Australian Institute of Criminology, Canberra.

Cunneen, C., (1994) 'Enforcing Genocide? Aboriginal Young People and the Police', in White, R. and Alder, C. (eds), *The Police and Young People in Australia*, Cambridge University Press, Melbourne.

Cunneen, C., (1997) 'Community Conferencing and the Fiction of Indigenous Control', *Australian and New Zealand Journal of Criminology*, vol 30, no 3, pp 292–311.

Cunneen, C., (1999) *Zero Tolerance Policing: Implications for Indigenous People*, ATSIC, Canberra.

Cunneen, C., (2001a) *Conflict, Politics and Crime: Aboriginal Communities and the Police*, Allen & Unwin, Sydney.

Cunneen, C., (2001b) *The Impact of Crime Prevention on Aboriginal Communities*, New South Wales Crime Prevention Division and Aboriginal Justice Advisory Council, Sydney.

Cunneen, C., (2002) 'Mandatory Sentencing and Human Rights', *Current Issues in Criminal Justice*, vol 13, no 3, pp 322–327.

Cunneen, C., (2005a) *Evaluation of the Queensland Aboriginal and Torres Strait Islander Justice Agreement*, Institute of Criminology, University of Sydney, Sydney.

Cunneen, C., (2005b) 'Consensus and Sovereignty: Rethinking Policing in the Light of Indigenous Self-determination', in Hocking, B. (ed) *Unfinished Constitutional Business? Rethinking Indigenous Self-determination*, Aboriginal Studies Press, Canberra.

Cunneen, C., (2006a) 'Racism, Discrimination and the Over-representation of Indigenous People in the Criminal Justice System: Some Conceptual and Explanatory Issues', *Current Issues in Criminal Justice*, vol 17, no 3, pp 329–346.

Cunneen, C., (2006b) 'Aboriginal Deaths in Custody: A Continuing Systematic Abuse', *Social Justice*, vol 33, no 4.

Cunneen, C. and Grix, J., (2003) 'Chronology: The Stolen Generations Litigation 1993–2003', *Indigenous Law Bulletin*, 5(23), pp 14.

Cunneen, C. and Grix, J., (2004) *The Limitations of Litigation in Stolen Generations Cases*, Research Discussion Paper 15, Australia Institute of Aboriginal and Torres Strait Island Studies, Canberra.

Cunneen, C. and Kerley, K., (1995a) 'Deaths in Custody in Australia: The Untold Story of Aboriginal and Torres Strait Islander Women', *Canadian Journal of Women and the Law*, vol 8, no 1, Spring, pp 531–552.

Cunneen, C. and Kerley, K. (1995b) 'Indigenous Women and the Criminal Justice System: Some Comments on the Australian Situation', in Hazelhurst, K. (ed), *Perceptions of Justice: Issues in Indigenous Community Empowerment*, Aldershot [England]; Avebury, Sydney, pp 71–94.

Cunneen, C. and Libesman, T., (2000a) 'An Apology for Expressing Regret', *Meanjin*, vol 59, no 1, pp 145–154.

Cunneen, C. and Libesman, T., (2000b) 'Postcolonial Trauma: The Contemporary Removal of Indigenous Children and Young People from their Families in Australia', *Australian Journal of Social Issues*, vol 35, no 2, pp 99–115.

Cunneen, C. and Libesman, T., (2001) 'Cultural Rights, Human Rights and the Contemporary Removal of Aboriginal and Torres Strait Islander Children from their Families', in Garkawe, S., Kelly, L. and Fisher, W. (eds), *Indigenous Human Rights*, Sydney Institute of Criminology, Sydney.

Cunneen, C. and Libesman, T., (2002) 'Removed and Discarded: The Contemporary Legacy of the Stolen Generations', *Australian Indigenous Law Reporter*, vol 7, no 4, pp 1–20.

Cunneen, C. and Luke, G., (2006) *Evaluation of the Aboriginal Over-representation Strategy*, Report to the New South Wales Department of Juvenile Justice, Sydney.

Cunneen, C. and McDonald, D., (1997) *Keeping Aboriginal and Torres Strait Islander People Out of Custody: An Evaluation of the Implementation of the Recommendations of the Royal Commission into Aboriginal Deaths in Custody*, Aboriginal and Torres Strait Islander Commission, Canberra.

Cunneen, C. and Robb, T., (1987) 'Criminal Justice in north-west New South Wales', New South Wales Bureau of Crime Statistics and Research, Attorney-General's Department, Sydney.

Cunneen, C. and Schwartz, M., (2005) *Customary Law, Human Rights and International Law: Some Conceptual Issues*, Background Paper 11, Law Reform Commission of Western Australia, Perth.

Cunneen, C. and White, R., (2007) *Juvenile Justice Youth and Crime in Australia*, 3rd edn, Oxford University Press, Melbourne.

Daes, E., (1995) 'Principles and Guidelines for the Protection of the Heritage of Indigenous People', Sub-Commission on Prevention of Discrimination and Protection of Minorities of the Commission on Human Rights, Economic and Social Council, United Nations: E/CN.4/Sub.2/1995/26.

Daes, E., (2004) 'Final Report, Prevention of Discrimination and Protection of Indigenous Peoples', Indigenous People's Permanent Sovereignty over Natural Resources, E/CN.4/Sub.2/2004/30.

Daly, K. and Marchetti, E., (2007) 'Indigenous Sentencing Courts: Towards a Theoretical and Jurisprudential Model', *Sydney Law Review*, vol 29, no 3, pp 415–443.

Davis, M. and McGlade, H., (2005) *International Human Rights Law and the Recognition of Aboriginal Customary Law*, Background Paper, Law Reform Commission of Western Australia, Perth.

Deane, W., (1996) 'Some Signposts From Daguragu', Paper presented at the Inaugural Lingiari Lecture, Darwin, 22 August 1996.

Dennison, S., Stewart, A. and Hurren, E., (2006) 'Police Cautioning in Queensland: The Impact on Juvenile Offending Pathways', *Trends and Issues*, no 306, Australian Institute of Criminology, Canberra.

Department of Aboriginal Affairs, (1976) *The Role of the National Aboriginal Consultative Committee—Report of the Committee of Inquiry*, Australian Government Publishing Service, Canberra.

Department of Environment and Heritage, (2002–2003) *Annual Report*, <http://environment.gov.au/about/publications/annual-report/01-02/outcome1-heritage.html> accessed 12 May 2008.

de Vattel, E., (1852) *Law of Nations*, T. & J.W. Johns, Philadelphia.

Dodson, M., (1994) 'The End in the Beginning: Re (De) fining Aboriginality', *Australian Aboriginal Studies*, no 1, pp 2, 13.

Dodson, M., (1995) *Aboriginal and Torres Strait Islander Social Justice Commissioner Third Report*, Australian Government Publishing Service, Canberra.

Dodson, M., (1996) Aboriginal and Torres Strait Islander Social Justice Commissioner Fourth Report, AGPS, Canberra.

Dodson, M., (1997) 'Launch Speech for the *Bringing Them Home* Report', speech delivered at the Australian Reconciliation Convention, Melbourne, 26 May, <http://www.hreoc.gov.au/about/media/speeches/social_justice/stolen_generation_launch.html> accessed 23 May 2008.

Dodson, M. and Pritchard, S., (1998) 'Recent Developments in Indigenous Policy: The Abandonment of Self-determination?', *Indigenous Law Bulletin*, 21.

Donaldson, M. and Park, Y., (2003) 'The *Racial Discrimination Act*: Does it have a Role in Native Title?', *Indigenous Law Bulletin*, vol 5, no 24, pp 8–11.

Douglas, H., (1998) 'The Cultural Specificity of Evidence: The Current Scope and Relevance of the Anunga Guidelines', *University of New South Wales Law Journal*, vol 21, no 1, p 27.

Drugs and Crime Prevention Committee, (2001) *Inquiry into Public Drunkenness, Final Report,* Parliament of Victoria, Melbourne.

D'Souza, N., (1998), 'Authors of Our Own History: The Challenge for all Australians', *University of New South Wales Law Journal Forum Stolen Children: From Removal to Reconciliation,* vol 4, no 5.

Eades, D., (1994) 'Aboriginal English in Court', *The Judicial Review,* vol 1, no 4, p 367.

Eades, D., (1995a) 'Cross Examination of Aboriginal Children: The Pinkenba Case', *Aboriginal Law Bulletin,* no 75.

Eades, D. (ed), (1995b) *Language in Evidence,* University of New South Wales Press, Kensington.

Eades, D., (2000) *Aboriginal English in the Courts: A Handbook,* Queensland Department of Justice, Brisbane.

Elder, B., (1988) *Blood on the Wattle: Massacres and Maltreatment of Australian Aborigines since 1788,* Child and Associates, Frenchs Forest.

Ellison, R. W., (1952) *Invisible Man,* Random House, New York.

Evans, R., Saunders, K. and Cronin, K., (1988) *Race Relations in Colonial Queensland,* University of Queensland Press, St Lucia.

Evatt, Hon. E. AC, (1996) 'Review of the *Aboriginal and Torres Strait Islander Heritage Protection Act 1984* (Cth)', <http://www.fatsil.org.au> accessed 10 May 2008.

Ferrante, A., Fernandez, J. and Loh, N., (1999) (2001) *Crime and Justice Statistics for Western Australia: 2000,* Crime Research Centre, Crawley.

Ferrante, A., Loh, N., Maller, M. Valuri, G. and Fernandez, J., (2005) 'Crime and Justice Statistics for Western Australia: 2004', Crime Research Centre, Crawley.

Fforde, C. and Ormond-Parker, L., (2001) 'Repatriation Developments in the UK', *Indigenous Law Bulletin,* 10.

Final Recommendations, (2003) *Building Effective Governance Conference,* Jabiru, Northern Territory, 4–7 November 2003, <http://www.nt.gov.au/cdsca/indigenous_conference/web/html/Final_Recommendations.pdf>.

Findlay, M., Odgers, S. and Yeo, S., (2005) *Australian Criminal Justice,* Oxford University Press, Melbourne.

Fitzgerald, T., (2001) *Cape York Justice Study November 2001,* Department of Communities, Brisbane, <http://www.communities.qld.gov.au/community/publications/documents/pdf/capeyork/01_cyjs_intro.pdf >.

Flynn, M., (2005a) 'Not "Aboriginal Enough" for Particular Consideration When Sentencing', *Indigenous Law Bulletin,* vol 6, no 9, pp 15–17.

Flynn, M., (2005b) *Reconciling 'Practical Reconciliation' with the Racial Discrimination Act,* paper delivered at the Castan Centre 'Human Rights 2005: Year in Review' Conference, 2 December, <http://www.law.monash.edu.au/castancentre/events/2005/flynn-paper.html> accessed 22 May 2008.

Flynn, M., (2005c) 'Why has the *Racial Discrimination Act 1975* (Cth) Failed Indigenous People?', *Australian Indigenous Law Reporter,* 2.

Gale, F., Bailey-Harris, R. and Wundersitz, J., (1990) *Aboriginal Youth and the Criminal Justice System,* Cambridge University Press, Cambridge.

Gallagher, P. and Poletti, P., (1998) *Sentencing Disparity and the Ethnicity of Juvenile Offenders*, Judicial Commission of New South Wales, Sydney.

Gayim, E., (1993) *The Eritrean Question: The Conflict Between the Right of Self-determination and the Interests of States*, Iustus Forlag, Uppsala.

Gaze, B., (2005) 'Has the *Racial Discrimination Act* Contributed to Eliminating Racial Discrimination? Analysing the Litigation Track Record 2000–04', *Australian Journal of Human Rights*, vol 11, no 1, <http://www.austlii.edu.au/au/journals/AJHR/2005/6.html> accessed 22 May 2008.

Gilbert, K., (1973) *Because a White Man'll Never Do It*, Angus & Robertson, Sydney.

Global Indigenous Peoples' Caucus Steering Committee, (2007) 'The Declaration on the Rights of Indigenous Peoples: Report of the Global Indigenous Peoples' Caucus Steering Committee', 31 August 2007.

Goldflam, R., (1995) 'Silence in the Court! Problems and Prospects in Aboriginal Legal Interpreting', in Eades, D. (ed), *Language in Evidence*, University of New South Wales Press, Kensington.

Goodall, H., (1996) *Invasion to Embassy: Land in Aboriginal Politics, 1770–1972*, Allen & Unwin, St Leonards.

Green, R. G., (1998) *Justice in Aboriginal Communities: Sentencing Alternatives*, Purich Publishing, Saskatoon, Canada.

Grotius, (1950) *De Jure Praedae*, Oxford University Press, London. Originally published in 1604.

Gungil Jindibah Centre, (1994) *Learning from the Past*, Southern Cross University, Lismore.

Gunn, L., (2004) '*De Rose v State of South Australia*', *Indigenous Law Bulletin*, 5, 930, pp 14–16.

Gunstone, A., (2006a) 'The Impact of the Howard Government upon the Formal Australian Reconciliation Process', *Journal of Australian Indigenous Issues*, 9(2–3), pp 57–72.

Gunstone, A., (2006b) 'The Howard Government's Approach to Indigenous Self-determination' *MAI Review Online*, 1, pp 1–3.

Gunstone, A., (2007) *Unfinished Business: The Australian Formal Reconciliation Process*, Australian Scholarly Publishing, Melbourne.

Gunstone, A., (2008) 'Unfinished Business: The Australian Reconciliation Process from 1991– 2000', in Gunstone, A. (ed), *History, Politics and Knowledge: Essays in Australian Indigenous Studies*, Australian Scholarly Publishing, Melbourne (forthcoming).

Haebich, A., (1992) *For Their Own Good*, University of Western Australia Press, Nedlands.

Hannaford, J., Collins, B. and Huggins, J., (2003) *Review of the Aboriginal and Torres Strait Islander Commission*, Department of Immigration and Multicultural and Indigenous Affairs, Canberra.

Hannum, H., (1996) *Autonomy, Sovereignty and Self-determination: The Accommodation of Conflicting Rights*, University of Pennsylvania Press, Philadelphia.

Harris, M., (2004) 'From Australian Courts to Aboriginal Courts in Australia—Bridging the Gap?', *Current Issues in Criminal Justice*, vol 16, no 1, July 2004.

Harris, M., (2006) 'A Sentencing Conversation: Evaluation of the Koori Courts Pilot Program', Department of Justice, Melbourne.

Hayes H. and Daly, K., (2004) 'Conferencing and Re-offending in Queensland', *Australian and New Zealand Journal of Criminology*, 37(2), pp 167–191.

Healy, C., (1997) *From the Ruins of Colonialism: History as Social Memory*, Cambridge University Press, Melbourne.

Hennessy, A., (2005) 'Indigenous Justice: Indigenous Laws at the Colonial Interface', Paper presented to *Law Asia Conference*, Bali, March 2005.

Hennessy, N., (1999) *Review of the Gate Keeping Role in the Young Offenders Act 1997 (NSW)*, Report to the Youth Justice Advisory Committee, New South Wales Attorney-General's Department, Sydney.

Hill, R., (1995) 'Blackfellas and Whitefellas: Aboriginal Land Rights, The Mabo Decision, and the Meaning of Land', *Human Rights Quarterly*, 17(2), pp 303–322.

Hill, R., (2000) *Decision on the Future of Boobera Lagoon*, Media Release (28 June 2000).

Holnbeck, C., De Jaegher, S. and Schumacher, F., (Metis Child and Family Services), (2003) 'Developing Child Welfare Services from the Ground Up: A Multidisciplinary Approach', *Envision: The Manitoba Journal of Child Welfare*, vol 2, no 2, pp 17–27.

Hookey, J., (1984) 'Settlement and Sovereignty', in Hanks, P. and Keon-Cohen, B. (eds), *Aborigines and the Law*, Allen & Unwin, Sydney.

House of Representatives Standing Committee on Aboriginal and Torres Strait Islander Affairs, (1994) *Justice Under Scrutiny*, Australian Government Publishing Service, Canberra.

Howard, J., (1989) 'Ministerial Statement: Administration of Aboriginal Affairs', *Hansard*, House of Representatives, Debates, 11 April 1989, <http://parlinfo.aph.gov.au> accessed 6 October 2008.

Howard, J., (2000) 'Transcript of The Prime Minister The Hon John Howard MP Menzies Lecture Series Perspectives on Aboriginal and Torres Strait Islander Issues', Canberra, 13 December 2000.

Howard, J., (2004) 'Transcript of the Prime Minister the Hon John Howard MP, Joint Press Conference with Senator Amanda Vanstone', Parliament House, Canberra, 15 April 2004.

Howitt, R., (2006) 'Scales of Coexistence: Tackling the Tension between Legal and Cultural Landscapes in Post-Mabo Australia', *Macquarie Law Journal*, vol 6, pp 49–64.

Human Rights and Equal Opportunity Commission, (1991) *Racist Violence*, Report of the National Inquiry into Racist Violence, Australian Government Publishing Service, Canberra.

Human Rights and Equal Opportunity Commission, (1997) *Bringing Them Home: Report of the National Inquiry into the Separation of Aboriginal and Torres Strait Islander Children from Their Families*, Commonwealth of Australia, Canberra.

Human Rights and Equal Opportunity Commission, (1999) *Sentencing Juvenile Offenders*, Human Rights Brief no 2, Human Rights and Equal Opportunity Commission, Sydney.

Human Rights and Equal Opportunity Commission, (2001) *Diversion of Juvenile Offenders*, Human Rights Brief no 5, Human Rights and Equal Opportunity Commission, Sydney.

Human Rights and Equal Opportunity Commission, (2005) *Federal Discrimination Law 2005*, Human Rights and Equal Opportunity Commission, Sydney, <http://www.hreoc.gov.au/legal/FDL/fed_discrimination_law_05/index.html> accessed 22 May 2008.

Human Rights and Equal Opportunity Commission, (2006) *Submission of the Human Rights and Equal Opportunity Commission to the Senate Legal and Constitutional References Committee on the Crimes Amendments (Bail and Sentencing) Bill 2006*, Human Rights and Equal Opportunity Commission, Sydney.

Human Rights Committee, (2000) Transcript—Meeting, 21 July 2000, 69th Session held in Geneva, <http://www.faira.org.au/hrc/articles/hrc_21_07_00.html> accessed 12 May 2008.

In the Hands of the Region—A New ATSIC, The Hon. John Hannaford, Ms Jackie Huggins, the Hon. Bob Collins, for Minister for Immigration and Multicultural and Indigenous Affairs, November 2003.

Intjartnama Consultants, (1994) *A Plan to Increase the Involvement and Employment of Aborigines in the Justice Process and the Delivery of Non-Custodial Sentencing Where They Live* [Intjartnama Report], Northern Territory Department of Correctional Services, Darwin.

Jackson, M., (1995) 'Justice and Political Power: Reasserting Maori Legal Processes', in Hazlehurst, K. (ed), *Legal Pluralism and the Colonial Legacy*, Avebury, Aldershot.

Janke, T., (1998) *Our Culture: Our Future*, Australian Institute of Aboriginal and Torres Strait Islander Studies and the Aboriginal and Torres Strait Islander Commission.

Janke, T., (1999) 'Our Culture: Our Future, Report on Australian Indigenous Cultural and Intellectual Property Rights', Aboriginal and Torres Strait Islander Commission, Sydney.

Janke, T. and Quiggin, R., (2005) *Indigenous Cultural and Intellectual Property and Customary Law, Background Paper no 12*, The Law Reform Commission of Western Australia, Perth.

Jochelson, R., (1997) *Aborigines and Public Order Legislation in New South Wales*, Crime and Justice Bulletin no 34, New South Wales Bureau of Crime Statistics and Research, Sydney.

Johnston, E., (1991a) *Royal Commission into Aboriginal Deaths in Custody, National Report, Five Volumes*, Australian Government Publishing Service, Canberra.

Johnston E., (1991b) *Royal Commission into Aboriginal Deaths in Custody, National Report, Volume 2*, Australian Government Publishing Service, Canberra

Jonas, W., (2002a) *Social Justice Report 2001: Aboriginal and Torres Strait Islander Social Justice Commissioner*, Human Rights and Equal Opportunity Commission, Sydney.

Jonas, W., (2002b) 'Reconciliation—Where to Now?', Aboriginal and Torres Strait Islander Social Justice Commissioner Launches: Social Justice Report 2001 and the Native Title Report 2001, 17 July 2002.

Jopson, D., (2002) 'First Compensation Win for the Stolen Generations', *The Age*, 18 October 2002.

Joudo, J., (2006) *Deaths in Custody in Australia: National Deaths in Custody Program. Annual Report 2005*, Australian Institute of Criminology, Canberra.

Joudo, J. and Veld, M., (2005) *Deaths in Custody in Australia: National Deaths in Custody Program, Annual Report 2004*, Australian Institute of Criminology, Canberra.

Keating, P., (1992) 'Redfern Speech' Redfern Park, Sydney, 10 December 1992, <http://www.keating.org.au/main/cfm>.

Kelly, L. and Behrendt, L., (2007) 'Creating Conflict: Case Studies in the Tension between Native Title Claims and Land Rights Claims', *Journal of Indigenous Policy*, issue 8, pp 73–93.

Kelly, L. and Oxley, E., (1999) 'A Dingo in Sheep's Clothing?', *Indigenous Law Bulletin*, vol 4, no 18.

Kersher, B., (1998) 'R v Ballard, R v Murrell and R v Bonjon', Australian Indigenous Law Reporter, no 3, pp 410–425.

Kerwin, D. and Leon, M., (2002) 'A Comment on Aboriginal Cultural Heritage Protection in Australia', in Indigenous Law Bulletin, vol 5, no 16.

Kidd, R., (2007) Hard Labour, Stolen Wages. National Report on Stolen Wages, ANTAR, Sydney.

Kimm, J., (2004) A Fatal Conjunction: Two Laws, Two Cultures, The Federation Press, Leichhardt.

Laing, N., (2006) 'Distinguishing Native Title and Land Rights: Not an Easy Path to Rights OR Recognition', Journal of Indigenous Policy, 8, p 50.

Lake, M., (2002) Faith: Faith Bandler, Gentle Activist, Allen & Unwin, Sydney.

Langton, M., (1991), 'Too Much Sorry Business', Appendix D(i), in Johnston, E., National Report, Volume 5, Royal Commission into Aboriginal Deaths in Custody, Australian Government Publishing Service, Canberra.

Langton, M., Palmer, L., Tehan, M. and Shain, K. (eds), (2004) Honour Among Nations? Treaties and Agreements with Indigenous Peoples, Melbourne University Press, Carlton.

Lateline Transcript, (2006) 'Prosecutor Reveals Sexual Abuse and Violence in Northern Territory Indigenous Communities', ABC, 15 May, <http://www.abc.net.au/lateline/content/2006/s1639133.htm> accessed 23 May 2008.

Law Reform Commission of Western Australia, (2006) Aboriginal Customary Laws, Final Report, Law Reform Commission of Western Australia, Perth.

Lawrie, R., (2002) Speak Out Speak Strong: Researching the Needs of Aboriginal Women in Custody, Aboriginal Justice Advisory Council, Sydney.

Laynhapuy Homelands Association Inc., (2006) Submission to the Community Affairs, Legislation Committee, Senate.

Lee, P., (2006) 'Individual Titling of Aboriginal Land in the Northern Territory: What Australia can Learn from the International Community', University of New South Wales Law Journal, 29(2).

Legal and Constitutional Legislation Committee, Senate, Canberra, 4 October 2005, Evidence of Michael Prowse, Central Land Council.

Legislation Council Standing Committee, (2006) Community Based Sentencing Options for Rural and Remote Areas and Disadvantaged Populations, New South Wales Parliament, Sydney.

Libesman, T., (2004) 'Child Welfare Approaches for Indigenous Communities: International Perspectives', Child Abuse Prevention Issues, Autumn, no 20, pp 1–39, <http://www.aifs.gov.au/nch/pubs/issues/issues20/issues20.html#author> accessed 23 May 2008.

Libesman, T., (2004a) 'Towards an Inclusive Early Childhood Agenda,' Balayi: Culture, Law and Colonialism, pp 62–72.

Libesman, T., (2007a) 'Can International Law Imagine the World of Indigenous Children?', The International Journal of Children's Rights, vol 15, pp 283–309.

Libesman, T., (2007b) 'Indigenising Indigenous Child Welfare', Indigenous Law Bulletin, vol 6, no 24, pp 17–19.

Lilles, H., (2001) 'Circle Sentencing: Part of the Restorative Justice Continuum', in Morris, A. and Maxwell, G. (eds), Restorative Justice for Juveniles, Hart Publishing, Oxford.

Lind, B. and Eyland, S., (2002) 'The Impact of Abolishing Short Prison Sentences', *Crime and Justice Bulletin*, no 73, New South Wales Bureau of Crime Statistics and Research, Sydney.

Locke, J., (1689), *Two Treatises of Government: In the Former, The False Principles and Foundation of Sir Robert Filmer, And His Followers, are Detected and Overthrown. The Latter is an Essay concerning The True Original, Extent, and End of Civil-Government.*

Locke, J., (1988) *Two Treatises of Government*, Cambridge University Press, New York.

Loh, N., Maller, M., Fernandez, J., Ferrante, A. and Walsh, R.J., (2007) *Crime and Justice Statistics for Western Australia: 2005*, Crime Research Centre, Crawley.

Luke, G. and Cunneen, C., (1995) *Aboriginal Over-Representation and Discretionary Decisions in the NSW Juvenile Justice System*, Juvenile Justice Advisory Council of New South Wales, Sydney.

Luke, G. and Cunneen, C., (1998) *Sentencing Aboriginal People in the Northern Territory: A Statistical Analysis*, Report to Northern Australia Aboriginal Legal Aid Service, Darwin.

Luke, G. and Lind, B., (2002) 'Reducing Juvenile Crime: Conferencing versus Court', *Crime and Justice Bulletin*, no 69, New South Wales Bureau of Crime Statistics and Research, Sydney.

Lynch, M., Buckman, J. and Krenske, L., (2003) *Youth Justice: Criminal Trajectories*, Research and Issues Paper no 4, Crime and Misconduct Commission, Brisbane.

McCausland, S., (1999) 'Protecting Communal Interests in Indigenous Artworks after the Bulun Bulun Case', *Indigenous Law Bulletin*, 4 (22).

McCorquodale, J., (1986) 'The Legal Classification of Race in Australia', *Aboriginal History*, 10, 1, pp 7–24.

McCorquodale J., (1987a) *Aborigines and the Law: A Digest*, Aboriginal Studies Press, Canberra.

McCorquodale J., (1987b) 'Judicial Racism in Australia: Aboriginals in Civil and Criminal Cases', in Hazlehurst, K. (ed), *Ivory Scales: Black Australia and the Law*, University of New South Wales Press, Kensington.

Mackay, M., (1996) 'Aboriginal Juveniles and the Criminal Justice System: The Case of Victoria', *Children Australia*, 21(3), pp 11–22.

McKenzie, B. and Morrisette, V., (2003) 'Social Work Practice with Canadians of Aboriginal Background: Guidelines for Respecting Social Work', in Al-Krenawi, A. and Graham J. R. (eds), *Multicultural Social Work in Canada: Working with Diverse Ethno-racial Communities*, Oxford University Press, Toronto, pp 251–282.

McKenzie, K., Horton, D. and Bancroft, R. (1994), *The Encyclopaedia of Aboriginal Australia [electronic resource]: Aboriginal and Torres Strait Islander History, Society and Culture*, Aboriginal Studies Press for Australian Institute of Aboriginal and Torres Strait Islander Studies, Canberra.

McKeogh, J., Stewart, A. and Griffith, P., (2004) *Intellectual Property in Australia*, LexisNexis Butterworths, Australia.

McNamara, L., (2000) 'The Locus of Decision-making Authority in Circle Sentencing: The Significance of Criteria and Guidelines', *Windsor Yearbook of Access to Justice*, 18, pp 60–114.

McNeil, K., (1989) *Common Law Native Title*, Oxford University Press, London.

McNeil, K., (1996) 'Racial Discrimination and Unilateral Extinguishment of Native Title', *Australian Indigenous Law Reporter*, vol 1, no 2, pp 181–221.

McNeil, K., (1997) 'Extinguishment of Native Title: The High Court and American Law', *Australian Indigenous Law Reporter*, vol 2, no 3, pp 365–370.

McNeil, K., (2004) 'The Vulnerability of Indigenous Land Rights in Australia and Canada', *Osgood Hall Law Journal*, vol 42, no 2, pp 271–301.

McRae, H., Nettheim, G., Beacroft, H. and McNamara, L., (2003) *Indigenous Legal Issues*, Thomson Law Book, Sydney.

Mahoney, D., (2005) *Inquiry into the Management of Offenders in Custody and in the Community*, Department of Premier and Cabinet, Perth.

Malcolm, D. K., (1994) 'Report of the Chief Justice's Taskforce on Gender Bias', Unpublished Report, Perth.

Manne, R., (2001) 'In Denial: The Stolen Generations and the Right', *Australia Quarterly Essay*, issue 1, Schwartz Publishing, Melbourne.

Manne, R., (2005) 'Aboriginal Child Removal and the Question of Genocide 1900–1940', in Moses, A.D. (ed), *Genocide and Settler Society: Frontier Violence and Stolen Indigenous Children in Australian History*, Berghahn Books, New York.

Mantziaris, C. and Martin, D., (2000) *Native Title Corporations: A Legal and Anthropological Analysis*, The Federation Press, Annandale.

Marchetti, E. and Daly, K., (2004) 'Indigenous Courts and Justice Practices in Australia', *Trends and Issues*, no 277, AIC, Canberra.

Marks, G., (2004) 'Human Rights Special—Australia, the Committee on the Elimination of All Forms of Racial Discrimination and Indigenous Rights', *Indigenous Law Bulletin*, vol 6, no 7, pp 11–13.

Marks, G., (2006) 'Australia, Indigenous Rights and International Law', *Indigenous Law Bulletin*, vol 6, no 22, pp 20–23.

Markus A., (1990) *Governing Savages*, Allen & Unwin, Sydney.

Markus, A., (1994) *Australian Race Relations 1788–1993*, Allen & Unwin, Sydney.

Markus, A., (2004) 'Thinking Black: William Cooper and the Australian Aborigines' League', Aboriginal Studies Press, Canberra.

Marr, D., (2007) 'His Master's Voice', *Quarterly Essay*, issue 26, pp 1–84.

Martin, D., (2005) 'Rethinking Aboriginal Community Governance: Challenges for Sustainable Engagement', in Smyth, P., Reddel, T. and Jones, A. (eds), *Community and Local Governance in Australia*, University of New South Wales Press, Sydney.

Mazower, M., (1997) 'Minorities and the League of Nations in Inter-war Europe', *Daedalus Journal of the American Academy of Arts and Sciences*, Spring, vol 126, no 2.

Mead, A. and Ratuva, S. (eds), (2007) 'Pacific Genes and Life Patents, Call of the Earth and United Nations', University Institute of Advanced Studies.

Meehan, B., (1984) 'Aboriginal Skeletal Remains', *Australian Archaeology*, 19, pp 122–127.

Mellor, D. and Janke, T., (2003) *Valuing Art, Respecting Culture, Protocols for Working with the Australian Indigenous Visual Art and Craft Sector*, National Association for the Visual Arts, Potts Point, New South Wales.

Memmott, P., Stacy, R., Chambers, C. and Keys, C., (2001) *Violence in Aboriginal Communities*, Attorney-General's Department, Canberra.

Meyers, G. D. and Raine, S., (2001) 'The Legislative Response to the High Court's Native Title Decisions in *Mabo v. Queensland* and *Wik v. Queensland*', *Tulsa Journal of Comparative & International Law*, 8.2, pp 95–167.

Mildren, D., (1997) 'Redressing the Imbalance Against Aboriginals in the Criminal Justice System', *Criminal Law Journal*, vol 21, pp 7–22.

Morgan, F., (1993) 'Contact with the Justice System over the Juvenile Years', in Atkinson, L. and Gerull, S.A. (eds) *National Conference on Juvenile Justice*, Australian Institute of Criminology, Canberra.

Morgan, N. and Motteram, J., (2004) *Aboriginal People and Justice Services: Plans, Programs and Delivery*, Background Paper 7, Law Reform Commission of Western Australia, Perth.

Morris, J., (2002) 'Sea Country—The Croker Island Case: *Commonwealth of Australia v Yarmirr*', *Indigenous Law Bulletin*, vol 5, no 14, pp 18–20.

Moses, A. D., (2000) 'An Antipodean Genocide? The Origins of the Genocidal Moment in the Colonization of Australia', *Journal of Genocide Research*, vol 2, no 1, pp 89–106.

Moses, A. D. (ed), (2005) *Genocide and Settler Society: Frontier Violence and Stolen Indigenous Children in Australian History*, Berghahn Books, New York.

Mowbray, M., (2005) 'If Indigenous Governance = Local Government, What are the Options?', *2005 Seminar Series: Indigenous Governance—Challenges, Opportunities and Outcomes*, 11 May, <http://naru.anu.edu.au/papers/2005-04-11Mowbray.pdf>

Munoz, H., (1946) *Address on the International Community—Its Law—Its Forms—Its Rights: According to Francisco de Vitoria*, University of Santo Thomas Press, Manila.

Murdi Paaki Regional Council, (2002) *Submission to the House of Representatives Standing Committee on Aboriginal and Torres Strait Islander Affairs, Inquiry into Capacity Building in Indigenous Communities*, 27 August 2002.

Nakata, M., Byrne, A., Nakata, V. and Gardiner, G., (2005) 'Indigenous Knowledge, the Library and Information Service Sector, and Protocols', in Nakata, M. and Langton, M., *Australian Indigenous Knowledge and Libraries*, ATSILIRN.

National Inquiry into the Separation of Aboriginal and Torres Strait Islander Children from Their Families (NISATSIC), (1997) *Bringing Them Home*, Commonwealth of Australia, Canberra.

Neal, D., (1991) *The Rule of Law in a Penal Colony*, Cambridge University Press, Melbourne.

Nettheim, G., (1981) *Victims of the Law. Black Queenslanders Today*, Allen &Unwin, North Sydney.

New South Wales Aboriginal Land Council (NSWALC), (2007) *Annual Report 2006–2007*, NSWALC.

New South Wales Anti-Discrimination Board, (1982) *Study of Street Offences by Aborigines*, New South Wales Anti-Discrimination Board, Sydney.

New South Wales Bureau of Crime Statistics and Research, (2006) *New South Wales Criminal Court Statistics 2005*, New South Wales Bureau of Crime Statistics and Research, Sydney.

New South Wales Department of Juvenile Justice, (2005) *Annual Report 2004–05*, New South Wales Department of Juvenile Justice, Sydney.

New South Wales Law Reform Commission, (2000) *Sentencing: Aboriginal Offenders*, Report no 96, New South Wales Law Reform Commission, Sydney.

New South Wales Office of the Ombudsman, (1999) *Policing Public Safety*, Office of the Ombudsman, Sydney.

New South Wales Office of the Ombudsman, (2005) *Working with Local Aboriginal Communities*, Office of the Ombudsman, Sydney.

New South Wales Victims Compensation Tribunal, (2002a) Reasons for Dismissal: File Ref 73123, 15 February 2002.

New South Wales Victims Compensation Tribunal, (2002b) Appeal Determination: Application no 73125, 30 September 2002.

Norberry, J. and Gardiner-Garden, J., (2006) Laws and Bills Digest Section and Social Policy Section: Aboriginal Land Rights (Northern Territory) Amendment Bill 2006, Parliamentary Library Information Analysis and Advice for the Parliament, *Bills Digest*, Canberra, vol 158: 3.

Northern Territory Government, (2007) 'Ampe Akelyernemane Meke Mekarle, Report of the Northern Territory Board of Inquiry into the Protection of Aboriginal Children from Sexual Abuse: Little Children are Sacred', Darwin.

North Queensland Land Council, (2005) *Submission to the Legal and Constitutional Legislation Committee*, Senate.

Nowra, L., (2007) *Bad Dreaming: Aboriginal Men's Violence against Women and Children*, Pluto Press, North Melbourne.

Nugent, M., (2008) '"To Try to Form some Connections with the Natives": Encounters between Captain Cook and Indigenous People at Botany Bay in 1770', *History Compass*, vol 6, no 2, pp 469–487.

O'Donnell, K., (2008) Speech, Tenth Anniversary of the Hand Back of the Mutawintji Lands to the Wiimpatja Owners.

Office of the Aboriginal and Torres Strait Islander Social Justice Commissioner, (1996) *Indigenous Deaths in Custody 1989–1996*, Human Rights and Equal Opportunity Commission, Sydney.

Office of Crime Statistics, (2001) *Crime and Justice in South Australia, 2000: Juvenile Justice*, Office of Crime Statistics, South Australian Attorney-General's Department, Adelaide.

Office of Crime Statistics and Research, (2005) *Crime and Justice in South Australia, 2004: Juvenile Justice*, Office of Crime Statistics and Research, South Australian Attorney-General's Department, Adelaide.

Office of Crime Statistics and Research, (2006) *Crime and Justice in South Australia, 2005: Juvenile Justice*, Office of Crime Statistics and Research, South Australian Attorney-General's Department, Adelaide.

Office of Indigenous Affairs, (1996) 'Towards a More Workable *Native Title Act*: An Outline of Proposed Amendments', Department of Prime Minister and Cabinet, Canberra.

Ofuatey-Kodjoe, W., (1977) *The Principle of Self-determination in International Law*, Nellen Press, New York.

Ormond-Parker, L., (2003) 'Aboriginal Remains Return Home', *Indigenous Law Bulletin*, vol 5, issue 24.

Pascoe, T., (2005) 'The Youth Justice System and the Youth Murri Court', Paper presented at *Our Shared Future Conference*, Brisbane Youth Detention Centre, 7 June 2005.

Patton, P., (1995) 'Mabo, Freedom and the Politics of Difference', *Australian Journal of Political Science*, vol 30.

Payne, S., (1992) 'Aboriginal Women and the Law', in Cunneen, C. (ed), *Aboriginal Perspectives in Criminal Justice*, Sydney University Institute of Criminology, Sydney.

Pearson, N., (2003) 'Land is Susceptible of Ownership', in Langton, M., Palmer, L., Tehan, M. and Shain, K. (eds), *Honour Among Nations? Treaties and Agreements with Indigenous Peoples*, Melbourne University Press, Carlton, pp 83–100.

Perkins, C., (1975) *A Bastard Like Me*, Ure Smith, Sydney.

Perkins, C., (1994) 'Self-determination and Managing the Future', in Fletcher, C. (ed), *Aboriginal Self-determination in Australia*, Australian Institute of Aboriginal and Torres Strait Islander Studies, Canberra.

Perry, M. and Lloyd, S., (2003) *Australian Native Title Law*, Thomson Lawbook Co, Sydney.

PIAC, (2000) *Submission to the Senate Inquiry into the Stolen Generation*, PIAC, Sydney.

Potas, I., Smart, J., Bignell, G., Lawrie, R. and Thomas, B., (2003) *Circle Sentencing in New South Wales: A Review and Evaluation*, New South Wales Judicial Commission and Aboriginal Justice Advisory Committee, Sydney.

Prakash, S., (1998) *Country Studies: India, Part 6: Local Species—Turmeric, Neem and Basmati*, World Trade Organization and World Bank Trade and Development Centre.

Pratt, A. and Bennett, S., (2004) 'The End of ATSIC and the Future Administration of Indigenous Affairs', *Current Issues Brief no 4, 2004–2005*, Parliamentary Library, Canberra.

Pritchard, S., (1992) 'The Right of Indigenous Peoples to Self-determination under International Law', Aboriginal Law Bulletin, 2(55), pp 4–8.

Pritchard, S., (1997) 'Native Title from the Perspective of International Standards', *Australian Yearbook of International Law*, 18, pp 127–173.

Pritchard, S. (ed), (1998) *Indigenous Peoples, the United Nations and Human Rights*, The Federation Press, Annandale.

Pritchard, S., (1999) 'Breaking the National Sound Barrier: Communicating with the CERD and CAT Committees', *Australian Journal of Human Rights*, vol 5, no 2.

Queensland Criminal Justice Commission (1996), *Aboriginal Witnesses in Queensland Criminal Courts*, Goprint, Brisbane.

Queensland Domestic Violence Taskforce, (1988) *Beyond These Walls: Report of the Queensland Domestic Violence Taskforce to the Minister for Family Services, Welfare and Housing*, Queensland Government, Brisbane.

Queensland Domestic Violence Taskforce, (1998) *Beyond These Walls: Report of the Queensland Domestic Violence Taskforce to the Minister for Family Services, Welfare and Housing*, Queensland Government, Brisbane.

Quiggin, R., (2001) 'Boobera Lagoon', *Indigenous Law Bulletin*, ILB 9, based on telephone conversations with Julie Whitton (16 February 2001) and Albert Dennison (15 February 2001).

Quick, J. and Garran, R. R., (1976) *The Annotated Constitution of the Australian Commonwealth*, 1901 ed, Legal Books, Sydney.

Race Discrimination Commissioner, (1995) *Alcohol Report*, Human Rights and Equal Opportunity Commission, Sydney.

Radding, R. J., (2003) 'Interfaces Between Intellectual Property and Traditional Knowledge and Folklore: A U.S. Perspective', <http://library.findlaw.com/2003/Mar/19/132644.html#textIIIA>.

Read, P., (1992) 'Unearthing the Past is Not Enough', *Island*, 52, 49.

Reay, M., (1945) 'A Half-caste Aboriginal Community in North Western New South Wales', *Oceania*, vol 15, no 4, pp 296–323.

Reconciliation Australia, 'Annual Report 2006–07', Canberra, 15 April 2008.

Reconciliation Australia, 'Reconciliation Actions Plans—Turning Good Intentions into Actions', Canberra, 25 July 2006.

Reilly, A. and Genovese, A., (2004) 'Claiming the Past: Historical Understandings in Australian Native Title Jurisprudence', *Indigenous Law Journal*, vol 3, pp 19–42.

Reynolds, H., (1981) *The Other Side of the Frontier*, Penguin Books, Ringwood.

Reynolds, H., (1989) *Dispossession*, Allen & Unwin, Sydney.

Richards, J., (2008) *The Secret War: A True History of Queensland's Native Police*, University of Queensland Press, St Lucia.

Richardson, J., (2007) Reflections on *Trevorrow v State of South Australia*, Unpublished paper on file with author.

Ritter, D., (1996) '"The Rejection of Terra Nullius" in *Mabo*: A Critical Analysis', *Sydney Law Review*, vol 18, no 5.

Ritter, D., (1998) '"The Rejection of Terra Nullius" in *Mabo*: A Critical Analysis', *Sydney Law Review*, 18, 1.

Robertson, B., (2000) *The Aboriginal and Torres Strait Islander Women's Task Force on Violence Report*, Queensland Department of Aboriginal and Torres Strait Islander Development, Brisbane.

Robinson, R., (2001) *The Debt: What America Owes to Blacks*, Plume Books, New York.

Rose, D., (1984), 'The Saga of Captain Cook: Morality in Aboriginal and European Law', *Australian Aboriginal Studies*, 2, pp 24–29.

Rotman, L. I., (1996) *Parallel Paths: Fiduciary Doctrine and the Crown–Native Relationship in Canada*, University of Toronto Press, Toronto.

Rowley, C., (1970) *The Destruction of Aboriginal Society*, Penguin, Harmondsworth.

Rowley, C., (1972a) *The Destruction of Aboriginal Society*, Penguin, Harmondsworth.

Rowley, C., (1972b) *Outcastes in White Australia*, Penguin, Harmondsworth.

Ryan, L., (1974) *Report to the Australian Institute of Aboriginal Studies on Truganini*, Unpublished manuscript.

Ryan, L., (1981) *The Aboriginal Tasmanians*, University of Queensland Press, St Lucia.

Rudd, K., (2008) 'Apology to Australia's Indigenous Peoples', House of Representatives, Parliament House, Canberra, 13 February 2008, <http://www.pm.gov.au/media/Speech/2008/speech_0073.cfm>.

Ruddock, P., (2002) 'ATSIC Review Panel Announced', Media Release, 12 November 2002.

Sadurski, W., (1986) 'Gerhardy v Brown v The Concept of Discrimination: Reflections on the Landmark Case that Wasn't', *Sydney Law Review*, vol 11, no 1, pp 5–43.

Saggers, S. and Gray, D., (1991) *Aboriginal Health and Society: The Traditional and Contemporary Aboriginal Struggle for Better Health*, Allen & Unwin, Sydney.

Sanders, W., (1995) 'Reshaping Governance in Torres Strait: The Torres Strait Regional Authority and Beyond', *Australian Journal of Political Science*, Australian National University, vol 30, no 3, pp 500–524.

Sanders, W., (2004) *Thinking about Indigenous Community Governance*, Discussion Paper 262, Centre for Aboriginal Economic Policy Research, Australian National University.

Saul, B., (2000) 'The International Crime of Genocide in Australian Law', *Sydney Law Review*, vol 22, pp 527–582.

Saunders, C., (1995) 'Constitutional Arrangements of Federal Systems', *Publius: The Journal of Federalism*, vol 25, no 2, p 61.

Saunders, C., (2006) 'The Use and Misuse of Comparative Constitutional Law', *Indiana Journal of Global Legal Studies*, vol 13, issue 1, p 37.

SCROGSP, (2005) *Overcoming Indigenous Disadvantage—Key Indicators 2005*, Productivity Commission, Melbourne.

Secretariat of National Aboriginal and Islander Child Care (SNAICC), (2005) 'Achieving Stable and Culturally Strong Out of Home Care for Aboriginal and Torres Strait Islander Children', Policy Paper, Melbourne.

Senate Legal and Constitutional References Committee, (2000) 'Healing: A Legacy of Generations', Commonwealth of Australia, Canberra.

Senate Standing Committee on Constitutional and Legal Affairs, (1983) 'Two Hundred Years Later', Australian Government Printing Service, Canberra.

Senate Standing Committee on Legal and Constitutional Affairs, (2006) *Unfinished Business: Indigenous Stolen Wages*, Commonwealth of Australia, Canberra.

Skrzypiec, G. and Wundersitz, J., (2005) 'Young People Born in 1984: Extent of Involvement with the Juvenile Justice System', Office of Crime Statistics and Research, Adelaide.

Smiles, S., (2008) 'Hostel Eviction of Aborigines "Not Isolated"', *The Age*, 12 March, <http://www.theage.com.au/news/national/hostel-eviction-of-aboriginesnotisolated/2008/03/11/1205125911267.html> accessed 22 May 2008.

Smith, D., (2002) 'Jurisdictional Devolution: Towards an Effective Model for Indigenous Community Self-determination', CAEPR Discussion Paper no 233.

Snowball, L. and Weatherburn, D., (2006) 'Indigenous Over-representation in Prison: The Role of Offender Characteristics', *Crime and Justice Bulletin*, no 99, Bureau of Crime Statistics and Research, Sydney.

Steering Committee for the Review of Government Service Provision, (2006) *The Report on Government Services 2006*, Productivity Commission, <http://www.pc.gov.au/gsp/reports/rogs/2006> accessed 23 May 2008.

Stephenson, M. A. and Ratnapala, S. (eds), (1993) *Mabo, A Judicial Revolution: The Aboriginal Land Rights Decision and its Impact on Australian Law*, University of Queensland Press, St Lucia.

Storey, M., (1998) '*Kruger v Commonwealth*: Does Genocide Require Malice?', *University of New South Wales Law Journal*, vol 21, no 1, pp 224–231.

Strang, H., (2001) *Restorative Justice Programs in Australia, A Report to the Criminology Research Council*, Australian Institute of Criminology, Canberra.

Strelein, L., (1996) 'The Price of Compromise: Should Australia Ratify ILO Convention 169?', in Bird, G., Martin, G. and Nielsen, J. (eds), *Majah: Indigenous Peoples and the Law*, The Federation Press, Leichhardt.

Strelein, L., (2005) 'Native Title Holding Groups and Native Title Societies: *Sampi v State of Western Australia*', *Land, Rights, Laws: Issues of Native Title*, vol 3, no 4, 1.

Strelein, L., (2006) *Compromised Jurisprudence: Native Title Cases Since Mabo*, Aboriginal Studies Press, Canberra.

Stuckey, M., (2005) 'Not by Discovery but by Conquest: The Use of History and the Meaning of Justice in Australian Native Title Cases', *Common Law World Review*, vol 34, issue 1, pp 19–38.

Taylor, N. and Bareja, M., (2005) *2002 National Police Custody Survey*, Australian Institute of Criminology, Canberra.

Taylor, N., (2006) *Juveniles in Detention in Australia 1981–2005*, Technical and Background Paper no 22, Australian Institute of Criminology, Canberra.

Tehan, M., (2003) 'A Hope Disillusioned, an Opportunity Lost? Reflections on Common Law Native Title and Ten Years of the *Native Title Act*', *Melbourne University Law Review*, vol 27, p 523.

Thompson, J., (2002) *Taking Responsibility for the Past, Reparation and Historical Injustice*, Polity Press, Cambridge.

Thompson, P. and Goodall, H., (2008) 'From Movement to Management: Aboriginal Assertion, Government and Environmentalist Responses and Some Ways Forward Regarding Conservation and Social Justice', *Transforming Cultures eJournal*, vol 3, no 1, <http://epress.lib.uts.edu.au/journals/TfC> accessed 30 October 2008.

Tomas, N., (1996) 'The Maori Language—The Chiefly Language of Aotearoa—The Long Struggle', in Bird, G., Martin, G. and Nielson, J. (eds), *Majah: Indigenous Peoples and the Law*, The Federation Press, Sydney.

Trimboli, L., (2000) *An Evaluation of the New South Wales Youth Justice Conferencing Scheme*, New South Wales Bureau of Crime Statistics and Research, Sydney.

Urbis Keys Young, (2001) *Aboriginal Child Welfare and Juvenile Justice Good Practice Project*, Urbis Keys Young, Milsons Point.

van Krieken, R., (2001) 'Case Notes: Is Assimilation Justiciable? *Lorna Cubillo and Peter Gunner v Commonwealth*', *Sydney Law Review*, vol 23, no 2, pp 239–260.

Vanstone, A., 'New Bill to Benefit Thousands of Aboriginal Corporations', (Press Release, 23 June 2005.

Ward, A., (1999) *An Unsettled History*, Bridget Williams Books, Wellington.

Watson, N., (2006a) '*The Corporations (Aboriginal and Torres Strait Islander) Bill 2005* (Cth): Coming Soon to a Community Organisation Near You', *Indigenous Law Bulletin*, vol 6, no 19.

Watson, N., (2006b) 'Howard's End: The Real Agenda Behind the Proposed Review of Indigenous Land Titles', *Journal of Indigenous Policy*, 8, p 20.

Watson, N., (2007a) 'Implications of Land Rights Reform for Indigenous Health', *Medical Journal of Australia*, vol 186, no 10, pp 534–536.

Watson, N., (2007b) 'Strewth Darryl, You Wouldn't Believe it! The Erosion of Aboriginal Land Rights', *Precedent*, 83.

Wearne H., (1980) *A Clash of Cultures: Queensland Aboriginal Policy (1824–1980)*, Uniting Church of Australia, Brisbane.

Weatherall, B., (1990) Foreword by the Chairman, Aboriginal Provisional Government, <http://www.kooriweb.org/apg/papersl.htm> accessed 6 October 2008.

Weatherall, B., (2004) *Repatriation of Indigenous Ancestral Human Remains: No respect, No Progress*, paper at the AIATSIS Conference.

Weatherall, T., (1989) 'Aborigines, Archaeologists and the Rights of the Dead', *Australian Archaeology*, 19, pp 122–147.

Webber, J., (1995) 'The Jurisprudence of Regret: The Search for Standards of Justice in Mabo', *Sydney Law Review*, 17, 5.

Westley, R., (1998) 'Many Billions Gone: Is It Time to Reconsider the Case for Black Reparations?', *Boston College Law Review* 40, 429.

Wilson, G., (1999) *Enhancing the Role of Aboriginal Communities in Federal Corrections*, Correctional Service of Canada, Ottawa.

Williams, G., (1999) *Human Rights under the Australian Constitution*, Oxford University Press, Melbourne.

Williams, G. and Blackshield, T., (2006) *Australian Constitutional Law and Theory: Commentary and Materials*, 4th edn, The Federation Press, Annandale.

Williams, G., (2006) 'The Victorian Charter of Human Rights and Responsibilities: Origins and Scope', *Melbourne University Law Review*, 30(3), p 880.

Williams, G., (2007) *A Charter of Rights for Australia*, University of New South Wales Press, Kensington.

Williams, N., (1987) *Two Laws, Managing Disputes in a Contemporary Aboriginal Community*, Australian Institute of Aboriginal Studies, Canberra.

Williams, R., (1986) 'The Algebra of Federal Indian Law: The Hard Trail of Decolonizing and Americanizing the White Man's Indian Jurisprudence', *Wisconsin Law Review*, 219.

Williams, V., (2003) *The Approach of Australian Courts to Aboriginal Customary Law in the Areas of Criminal, Civil and Family Law*, Background Paper no 1, Law Reform Commission of Western Australia, Perth.

Wilson, J. Q. and Kelling, G., (1982) 'Broken Windows', *The Atlantic Monthly*, March 1982, pp 29–38.

Windshuttle, K., (1994) *The Killing of History*, Macleay Press, Sydney.

Windshuttle, K., (2002) *The Fabrication of Aboriginal History, Volume One: Van Dieman's Land 1803–1847*, Macleay Press, Sydney.

Woodward, E., (1973) Aboriginal Land Rights Commission, First Report.

Woodward, E., (1974) Aboriginal Land Rights Commission, Second Report.

Wootten, H., (1989) *Report of the Inquiry into the Death of Malcolm Charles Smith*, Australian Government Publishing Service, Canberra.

Wootten, H., (1991a) *Royal Commission into Aboriginal Deaths in Custody, Regional Report of Inquiry in New South Wales, Victoria and Tasmania*, Australian Government Publishing Service, Canberra.

Wootten, H., (1991b) '99 Reasons ... The Royal Commission into Black Deaths in Custody', *Polemic*, 2(3), pp 124–128.

World Intellectual Property Organization, (2001) *Intellectual Property Needs and Expectations of Traditional Knowledge Holders*, Report on Fact-finding Missions on Intellectual Property and Traditional Knowledge 1998–1999 WIPO Geneva 2001, <http://www.wipo.int/tk/en/tk/ffm/report/final/pdf/part1.pdf>.

Wright, L., (2003) 'An Analysis of the Ward Decision: Part 2', *Indigenous Law Bulletin*, vol 5, no 26, pp 17–23.

Yu, P., (2001) 'Unfinished Business—National Responsibilities and Local Actions', in Garkawe, S., Kelly, L. and Fisher, W. (eds), *Indigenous Human Rights*, The Federation Press, Annandale.

Yunupingu, G., 'What the Aboriginal People Want', *The Age*, 26 August 1987.

Index

Printed in Australia
16 Jul 2015
424101